Landscaping with Herbs

Landscaping with Herbs

by

James Adams

TIMBER PRESS
Portland, Oregon

Front cover:
A replica cottage garden at Fall City Herb Farm,
Fall City, Washington. Photo by James Adams.

Paperback edition printed 2001.

ISBN 0-88192-514-4

Designed by Sandra Mattielli

Printed in Hong Kong

TIMBER PRESS, Inc.
The Haseltine Building
133 S.W. Second Avenue, Suite 450
Portland, Oregon 97204, US.A.

Library of Congress catalog card number 87-163339

Contents

To My Wife, Jeanne
and
Jeff, Jenny, Andy, Becky & Paul
Who Forage In My
Herb Garden.

Acknowledgments

Very simply, this book would not have been written without the support of my wife, Jeanne. Not only was she a fine editor that saw to it I sent off polished work, but she was also an invaluable listener. She is a very remarkable and wonderful person.

There are many people who have assisted me over the past two years, too many to list them all and their contributions of thoughts and design suggestions. It has been a privilege to work with three special people who helped me from the beginning—and even before that: Mary Medalia, Betty McSorley and Judy Zugish. Mary is known fondly as the Herb Lady at Seattle's Pike Place Market, where she has been selling the finest herbs in the Northwest for some 30 years. No finer herbs can be found anywhere, and no finer lady either. Betty McSorley, like Mary, was an unwavering source of enthusiasm. It seemed both had the answers every time I came knocking. I can't thank Betty enough for her moral support and all-consuming interest in the secrets of herbs that rubbed off on me the very first time we met. You may find her at the *GARDEN GATE* in Rochester, WA. Judy is someone you just have to meet. She's like an effervescent herb tea, an exciting package of herbal mysteries you simply can't tire of. She is owner of the *BOUQUET BANQUE* in Marysville, WA. Many invaluable thoughts and ideas about the herbs in this text were offered by Mary, Betty and Judy.

A group of people that deserve specific mention are the many library staff employees that ran their tails off searching for obscure and little used books. They like that sort of thing I understand. My special thanks to Rivka and Darlene and Kitty and Jim and Ardith and Eddie at the Chehalis Library. Many thanks to Heidi Mercado, Librarian of the Chemistry Library at the University of Washington, and I can't begin to thank enough Anna Zeigler for her assistance from the depths of the University's Herbarium. Joy Mastroguiseppe of the Marion Ownbey Herbarium of Washington State University identified nearly 120 weird worts, so that correct natural histories could be compiled about the herbs in this text. Between Joy and Steve Gibbs, also from the Washington State Cooperative Extension Services, I was able to gather a remarkable amount of inside data about herbs.

Growers, sellers and nomenclature buffs as I am can be grateful for Dr. A. O. Tucker's input on the accepted scientific nomenclature of the herbs. Dr. Tucker, Co-Curator of the Delaware State College Herbarium, has done extensive research in nomenclature of herbs, particularly those stubborn families like Oregano, Mint, Lavender and Rosemary. We should all be indebted to him for this exhaustive research. (See, "Nomenclature of the Culinary Herbs and Potherbs," Chap. 3 in *Herbs, Spices & Medicinal Plants*, Vol I, Cracker & Simon, 85.)

Other valuable people include the Zimmerman's of the Fall City Herb Farm, Michele Nash, Gail Schilling, Angelo Pellegrini, Irving Scherer, John Eccles and many more who shared their gardens with us. I am grateful to Kelly Powell for his interest, time and equipment which most certainly helped me provide better pictures than I would otherwise have composed. And if it were not for Leone Seidel, on her typewriter and computer, who made writing fun, I'd have lost my patience and courage long ago.

Table 1
Key to Plant Symbols

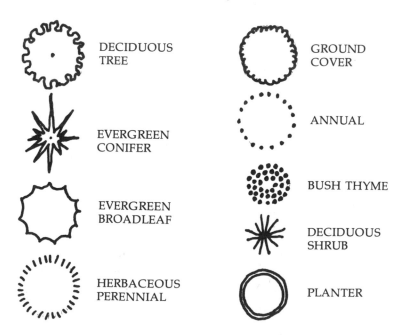

DECIDUOUS TREE

EVERGREEN CONIFER

EVERGREEN BROADLEAF

HERBACEOUS PERENNIAL

GROUND COVER

ANNUAL

BUSH THYME

DECIDUOUS SHRUB

PLANTER

How to Use This Book

Because I am so involved in the lives of herbs, people expect me to know what an herb is. I can only answer, "any plant that you find useful". The definition of an herb has changed through the centuries, replaced in some cases by more specific terminology: vegetable, grain, fruit, etc. and recently, "ornamental". Many plants with an historical use, and once considered herbs, are now merely ornamental plants to many gardeners. You would be surprised at the number of medicinal gems in your gardens, a pharmacy by medieval standards: Quince, Christmas Rose, Honeysuckle, Hollyhock, Pussywillow, Trillium, Oregon Grape, Alder, Oak, Larkspur, Lily of the Valley, Juniper berries. You name it, someone classified it as a medicinal. This indiscriminate labelling has not simplified the herbalist's task of sorting through the real from the imaginary medicinal plants. But they remain with us in our gardens because someone once found them useful.

They are pretty. That is sufficient for me. We may grow some herbs because they scent our environment. Is that stretching the term a bit? Not at all. Jasmine and Mock Orange have been used this way for centuries. My point is that plants are herbs if you use them— even to surround your home as screens, or use them for shade, fragrance or food for the birds—no matter what end use is in store, they are being applied to your daily life.

What then is this book doing describing only a selection of herbs, predominantly culinary, out of the multitude? Two reasons: 1) I am interested in those herbs that are less thought of as ornamentals than they should be, plants that are left out of most landscaping texts and designs for lack of data about their qualities, other than culinary; and 2) I am restricting myself to herbs with which I have had experience. There are literally thousands of true medicinal herbs that could be included. Some you know, such as Foxglove. But many you possibly don't recognize as herbs, but still cultivate for their beauty, such as Peonies, St. John's Wort and the Passion Flower. After reading this book I hope you will be more venturesome. Just because someone says it's an herb shouldn't ruin the fun of growing a new plant you have found. Instead, look up its history. Like Yarrow it might have saved an empire, like Hyssop bathed the wounds of our Lord Jesus Christ, like Monarda blushed m'lady's cheeks, or like Dyers Camomile supplied the khaki color for camouflaged uniforms. Herbs are special, or they wouldn't be herbs.

Each chapter of this book is divided into three sections. The first section describes a form of landscaping. This is a general overview, the purpose of which is to introduce you to the theme of such a landscape so you can choose ornamental herbs more wisely. Certain restrictions on plant uses are described and must be examined before designing or redesigning the gardens of a homesite. Use Table 1, Key to Plant Symbols, when examining the architectural designs in this book.

The second section closely examines a selection of herbs. This selection is by no means exclusive. They are chosen to some extent to emphasize the chapter's theme. In this way the basic landscape covered by each chapter is better understood. Other ornamental plants that are chosen as companions to herbs in feature gardens are only mentioned throughout in order to simplify the comparisons that are made between the habits and ornamental characteristics of herbs. They are more easily visualized when only a small number of comparisons are used. Forgive me if I did not use your favorite ornamental. Remember this book is intended to spur you to experiment and adventure.

In order to get the most from this book first decide objectively what landscape you have or are interested in looking at. If you are undecided then read all of the first sections of each chapter for insight and certainly follow this with readings from some of the many books listed in the bibliography. Then read again the first section of the chapter that most closely defines what you seek. Can you see your homesite in that context? The more easily definable your landscape is the easier it will be to choose ornamental herbs that fit.

Now make an inventory of the valuable ornamental plants in your landscape or those that you want to have as neighbors to herbs. Study the tables in the appendices and select six to a dozen herbs that exhibit similar characteristics or sound intriguing. Locate them via the index and read about their needs and desires. Examples are given that compare or contrast other plants so you can get a grasp of the herb's nature. Consider their value to you as well. You may prefer a culinary herb to a pretty one.

Once you have your list, read the last section of the chapter that corresponds to your landscape. This will give you an idea of how some herbs have been used in actual settings. Some landscapes can accommodate many herbs, others are able to adequately present no more than a dozen. Purchase those that remain on your list and let them loose in your landscape to entertain you and your guests.

Remember, an ornamental herb doesn't require use. Certainly I recommend that you experiment with using it, for to make it valuable you must know what it is capable of doing for you. Once you have shared that knowledge with other gardeners you will then know why herbs are exciting ornamentals. Be a bridge between the past and the future, experiment with herbs.

I have limited the use of uncommon terminology or scientific terms to those in the following glossary:

CHEMOTYPE/CHEMOVAR—a chemically distinct variety or cultivar that is identical to the species but distinguished only by its fragrance or chemical make-up.

CULTIVAR—horticulturally derived variation of a species.

CUTTING—portion of plant (severed by a sharp knife) for purposes of propagation.

DRIFT—a grouping of identical plants arranged in a variety of shapes combined with other drifts of plants in such a way to encourage the sense of motion in a planting.

ESPALIER—woody herbs (including trees) wired to a trellis or wall, sometimes in decorative patterns.

"FORMAL"—a garden designed geometrically but included in another landscape form as a separate, and often isolated, garden.

FILTERED SHADE—Partial shade found in forests where patches of sun brighten the scene only momentarily.

INFLORESCENCE—the flowering or reproductive part of a plant.

INFORMAL BORDER—plants natural, not pruned to decorative or geometric shapes.

LIVING SCREEN—barrier over 3' of plants (may include espaliered).

MEAD—region where low grasses, wildflowers and herbs compose the lawn.

PARTIAL SHADE—sun for part of the day.

POTPOURRI—fragrant mixture of herbs in a container that is stoppered and used as an air freshener.

QUAD—garden arrangement of four square beds surrounded by a hedge or fence.

ROOT DIVISION/CROWN DIVISION—severing of reproductive roots or a plant's crown into pieces for purposes of propagation.

POLYMORPHIC—variable in habit and foliage characteristics (occurs within a species).

RUGOSE—wrinkled and pitted (usually refers to a leaf texture).

SIMPLES—simple herbal remedy for a simple ailment.

START—rooted cutting.

SPORT—branch or foliage with atypical characteristics.

SACHET—cloth bag containing fragrant herbs, usually used as is to scent articles of clothing or fabric.

STREWING HERBS—fragrant herbs thrown to the floor and crushed underfoot to scent rugs and freshen the air.

STANDARD—a form of topiary that makes a woody perennial herb represent a tree, with a ball of foliage atop a bare trunk.

TISANE—mixture of fragrant and flavorful herbs in a cloth bag (tea bag) to be used to make an infusion for medicinal purposes (a medicinal tea).

TOPIARY—pruning and training evergreen woody herbs to take on recognizable shapes or characteristics.

VARIETY—variation of the species with stable characteristics.

VOLATILES—chemicals that escape from a plant under normal conditions that we perceive as scent.

Virtually every plant mentioned in this book has been used in some fashion to let it qualify as an herb. I dwell only on the significant ones. But where in the botanical world do all of these herbs and plants fit? Without man they are unlabeled but still have a history to tell, one of the most fascinating histories imaginable, evolution. The plant kingdom is at least one billion years old, and many scientists say as old as four billion years if unicellular plants (Algae, etc.) are added. They came from nothing and created an Eden.

Let's take a quick look at how plants fit together; who their relatives are. Table 2 is a family tree of the herbs. A few plants other than those in this book are added to give a better picture of their family life. When these herbs evolved in history is another story and a long and controversial one. Suffice it to say the wind pollinated plants were some of the oldest plants, Sweet Bay, Witch Hazel, Birch, Magnolias, etc. The daisied flowers so plentiful today were relatively late in coming, relying as they do on the pollinators such as insects and birds. You may want to refer to this table as you are reading to see how an herb evolved, who its cousins are and which ornamentals could be joined in a feature garden that's all in the family.

Table 2
Key to Botanical Classification of Herbs
Family Tree of Herbs

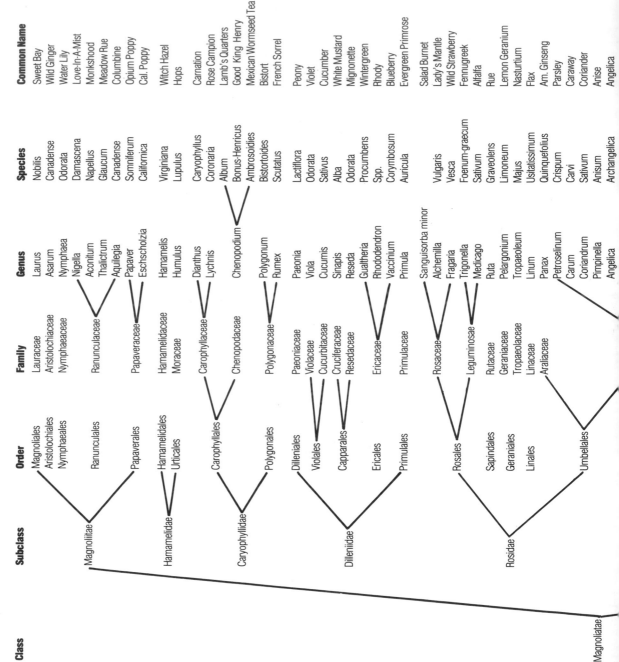

Class	Subclass	Order	Family	Genus	Species	Common Name
		Magnoliales	Lauraceae	Laurus	Nobilis	Sweet Bay
		Aristolochiales	Aristolochiaceae	Asarum	Canadense	Wild Ginger
		Nymphaeales	Nymphaeaceae	Nymphaea	Odorata	Water Lily
				Nigella	Damascena	Love-In-A-Mist
		Ranunculales	Ranunculaceae	Aconitum	Napellus	Monkshood
				Thalictrum	Glaucum	Meadow Rue
				Aquilegia	Canadense	Columbine
		Papaverales	Papaveraceae	Papaver	Somniferum	Opium Poppy
	Magnoliitae			Eschscholzia	California	Cal. Poppy
	Hamamelidae	Hamamelidales	Hamamelidaceae	Hamamelis	Virginiana	Witch Hazel
		Urticales	Moraceae	Humulus	Lupulus	Hops
			Caryophyllaceae	Dianthus	Caryophyllus	Carnation
		Caryophyllales		Lychnis	Coronaria	Rose Campion
	Caryophyllidae		Chenopodaceae	Chenopodium	Album	Lamb's Quarters
					Bonus-Henricus	Good King Henry
					Ambrosoidies	Mexican Wormseed Tea
		Polygonales	Polygonaceae	Polygonum	Bistortoides	Bistort
				Rumex	Scutatus	French Sorrel
		Dilleniales	Paeoniaceae	Paeonia	Lactiflora	Peony
		Violales	Violaceae	Viola	Odorata	Violet
			Cucurbitaceae	Cucumis	Sativus	Cucumber
		Capparales	Cruciferaceae	Sinapis	Alba	White Mustard
	Dilleniidae		Resedaceae	Reseda	Odorata	Mignonette
		Ericales	Ericaceae	Gualtheria	Procumbens	Wintergreen
				Rhododendron	Spp.	Rhody
				Vaccinium	Corymbosum	Blueberry
		Primulales	Primulaceae	Primula	Auricula	Evergreen Primrose
				Sanguisorba minor		Salad Burnet
		Rosales	Rosaceae	Alchemilla	Vulgaris	Lady's Mantle
				Fragaria	Vesca	Wild Strawberry
			Leguminosae	Trigonella	Foenum-graecum	Fennugreek
	Rosidae			Medicago	Sativum	Alfalfa
		Sapindales	Rutaceae	Ruta	Graveolens	Rue
		Geraniales	Geraniaceae	Pelargonium	Limoneum	Lemon Geranium
			Tropaeolaceae	Tropaeoleum	Majus	Nasturtium
		Linales	Linaceae	Linum	Ustitatissimum	Flax
			Araliaceae	Panax	Quinquefolius	Am. Ginseng
		Umbellales		Petroselinum		Parsley
				Carum	Crispum	Caraway
				Coriandrum	Carvi	Coriander
				Pimpinella	Sativum	Anise
				Angelica	Anisum	Angelica
Magnoliatae					Archangelica	

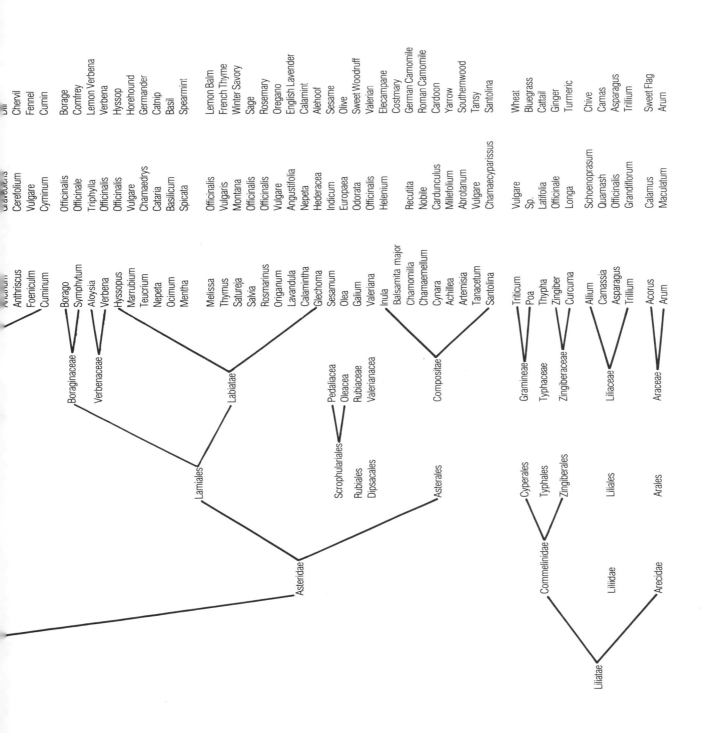

Chapter 1 / INTRODUCTION

All gardeners including herbs in their gardens do so for the same reason: they are more than pretty plants. Even if you haven't raised one, the word "herb" still conjures images of ancient mages and contemporary apothecaries apportioning plant parts for innumerable and frequently unfathomable reasons.

Quickly off the tip of the tongue come recollections of many commonly encountered herbs: annuals such as Summer Savory, Chervil and Dill; herbaceous perennials such as Lovage, Roman Camomile and Fennel; woody perennials like Sage, Thyme and Rue; vines like Hops and Jasmine; bulbs of Chives and Saffron; and the winter-blooming shrub Witch Hazel.

Included in herbal gardens could be Snakeroot, Felon Herb, Hindheal, Herb-of-Grace, Rattlesnake, Mosquito plant, Five Fingers, Lion's Mouth, King's Cure-All, Starwort, Alecoast and Bugloss—names not easy to remember but coined by centuries of use.

Mankind has always put great value on herbs and flowers. In past times they were valued ornamentally as well as for more practical reasons. Only recently, due to the declining use of herbs in medicines and the wide selection of rugged ornamentals gathered from all over the world, have the lackluster herbs fallen by the wayside to become, in many cases, unappreciated weeds.

Before the evolution of a settled society, man's chief interest in plants was for nourishment, with other uses arising quickly as men established homesites. In the Paleolithic Period of the Stone Age (30,000–11,000 B.C.) men were nomadic, following grazing herds of large mammals. With them, either accidentally or by choice, went the seeds of plants they used most often. Ruins from the Mesolithic Period (11,000–5,000 B.C.) have revealed much about the developing dependence upon plants. For example, evidence found at archeological sites showed that Mesolithic fishermen in southeastern Asia began propagating roots and cuttings of specific plants in order to supply themselves with plant dyes, extracts for fish poisons, fibers for nets and bark for textiles.

Food, shelter and religious rituals were the first uses of herbs, followed quickly by clothing and eventually cure-alls. When it was discovered that some plants could combat diseases, our ancestors began to investigate the world around them in more detail in hopes of finding the "bread of life" that would sustain them forever. Since the search began, less than a few hundred out of hundreds of thousands of plant species have proved valuable as either a medicine or a producer of quality seeds, fruits, bark, roots or leaves. Improvements from selective breeding techniques, that is, planting the seed of only the finest of each year's stock (e.g. the hardiest, a heavy producer or one that shows special new traits) have evolved many new forms and adapted herbs to fit every environment in the world.

One of the first uses of herbs was as an element in sacrificial rites performed on altars.

For primitive man a beautiful flower was a powerful talisman, the bearer of magical abilities, a ward fending off devils and demons in the dark of night. Though many of the powers associated with herbs are certainly fantasy, deep within this convoluted world of herb lore are true powers. Even today 40% of the medicines prescribed by doctors are derived from plants.

Undoubtedly the most significant role herbs have played throughout man's history is in medicine. Every culture, past and present, has relied on the widely varied philosophies of its shamen and physicians to keep the human body free from disease and discomfort. The Greek scholar, Theophrastus, a pupil of Aristotle in the fourth century B.C., first classified over three hundred simples (herbal remedies for simple ailments). Dioscorides, a Greek physician in the first century after Christ, compiled an herbal that for 15 centuries was a standard tome for those practicing the art of medicine.

Other scholars such as Hippocrates, Aristotle, Galen, Dodens, and master gardeners Charlemagne, Gerarde, Parkinson, and learned writers Jon Gardener, Dr. William Turner, Culpepper and Sir Francis Bacon were all involved with the evolution of the art of healing into the science of medicine.

Because diet has always been a controlling factor in man's pursuit of a more healthful life, herbs have played a significant role in reaching that goal. Many positive effects of herbal remedies once attributed to magic can be explained by the presence of vitamins and minerals. The diets of our forebears chronically lacked many vital nutrients. The results from consuming herbs containing these nutrients were often dramatic. The mystery of Scurvy Grass, *Cochlearia officinalis,* its ability to heal the bleeding gums formerly developing in late winter, lies in its high concentration of Vitamin C and its early appearance in spring just when needed. Such positive effects helped bolster the notion that herbs were indeed magic. The vast, worldwide health food industry thrives today, in part, because of this notion.

We need not believe all the tales we hear about miracle or magical herbal remedies but we should respect the herbs for the history they represent. Although mysticism has been replaced by the demands of a consumer society, still with us after untold centuries are herbal products such as cosmetics, perfumes, candies, liqueurs, vitamins, foods, medicines, gums, teas, tobaccos, dyes, soaps, oils, incense, disinfectants, toiletries, decorative gifts, fermented beverages and fragrances for stationery and fabrics.

There are also unlimited culinary uses of herbs to consider. Herbs such as Lovage and Parsley flavor soups while Salad Burnet adds zest to a salad. Saffron and Chives flavor cheese, Dill and Basil perk up a butter. Rosemary and Savory go well with all meats, but Fennel and fish are a match to remember. Borage finds a place in cake decorating while Poppy and Caraway seeds make delicious candy. Hosts of Mints create hundreds of hearty summer ices.

Herbs have innumerable cosmetic uses: wash waters and ointments for skin and hair care and fragrances for perfumes are by far the most popular. As decorations the various plant parts such as seeds, seed pods, leaves and flowers provide interesting dried materials for floral arrangements that range in design from simple swags hung over doors and flower petal designs on greeting cards to concerted works of art.

Herbs have an ageless quality that is still appreciated. Because they are a vast kingdom of riches which can readily be exploited there is magic in herbs even to this day. It is this magic that lures poets and playwrights to praise and glorify herbs. Religions deify them. Mages and scientists philosophise on them. Herbalists and cosmeticians swear by them. Gourmets relish them. Artists portray them. Cosmologists predict by them. Gardeners adore and pamper them.

For at least 12,000 years man has been a farmer, a gardener and a landscaper. Like native trees and shrubs, herbs were used in landscaping around primitive dwellings. Herbs were chosen for their utility in medicines, religion, cooking and food preparation; whereas trees and shrubs were usually chosen for protection from enemies and weather. The earliest landscapers attempting to confine and recreate natural settings quickly learned that gardens were more manageable when only one small niche in nature was captured and defined within the boundaries of a given plot of land. Even the most minute garden became a milestone for mankind. Each one embraced nature and defined life over and over and over again through good times and bad, reminding people how much they are a part of the world, how much they need it. Through those centuries the occupants of castles, cabins and condominiums have conspired to copy this ancient rite.

As people, politics, and plant lore changed so did the design of gardens. Gardens became sanctuaries not only around individual homesites but for community parks, commons, church yards, and governmental precincts as well. As communities grew the need for protective cover gave way to enticing gardens, signatures of influential people. The huge herb gardens of Charlemagne tended by hundreds of gardeners in the early 9th century are an example.

Natural terrain in many new lands engendered new ideas. Rocky Mediterranean coastlands and mideastern deserts, the Asian Steppes and European mountains, African tropics and the misty British Isles all yielded to the touch of gardeners and joined the ranks of landscape forms. Landscaping today reflects the amalgamated history of hundreds of nations and countless people and customs.

Plants have been such an intimate part of human evolution that whether we are the student or the teacher of herb lore, we can all be comfortable collecting and arranging them according to our tastes. The tastes of some may run to rigid geometric designs based on perfect symmetry, as in the *formal* landscape. Others, however, are enamored of imitating nature's randomness and so fashion an *informal* landscape.

Gently winding paths, intersecting in great hyperbolic arcs with patios and plantings, are the stuff of the practitioners of *contemporary* landscaping. A smattering of this and a bit of that neatly yet naturally snuggled into beds of bark and crushed rock suits them fine.

Like a flood ravaged valley, the *rock garden* landscape is strewn with boulders large and small. Randomly scattered tuffets of bold color add a sense of brightness to the scene. Nearby in a secluded meadow, flowers, as though sown midst the frenzy of a gypsy dance, create chaotic drifts of color characteristic of the *wild garden* landscape.

Those who prefer to square dance, tame this natural chaos into a checkerboard of raised beds, then summarily surround and subdue it all with a low fence or hedge. Contrast in this *dooryard* landscape is seen in textures and heights and greens and golds. It is a garden where beneficial herbs are favored over ornamentals.

As our megalopolises grow and engulf us, landscapes diminish in size, yet even the smallest space can be enhanced by walk enveloped *ponds*. Here a tiny spring and a few aquatic herbs suffice as a soliloquy on life. The last watering place a refreshing landscape reflecting serenity and constancy, emphasizes for us again the depth of the bond between man and nature.

When the decision to landscape is made, we necessarily design before planting. It is important to read about and study the various landscape forms—to venture out on weekends to see what the neighbors have done or what types of plants we prefer, visit nurseries and garden centers to determine what is actually available and at what price. This planning stage can take months to years.

Once the desired form of landscape is decided upon we are a giant step closer but a significant amount of planning, not to mention work, remains ahead. The first task takes us to the library, or the bookstore, again, where ideas for garden and landscape designs may be found. From there, with notes on preferences and availabilities determined in earlier explorations we can begin to sketch in our minds and on paper what we want to create. In the final stages the development of a sustainable budget is required.

It is now necessary to obtain the herbs that have been chosen for a design. To be frank this task can become troublesome. Herbs have an overabundance of names which at their best are confusing when the time comes to order a particular plant. Oswego Tea, Beebalm, Mountain Mint and Mountain Balm are all common names for the popular North American flower *Monarda didyma,* used by the Oswego Indians long before the Americas were discovered by Europeans. Other species of this genus are *M. punctata,* sold as Horsemint, and *M. fistulosa,* sold as Wild Bergamot. Cultivars include 'Prairie Night', 'Salmon Queen', etc. Though they add to the list of names, cultivar names often solve some of the "which is which" problems that arise with closely related varieties.

Further confusion of genus and species assignments by botanists have shifted in a game of botanical musical chairs with the new names not yet widely known or even accepted. A good example is Marjoram, or we should say Oregano. Not affecting the plant in the least, but confusing us is the switching of the *Majorana* genus to *Origanum.* Therefore, *M. hortensis,* known as Sweet Marjoram, is now *O. majorana* and *M. onites,* Pot Marjoram, is *O. onites.* Other Oreganos with a confusing assortment of botanical and common names are *O. vulgare,* Wild Marjoram; and *O. dictamnus,* Hop Marjoram. All are often sold simply as Oregano.

In order to purchase by mail it is often best to first know well the exact genus and species of each plant desired. Plant identification will be important when your search for seeds yields packets labeled only by genus: Lavender, Thyme, Oregano, Calendula, Savory. Often more than one species or variety of plant can be grown from a packet of seed labeled in such a roughshod way. Results are generally more exciting than a nuisance.

Preferable for landscaping are potted starts of exactly the species we want. Only a few nurseries and fewer garden centers stock more than a dozen herb starts suitable as ornamentals. Gardeners living in large metropolitan areas have more, but still inadequate opportunities. However, thanks to garden catalogs and especially herb and native plant sales sponsored by enthusiasts, desired materials can be found.

With the selected plants in hand you can begin propagating. Propagation is required for two reasons. First, because several of the same species will usually be required, you must propagate for quantity. Secondly, different sizes, shapes and types of conditioning may be needed to fit a particular herb to a design and they will not generally be available the way you would like them.

Many herbs also have more bad growing habits than do "plastic" ornamental plants purchased from nurseries. So even if you can find the species you want it may need taming, or perhaps a little understanding, before it is transferrable to the landscape. Let us not forget that a considerable amount of effort goes into taming all ornamental plants by the growers before they are put on sale for landscape use.

Propagation is an important step because it helps us fully understand the plants we will be dealing with and enjoying. Learning to recognize the seasonal changes an herb goes through as well as the variances throughout its life cycle will be very useful. Cultural problems can more easily be distinguished from disease and unexpected insect damage. Constant vigilance will allow you to catch the creation of a "sport", or new variety. Many sports can only be propagated by cuttings. Just as valuable is the benefit from being able to identify seeds and seedlings. Later when the garden is flourishing, weeding will repay you for all the toil expended in creating your landscape through sales of these "exotic" herbs at plant sales.

Whether a garden's design is functional, such as a play yard, patio, entrance way or service yard, or fictional, with a pond, rockfield, or miniature meadow enveloped by a small forest, one of the basic landscape forms must be adhered to as a framework. An integrated landscape plan is the background in which one or more garden designs are woven. The whole bears the creative signature of its owner.

The landscaped garden is the evidence by which neighbors and visitors judge gardeners. The more expressive a design, the more viewers will be impressed, whether or not they themselves are gardeners, for it will be obvious to them that this ground has been shaped by a skilled hand. Choosing ornamental herbs for special plantings in a landscape will multiply the homeowner's pleasures because of the many and more favorable comments from fascinated visitors.

The landscaped homesite is a piece of art, a creative work with form and beauty and benefit. It is possible to dwell here on a dozen different methods to describe how landscaping is brought into focus and metamorphosed from thoughts and things into an artistic design. Hundreds of books are available on just that subject. However, whatever words are chosen to describe beauty and artistry, and whatever method is taken to achieve them, neither is important unless we really enjoy landscaping, reading about techniques and designs and above all, enjoy what gardeners have done throughout history, *experimenting.*

The concepts for using herbs in landscaping must be dug spadeful by spadeful out of bygone tomes on lore and sifted carefully for meaningful ideas that can be reoriented to the needs of today's gardeners and their homesites. Tables and charts of ornamental plants rarely include even a few herbs and too much reading can lead to disinterest. Experimenting is an exciting and more rewarding solution.

Experimenting begins when the herbs are finally introduced to the landscape. Now we must take a trip back in time as we become involved in integrating ancient herbs with a 20th century landscape. By definition they are beneficial as well as beautiful. They are a delightful, ofttimes eccentric "old family" of plants, containing annuals, biennials, herbaceous perennials, woody and evergreen perennials, vines, bulbs and shrubs.

Herbs can be used to influence or enhance garden designs in many ways. In our landscape we may either recall ancient moments with carefully chosen and arranged herbs or merely make use of their gifts for ourselves and enable us to share with others the rich knowledge we have garnered. We may wish to recreate historical periods and places using garden designs of those times as well as the precise species of plants grown by the people of the century represented. Many of the culinary and medicinal herbs are no longer used and may be difficult to find, but well worth the search if only to preserve a portion of history as a living plant. Though many medicinal herbs are no longer recognized as possessing therapeutic value, they are a glorious flora that can be displayed ornamentally in physick gardens. Herbs can also be planted to individual themes according to their use as fragrant, culinary, cosmetic or decorative material sources.

If we choose to accent the use of herbs, then plantings such as salad greens like Salad Burnet, Caraway, Chervil and Chives would be good choices. Or perhaps our favorite teas of Mint, Anise, Lemon Balm and Camomile. Other groups may contain heady spices like Sage, Savory, Basil and Oregano.

We may want to combine herbs useful in floral arrangements using seeds of Dill, Calendula and Borage, or seed pods of Violets, Coriander and Rue, or the bamboo-like stalks of Lovage which, when cut, become cylinders and circles. Flowers from silvery Wormwood form tall backgrounds for sunny buttons of Santolina and spikes of Wooly Betony and mauve-stained Sage.

Some may design a garden that will tell a story using herbs that help recreate historical periods, such as the formal gardens of the Governer's Palace in Colonial Williamsburg, VA, reminiscent of 18th century gardens in Europe and America. Others recreate gardens of historical places such as a reconstructed village: Plymouth Plantation,

Plymouth, MA landscaped in the style of 17th century American dooryard and kitchen gardens, or the Hancock Shaker Village, Pittsfield, MA with replicas of Shaker gardens. Physick gardens contain only medicinal plants. They are abundant today as historical gardens or active centers of research at universities around the world. The University of Washington, Seattle, WA displays hundreds of medicinal herbs in its four acres of formal gardens. Designed in 18th century style is the Pennsylvania Hospital physick garden, Philadelphia, PA, the first American hospital. Often these gardens are used as living laboratories and reference libraries for studies ranging from history and anthropology to biochemistry and pharmacognosy (the study of drugs obtained from nature).

Observing another world from our doorstep is a common desire and choosing ornamental herbs can help achieve that goal. Landscapes using herbs give us gardens embedded in history. We can enter into fantasy among the herbs in our garden. We can enjoy a refreshing patch of grey nestled in light green and see peasants stooping to pick delicate yellow and blue flowers for fragrant herbal potpourris destined for noble courts in Rome and Athens. These herbs are Camomile and Lavender. The market for their flowers remains unchanged since ancient times. In the distance, rolling drifts of purple foliage break against a wall of tall green giants with beaded hair. Brown-skinned workers harvest these crops so they may be consecrated by priests and entombed with pharaohs. These workers are Egyptian slaves harvesting 'Krishna' Basil and Coriander seed.

Some gardeners may simply wish to include a few herbs here and there that they use on occasion, very likely for cooking, such as Thyme, Marjoram, Rosemary, Basil and Sage; simple herbs easily raised and endlessly enjoyed season after season.

There are a few who will choose to design the essence of a dreamworld with fabulously foliaged plants exuding rich and exotic scents, a garden designed to ensorcell, a garden that provokes you to wonder at the beauty of those lifeforms we call herbs. Wandering in this Eden your senses are forever on the verge, but just out of reach, of being satiated by the myriad of miracle plants you can see, touch and smell. Thoughts that at one time kept you from believing in the mystical power of herbs are winnowed from your wonderment by a crafty guide. You leave knowing your hands could also create this dreamworld and all the elixirs of the ancient herbalists. You feel kindred to them.

Fragrance is an important ornamental characteristic. Perfumes, cosmetics, mouth washes and body soaps all conspire to invoke sensual reminiscences by copying the herbal scents of Jasmine, Lavender, Lemon Balm, Lemon Verbena, and Patchouli. Gardens devoted to fragrant foliages and flowers are the most delightful of any that can be designed. Thick and rich herbal odors, sweet and spicy scents seem to resurrect for us our youthful, carefree days and tender memories of moments our hearts had carefully hidden.

You may ask what all that has to do with the ornamental aspects of herbs. *It is the other half to a whole.* You can always buy an ornamental plant but you do not have an herb unless you know its heritage. There are a few fortunate herbs, though planted with no eye to utility, which have qualities that have let them get by as ornamentals; Wormwood, Rue, Germander and Santolina. However, without a use or a history, an herb is usually not an ornamental but a weed.

Landscaping is one of man's proudest pursuits. Its ancient roots are so deep in our history that it has become an integral part of our lives. From time to time changing customs devalue certain plants or artistic forms but the varieties of designs and materials always increase with each new generation of gardeners. Because the garden is a necessary part of our lives we expend a vast amount of effort in making it into something in which we can find our place in nature, appreciate and utilize. Today in our landscapes it is possible to combine the world's most beautiful flowers with the most honorable of all plants, the herbs. A landscape that includes herbs is a constant reminder of how much the kingdom of plants has become a part of our lives.

Next time you are strolling past a neighbor's think about what you are really seeing. In truth it is another world, small and separate from the real world, a wellspring of comfort and passion and security in troubled and unsettled times—a companion. When this other world includes herbs it is a sign that someone has sought beyond the beauty of nature and chosen to interweave a little of the history of man into his living space.

Herbs are more than plants. They simultaneously spice the food we eat and provide our bodies with nutrients vital for healthful living. They scent every minute of our day. They can cure melancholy as well as cancer. They are friends that are growing among the plants in our garden making life more enjoyable and more livable.

Chapter 2 / SECTION 1

The Fragrant Garden

The distinguishing quality of many herbs is their fragrance. Because of their characteristic odors, even after a single encounter, fragrant herbs are never forgotten. Enchanting, arousing, sensational, sublime, erotic, and heavenly are usual descriptions by visitors to fragrant gardens who have for the first time experienced the odors of many common herbs that they can grow in their home garden.

Fragrant plants and herbs enable the home gardener to enjoy a multitude of scents. Lemon scents can be found in Lemon Balm, *Melissa officinalis;* Lemon Verbena, *Aloysia triphylla;* Lemon Grass, *Cymbopogon citratus;* Lemon Thyme, *Thymus* × *citriodorus;* Lemon Geraniums, *Pelargonium limoneum; Eucalyptus maculata* var. *citriodora;* and Mock Orange, *Philadelphus* × *lemoinei.* Pineapple can be had by growing Pineapple Mint, *Mentha suaveolens;* Pineapple Weed, *Chamomilla suaveolens;* Pineapple Sage, *Salvia elegans;* and Mock Orange, *Philadelphus* 'Enchantment'. Minty scents can be enjoyed as shrubs such as Mintbush, *Prosanthera;* American Pennyroyal, *Hedeoma pulegioides;* Bible Leaf *Balsamita major;* Korean Mint, *Agastache rugosa;* and Calamint, *Calamintha nepeta.* The fragrance of Caraway seed can be enjoyed as a garden herb in Caraway Thyme, *Thymus herba-barona.* A clump of Basil provides a sweet cinnamon, ginger or clove scent. Anise scents are produced by Fennel, *Foeniculum vulgare;* Anise Hyssop, *Agastache foeniculum;* Sweet Cicely, *Myrrhis odorata;* and Goldenrod, *Solidago odorata.* These herbs have been a source of the spice of life for untold millions of housewives, peasants and industrious lords and ladies in every century past. What treasures they are, to be able to please so many people for so long. Let them please you too.

Most people become interested in growing fragrant herbs simply because they are traditional herbal scents; Spearmint, Peppermint, Lemon Verbena, Rose, Wintergreen, Lemon Balm, Camomile, Lavender, Rosemary and Ginger. Sometimes a small gift of a potpourri or bouquet carried home from a friend's garden is enough to entice another gardener into growing herbs, if only for their scent. Secreted away in sachets or potpourri jars, collections of dried herbs can enliven and purify the air indoors with just the shake of a hand. It is certainly possible to do the same from a pressurized can filled with an herbal fragrance but not with the same satisfying effect, nor the same sense of self achievement. Because we have grown the herbs ourselves, the room smells of our success as a gardener and herbalist, in the same way that a bright bouquet of dazzling flowers rewards our gardening talents.

More precious than potpourris are the essences of herbs. These are the herb's fragrant oils. They have been extracted and captured in tiny, dram vials. The essences of Rosemary, Pennyroyal, Rose, Clove and Jasmine are but a few. These and many more are used to scent potpourris and sachets, herb pillows, linen, and clothing. For elegant dining, essences can be used to scent tablecloths, napkins, artificial or dried flowers in a bouquet, fingerbowl water and candles. Furniture, drapes and carpets can be scented for special effects. Essences can also be used to scent stationery and writing inks, party costumes, talcum powder and soap, dried arrangements, decorative ornaments, macrame and embroidered fabrics. Commercial products containing herbal scents and flavors include toothpaste, candy, gum, mouthwash, room spray, shampoos, bath powders and cosmetics.

The sweet herbs: Mint, Lavender, Lemon Balm, Sweet Cicely, Rosemary, Costmary, Southernwood, Camomile, Sweet Flag, Santolina and Thyme have been in household use for millenia, primarily in wash waters and for strewing. Strewing herbs were thrown to the floor and trod or sat upon in order to enjoy their fragrance. For wash waters they were enclosed in a cloth bag and steeped in boiling water for a few minutes. The scented water was then used as a rinse water for dustcloths and floor mops. There is no reason to avoid strewing herbs today. Prior to vacuuming, strew your favorite fragrant herb near doorways or in halls, or in bedrooms and baths. Crush the herb underfoot then sweep or vacuum. The scent will cling to carpets and refresh the air for hours, masking the unwanted dusty odor that accompanies vacuuming. Three herbs are recommended: Pennyroyal, Lemon Geranium and Basil. All three are also repellants and may deter fleas from traveling through carpets.

A few herbs are grown for their use in food preparation, added to give a special dish a delicious taste and odor; Basil, Sage, Thyme and Oregano for example. These herbs are easily grown in any garden soil and may be used either fresh or dried. The drying process invariably reduces a significant proportion of the fragrant component of an herb's essence. Fresh herbs should be preserved by freezing them whole in either water or oil or ground into a paste. In the same way an oil will extract a flower's fragrance for perfume, that same desirable chemical fraction will be held in an oil for use in cooking. Freezing will extend the storage life of an oil herb paste indefinitely.

A fragrant herb garden becomes a large perfume vat where scents are mixed by breezes, wafted on the wind to our noses, forever varying. Formulas are being created spontaneously. For the gardener, our whole life's work is not unlike that of a professional perfumer. Careful combinations of several herbal fragrances can create floral perfumes and pockets of single scents that can please and entertain anyone. In a fragrant garden, we can see all the components of our perfume vat. We can amble along and touch them, call them into life as they are needed.

There are a few steadfast guidelines to follow and this chapter will present them for you to consider next time you have a new plant in hand and wonder where to place it in the landscape. First, the highly fragrant herbs should be used as magnets, to draw attention to less spectacular herbs. To design a garden that projects an aroma that is self-generating and inviting we need to use those few herbs that provide remarkable results: Lavender, Sage, Mint, Rosemary, Camomile, Basil, Coriander, Wormwood, Southernwood and Savory. Thyme is indeed fragrant but not without crushing the leaves. So too are Catnip, Monarda, Anise, Costmary and most of the common herbs.

One approach to planning a fragrant magnet is mixing herbs of similar fragrance for a combined effect that is more intense that any individual herb by itself. In this case, anise-scented herbs such as Fennel, Sweet Cicely and Chervil may be grouped to join forces, producing a penetrating fragrance noticeable at some distance. Another approach uses an intensely fragrant herb in a grouping of many others, such as a border of daisy-like flowers of *Celmisia, Anthemis* and *Senecio* alternated with clumps of German Camomile.

Plant fragrant herbs as the focal point of a garden feature. (Fig. 1) Once visitors have discovered the whereabouts of the inviting scent, the handling begins, and sometimes never stops. Making sampling worthwhile is important for it encourages further handling. This, of course, multiplies the aroma, making the stop worthwhile. It is here that other aromatic plants and herbs are planted, ones with equally surprising fragrances but a bit more secre-

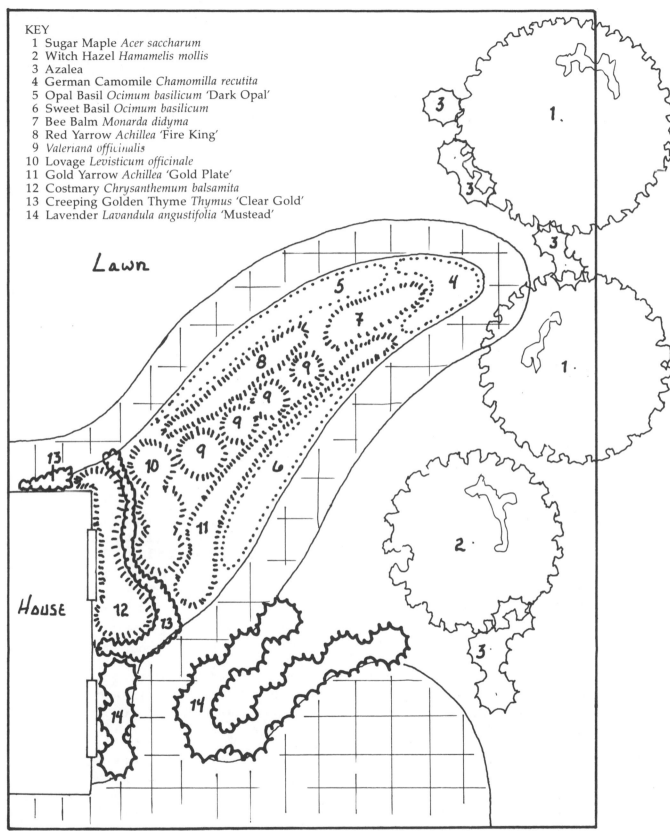

KEY
1 Sugar Maple *Acer saccharum*
2 Witch Hazel *Hamamelis mollis*
3 Azalea
4 German Camomile *Chamomilla recutita*
5 Opal Basil *Ocimum basilicum* 'Dark Opal'
6 Sweet Basil *Ocimum basilicum*
7 Bee Balm *Monarda didyma*
8 Red Yarrow *Achillea* 'Fire King'
9 *Valeriana officinalis*
10 Lovage *Levisticum officinale*
11 Gold Yarrow *Achillea* 'Gold Plate'
12 Costmary *Chrysanthemum balsamita*
13 Creeping Golden Thyme *Thymus* 'Clear Gold'
14 Lavender *Lavandula angustifolia* 'Mustead'

Lawn

House

Fig. 1. A fragrant garden using the most fragrant herbs for a self generating scent. A short cut is provided by a ground hugging mat of Creeping Thyme (13) that clambers over and around stepping stones.

tive about showing them.

Walking close to a fence along which Fennel is grown as a screen, the fragrance of anise is apparent. If Fennel is mixed with Camomile, Catnip and annual pinks in the sun, or Violets, Primroses and Mint in partial shade, the scent is divine. Surround small gardens with a border of fragrant herbs by using a frame of Lavender, Basil, German Camomile or Santolina. A circular frame of Chives, with purple globes cavorting about in the air, is a dramatic strategy for a simple arrangement of fragrant plants in a small yard.

Second, for the best results fragrant herbs must be located in strategic spots and planted where they can be touched. Pockets of fragrant herbs should be located close to leisure areas such as paths, barbeque pits, patios, home entrances, entrances from the street or driveway, around gates, swings, home foundations or in pass-throughs of fences and hedges within the landscape. These are places where a visitor may chance to brush the foliage of nearby herbs or stop to take a deeper breath of a scent on the wind. Plants we can brush past and caress fondly with our hands or feet, filling the air with their freshness, is what a fragrant garden is all about.

The highly fragrant herbs should be the primary elements of an entrance design. (Fig. 2) Patios, porches and doorways provide many alternatives for the lover of fragrant herbs. These are areas where people stop to admire your gardens, move about leisurely and rest for a moment, enjoying the scents that come their way.

For the simple open and uncluttered porch, low, mounded perennial and annual berbs are best. They should be placed at the junctions of the incoming walks. Contrasting foliage may be added according to the demands of the landscape design. But the overall design should take into account that the most fragrant herbs should be placed adjacent to the walks and porch edges where they will be brushed and handled. Steps leading up to the porch are candidates for those herbs that can be planted in the cracks or to the side that creep in and out and are trod upon, releasing an inviting aroma. Along the porch, low bushes that do not obstruct the view of the garden but still provide some cover for those sitting on the porch are needed: Lavender, Southernwood, Santolina, Rosemary, Sage and Wormwood are examples.

If a walk leads to the street or sidewalk, a procession of these fragrant herbs should flow with it, extending part way down the walk for an enjoyable entrance theme. At the sidewalk, Wormwood or Winter Savory, both neatly trimmed and contrasted with low growing junipers, and a ground cover of bark or gravel, provide a fragrant welcome for those approaching from the street. A popular, living ground cover is the blue-flowered *Nepeta mussinii*, a dwarf species of Catnip. Moderately low herbs should be planted near the driveway, punctuating the entrance that will be used by guests arriving by car. The evergreen herbs Southernwood, Wormwood, Santolina, and Bush or Creeping Thymes are appropriate.

Fragrant herbs can also make a rewarding gatestop. (Fig. 3) Whether planted around the gate post, in the path of the swinging gate door, or in a direct line of foot traffic, they will release cheery notes of fragrance to anyone entering. Guests will go out of their way to use such a splendid entrance precisely because of the regaling greeting. Useful herbs for this gate stop task are Lavender, Hyssop, Santolina, Sage and Winter Savory. They all form dense clumps of woody parts that can handle rough useage quite well but can be pruned at any time to keep a neat and trim appearance. For heavy gates it is wise to drive a stake close to the center of the clump where the gate is required to stop. A few non-woody herbs for this use are the Mints, Lemon Balm, Costmary and Roman Camomile. A Rosemary standard in a heavy pot can also be used. Fragrant vines of Jasmine and Honeysuckle, *Lonicera*, growing along the gate door or over it in an arch add heavy floral scents to the gate stopper's contribution each time the gate is used.

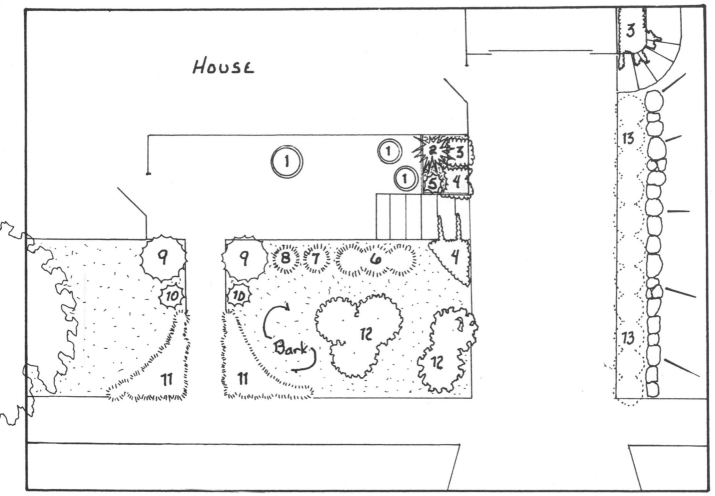

Fig. 2. Entrance ways cloaked in fragrant herbs and a patio surrounded by highly scented plants for an enjoyable rest stop.

KEY
  1 potted herbs
  2 *Thuya orientalis*
  3 Oregano Thyme *Thymus pulegioides* 'Oregano-scented'
  4 Cr. Red Thyme *Thymus pulegioides* 'Kermesinus'
  5 Southernwood *Artemisia abrotanum*
  6 Lemon Balm *Melissa officinalis*
  7 Peppermint Geranium *Pelargonium tomentosum*
  8 Variegated Lemon Balm
  9 Lavender *Lavandula angustifolia* 'Hidcote'
 10 Dwarf Lavender *Lavandula angustifolia* 'Nana'
 11 Dwarf Catnip *Nepeta mussinii*
 12 Grey Birch *Betula populifolia*
 13 German Camomile/bulbs/Calendula

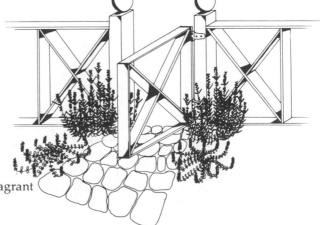

Fig. 3. Gate entrance that entertains the visitor with fragrant herbs Lavender and Thyme as the door is opened.

Back doors, kitchen doors and patios have a need of a special group of fragrant herbs: the Mints, Artemisias, Fennel, Lovage, Lemon Balm, Lavender, Camomile and Chives. Since most herbs are grown to be used as samples and simples, all of these provide household potions and necessities. The Mints and Camomiles for teas and cool drinks, icings and candies. Fennel, Lovage and Chives find their way into virtually every meal whether a salad, a soup, main course or dessert. Lavender, Lemon Balm and the *Artemisias* such as Wormwood, Southernwood and White Mugwort become indispensable scents for room deodorizers, baths and washwaters.

Along frequently used paths, fragrant herbs may be featured as borders or mass plantings. (Fig. 4) Mass plantings should be located on curves or junctions of paths where a pause in the stroll is customary. Borders should feature a mixture of the most colorful and fragrant herbs. In general both sides of a path should have an identical fragrant planting for the fullest effect. In a small garden, this may be impractical as well as limiting the number of fragrant herbs that can be employed. Matched borders of mixed species at either side of a path are attractive and an ideal solution to limited space problems. Along curving walks from the public sidewalk to the main entrance of a home, a line on both sides with mixed fragrant herbs adds an inviting aromatic note in any landscape. The changing foliage, colors, and the coming and going of flowers ensures an entertaining arrangement the year around.

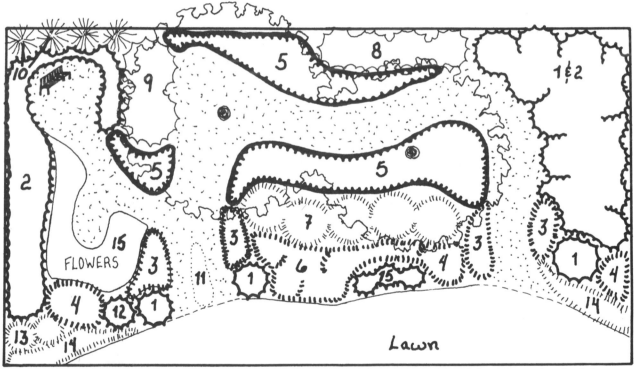

Fig. 4. Massed plantings for self-generated fragrant airs and a dazzling array of colorful flowers for an enchanting garden.

KEY

1 Lavender *Lavendula angustifolia* 'Hidcote'
2 *Santolina chamaecyparissus*
3 Bible Leaf *Balsamita major*
4 *Valeriana officinalis*
5 Florists' Violet *Viola odorata*
6 herbaceous perennials
7 Sweet Cicely *Myrrhis odorata*
8 Rhododendron
9 Rhododendron
10 Mock Orange *Philadelphus* sp.
11 German Camomile *Chamomilla recutita*
12 Southernwood *Artemisia abrotanum*
13 *Astilbe* spp.
14 Scented Geraniums *Pelargomium* spp.
15 Fragrant annuals

The third guideline for planting highly fragrant herbs in the landscape is to use containers. (Figures 8, 28 and 51) For over 8 centuries Venetian housewives have nurtured thriving gardens in simple clay pots on slender balconies overlooking the canals. Then, as today, fragrant herbs were used to purify and mask unwanted odors in the air that entered the house. Containers are practical because they can be carried wherever a certain scent is desired. Windows should be graced with fragrant plants, either in a garden or in a container such as a window box. Window boxes were most popular during the 17th and 18th centuries. Flowers and fragrant herbs such as Mignonette, Violets, Gilliflowers (the Carnations and Pinks), Basil, Camomile, Scented Geraniums, Dwarf Lavender and Mints were grown.

Containers have always been used in landscaping to accent a particular plant. Fragrant turf seat covers of Roman Camomile were a medieval treat. Other mat-forming herbs such as Thyme and Corsican Mint were also used. One container is asking a lot of any scented plant, so to be effective it must not only be highly fragrant but also easy to grow and hardy. The Mock Orange and Lime are classic examples of a single plant used to scent a small courtyard or secluded patio. Whether the container used to emphasize a fragrant plant is a fashionable urn, window box, turfed seat or hanging planter, several herbs are quite suitable: Roman or German Camomile, Lavender, Rosemary, Basil, several Mints, Pennyroyal, Calamint and the Jasmines. (Figures 12 and 50)

A fourth guideline for planting a fragrant garden is to use fragrant herbs as prominent borders, hedges, ground covers or screens. A border is a general term implying a demarcation in the landscape using plant materials. Borders are used on edges of open areas such as lawns and patios. They are used as a frame around gardens or as a line of foliage paralleling paths and fences. The term "hedge" refers to the use of woody perennials. Hedges are commonly used for major divisions between garden patterns within the landscape.

Often a tall dense border will achieve the same screening effect as a fence. A living screen, which implies a background border plant that is over 3 ft. high and used to hide something from view, provides a natural barrier in the landscape. Maintenance of an herbaceous screen, one that is gone in winter months, is far less demanding than hedges of evergreen or espaliered plants. During the growing season, little or no pruning is needed to keep the screen looking neat and natural. Herbs that make useful fragrant screens are the herbaceous perennials: Tansy, Giant Alliums, White Mugwort, Fennel, Meadowsweet, *Filipendula ulmaria,* and Valerian.

Ground covers are one of the most popular uses of fragrant herbs. New varieties are steadily being developed labeled "mat-forming" or "procumbent". They can immediately be put to use as ground covers. A thin crack between bricks or stones in a path will accommodate many. Under or amidst larger plants and in open expanses, these low-growing forms will spread into one another to create dense covers, from knee-deep to thinner than the sole of a shoe. Consider a fragrant ground cover effective when an acceptable scent comes naturally to passersby. Increase the number of plants or the area involved as necessary. For most fragrant herbs, 25 sq. ft., a patch 5 × 5 ft., is a minimum and many patches should approach 100 sq. ft. if a dominating scent is desired in the landscape.

A fifth guideline in landscaping with fragrant plants is to assist them in their task of releasing an identifiable scent by taking advantage of air currents. (Figures 5A, 5B and 5C) Before any landscaping is begun, the prevailing wind directions should be determined. Wind breaks and shade plants are designed into the landscape from this data. Slowing or stopping winter winds, but not sunlight, keeps a home warmer with less energy. Directing summer breezes to where we want them will cool outdoor leisure areas as well as funnel fragrant air from special beds. If possible, they must be directed to perform in a reliable manner, such as generating a wind through a breezeway or trapping warm air with an

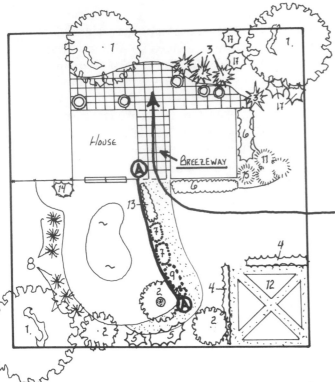

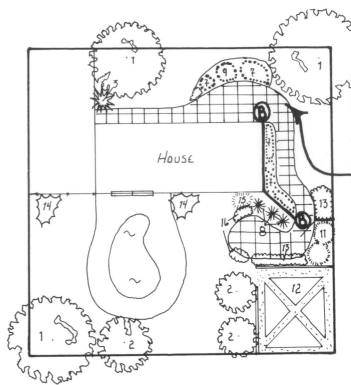

Fig. 5A. Direct breezes along a screen AA and through a breezeway to front patio. A paved patio warmed by the sun assists in drawing a parcel of air toward it through the breezeway.

Fig. 5B. A gate at the upwind edge of the screen BB forces wind down the beds to where it is wanted. Wind currents breeching the screen become turbulent passing over and pick up more scents from foliage while delayed over the warmed patio.

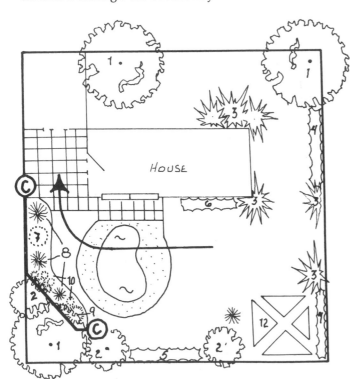

Fig. 5C. Shrubbery and trees upwind direct breezes toward the house and courtyard. A hot driveway beyond is effective in drawing a breeze through the courtyard.

KEY
 1 Fl Cherry *Prunus* sp.
 2 Dwarf Apple *Malus* spp.
 3 *Juniperus horizontalis*
 4 Holly *Ilex aquifolia*
 5 Barberry *Berberis darwinii*
 6 Yew *Taxus*
 7 Fragrant annuals
 8 Roses
 9 Carnation *Dianthus*
10 Basils *Ocimum basilicum*
11 *Valeriana officinalis*
12 KITCHEN GARDEN
13 Roman Camomile *Chamaemellum nobile* var. *florepleno*
14 Southernwood *Artemisia abrotanum*
15 Lemon Balm *Melissa officinalis*
16 Oregano Thyme *Thymus pulegioides* 'Oregano-scented'
17 Azaleas

enclosed patio. The task is not simple and often not possible due to existing vegetation or predicted interference from plants growing in neighboring yards. It is best to design for the prevailing winds of the summer months, the time of year that most fragrant plants abound. Wind direction may change throughout the seasons so be thoughtful about where a screen might be best put to use.

In the landscape, wind screens of living hedges create turbulence, divert breezes and stir foliage gently, helping it release its scent. Upon encountering a barrier, the flow of air will rise creating turbulence on either side. On the leeward side of a fence, a parcel of air is trapped, warmed slightly, and given a chance to pick up more of a fragrance and hold it longer. If the fence sits at a slight angle to the wind's direction of travel, the breeze turns and follows the fence, picking up any odors from foliage planted along it. Obstacles upwind can be added to stop the wind from moving in that direction also, such as a slight cant to the tip of the fence or shrubbery.

At the downwind side, we must give the wind a chance to move freely away or if possible, to draw it along. A breezeway may be designed into the home through which fragrant air will be vented. In the front garden a large entrance patio of stone will act as a hot spot to help draw air through the breezeway. Foliage planted along the perimeter of the patio will slow incoming winds from other directions. During the summer months, delicious scents winnow through the breezeway and across the patio, providing enjoyment as well as entertainment. Large areas of concrete, patios of brick, sand or gravel, driveways, or expanses of lawn unshaded by trees, create warm surfaces that help drive a breeze. Hot air rising from these areas must be replaced by nearby air currents and it is those we have diverted to move in this direction. Sunny spots also give the warmer air an opportunity to extract more odor-producing substances from any herbs within its bounds.

To better enjoy fragrant plants let's look at some of the volatiles that we perceive as odors released by both flowers and foliage. Although the term fragrance is easily defined it is extremely difficult to identify the chemicals we are smelling. It is even more difficult to categorize herbs or flowers by their odor. Many produce several fragrant compounds. The Mint family is a good example of a multitude of odors, from subtle apple to spicy lime, yet all are only overtones to the predominant mint scent. As an example, in the essence of Peppermint, *Mentha* $\times$ *piperita,* are the spicy, mint-scented chemicals menthol and menthone as well as pinene and eucalyptol, which have a camphoraceous scent.

The herbs discussed in this book will be given an odor classification according to Table 3. This is intended for those who have never had an opportunity to sniff a particular herb and may be curious. The herbs were chosen to be representative of the odor of the fragrance chemicals listed. Chemicals are mentioned in the text for each herb if they are known so that a better understanding of the fragrance of an herb is possible. A table certainly does not substitute for the real adventure, but it may spark curiosity.

A fragrance is merely one component in a plant's arsenal of chemicals that protect and defend it. An herb releases a fragrance as a measure to ensure its reproductive success. Like petal colors, flower odors attract pollinators—moths, flies, butterflies, wasps and many birds. On the other hand, fragrant foliages act as cautionary signs to animals indicating that this plant is not to be nibbled. Quite often these foliages have a disagreeable taste reinforcing the signal to browsers and grazers.

Two such chemicals that have ulterior motives are camphor, produced by some of the Artemisias, and methylepijasmonate, the major scent-producing chemical in the flowers of Jasmine. Camphor is allelopathic. It is an herbicide that when washed to the ground, effectively kills germinating seeds around the plant, thus eliminating herbaceous competition. Methylepijasmonate is one of the most highly regarded fragrant chemicals. It is a scent particularly attractive to many flying insects. Although man does not resemble a bug in any

Table 3
Odor Classification and Chemicals Responsible for Some Herbal Fragrances

Odor Class	Fragrance Chemicals	Herb
SPICY	Asarole	Ginger
	Anethol	Anise
	Carvone	Caraway
	Cinnamonaldehyde	Cinnamon
	Citral, Citronellal	Lemon Balm
	Cuminal	Cumin
	Eugenol	Clove
	Fenchone, Chavicol	Fennel
	Farnesol	Lime
	Limonene	Pineapple Mint
	Menthol, Menthone, Piperitone	Pepper Mint
	Methylsalicylate	Wintergreen
	Myrcene	Hop
	Pulegone	Pennyroyal
	Cymene, Terpinene, Linalool*	
CAMPHORACEOUS	Pinene	Hyssop
	Camphor, Borneol	Rosemary
	Thujone, Eucalyptol	Sage
	Thymol	Thyme
	Farnescene, Cedral, Bisabolol*	
FLORAL	Azulene, Chamazulene	Camomile
	Geraniol	Rose
	Irone	Violet
	Methylepijasmonate	Jasmine
	Phenylethylalcohol, Benzyl acetate*	
HERBACEOUS	Carvacrol	Oregano
	Coumarin	Woodruff, Hay
	Phenylacetic acid	Honey
	Umbeliferone, Phellandrene, Ionone*	
ALLIACEOUS	Allyldisulfide, allicin	Garlic

*Not found in sufficient quantity to impart its odor to a specific herb.

way, human chemistry also utilizes this attractant scent. We do not understand it, but the fragrance apparently evolved over many millions of years to lure and is so successful that even man finds these scents enticing, and uncommonly attractive often to the point of being sensually arousing.

There are also many herbs that contain fragrant and tasty chemicals for us to enjoy when we eat. When we use an herb in cooking some of its fragrance is lost immediately. We can smell it. Yet some is retained in the fat and oil of the concoction before us. What is most important is to retain the true fragrance and flavor of the herb by harvesting, preserving and storing it in the best way possible. We know this is not always possible. In many cases we are accustomed to the odor and taste of the herb only in its preserved state. Odor chemicals are odoriferous simply because they are volatile, that is they are easily released to the air from the plant material. To enjoy these special aromas, evident only at harvest, careful procedures

Plate 1

Harvest of gold. Ornamental herbs from the garden for decoration. Flowers of Lavender Cotton, Feverfew, Calendula and Green Santolina.

ELECAMPANE

" Excellent herbs had our fathers of old—
Excellent herbs to ease our pain—
Alexander and Marigold,
Eyebright, Orris and Elecampane,
Basil, Rocket, Valerian, Rue,
(Almost singing themselves they run),
Vervain, Dittany, Call-me-to-you—
Cowslip, Melilot, Rose of the Sun.
    Anything green that grew out of the mould
    Was an excellent herb to our fathers of old.
                                RUDYARD KIPLING.

In no haven other than an herb garden can reading be pursued with more enjoyment especially when true scents can be called forth to supplement fine poetry.

Fragrant magnet of Valerian in the center square in a formal garden, Medicinal Herb Garden, Univ. of Washington, Seattle, WA.

Fragrant magnet in dooryard design using 'Cinnamon Basil (lower right) at waist level where it is accessible to hands and Roman Camomile (center) that signals its presence from a turf seat that doubles as the raised bed's frame.

Luring the visitor to closer inspection in a fragrant garden is Southernwood. Here where a path encounters a perennial bed the garden also displays Ginger Mint and Oregano (in bloom behind).

Plate 2

Fragrant frame of spicy 'Dark Opal' Basil around a bed of fragrant Roses at the home of Irving Scherer, Chehalis, WA.

Fragrant herbs jutting into a rocky pathway where they will be brushed by passersby. Blue and pink Hyssop, Creeping Savory, Roman Camomile and Thyme are visible.

German Camomile lounging on a walk where it will be stepped on, releasing its apple scent to the entire yard.

Wooly Thyme plunging over a precipice just behind a sitting chair at the home of Michele Nash, Mercer Island, WA.

Fragrant gate stop of *Santolina* 'Nana'.

Entrance theme from driveway. Evergreens, Southernwood, Lemon Balm, Creeping Thyme, Dwarf Catnip and Violets decorate this compact feature.

must be followed to retain more volatile chemicals as well as preventing others from degenerating during storage.

There are countless ways to preserve herbs: candy, cheese, vinegar, butter and, of course, drying are most common. Which is best? Let's find out. First, it must be remembered that the volatile, odoriferous chemicals are for the most part not water soluble. Dropping them into hot stew will be quite rewarding but only briefly. Preserving the herb in oil and cooking at a low heat for a short period ensures the trapping of aromatic chemicals.

Second, most herbal aromas are not single chemicals but conglomerations of several or more. During preservation some are lost and others, that are more stable, become prominent. Take, for example, the ripening of Coriander seed. When picked slightly green, it is spicy but muted by a heavy waxy odor. When fully ripe its scent is sharp, spicy and sweet. The task before every gardener of herbs is to experiment with different methods of preservation to determine how you like your herbs stored in order to yield the aroma you enjoy the most.

Third, pick no herb before its time. That is very easy for me to say but I am the first to violate this principle by slipping out of my kitchen any day of the year to snip off a piece of fresh herb. Nothing can compare. Not even the best stored product. But to be sure that the material being stored is at its very best, know when to harvest it. Taste it. Smell it. Dry a little and see if it's bitter or musty. When it smells the way you want it to, harvest it. To give you a little help there are three rules of thumb. 1) Never harvest when water or dew are on the plant. They must be air dry. You may have to compromise with the weather on this one. 2) Harvest before the heat of the day. Transpiration reduces the levels of an undetermined number of the herb's constituents during the late afternoon. Never harvest (for storage) in the evening. 3) Harvest just prior to blooming.

Some of the chemicals stored are attractants for pollinators, they are pleasing to us as well as bugs, and they are present in their highest concentration prior to and during blooming. However, once an herb blooms other chemical changes occur that often decrease the quality of its fragrance and interfere with its storage ability. Let's take Basil as an example. The fresh herb is highly fragrant, but exceedingly so just prior to blooming. More than 15 chemicals are responsible for the aroma of Basil as you smell it out in the garden. Basil produces some chemicals that attract pollinators; they are concentrated on the flowering tops, on bracts and calyxes. Chemicals that repel flying insects are found on leaves and stems, while other repellant chemicals on leaves taste badly, inhibiting chewing insects. Many other fragrant chemicals that are part of the herb's machinery for life are exuded along with water during periods of rapid transpiration in late afternoon. This process can be rapid enough to cause wilting on hot sunny afternoons.

Basil is best harvested at midday and in mid-to late summer when its flowers have just opened. Flower tops are included because of their contribution of floral and sweetly spiced scents. But to fully preserve all of these chemicals there is little to do but freeze the harvested material. This is a costly option. Second to that is pesto. Although, if you do not choose to entertain recipes that call for pesto, because of the cheese (milk-free diets) or salt (low-sodium diets), the best preservation method is an oil paste.

Let's discuss some of the ways to preserve herbs. Table 4 shows the four basic types of preservation. In decreasing order of energy requirement they are freezing, solvents, absorbents and drying. Each is accompanied by specific methods.

Freezing requires considerable energy. Freeze dried herbs are essentially a commercial product only. Storing whole herbs in air-tight containers in the home freezer is the most satisfactory way of preserving the true nature of an herb. However, it is costly and worth the expense for only two herbs, French Tarragon and Lemon Verbena. Loss of volatiles still occurs but at a reduced rate. Storage is limited to 6–8 months. Freezer storage is valuable

Table 4
Methods of Preserving Herbs

High Energy ⟶ *Low Energy*

FREEZING	: Freeze Dried		Freezer Storage
SOLVENT	: Alcohol, Vegetable oil, Vinegar, Cheese, Butter, Syrup		
ABSORBENT	: Sugar		Salt
DRYING	: Oven	Microwave	Air

Low Energy

only to those who enjoy a refreshing cup of herb tea. Make your herb blends for teas before freezing. Go so far as to put the materials in tea bags (which provide extra protection). Herbs that must be preserved this way to yield a true off-the-plant flavor and fragrance are German Camomile, Catnip, Fennel, Sweet Cicely, Anise, Lemon Verbena, Mint, Anise Hyssop, Calamint, Chervil, Lemon Balm and Pineapple Sage.

The Solvent method offers the widest variety of options. Alcohol preservation is least common because of the cost and limited culinary use. It is an excellent method to extract fragrant oils and volatiles from herbs however. Most, if not all, alcohol products are in fact already herbally flavored. Rosemary, Mint, Thyme and the green seeds of Sweet Cicely, Lovage, Anise and Fennel are preserved nicely in whiskey or Vermouth for use in marinades, candies, mixed drinks and punch.

Vinegar is used for certain salad and marinade herbs such as Basil, Tarragon, Savory, Rosemary, Sweet Marjoram and Garlic Chives. Use only distilled white vinegar and do not use wet material or too much. A vinegar extraction is strengthened by repeated changes for fresh material. It may be necessary to filter the vinegar to keep it clear.

Cheese is a solvent of sorts. It contains many fats, sugars and oils that can retain a significant proportion of an herb's chemical signature. Of course, the cheese itself has a major influence on the product. Cream cheese, Brie, Mozarella and other soft mild cheeses are best to blend with fresh herbs. Allow some period of aging, 1 week to 10 days, before using. The shelf life is usually less than 1–2 months. Herbs are either folded into the cheese or blended at low speed.

An herb butter can effectively preserve an herb for several months. Fresh herbs are chopped, or better yet, blended into butter (margarine for milk-free diets) in a ratio of 1 Tbsp. herb to 2 Tbsp. butter. Heat the mixture to boiling and simmer for 8–10 minutes. Pour into a mold and refrigerate. The mixture will separate, yielding a colored top layer that retains the herb's fragrant signature. This layer is good for spreads and pastries. The herb-rich bottom layer is good for stews, soups and basting broths. Powdered herbs can also be used. Mix them 1:4.

Preserving herbs in vegetable oil is another choice method for retaining natural freshness. For dishes such as salad dressings, oriental stir-fries, gravy and sauces or marinades, the oil method proves this point. The bite of Basil, mellow richness of Tarragon and sweet perfection of Sweet Marjoram remains intact. Mix fresh herbs 4:1 and puree in a blender. Use soybean, sesame, peanut or safflower oils. A little sugar and salt can be added to extend shelf life, preserve color and to some extent, extract fragrant oils. Ascorbic acid (Vitamin C) can also be added to extend shelf life and preserve color. Use ½ teaspoon of each to 1 pint of puree. This product should be refrigerated, and has a shelf life of 3–4 months (without additives) or up to 6 months (with salt and/or ascorbic acid).

When using solvent methods to preserve do not overlook the advantage of herb blends. Not only can remarkable products emerge but some extra shelf life will result when herbs such as Basil, Sage, Savory, Rosemary and Thyme are added. These herbs all confer some antimicrobial activity to herb mixtures. Favorite recipes can be made more quickly by having the herb mixture at hand in oil or butter form, such as for soups and stews.

Herb syrups are in essence the same as fruit syrups. Sugar becomes the preserving material. Herbs are prepared by using either an infusion (steeping herbs in boiled water for 5–10 minutes) or a decoction (bringing herbs and water to a boil and simmering for 5–10 minutes). A little sugar (1 tsp. per cup) may be added to facilitate extraction of aromatic oils. The strained liquid is then converted to a syrup by adding 2 c. of sugar per cup of liquid and boiling to desired consistency. Mint Syrup is most famous but Basil, Ginger and Violet Syrup are just as easily prepared.

Sugar and salt are absorbent materials that trap volatile chemicals. Layer herbs and either absorbent in pint jars and seal tightly. Salt preserves for a longer period of time but is not as useful for those on salt restricted diets. Sugar, flavored by Lemon Verbena, Lemon Balm, Rosemary, Mint, Scented Geraniums, Lemon or 'Krishna' Basil and Chervil is excellent for cookies, pastries, oriental cuisine and teas.

Drying is the most popular method of preserving herbs. Air drying removes about 80% of a plant's moisture and is used for large volumes of material. Oven drying can remove up to 90% although its main advantage is to dry a small amount of herbs quickly. A microwave oven can be used to dry a minute amount of herb extremely quickly.

Air drying should be done in the shade. Herbs producing seeds are bound and covered by paper bags which are then hung under eves or on a covered porch. Check them periodically for dryness. Oven drying is accomplished with either a wire screen to hold plucked leaves or a rack of slim dowling for whole plants. The latter yields a coarse product that may require cleaning to remove stems before use. Three temperature levels are used in this book to indicate how warm an oven should be to adequately dry a specific herb: Low 80–90°F, Medium 90–110°F, and High 110–140°F. It is not practical to offer an average drying time for all herbs but expect oven drying to require from 4 to 12 hours. A convection oven will usually halve the drying time.

The microwave oven is useful for drying very small amounts (1 teaspoon to a few tablespoons) of an herb for either immediate use or simply because no more can be harvested. A gardener cultivating only one French Thyme does not need to spend 2–4 hours drying a handful when 10 minutes in a microwave will suffice. In addition, some recipes, particularly something quick, call for powdered herbs as opposed to whole fresh herbs. When no dried herb is available the microwave comes to the rescue with dried material that is easily powdered in no time at all.

When using a microwave to dry herbs be sure to place them on a paper towel. Do not cover them. Give branches room to wilt so that they do not cross. Set the microwave on *Defrost*. Do not use a normal setting unless the oven is designed to handle dehydration. Most fresh herbs require from 8–15 minutes on defrost to dry fully. Resetting for successive 3–5 minute periods is recommended so neither the herb nor the oven is overheated. Microwave dried Chives, Lemon Balm, Calamint, Savory, Rosemary and French Thyme are superior to the radiant-oven dried product.

Let's take a look at some of the world's most fragrant herbs; evergreen herbs such as Creeping Thyme, Roman Camomile, Creeping Rosemary and Lavender; semievergreen shrubs such as Wormwood, Creeping Savory and Southernwood; herbaceous perennials Valerian, Mint and Fennel; vines of Jasmine; and annuals German Camomile, Coriander and Basil.

Chapter 2 / SECTION 2

Herbs for a Fragrant Garden

Many of the most popular fragrant ground covers come from the Thyme family. Creeping Thyme comes in many forms to suit all tastes and fit all designs. They all tend to grow more densely if heavily pruned in early spring and a sunny, warm niche is necessary for a full fragrance. Although their flowering periods vary it is their most fragrant period and must not be discouraged. Masses of Thyme flower spikes, however, create a traffic jam of bees and butterflies so beware of planting them in leisure areas if you are not a fan of bees, or they of you.

Some Creeping Thymes produce an abundance of fertile seed that may be sown along sidewalks or between steps or paving stones. An easy tool for simplifying the transfer of seedlings to the garden walk is a seed tray composed of a dozen parallel troughs, ⅜ in. wide and ¾ in. deep. Slender rows of well rooted, healthy plants, one seedling to the inch, may be transplanted directly into the cracks between paving stones or steps using this technique.

A mixture of more than two species is best, as it provides more color and foliage contrast as well as a margin of safety in any one spot. Combinations always appear to be wrestling in a confusion of intermingling colors in joyful pursuit of one another. If kept trimmed in early spring with a lawn mower set high, cultivars of *T. praecox* and *T. pulegioides* form dense mats valuable for the fragrant mead. Do not forget to plant a significant quantity of spring and fall bulbs along with Creeping Thyme covers to produce a year round show of color and fragrance.

The genus *Thymus* is easily the most confusing of all the culinary herbs. Over 150 species, varieties, and cultivars exist world-wide and taxonomic data is difficult to find or interpret. The classification used for Thyme in this text is based on the fabulous work of Harriet Flannery, *A Study of the Taxa of Thymus Cultivated in the United States.*

The Creeping Thymes covered in this discussion are: Moroccan Thyme, *T. brousonetti*; Tuffeted Thyme, *T. caespititius*; Caraway Thyme, *T. herba-barona*; Peter Davis Thyme, *T. leucotrichus*; Mother-of-Thyme, *T. pulegioides*; and Wild Thyme, *T. praecox* ssp. *arcticus*. Several Thymes have only cultivar designations. Those discussed here are 'Clear Gold', 'Doone Valley', 'Linear Leaf Lilac' and 'Long Leaf Gray'. There are an unlimited number of discrepancies in popular nomenclature. For example, the legendary *T. serpyllum* is rarely cultivated and is unknowingly represented (or substituted for) by *T. pulegioides* or *T. praecox*. *T. nummularius* is invariably *T. pulegioides*. Of those Thymes that have no species designation, 'Long Leaf Gray' is sold as *T. glabrous loevyanus*, *T. lanicaulis* and *T. thracicus*, while 'Linear Leaf Lilac' is sold as either *T. panonnicus* or *T. marshallianus* (Marshall Thyme).

In order to assist you in choosing a Creeping Thyme to experiment with, those discussed here will be separated by approximate height into two categories: prostrate (less than 3 in. and rooting along branches at nodes) and mounding (forming either procumbent or decumbent spreading mounds over 3 in. high). Procumbent (branches lying flat on the ground) and decumbent (branch tips ascending) habits do not always root at every node, but at the branch ends.

Several handsome prostrate Creeping Thymes are widely available from herb growers. In general, these are less then 3 in. high, including flowering stems: *T. caespititius* and its cultivar 'Tuffet', and *T. praecox ssp. arcticus* and its cultivars 'Mayfair', 'White Moss', 'Pink Chintz', 'Coccineus', 'Languinosus', and 'Halls Wooly'.

The prostrate Creeping Thymes are characterized by tiny leaves, compact habit, and dense mats that are scarcely higher than the pebbles they may find themselves growing among. The most popular are *T. praecox* ssp. *articus* 'White Moss', with shiny, green leaves, and 'Languinosus', or Wooly Thyme, with exceedingly hairy leaves and stems. They grow no higher than the thickness of stem and leaves as they creep along in hot, sunny sites. They are tough herbs that can take considerable traffic and as such, are perfect for dampening footfalls on stony ground. Such a heavenly soft walk is also fragrant as these two Thymes release their aromas when crushed. 'Languinosus', with its fuzzy, grey-green leaves, is not hardy in damp soils during winter months so should be grown in a well drained, sandy soil in full sun or partial shade. In the latter it tends to thicken into a fluffy 2 in. carpet but loses its resilience to foot traffic. 'Halls Wooly' is quite similar to 'Languinosus', growing as a somewhat thicker blanket but it is highly regarded for its prolific flower production.

Two other highly ornamental and pancake-thin ornamental Creeping Thymes of this subspecies are 'Pink Chintz' and 'Coccineus'. They display prominent pink and magenta flowers on shiny, dark green mats of exceptional beauty. These two herbs look their best slithering among fissures in rocks or paving, their flowers crowding the cracks so colorfully at bloomtime it is as if someone had spilled cherry frosting in the garden. Add to this their delicious Thyme aroma and it's an experience you will want to share with everyone.

T. Praecox ssp. *articus* 'Mayfair' also has an admirable, dark green foliage but it has butter-yellow spots on some leaves, in no regular pattern, that often engulf entire leaves yet avoid others completely. In some cases, a whole branch is dressed in gold with nary a spot of green. 'Mayfair' has a splendid, thick garment of rose in midsummer.

As its name implies, *T. caespititius* is caespitose. Rather than quickly spreading it stops to form small tuffets or mounds; the cultivar 'Tuffet' decidedly so. This striking habit and its light green, needle-like leaves make it an uncommonly beautiful Creeping Thyme for open rocky areas, dry bed streams, as a border in knots and parterres or part of a contemporary feature. Not only does this Thyme look better emerging from a sandy bed, it grows and spreads faster. In average garden soil, use ½–1 in. layer of sand where it is to grow.

'Doone Valley' is best described as a harlequin Thyme because of its uncertain origin, fleeting lemon scent, splashy colors (glossy, dark green leaves with some branch tips dipped in gold), its summer cloak of rose-purple so thick the plant is barely visible, and the shedding of its golden variegation in the summer. This prostrate mat is temperamental about soils, particularly damp ones, so during winter a layer of sand will help see it through. 'Mayfair' closely resembles 'Doone Valley' but has more widespread variegation that does not vanish in summer. Both are sold as Golden or Creeping Golden Thyme.

The Creeping Thymes, forming spreading mounds that are generally over 3 in. high, and as much as 8–10 in., are divided into two categories: 1) a compact spreading mat, and 2) a mound. The first contains *T. leucotrichus* and *T. pulegioides* and its cultivars 'Fosterflower', 'White Magic', 'Oregano-scented', and 'Kermesinus'. Those of the second category that form slow-spreading mounds are *T. brousonetti*, *T.* 'Clear Gold', *T. pulegioides* 'Gold Dust', *T. herba-barona*, *T.* 'Nutmeg', *T.* 'Linear Leaf Lilac', and *T.* 'Long Leaf Gray'. These categories are not clearly defined because many Thymes are polymorphic, that is, quite variable in habit. A significant factor interfering with their habit is sexual variability; some plants bear only female flowers. This proclivity results in a slightly different appearance of the herb from its male/female counterpart.

A spreading mat may be either procumbent or decumbent and forms a loose, rapidly spreading ground cover. Most representative of this habit is *T. pulegioides* and its cultivars. All are incorrectly sold as *T. serpyllum.* Mother-of-Thyme is the correct common name, however. The spreading mats of Mother-of-Thyme include the beautiful cultivars 'Fosterflower', named after Gertrude Foster, and 'White Magic', both white-flowering, and the lavender or purple-flowering 'Oregano-scented'.

Both white-flowering cultivars are very hardy Creeping Thymes with a good Thyme fragrance. 'White Magic' is somewhat lemon-scented. These 3–6 in. mats are two of the finest mead herbs because of their hardiness and resilience to foot traffic. They will both do well in partial shade with a well drained soil of average fertility.

'Oregano-scented' is also sold as Oregano Thyme, *T. serpyllum* or *T. nummularius.* The name 'Oregano-scented' is a bit presumptuous, but it does have a pleasant Thyme scent with a rich, woodsy note. It has fairly large, dark green leaves and produces a moderate supply of lavender flowers. 'Kermesinus' resembles 'Oregano-scented' except for a heavier flower spike of rose-purple and a somewhat less dense habit.

A less commonly cultivated spreading Thyme is Peter Davis, *T. leucotrichus.* It forms a grey-green, open mat 3–4 in. high. It blooms very early with colorful flower spikes of showy pink flowers marked by especial beauty. Its biting, spicy scent and flavor is a result of thymol mixed with borneol, camphor, and limonene. This Creeping Thyme and *T. brousonetti* create a dazzling pink carpet when in bloom about mid-May and are best as ground covers along paths, in sunny meads, rock gardens, and design motifs in parterres.

The slow spreading, mounding Thymes are often simply rangy sub-shrubs only 6–10 in. high, but they tend to root at branch tips and carry on as though not satisfied to stay in place like bush Thymes.

The Thyme just mentioned, *T. brousonetti,* or Moroccan Thyme, bears the most glorious flowers of any Thyme, shooting out in ½ in. trumpets clustered into a pastel pink pompom. Its foliage is green with a medicinal or resinous odor composed of cymene, myrcene, and carvacrol. This Creeping Thyme is hardy to Zone 8 with protection and should be given a sandy soil and a thick sandy layer beneath to protect it in winter.

Two Creeping Thymes, *T.* 'Clear Gold' and *T. pulegioides* 'Gold Dust', are both sold as Golden or Creeping Golden Thyme. They have mottled leaves of yellow-green and lavender flowers. The basic difference between them is the more compact habit of 'Gold Dust'. Both form a 4–8 in., slowly spreading ground cover of a decumbent habit. They are best used in a mixed planting ground cover where only modest color contrast is desired. Their lavender-pink flowers do not become them; the combination of pink and yellow-green is not complimentary.

Caraway Thyme, *T. herba-barona* and *T.* 'Nutmeg', are two fairly compact mounding herbs that from one whiff you would think could only be harvested in a dreamland. They are strongly fragrant and quick to spread into an 18 in. wide prostrate mat from 2–6 in. high. They contribute a heavenly odor to the garden air as they flow beneath our feet, spreading from cracks between paving stones on a sunny walk. The chemistry of both is similar, a pure caraway fragrance from carvone and a spicy note of limonene. Either of these Thymes are exciting culinary spices for spaghetti sauces, chili, and pot roast or other stewed meats and vegetables.

Two Thymes that spread slowly in diffuse, thinly foliaged mounds, are *T.* 'Linear Leaf Lilac' and *T.* 'Long Leaf Gray'. These two unique Thymes have hairy or ciliated grey-green leaves that are long, slender, and on the former, somewhat curved. Their purple or lilac flowers are a prominent feature in early summer and both combine well in a widespaced mixed border with Dwarf Catnip, *N. mussinni,* to provide a silver lining along a driveway or sunny walk in winter as well as summer. Their sparsely foliaged branches do not form a simple rosette (spider web), resembling instead the writhing tentacles of a sea monster groping about indiscriminately. They give character to any rock garden or austere contemporary garden feature and should be grown to contrast with other slow spreading herbs and plants such as *T. caespititius* and *T. leucotrichus* in an informal border. For contemporary designs they can be paired with Dwarf Germander; Incana Santolina; and Speedwell, *Veronica prostrata,* for a spectacular foliage and flower show as well as a neat and attractive blend of textures in winter.

Once a highly revered medicinal of Egyptian physicians, Camomile has never strayed more than a doorstep away from man's needs. In more than one language the name given this herb implies apple-scented. From castle lawns, bench seats, and window sills via medieval Venice to 16th century London then in wooden buckets strapped to the sides of Conestoga wagons that crossed America, Camomile is one of the most desirable of all herbs.

Many forms of Camomile exist, from sweet-flowered cultivars for teas and tisanes to the flowerless turfs that adorned castle keeps. More than one genus is involved and there is still much confusion on botanical placement. For simplicity it is important to remember that the annual Camomile comes from the *Chamomilla* genus, *C. recutita [Matricaria recutita, M. chamomilla]* and is commonly called Roumainian or German Camomile. The perennial Camomile comes from the genus *Chamaemelum. Chamaemelum nobile* is the popular creeping species called Roman Camomile. Other Camomiles include Pineapple Weed, *Chamomilla suaveolens,* smelling of tart pineapples; fruity scented *Matricaria suffruticosa,* from S. Africa; *Anthemis cotula,* a medicinal weed called Stinking Camomile, Mayweed or Dog Fennel; *A. cupaniana,* an aromatic grey-foliaged herb resembling Roman Camomile; and two other *Anthemis* species, *A. sancti-johannes* and *A. tinctoria,* the Marguerite, that are not scented but common ornamentals in the perennial garden.

Chamaemelum nobile, Roman Camomile, is a mat-forming perennial that has the sweetest, most deliciously scented foliage of any plant. There are rayless, single and double-flowered cultivars. A cultivar, Lawn Camomile, *C. n.* 'Trenague' is a non-flowering turf variety that can be mown to form a lawn of spongy carpet smelling of apples right out of an oven. This cultivar forms attractive tight rosettes of foliage like verdant spiny starfish. Roman Camomile was popular in medieval days as a covering on benches.

Flowers may be discouraged on Roman Camomile, except the double flowered forms, which are the most pleasantly scented, to improve the fragrance of the foliage. It must not be allowed to become rangy as it cannot spread effectively unless firmly pressed into the soil. Planted in loose moist soils and kept mown to no more than 2 in., Camomile will develop into a dense mat suitable for sitting. Either full sun or partial shade are acceptable to Camomile.

As a fragrant perennial ground cover, Roman Camomile should, and can be, a part of every landscape. Its phenomenal fragrance is a special feature to which few plants can lay claim. Use it as a path covering in a wilderness, dry bed ravine in wild and informal settings, an aromatic entrance theme around the paving stones leading through a contemporary homesite to the door, a floor covering in an open forest glade, a mead herb, or a turf bench or lawn manicured to furry softness in a formal garden.

During medieval days a bench was usually a flat-topped pile of earth pushed against the side of a castle wall or into a mound elsewhere. On top was Roman Camomile, essentially a fragrant plant grown as a seat cover. 'Trenague' developed as a turf variety and was most popular because of its dense habit and lack of flowers. As a cover it must be cut back regularly and grown in full sun in cool climates, or partial shade in hot.

Because it can be mown and trimmed, Roman Camomile is a valuable counterpart to turf grass even in the most formal, feature garden. In fact, its aromatic gift makes it so superior to grass in formal design that grass just cannot compare.

Spilling uncontrolled across a rocky barren slope, Roman Camomile creates a bold dendritic pattern like the many fingers of a river reaching out into the sea. In an intermittent stream-bed it will keep to the moist areas and thicken beautifully in wet depressions in full sun. Rock walls or escarpments, provided with planting pockets full of rich soils, clothed all in Roman Camomile, are thrilling sights and a splendid treat for the nose.

The annual German Camomile is a highly aromatic, flower-bearing herb used to scent wash waters for hair rinses and medicinal baths, in medicinal ointments or teas and candies. Camomile tea has been a favorite nightcap for thousands of years. It is a weedy, profusely blooming annual that will self-sow in any soil, exposure or climate. It is frost hardy and in cooler climes will grow surrounded by snow, provided the ground does not freeze. It excells in full sun, developing small 12 in. diameter bushes that become encased under hundreds of ½ in. daisies. Its talent for self-sowing is unsurpassed by any herb, and possibly most weeds. If it were not for its unequalled fragrance it would certainly rank with Chickweed. For unmixed borders or mass plantings give each plant 12 in. from center. Overcrowding simply ruins its handsome bushy nature so avoid it. Be sensible—be ruthless when thinning.

A limed clayey soil produces the most fragrant flower, which is the result desired. The apple-scent comes from the flower, not the foliage, and is strongest when planted in groups of several or more plants. No agitation is required for German Camomile to scent an entire yard day and night. Its apple-scent, created by a combination of camphoraceous, herbaceous and spicy scents that include the chemicals azulene and anethol, is best in mid-afternoon, which is the time of day the flowers should be picked. For the finest aroma in a tea, flowers should not be allowed to age more than a few days after first opening. To protect successive crops of German Camomile from losing their fine fragrance, be sure no Mayweed, *Anthemis cotula,* grows in any abundance near your garden. German Camomile readily crosses with Mayweed, to its disadvantage.

German Camomile lends itself well to hard, dry areas where little else will grow without extensive soil renovation. Rocky banks, ravines, rock walls, brick walks, and along driveways and sidewalks where afternoon sun may produce intense heat are favorite spots of this delightful weed. Its seed may be sown where it is to grow and in poor soils this is recommended. It transplants well, even when in full bloom, if plenty of soil is taken up and water applied after planting. Sown in spring it will bloom by midsummer and continue for two months or more. Left on the plants, the flowers retain their scent through most of the season.

German Camomile is a versatile herb for a medium to low border or ground cover use in wild and informal designs on hot, dry sites. Given free reign, its light tolerance and frost hardiness both improve with time from self-sown individuals. Be careful. Its shade tolerance will allow it to germinate under other plants, grow through them rapidly, and emerge into the light to flourish, eventually bestowing its host with what appears to be a cloak of daisies but also robbing it of water and nutrients. Take care in the wild garden where it is allowed to sow and grow freely as it will overtake other slower germinating and maturing plants. Thin a stand early to improve the chances of other self-sowing, wild herbs. In rich soils it may grow tall and slender instead of bushy, so be sure to thin into clumps, not singles, so they will support themselves without staking or toppling over in heavy rain.

German Camomile has been used in exceedingly long or intricate borders in formal parterres where its self-sowing attribute, a time and labor saving boon, provide a profusion of highly fragrant daisies all summer giving it a stature no other single annual herb enjoys. It is an easily established ground cover in meadows and sunny glades or as an area of color balance in the contemporary garden that features other annuals or biennials, such as the vegetable garden. In the informal perennial bed it is an excellent transition planting.

In any vegetable garden German Camomile is a valuable bee plant that attracts many winged creatures, thus improving yield. In the dooryard garden it is grown along paths where it can be easily harvested and its seeds will drop harmlessly to the path where trodden underfoot, they are unlikely to propagate uncontrollably or at the expense of a pampered neighbor.

German Camomile can be seeded directly into containers for displays around doors, porches, and patios. It can be sown repeatedly all year for a continual show of bloom from early spring, if plants are begun in cold frames, through late fall. The pleasant ah-inspiring, apple-scent of German Camomile in full bloom is an event that must be experienced. Rich soils beget slender plants and should be avoided. Do not overfertilize. Do not cut plants back but allow long cascading branches to form.

The flowers of German Camomile are the source of Camomile tea and yield the best flavor of all the Camomiles. What a treat it is to be able to step out onto the patio and pluck a few flowers from a hanging planter of Camomile for a quick cup of one of history's most famous teas.

On the other side of that Conestoga wagon going west, in another part of the castle near a pond, or powdered and sealed in a pharaoh's tomb for spiritual defense, Mint, in any of its hundreds of guises, never left its master's side. The *Mentha* are among the finest aromatic plants in the world. They come packaged as hardy perennials that can literally be chopped into pieces and easily regrown spreading indefinitely in all directions. They must be allowed to fall onto walks and pavement, which they will do with nary a second thought, so foot traffic will trample and crush their succulent leaves, releasing their scent—pulegone, menthol, piperitone and carvone. If left alone, they will sprout tall thin stalks with fuzzy spires of honey-and mint-scented flowers in midsummer. To determine how good a stand of Mint is, count the bees; if you lose count, it's good.

Mint adds sparkle to any niche, doing best in filtered shade where the soil remains moist, humusy and slightly acidic. Variegated foliages and a multitude of fragrance highlights are possible: fuzzy, light green, apple-scented leaves of Applemint; cream-splashed leaves smelling of pineapples in Pineapple Mint; leaves with emerald and gold stains and a spicy hint of ginger in Ginger Mint; round, purplish leaves with a fragrance of oranges in Orange Mint; the aroma of limes, lemons, melons, Creme-de-Menthe, and many more are possible. Of the Mints available, Silver Mint is the least useful, being unornamental and marginally fragrant.

Many Mints may be sown where they are to grow, although cuttings are required for most cultivars. They multiply rapidly in any case but need uprooting and replanting every 4 years, or when the foliage becomes spindly or diseased. In warm, moist climates where wilt, caused by the disease organism Verticillium, is possible, a cultivar series of the Peppermint species called 'Mitcham' is a valuable resistant form. Two commonly available are 'Todd's Mitcham' and 'Murray Mitcham'. 'Black Mitcham' *M.* × *piperita* var. *piperita*, is a commercial cultivar. They are all powerfully menthol-scented and superior to Spearmint and Peppermint. Crossing occurs in gardens with many species or cultivars so strangers will suddenly appear in older stands. Literally hundreds of species and cultivars of Mint are known. Some of the finest ornamentals were discovered in mixed Mint plantings.

Cultivating Mints can be quite distressing, or remarkably easy, to propagate depending on your point view. In any case, to succeed the first time and prevent Mint from achieving the status of Bermuda Grass or Morning Glory in your garden, plant it in a container that is embedded at least 6 in. into the soil. The boundary should be unbroken, in other words, bricks are not sufficient, and must extend 2 in. or more above the soil surface.

Very few of the Mints are not hardy, and in general all will thrive for many years if well mulched. A top dressing of manure each spring and fall is beneficial. Many are marginally scented for a fragrant garden unless crushed and passed under the nose. Those with the finest fragrance are English Pennyroyal, *Mentha pulegium*; Pineapple Mint, *M. suaveolens*; Water Mint, *M. aquatica*; Spearmint, *M. spicata*; 'Orange', 'Lime' and 'Lemon' Mints, *M. × piperita* var. *citrata*; Corsican Mint, *M. requienii*; and Black Mint, *M. × piperita* var. *vulgaris*.

Orange, Black, Lime, Ginger and Pineapple Mints are the most valuable members of this genus for both landscaping and culinary uses. Orange, Lime and Lemon are all cultivars of the same species *M. × piperita* var. *citrata* and vary only in the citrousy pique. Orange is by far the most pleasant. They are tolerant of full shade, emerge early and form robust masses in short order. Lime has a larger leaf and darker color, which is a rich purple-green. They have rose-colored flowers that smell divine.

Black Mint is a rapidly spreading, dark purple Mint cultivated for menthol, which can constitute 90% of its oil. This Mint can literally numb the tongue. Confine it, for it is a vigorous and adventuresome herb that develops beastly stolons (a trailing shoot) that can easily breech a 4″, above-ground guard and burrow 10–12 in. to escape. Fortunately it is far superior to most other culinary Mints and is an exciting cultivar of Peppermint to grow.

The golden hue of Ginger Mint, *M. × gracilis* var. *variegata,* changes in intensity with the seasons and the amount of sunlight it receives. At its peak in late summer it is a superb, low-growing, quickly spreading ground cover in a sunny or semi-shady spot in gardens with both light and dark ornamentals. Its leaf is attractively serrated and its "ginger" scent is indeed spicy and delicious.

Pineapple Mint, *M. suaveolens,* is apparently the rich cousin of Apple Mint, *M. villosa* var. *alopecuroides*. The latter is a pleasant herb, but Pineapple Mint is racy. It likes full sun and an ultra-rich, moist soil. It is much slower growing than its cousin, and its light green leaf with creamy or white markings makes it an excellent feature or a ground cover in high visibility areas. Pair it with dark green companions, avoiding the yellows. Entirely white sports are commonplace. Replant it periodically for finest fragrance. Pineapple Mint's fragrance will diminish as a planting crowds so choose fragrant cuttings wisely to propagate only the best.

Corsican or Creme-de-Menthe Mint, *Mentha requienii,* has a cool, minty aroma that causes considerable searching by visitors for it is hard to find once its penetrating mint scent has been detected. A small patch will give a false impression of huge expanses of Mint nearby. These bright green mats often resemble a clump of *Sedum* from a distance. Growing at times to one or more inches, though normally less, the dense tight mats are smooth enough for marbles to roll across with ease. Damp, rich soils in full sun are recommended and light foot traffic will not set it back too much. In midsummer a film of miniscule blue flowers appears suddenly, lasting a month or more.

A perennial in warmer climates, Corsican Mint will die back in late fall after a hard frost but reseeds itself and reappears by early summer from the tiniest amount of material, to grow again next season. It spreads rapidly during early summer. A small handsized clump may spread 12 in. outward by the end of summer in ideal locations and travel in tiny, bright green rivulets along cracks to spread into an open area between paving stones. Clumps may be lifted with ease and replanted by pressing them into loose soil.

Corsican Mint is a valuable ground cover among plantings of dwarf materials. Fascinating miniature effects can be created using this Mint as a "grass". Dwarf plants appear to be of real proportions from a distance. It lends itself well to soil contouring for dwarf displays imitating grassy mounds, or meadows with a meandering stream of colored stones, or miniature parterre designs using Corsican Mint and inert materials in convoluted designs with heavenly scents.

Corsican Mint is also a candidate for turfed seats. Simply consider the bench as a large container and treat the Mint as a potted herb. It must be grown as a tightly packed ground cover no higher than half the depth of a finger nail. Do not use a rich soil. This Mint should be watered daily and to compensate for frequent watering, mineral supplements, particularly iron, should be added to keep the foliage a verdant green. It may be grown in the same pot with other plants provided there is not competition for nutrients. Large containers with fair-sized shrubs and trees, such as Sweet Bay and Lemon Verbena, are best.

English Pennyroyal, *M. pulegium,* is evergreen to Zone 6. Like most mints it spreads slowly during warm spells in winter months. Its dense habit makes it valuable as a fragrant winter herb for walks and patios where it should be encouraged to spread between cracks directly in the line of foot traffic. Although mouth wateringly fragrant, a tea of English Pennyroyal is relatively toxic because of the chemical pulegone. It is, however, an effective insect repellant when rubbed on the hands and face and is the most valuable herb for strewing or in wash waters for home use.

A variety of English Pennyroyal, Hoary Pennyroyal, *M. pulegium* var. *gibraltarica,* is sold as Gibraltar Mint. It has fuzzy narrow leaves and bears much of the Pennyroyal fragrance. This herb is of somewhat more erect habit and can grow in full sun in moist spots. This herb is sometimes incorrectly sold as Silver Mint.

Two less commonly cultivated herbs, also with delicious minty aromas worth investigating, are Lesser Calamint, *Calamintha nepeta,* and American Pennyroyal, *Hedeoma pulegioides.* Calamint resembles Pennyroyal, *Mentha pulegium,* in habit including its leaves, which are somewhat fuzzy and serrated. It has a strong, sweet flavor and minty odor, not at all camphoraceous. As such, it is well suited as a culinary spice on fish and pork, in sauces, gravies, potato salad and fresh in a green salad accompanying pickled condiments. It is much more fragrant during bloom and thick clumps should be cultivated, spreading onto walks and patios, over low retaining walls or into any damp, sunny or partly shaded area that is well traveled. Two species, *C. nepeta* and *C. sylvatica,* and four subspecies exist. *C. nepeta* subsp. *nepeta* is the most commonly cultivated Lesser Calamint. *C. nepeta* subsp. *glandulosa* has a more delicate flavor and is sometimes referred to as Nepetella.

American Pennyroyal, *Hedeoma* spp., are perennials and annuals native to North and South America and a number of species are often substituted for one another. Although Hedeoma means "sweet odor," only one species, *H. pulegioides,* resembles the strong, pleasant Pennyroyal aroma from *Mentha pulegium.* Its wiry, Summer Savory-like habit makes it difficult to place in the ornamental garden but in a good soil and full sun it yields a fine mint scent for strewing or wash waters. It prefers a dry, sandy soil, flowers profusely, and reseeds itself, growing rapidly in a single season to full size. It is a perennial but does not often survive cold winters, as will English Pennyroyal. Several species of *Hedeoma* are used as oregano in the tropical Americas. *Hedeoma floribundum,* is one example, and called Mexican Oregano because of its prominent scent.

Another deliciously fragrant herb is Winter Savory, *Satureja montana.* A subspecies, Creeping Savory, *Satureja m.* ssp. *pilosa,* stands about 4 in. high spreading to a 24 in. wide clump. In late summer, tiny flowers, giving the impression of a light snowcover, give a boost to its camphoraceous fragrance with a honey-sweet note. The latter has much less foliage than the bush form and is, therefore, better suited as a fragrant herb. It excels in a poor, dry, sandy soil and may best be used falling from walls and over rocky ledges where its dangling branches are tousled by the wind and are all the more fragrant.

The larger form of the species, *S. montana,* is a dense mound resembling a hedgehog.

It has a mellow camphoraceous aroma. Its neat appearance and slick shiny leaves are bright and attractive. It is a variable species so plants from 6 to 14 in. will emerge from the same package of seed. The most entertaining form is Pygmy Savory, *S. montana* ssp. *pygmaea*. It forms a dense, very dark green bush 8–10 in. in diameter. Its shiny savory leaves are more sharply pointed than the species and not a fraction of an inch on any branch is leafless. Varieties and subspecies occur frequently in purchased seed. Cuttings are easily rooted however, so if a choice specimen is cultivated, cuttings, not seed, should be used for propagation. Plenty of deep water and a rocky, well drained, limed soil will produce the most fragrant plants.

Although the culinary value of Winter Savory is not as fine as that of the annual Summer Savory, it is evergreen, can be harvested year round, and is significantly more ornamental. It grows several inches per year up to its full size. For a healthy, dense bush prune heavily in early spring and again lightly after blooming.

Winter Savory is best planted among evergreen borders that run in and out of the sun. It savors the drip line on the sunny side of trees and hotspots in rock fields in northern exposures that receive little afternoon sun. It is a long-lived, hardy herb with glossy, dark green foliage used to create accents in ornamental gardens with conifers and other broadleaf evergreens. It often shares the limelight with other small-leaved herbs such as Bush Thyme, Hyssop, and Germander, and ornamentals such as Box, Bayberry, and Miniature Roses. It has long been a formal garden herb for natural form borders of mounded bushes or neatly trimmed hedges and topiary.

The small stature of Winter Savory makes it a valuable rock garden herb, where it appears to be most at home. Whether perched on a stone escarpment, among boulders its size or greater, or scattered over rocky expanses, it needs to be seen and smelled so keep it close enough for curious hands to caress it as visitors wander past. Its branches are slow to heal so plants should be pruned and not jut out onto paths.

Prostrate or Creeping Rosemary, *Rosmarinus officinalis* var. *prostratus,* looks for all the world like Creeping Savory but for its larger, more spicily scented leaves that have a downy backside. It is perfect for the entrance gate that must swing through a patch, releasing its pungent aroma as a gay greeting. It is not generally tolerant of foot traffic so it is best grown on ledges and along open, sunny banks that have a path close enough for groping hands to find a fragrant purchase with every grasp. In most climates Prostrate Rosemary must be grown in containers to be brought indoors for the winter. The plant must be trimmed of unsightly or damaged branches and potted in late summer. They may be left outdoors only in Zones 8–10. Numerous varieties are available. 'Lockwood de Forest' has a lighter green foliage than others and keeps its dark blue flowers longer. Other cultivars include 'Golden Prostrate' and 'Kenneth Prostrate.'

All of the Prostrate Rosemarys should be seen cascading down wide-stepped entrances and grouped so that their warm, camphoraceous fragrance dominates the site. Use them at the feet of patio benches, flowing from containers, planted between paving stones, in rock gardens or among dwarf materials in contemporary features. Around the kitchen doors or barbeque grills it is easily plucked and savored in grilled foods, salads, and meat stews. Sausage and meat can be smoked to a tangy flavor using a cup of leaves thrown onto the hot coals when cooking outdoors. Rosemary has been used as an incense for more than 5000 years. Until early in this century, Rosemary Oil was burned to prevent the spread of disease by insects. Rosemary's "intoxicating fragrance" (which is its name in Chinese) is from an exhilarating combination of camphoraceous and spicy chemicals—borneol, eucalyptol, camphene, camphor and pinene.

ROSEMARY CHIPS

10 fried tortillas (broken into "chips")
2 Tbsp. butter or margarine
1 tsp. powdered Chives
½ tsp. Paprika
½ tsp. powdered Rosemary

Mix ingredients in pan. Bring to boil and pour over chips to coat them. Spread chips on baking sheet and bake in oven at 425° several minutes or until crisp. Serve alone or with fresh Chive Dip.

For a low maintenance border in either formal or informal settings, Lavender, *Lavandula* spp., is choice. One of the best known herbs due to its penetrating, yet perfume-quality fragrance, Lavender is available in many cultivars and species for use in the landscape. The differences are not major, limited to leaf size and shape, flower color and flower stalk length.

The hardy perennial Lavenders include English Lavender, *Lavandula angustifolia,* Spike Lavender, *L. latifolia* and Lavandin, *L.* × *intermedia,* a hybrid of the former two. A selection of cultivars of English lavender include: those with dark violet flowers, 'Munstead', which is lower growing and more compact, 'Hidcote', 'Mitcham Gray', a form quick to reach a full height of 18 in., 'Lodden Blue' and 'Nana Atropurpurea'; those with lavender blue flowers include 'Compacta', 'Gray Lady', 'Irene Doyle' and 'Twickle Purple'; a pink-flowered cultivar 'Rosea'; and white-flowered 'Alba' and 'Nana Alba'. Lavandin cultivars Dr. A. O. Tucker considers choice for landscaping include 'Dutch', 'Grappenhall', 'Grosso' and 'Hidcote Giant'.

Many Lavenders are tender perennials and restricted to the southern landscape unless they are potted and brought indoors in winter. In general, these species are not hardy below 10°F, regrowing poorly from damaged wood and most certainly dying if their roots are frozen. The most decorative and hardiest is *L. stoechas,* Stoechade or Spanish Lavender. It was once known as Stickadove. It is a sweet scented lavender, with short, narrow leaves and flowers that form a compact inflorescence about ½ in. thick and from 1–2 in. long with pink or lavender colored bracts and purple flowers. Of the six subspecies, *L.s.* ssp. *penduculata* has flower spikes shooting out on 6–8 in. stalks that bob around in the wind like tiny purple balloons, and *L.s.* ssp. *stoechas* 'Alba' has white flowers.

French Lavender, *L. dentata,* has fuzzy leaves serrated their entire length, giving the plant a soft appearance. Its lax growth habit gives it an unkempt look so prune early each spring and again in the fall. New growth improves its fragrance as it is not as strongly scented as other Lavenders. French Lavender is a winter-blooming species and in cooler climates (Zone 8 and colder) must be potted so its beauty can be enjoyed indoors. It is sometimes sold as Fringed Lavender.

Other species, less commonly available but fascinating ornamentals, include Wooly Lavender, *L. lanata,* with soft, downy-white leaves; the strangely scented Fringed Lavender, *L. multifida,* with light green, fern-like foliage and tufts of blue flowers; and *L. pinatta* which resembles the latter (including the common name) except for a pine-like scent. Neither is hardy below 20°F.

Lavender most commonly cohabits in an ornamental garden with other grey foliaged herbs and plants. Its tall, slender, purple flower spikes seem to be the perfect contrast for the thick, silvery, blue and pink-spotted spikes of Veronica Incana and Wooly Betony. Silver Thyme and Dittany often share a site with Dwarf or 'Mitcham Gray' Lavender in rockeries, knots, and narrow informal borders. Its neat, low maintenance style is indispensable and particularly noteworthy for its "ever-grey" winter use in a deciduous planting.

Lavender's optimum use is in matching borders along entrance paths, the perimeter of patios and along sunny walks and fragrant stops by benches in the secluded sections of a garden. Along paths they must fall onto the paving. Planting Lavender near hot dry surfaces extends their life and assists them in growing more densely and compactly. Like Thyme, Lavender must be protected from dampness by a layer of sand beneath its foliage. At least 2 in. is recommended. Part of this depth may be provided by porous paving materials such as brick, gravel, and stone. A sandy, well limed soil helps Lavender project a dependable fragrance and prolong its blooming season. 'Irene Doyle' Lavender can be cut immediately upon flowering and will develop a second crop of flowers lasting late into fall.

As a contemporary landscape herb, Lavender is becoming more popular. Try it in a sand feature for the front garden. Use a compact cultivar, 'Hidcote' or 'Twickle Purple' and gather around it a small collection of Clove Pinks with a bevy of Birdsfoot Violets scattered hither and thither across the dune-like expanse. Beach Wormwood, or Cinquefoil, with yellow or red flowers, can be used as well for more color and variety if desired.

Lavender has been used in formal arrangements as a perimeter border hedge on banks that surround knots and parterres to restrict entrance and encourage the visitor to enjoy the garden within. As such, it is a fragrant and colorful boundary.

In the wild or informal garden, Lavender should be a back border, providing a light background for dark foliaged herbs and ornamentals or clumped in several groups of 2, 3, and 5 for bright patches of blue and grey, looking like whales basking in the sun at the surface of an ocean of flowers.

The chemicals chiefly responsible for that legendary Lavender scent are linalool, borneol, eucalyptol, and fenchone. Citrousy notes in English Lavender are from limonene and pinene and its spicy notes from geraniol and ocimene. Stoechade Lavender and Spike Lavender, *L. latifolia,* contain camphors and terpenes yielding a strong medicinal odor. The sweet floral scent of French Lavender, *L. dentata,* is due to fenchone and geraniol.

In late summer, tall blue and purple flower spikes add immensely to the power of Lavender's clear, invigorating scent. They remind us of bath salts and perfume, fine stationery and room deodorizers. Not all Lavenders smell alike, though none is unpleasant. They all deserve to be experimented with for first-hand experience by the gardener they are intended to please. Lavender was once called the herb of war, a strange title considering its fragrance, but was once used as an antiseptic. Its oil was used on surgical incisions or mixed with the oil of Rosemary and burned as incense to purify the air in surgeries. Valuable as potpourri material today, Lavender flowers retain their fragrance for many years after drying.

Wormwood, *Artemisia absinthum,* is a hardy, semi-evergreen perennial with a fragrance that is bitter and pine-like. It is a scent that can be overpowering and is often described as medicinal. Thujone and terpenes are the primary camphoraceous chemicals in Wormwood, yet from a distance the scent is fruity and similar to the fragrance of Roman Camomile. When in bloom, the flower spikes form a yellow haze of tiny, button flowers that add a pure camphor highlight to the Wormwood scent. Wormwood plumes dry easily and are fine arranging material, doubling as an air deodorizer. Beware, however, of its proclivity to cause an allergenic response both in the respiratory system and the skin. Indoors the scent of Wormwood is less pungent and suggests a medicinal cleanliness pleasant in kitchens, bathrooms, and moldy basements. Wormwood's strange scent should not cause it to be banished from the fragrant garden. It is an invaluable accent to many evergreens in simple arrangements, its fragrance mingling with theirs to yield an overall richness. The odor of Wormwood is often more appealing when it can mingle with the heavier scents of Roses, Carnations, and Camomile. Wormwood contributes a tingling surprise hard to create otherwise.

Although a single Wormwood bush is dense, its feathery appearance may grow ragged unless trimmed back each spring and again after blooming. Wormwood may be kept cut to any desired height during the growing season if pruning is not severe. Planted about 18–24 in. apart, and regularly pruned, Wormwood forms a dense, medium height border from 24–30 in. Although it can grow to 48 in. during flowering and be a bit messy, the flowers heavy with pollen give a sunny contrast to dark spires of other fragrant flowers in a mixed border. Roman Wormwood, *A. pontica*, resembles Wormwood but for its extremely delicate foliage. It is less hardy, requires full sun and is not evergreen. Roman Wormwood is at its formal best as a small potted herb or in a grey garden.

Wormwood adds a silver lining in any ornamental garden. Its satiny, grey-green foliage stands out on glum, overcast days, providing relief from the many monotonous dark green evergreens of winter gardens. Due to its feathery foliage, Wormwood resembles some conifers and thus fits well in ornamental designs that use weeping or pendulous elements in evergreen features. Its natural, untrimmed habit is the one most easily managed and the best way to feature it. When trimmed into a neat hedge, it is becoming only in a formal garden as a border and requires constant attention, although there it will be in close company with other plants in need of constant attention. In the informal or wild garden, Wormwood should be grown as a back border snug with the forest front. It is most appealing intermingling with a woodland of spruce and fir. Use it as a patchy, traversable ground cover between widely spaced trees. Let it spill abruptly from the forest's edge onto a lawn without benefit of a perennial bed. This recalls the pattern of sparsely vegetated conifer forests in the mountainous regions of the western U.S.

For a wild effect, intersperse into the latter example a smattering of tall and slender wildflowers and herbs such as Foxglove, Monkshood, Lupine, Clary or Silver Sage and Kniphofia. In wide expanses of wilderness combine Wormwood and other larger, grey-foliaged, gaily-flowered shrubs such as Garden Sage and a mixture of its ornamental cousins of the genus *Salvia*; Lavender; Russian Sage, *Perovskia*; Carnations; Incana Santolina; and Pearly Everlasting, *Helichrysum lanatum*.

Wormwood is grown in the dooryard garden for its double value as a repellant. It can be a chemical repellant or a companion plant in the vegetable garden. An infusion of 1 c. Wormwood, 1 tsp. vegetable oil, and 1 c. water diluted and sprayed onto foliage acts as a short term insect repellent and will also prevent dampoff. It is important to keep the strength of such a solution quite weak (diluted until the Wormwood odor is just apparent) or it is toxic to seedlings as well as the fungus it is intended to control. The use of Wormwood medicinally as a vermifuge for either animals or man is not advised because of its toxicity.

'Silver Mound' Artemisia is a desirable ground cover for the fragrant garden. A number of ornamental Artemisias can be substituted; all are attractive and aromatic particularly along paths in sunny, hot recesses and rockeries. *A. frigida* 'Silver Mound'; *A. lanata*; *A. genipi*; and *A. schmidtiana* 'Nana' are all sold as Silver Mound and form handsome mounds that appear to be silvery furballs growing from 6–18 in. Another handsome ground cover, Beach Wormwood or Old Woman, *Artemisia stellerana*, has wooly white leaves shaped like the leaf of White Oak. It grows from 6–12 in. in full sun or part shade but needs a sandy or well-drained soil. It is deciduous and bears modest yellow flowers in summer.

Fennel, *Foeniculum vulgare*, spontaneously comes to mind as a screening herb. It is tall, approaching 5–6 ft. in good soils, and will grow in thick clumps without diminishing its fragrance. Fennel foliage exudes the most marked anise scent of all *Umbelliferae*, including Anise. (Though perhaps if Anise, at a diminutive 1 ft., could grow to 6 ft., it too might contribute more of its essence to the garden's atmosphere.) Its genus name, *Foeniculum*, means fragrant hay. Fennel contains some of the chemicals that give Anise its fragrance: anethol, fenchone, and pinene. Fennel Oil also carries camphene, myrcene, limonene and ocimene.

Sweet and Bitter Fennel differ in fragrance. Wild or Bitter Fennel, *Foeniculum vulgare* ssp. *vulgare,* contains more fenchone and limonene and less anethol than Sweet Fennel.

Fennel is a rapid grower in rich, damp soils. Foliage color varies with soil conditions, being yellow-green in poor, sandy soils and dark blue-green in rich clays. Soils little change its fragrance, however. A spring application of manure should not be forgotten. A single plant may self-sow into a sizable patch in 1–2 years, although close planting in the beginning will achieve the same results. Plants may be set 6 in. apart for a very dense screen. It is often treated as an annual because of its rapid growth from seed sown in early spring to full-sized plants in one season but yields significantly more seed in following years. Fennel is far more fragrant during flowering, from late summer throughout autumn. Its umbels grow very large with bright yellow flowers and fruits tasting of anise seed.

Fennel is an excellent fragrant herb for screening or along the back border. Its habit is somewhat unkempt when grown as a single plant in a perennial border but becomes quite elegant when packed into a dense back border drift with an entourage of Fernleaf Tansy, White Mugwort, Valerian, Astilbe, Foxglove, *Digitalis* spp., and Meadow Rue, *Thalictum aquilegiifolium* 'Purple Cloud'. This combination provides a dark green back border 3–4 ft. high and a flower display from spring through fall. For a thicker screen, Fennel can be cut back in early summer to as low as 18 in.

In a contemporary fragrant garden or a kitchen garden, Finocchio, *F. v.* ssp. *vulgare* var. *azoricum,* or Sweet Fennel, *F. v.* ssp. *vulgare* var. *dulce,* can be surrounded with Southernwood and Blue Sage with a low accenting border of either *Santolina neapolitana* or an assortment of ornamental and edible Alliums including Chives, *A. schoenoprasum;* yellow *A. moly* and *A. flavum; A. pulchellum;* the delightful *A. karataviense;* and the white Garlic Chive, *A. tuberosum.*

A red variety of Fennel can be substituted for a change of color using Red or Bronze Fennel. *F. v.* ssp. *v.* 'Rubrum'. Red Fennel has a purple or reddish-brown hue and readily replaces the species in any design. It is especially useful for bold and colorful vertical balance in an informal or contemporary landscape. It is as hardy as the species but does not take to partial shade and should be grown in rich, moist soil in full sun for the best color development. The dried herb is indistinguishable from the species. Sweet Fennel is a commercial variety with larger fruits having a higher essential oil content. This variety can grow to 7 ft.

At the base of the stalk of Finocchio just at ground level, the stem is swollen into a 3–6 in. "bulb" that is served as a steamed or baked vegetable. It imparts a sweet, delicate Anise flavor to combination vegetable dishes, soups, and stuffings or may be eaten alone as a side dish. It may be purchased at grocery stores under the names Finocchio or Anise Root. To encourage bulb formation wait till midsummer to plant out.

FINOCCHIO SIDE DISH

Surround a beef roast in last hour of cooking with:

> 2 c. Finnocchio (large wedges)
> 3 c. Mushrooms
> 2 Green Peppers (sliced into rings)
> 1 Red Pepper (sliced into rings)

Remove from juices and serve separately.

Plate 3

Path junction planted on both sides with identical low growing Lavender for a fragrant greeting at the Medicinal Herb Garden, Univ. of Washington, Seattle, WA.

Mass planting of Garden Sage to create an extravagant atmosphere behind a bench in the Medicinal Herb Garden, Univ. of Washington, Seattle, WA.

Decorative containers of herbs at the entrance to the home of Michele Nash, Mercer Island, WA.

Containers on an out building at the Bouquet Banque, Marysville, WA.

Fragrant turf seat composed of Creeping Golden Thyme backed by Orange Mint, Peppermint and a potted Lemon Verbena.

Fragrant screen of Sweet Fennel in kitchen garden of John Eccles, Winlock, WA.

Plate 4

'White Moss' Thyme creeping around rocks on a step.

Young plant of Crimson Thyme trying hard to show off in early summer.

Looking down on a patch of 'Mayfair' Thyme.

Patch of 'Pink Chintz' Thyme working its way down a rock wall.

A bright fragrant border of 'Clear Gold' Thyme creeps beneath a turf seat. The rose flowers belong to a clump of Wild Thyme which is part of the turf seat.

Plate 5

'Oregano-scented' Thyme cultivated in the kitchen garden at home of Judith Zugish.

'White Moss' Thyme in bloom. It is neighbor to 'Long Leaf Gray' Thyme with French Thyme behind in the garden of Michele Nash, Mercer Island, WA.

A bed of Orange Mint in bloom.

A carpet of Creme-de-Menthe Mint creates a flower-studded meadow beneath a 6 in. tall Dwarf Sage and a globe of *Santolina* 'Nana'.

Pineapple Mint frequently produces all white sports among its creme-on-lime variegated foliage that truly smells of pineapples.

A barrel of English Pennyroyal in bloom reaches out to passersby.

Plate 6

Calamint in early spring before a growth of tiny pink flowers on pendulous stalks, Medicinal Herb Garden, Univ. of Washington, Seattle, WA.

Pygmy Savory in a border of containers that provides support for a raised bed in a dooryard garden. Its neighbors include Chive, Dwarf Snapdragons and Dwarf Lavender.

Spanish or Stoechade Lavender in regal splendor at its post by a gate.

Silver Mound, *Artemisia lanata* forms a cheerful flowing mound for steps and terraces.

Wormwood and Chives form a fragrant frame around Comfrey in this contemporary feature.

CHICKEN SOUP

1 c. Noodles	1 Tbsp. Fennel
Boullion	1 Tbsp. Calendula
1 c. Water	½ tsp. Chives
1 c. Tomato quarters	½ tsp. Oregano
1 c. Green Pepper	1 tsp. Lovage
1 c. diced precooked Chicken	

Fennel foliage is dried easily at a medium temperature (90–110°F.). If 1 tsp. of Fennel is needed, dry ½ c. (packed) of fresh foliage in a microwave oven on *defrost* for 5–10 minutes. Then it can be more finely ground and evenly and esthetically applied to many recipes. Fresh Fennel is used on baked fish, lamb, or pork cuts by covering the meat in a relatively thick layer of 2–3 fronds. In other recipes Fennel is used dried to spread it evenly and avoid tangled, seaweed-like clumps of soggy Fennel.

Fresh Fennel can be eaten as a pot herb. Boiled in the gravy from the meat main course it yields a sweetened gravy and a tasty vegetable dish. Fresh Fennel can be used to make a butter by blending 1 c. of foliage in ½ c. butter, but the dried product powdered and boiled for 3 minutes is superior. A sweet butter can be made by plucking ½ c. of Fennel flowers and boiling for 3 min. in butter and straining. Fennel butter will keep for 3–4 months in a refrigerator.

Fennel seed can be used as well, providing a strong Anise flavor, but they require long cooking to soften. Green seeds, however, are easily crushed and used in recipes for rice, steamed vegetables and pudding to add sweetness. Green Fennel seeds make one of the finest herb teas that can come from a garden. Use 1 tsp. of crushed green seeds per cup or 1 Tbsp. of Fennel flowers.

CHICKEN HEARTS

1½ lbs. Chicken hearts
4 Tbsp. Fennel butter
Boullion
½ tsp. Fennel
½ tsp. Basil
½ tsp. Sweet Marjoram
½ tsp. Chives

Use no water, but add ¼ c. sherry after hearts are fully cooked in butter. Then add herbs, etc.

BAKED CHICKEN

Baste 1 chicken in 4 Tbsp. Fennel butter combined with 4 Tbsp. honey, ½ tsp. boullion, and ½ tsp. Fennel.

Place chicken in covered baking dish with ¼ c. sherry.
Add 4–6 cloves garlic.
Continue to baste while baking at 275 F. for 1½–2 hours.
Add 1 tsp. Lovage and ¼ tsp. Rosemary to juices to make gravy.

Many canned foods can be enlivened with a liberal dose of Fennel when cooking: soups, stews, noodles, and rice or potato entrees. Breads and biscuits benefit from an addition of crushed green seeds and apple, peach, or rhubarb pies sprinkled with the same become a new treat.

GUACAMOLE

2 Avocados
1 Tomato
¼ c. Chives (fresh chopped)
¼ tsp. salt
1 Tbsp. lemon juice
1 Tbsp. Fennel
½ tsp. Sweet Marjoram

Mix ingredients on slow speed to chunky consistency. Let stand at least 3 hours (in refrigerator) before serving.

CHIP DIP

6 oz. non-dairy dressing or sour cream
1 tsp. Honey
1 Tbsp. Fennel
½ tsp. Rosemary
1 Tbsp. Chives (fresh chopped)
1 Tbsp. Red Bell Pepper (finely chopped)

Refrigerate 24 hours before serving.

Coming with the highest recommendation as an annual border for a fragrant garden is Basil, *Ocimum spp.*—one of the world's most fragrant herbs. Although not always highly revered for its flavor, Basil has been in cultivation for thousands of years. Before the Egyptians farmed it along the Nile in 2500 B.C., Holy or Sacred Basil, *O. sanctum,* had been a sacred herb of India many centuries, perhaps millenia, earlier. Grown for food, spice, incense, and perfume, Basil is renowned for its ginger, clove, or licorice fragrance, three of the most widely traded spices in man's history. Basil is not a substitute for them but an herb with a fragrance all its own, at once strong and delicious.

The fragrant garden is imperfect without a border of Basil bolting to flower in the hot, summer sun. The peak of Basil's power comes just as flowers begin to open in mid-summer and the hotter the climate the more fragrant Basil will be. An enclosed patio will be saturated with its aroma using only 20 plants, penetrating the air regardless of wind or rain. Indoors, a half dozen or more plants hanging to dry send their spicy scent to every corner of the home. Basil, planted with Coriander, Camomile, and Summer Savory, recreates in any landscape the aroma of the spice markets of ancient times.

Basil requires a dry, well-drained soil. The source of water should be infrequent on the surface but available at depth. In the border, Basil plants should be underlain by bark or gravel to keep the surface dry—sawdust and mulch keep the soil too cool so are unsuitable. It is important to remember that poor soils will give the sweet Basils a pungent clove-like accent while rich soils and excess moisture impart a sweeter, licorice odor.

Most of the cultivars of Basil can be assigned a scent based on their chemical makeup. Although there will be some variation from soil to soil and climatic factors, the chemotypes of Basil are relatively stable.

The cultivated Basils include Lemon Basil, *Ocimum americanum*; Spice Basil, *O.* 'Spice'; Hoary Basil, *O. canum*; Sweet Basil, *O. basilicum*; Sacred Basil, *O. sanctum*; and Camphor Basil, *O. kilimandscharicum*.

There are two cultivars of the *O. sanctum* group: the green, ginger-scented 'Sri' Tulsi and the purple, clove-scented 'Krishna' Tulsi. They are both holy herbs in the Hindu religion. The purple foliaged Tulsi also has beautiful purple flowers and 'Sri' Tulsi, yellow-green.

The cultivars of *O. basilicum* are organized by Helen Darah in her manuscript *THE CULTIVATED BASILS,* into four categories: 1) tall, 3 ft., and slender; 2) large-leaved, to 2½ ft.; 3) dwarf, small leaves; and 4) compact, thyrsiflora.

The most commonly cultivated Basils fall into the two middle categories. The second includes 'Lettuce Leaf', 'Italian', and 'Crispum', the widely recognized culinary Sweet Basils with large glabrous green leaves, which may be "much puckered and crumpled" as Parkinson wrote of them centuries ago. The only pure purple cultivar is in this category, *O. b.* 'Dark Opal'. *O. b.* var. *minimum*, Bush Basil, is a cultivar of the dwarf category. It has small leaves, ½–1 in., and a handsomely dense habit.

An exquisite new Basil with a silver lining comes to us from Fox Hill Farm, Parma, MI. 'Silver Fox' is a variegated cultivar of the fine leaf Basil variety *O.b.* var. *minimum*. 'Silver Fox' has a touch of white on the margin of its pea-green leaves and is well endowed with a rich gingery scent. Give it a decorative container and feature it on a hot, sunny patio or in a fragrant garden for the summer, but invite it in for the winter to charm your guests with its abundance.

The fourth category is represented by a Sweet Basil whose flower spike grows into a crowded arrangement of lavender flowers that tend to form a spiral called a thyrsus. The 'Thyrsiflora' Basil, *O. b.* cv., is exceptionally beautiful, growing from 12–18 in. as a sturdy bush. It is an exceptionally useful culinary cultivar with an anise flavor and fragrance formed by two delicious chemicals, methylchavicol and linalool.

O. canum, Hoary Basil, and its cultivars are identified by chemotype only (fragrance chemicals). They do not appear to be different otherwise, distinguished by lemony (citral), camphor (camphor) and spicy (methyl cinnamate) scents. 'Lemon', 'Camphor' and 'Licorice' are common names for these cultivars. They are all identical, characterized by elliptic-lanceolate leaves pointed at both ends, hairy and pale green. Flowers are cream colored.

Lemon Basil, either *O. basilicum* 'Citriodorum' or *O. americanum*, which are identical, grow to 18 in. with a less bushy habit than Sweet Basil. Their leaves are narrow, light green, and inflorescences are lax and unattractive. Its pleasant lemon taste and fragrance has a gingery note.

'Spice' Basil has a complicated history of hybridization, so much so that no botanical name has been assigned to this diverse group, recognized by green, serrated leaves that are delicately scented and often mottled with purple. Its flowers are pink, quite large and showy. The aroma of the plant is delightfully spicy in a way no other Basil can compare.

A woody perennial Basil sold as Tree Basil may be any of 3 species *O. gratissimum*, a large shrub; hoary Basil, *O. canum*, a clove-scented cultivar; and 'Sri' Tulsi, *O. sanctum*. The first species is generally regarded as Tree Basil. None are spectacular as ornamentals.

Although the cultivated Basils are grown as annuals throughout the northerly latitudes, a large number of them are short-lived perennials that can be potted, wintered indoors, and replanted again the following spring, and the next, etc. The gardener needs only to give each specimen a try as a houseplant. It will need good illumination and a cool, dry soil that is not overly fertilized to keep them robust and slow growing. Begin their internment with a heavy pruning, before they are transplanted from the garden in mid-summer. Bring them in while the weather is still warm.

Not all of the Basils are suitable as ornamentals. The most popular cultivars used in landscape design are the Sweet Basils including 'Crispum', 'Bush' and 'Dark Opal', the purple 'Krishna' Tulsi, 'Spice' Basils, and 'Thyrsiflora'. Basils listed by their fragrance such as 'Cinnamon', 'Lemon', 'Camphor', or 'Licorice' can be any species, although they most commonly are cultivars of *O. canum* or hybrids of *O. canum* and *O. basilicum*. The seeds a gardener receives virtually always contain at least a few plants not identical with the majority. To the Basil grower this can be an enjoyable discovery, to the landscape gardener, a nuisance. Two frequent substitutions are 'Camphor' Basil, *O. canum* for Camphor Basil, *O. kilimandscharicum*, and 'Sri Tulsi' Basil, *O. sanctum* for Tree Basil, which most commonly refers to *O. gratissimum*.

The kitchen garden in any landscape is the proper environment for the Basils of leggy, obese, or sloppy habits, such as 'Lemon', Cinnamon', 'Licorice', 'Camphor', 'Lettuce Leaf' or the black sheep that is not representative of the package label. The latter should be set aside if they are remarkable, protected from cross pollination and either propagated from cuttings or seed.

The ornamental Basils are fabulous border herbs. Their powerful fragrance readily percolates into the garden air come rain or shine. Dense, solid color borders are as easy as planting seeds where they are to grow. Formal gardens and courtyards, as ancient as Egypt, relied on Basil to cleanse and refresh the air. Knots and parterres benefit from Basils since a number of contesting cultivars may be played one against the other. Opal is frequently used in formal or contemporary landscaping with 'Bush' and 'Spice' Basils.

Borders of Basil from giant swaths 2–3 ft. wide along palatial entranceways, to simple frames around beds of fragrant ornamentals circumscribed by a patio are possible. Plants should be spaced 8–12 in. for the Sweet Basils, 6–8 in. for 'Bush', 'Lemon', and 'Dark Opal' to give a dense, unbroken border. Planted closely, Basil becomes somewhat leggy so keep the spacing wider in less sunny sites to encourage sturdier growth. Double wide rows, set 12 in. apart on center, strengthens the bold color of Sweet Basils and magnifies their rich and spicy aroma.

The chemovars and hybrids of *O. canum* are suitable for dooryard and wild gardens. Some have glossy leaves with purple markings or purple stems and pink flowers. They require fair-sized clumps of 6–8 plants to provide a good garden fragrance. These are the cultivars known by their fragrance; i.e., 'Cinnamon' Basil, etc. They are tall, to 3 ft. or more, and really need constant pruning to give them shape. Place them where they will be brushed by visitors. Plant at their feet a ground cover that is exceptionally low and fragrant, such as Creeping Thyme, Corsican Mint, or Lawn Camomile.

In the contemporary setting, 'Dark Opal', 'Spice' Basil, 'Thyrsiflora', and 'Krishna' Basil are suitable for feature gardens. With ingenuity others can certainly be tried but these four are more easily worked into designs because of their purple hues and pink flowers. Combine them with grey-foliaged herbs and plants such as *Santolina* 'Nana' pruned to smooth globes, Dwarf Sage, Clove Pinks, Dittany, or *Origanum microphyllum,* or as a free style feature with ground covers of Beach Wormwood, Veronica Incana, Wooly Betony or *Cerastium tomentosum.* Gold or yellow-green foliages also go well with the purple Basils: herbs such as Golden Sage, Golden Oregano, Gold Lemon Thyme, Dwarf Feverfew, and *Santolina viridis.*

'Dark Opal', 'Krishna', 'Bush', 'Spice', and 'Crispum' should be planted in thick drifts in informal borders. Use at least 2 cultivars and keep them adjacent to one another for better appreciation of flowers and fragrance.

The black sheep of the fragrant herbs is Coriander, *Coriandrum sativum.* Its unfortunate name, meaning bug-like, referring to its odor, is a misnomer. The Coriander scent is indeed a fragrance and not goat-like or foul as some have described it. Of course, as odors go, not everyone agrees. Linnaeus, in his pioneering work on fragrance, categorized Coriander in 'hircine' company and added aside, "*aliis grati aliis ingrati*", that is, "pleasant to some, unpleasant to others".

Coriander leaves and the seeds when unripe are a bit off, but the odor is best described as a heavy, waxy scent that is only unpleasant when stuffed under the nose. It is a rich, warm, old wax aroma when used in a planting with other fragrant herbs and flowers and should be included, for it supplies an important fraction to the overall fragrance just as do civet and musk in perfumes. The odor of Coriander is a combination of scents from spicy terpinene (common to Caraway and Cumin), citrus and camphoraceous notes from pinene and other terpenes, and spicy overtones due to linalool (which can comprise as much as 80–90% of the oil). Coriander should not compete with musk or onion-scented herbs and flowers. Choose floral and spicy scents and keep the population of Coriander to less than half that of any of the other herbs in a mixed planting. You will be surprised at its performance.

The best Coriander comes from the central part of Russia and China where unknown natural factors are present that give us the sweet and spicy Coriander seed used in fine culinary recipes for pizza and pasta sauce. They are a rare sweet treat just off the plant before fully dry, becoming a dried spice that has been desired by cooks for as long as the spice trade has been in existence. Hot summers are an important prerequisite so time the planting of this annual so that seeds ripen during the heat of summer. It is generally recommended that ripe Coriander be harvested in early morning with the dew clinging to the seeds preventing them from bursting open explosively during handling. Plants should be pulled and bound then covered with paper bags and stored in a dry location. The foliage of Coriander (Cilantro) can be used fresh or dried at medium or high heat.

Thickly-sown drifts in wild gardens and wild retreats in kitchen gardens are the finest ways to enjoy the many talents of Coriander. Until it flowers and sets seed it is a weedy fellow with a funny odor. Its continuously emerging flocks of small pinkish flowers slowly metamorphose in the summer heat into glistening green globes that are crispy and sweet. By late summer, thousands of decorative tan beads bob about on rapidly thinning plants. Eventually the entire plant browns, remaining erect and proud, awaiting the gardener to pluck it from the ground at harvest time.

This sequence is quite ornamental when the proper design criterion are taken into consideration. First, light green backgrounds or contrasting materials are needed to accent the green or dark green foliage of Coriander as well as inhance its tan, beaded skeleton in late summer. Second, Coriander requires full sun and plenty of room. Close spacing makes for spindly plants susceptible to wind and rain damage. In any garden, give Coriander plants 12–18 in. of growing room. Third, locate a bee plant, an herb well endowed with nectar-rich flowers, close by to attract pollinators. Flies and wasps adore Coriander. Bees do not avoid it, but do not go out of their way to patronize it either. Monarda, Basil, German Camomile, and Borage are 4 bee herbs, any one of which can accompany Coriander in an arrangement.

In the kitchen garden, Coriander can be grown as a border. A double border, rows 12 in. apart, should be planted on the south side of a back border of Crinkled or 'Lettuce Leaf' Basil, or as a screen behind a front border of 'Dark Opal' or 'Krishna' Basil. Or it can be used to encircle a central patch of pole beans with an outside border of ornamental Kale or a red-leaf Lettuce. In a wild patch in the kitchen garden, combine Coriander, German Camomile, *Nigella*, Dill, Summer Savory, and Lemon Basil for a highly fragrant and beneficial garden of tasty seeds and foliage.

The perimeter bed in a dooryard garden is a safe site for Coriander. Let it share a mixed border with medium height, red and pink Yarrows, tucked in a narrow bed behind Miniature Roses, Feverfew and German Camomile. Here it can also be grown with 'Cinnamon' and 'Licorice' Basils and German Camomile, with a background of Garden Sage. These gardens exude perfumes that are easily described as enticing.

The most fragrant of the herbs recommended for growing in containers are the Jasmines. Their ability to arouse the emotions is legendary. One of the greatest treasures of history's mightiest monarchs was the essence of Jasmine. It has been used to scent everything from the lace cuffs on King Herod's royal robes to the sails of Cleopatra's ships. In centuries past, fields of Jasmine were grown only for the wealthy and powerful. Today they belong to every gardener.

Most Jasmines are not hardy in northern climates. Gardeners in these latitudes shrug their shoulders and sigh at their misfortune. Yet all the Jasmine species may be successfully grown in containers, from the minute *J. polyanthus,* whose evergreen foliage drapes daintily over pots with hundreds of fragrant white flowers, to the large twining bush *J. odoratissimum* and the heavy vines of *J. officinalis.*

J. officinalis, hardy to Zone 6, is a rapidly growing vine easily woven or wired onto a trellis anchored in a container. It blooms from early summer through fall and needs no trimming until through flowering in late fall. Flowers form predominantly on new wood. Therefore, last year's wood must be pruned off each fall, leaving young branchlets on one or more permanent trunks that may reach a total length of 15 ft.

J. grandiflorum is the most valued by perfumers, having the highest concentration of those chemicals that give Jasmine its beguiling power, methylanthranilate and benzyl esters. It blooms from July to October. Flowers should be picked during August for the most satisfying results in potpourris and sachets. This species can also be grown on a trellis.

J. sambac, Arabian Jasmine, is an evergreen that will bloom for most of the year. Move the container indoors during colder months and enjoy its perfume throughout its long blooming season. *J. sambac* is one of the Jasmines used for blending with Chinese tea. (There may be, perhaps, some use for such a blend since the flowers offer some antimicrobial activity to the mixture.) Another delicious, homemade, after-dinner tea is made with equal proportions of fresh *J. sambac* flowers and Camomile with a dash of roasted Chicory.

Containers should be located near windows and doors frequently open, in sunny breezeways, courtyards, or partially enclosed patios. A featured area in the garden consisting of a bench in a cul-de-sac surrounded by dense foliage, so as to seclude the site, is ideal for several pots of flowering Jasmines secreted away to create a bewitching atmosphere.

One of the most easily cared for and reliably fragrant herbs is Valerian, *Valeriana officinalis.* The flower plume of Valerian is referred to as having "heliotrope-like breath", an intoxicating fragrance, variously described, but most certainly floral and fruity. The legendary perfume Spikenard contained Valerian predominantly from the species *V. celtica.* Over one hundred species are known and though some are valuable for their fragrant flowers, other produce a spicy, luxuriantly aromatic root cherished by perfumers. Still others, such as *V. officinalis,* are grown commercially for their medicinal value as a powerful, non-addicting sedative.

Generally called Valerian today, instead of Fu, a handle from Greek times alluding to its malodorous airs during the drying process, this herb is still valuable today as a sedative. A few species commonly cultivated include Speick or Celtic Nard, *V. celtica,* which harks from the Alps and provides the ingredients for perfumes; Indian Valerian, *V. wallichii;* and Japanese Valerian or Kesso, *V. officinalis* var. *latifolia. V. sitchensis* from the steppes of Russia is considered the most important species for medicinal preparations, a reputation shared with *V. mexicana* from the New World. Some novel species include a 12 in. dwarf form, *V. arizonica;*

Elder-leaved Valerian, *V. sambucifolia;* and a low growing Marsh Valerian, *V. dioica* from Great Britian. These are mentioned because the many suppliers of Valerian do not always identify the species of the roots they sell for horticultural purposes.

The root oils contain pinene, camphene and limonene as well as a number of aromatic bornyl esters that are created during drying. The fragrance, which can be imitated by valerianic ether, is prized in India and the Mid-East. Strangely enough, it is the unpleasant smelling valerianic acid in the oil that is used as an intermediary in perfume manufacturing. It is one of those scents that is necessary to the final product's wide spectrum of odors, appealing to our sense of smell because it is more pleasing to encounter a mixture of fragrances than any single one. This is undoubtedly why a fragrant garden is so hypnotic— perhaps more so with Valerian about because of its sedative properties. Research indicates the active principles in Valerian root are truly central nervous depressants, but they are also highly unstable. The shelf life of the root is little more than a few months and any preparation that involves more than a simple infusion will destroy these active chemicals, rendering the medicine useless (except for the placebo effect which has also been studied and found to be a significant factor in successful treatments with Valerian).

Valerian's place in the fragrant garden is as a background herb. Its flowers are white or pink, highly fragrant, easily dried and everlasting. It blooms in early summer and lasts for several weeks. Do not get too close or the odor becomes heavy and can be regarded as putrid. From a distance the disgusting odors are diluted and the legendary heoliotrope fragrance dominates. To work an enchantment in your garden use at least 6 clumps. Arrange them along a pathway where they will be sheltered from winds or unite them at a central spot. Provide each clump at least 24 in. spacing and several years of maintenance-free flowering will be forthcoming. It is a hardy, herbaceous perennial that for the most part appreciates a heavy moist soil. *V. mexicana* and *V. sitchensis* can handle drier soils. It tolerates partial shade but is more fragrant in full sun. Depending upon the species, Valerian should be replanted every 4–6 years to thin the root system. It will grow from 3–6 ft. and makes a thin screen or border.

As a fragrant herb Valerian gives a special touch to compact features in formal or contemporary landscapes. Every garden needs a fragrant drift of Valerian and it is especially suited to wild and informal designs fitting into an arrangement with Meadow Rue, *Thallictrum glaucum,* Fennel and Astilbe. Valerian is a natural component along the forest front. In an informal landscape it should be tucked into a thicket of shrubbery or low trees.

A dapper herb for the fragrant and/or formal garden is the Curry Plant, *Helichrysum italicum* ssp. *siitalicum,* which entertains us with its near spherical shape, 12–18 in., and long-fingered, blue-silver foliage. One or two, wintered over in a cold frame (it is hardy to about 28°F) or greenhouse, are useful for turning a dull feature of conifers into an eye-catching arrangement. Its spicy scent is unquestionably that of Curry spice. Though most popular as a fragrant, silvered decorative material for wreaths and swags it can be used to spice an omelette or in breading fried chicken.

It prefers full sun and a sandy or a rocky, alkaline soil that remains dry. Its wispy, carefree habit adds a little informality in a formal arrangement with the Santolinas and Bush Thymes neatly trimmed into manageable mounds of comfortable size. Let *Origanum microphyllum* and Bush Basil share the scene for an immensely useful, fragrant and attractive feature garden.

Chapter 2 / SECTION 3

A Walk Through a Fragrant Garden

Visiting a fine garden is always an adventure. Examining the prize possessions of another gardener and enjoying the fruits of someone else's labor is a joy for anyone whether a gardener or not. Let's take a stroll through a small fragrant garden now. (Fig. 6) Descending the stairs from a deck to the garden in the early evening we feel the punch of a warm and spicy breeze wafting back over us. Our last step is cushioned by deep sand. The sand, as a source of the heat, draws air into the narrow garden keeping the air in motion even on calm days. It is an enclosed garden with a bowling green inside an oval path. Raised beds around the perimeter are stuffed with everchanging herbs and flowers, many of which are highly fragrant, scenting the entire yard during their reign, while others offer up their aromas to gentle carressing. "They are like shy people", Louise Beebe Wilder wrote, in *The Fragrant Garden,* "who find it difficult to open their hearts save at the magic of a sympathetic touch." If we delved no further in this garden than the drawing of deep breaths we would still go away enlightened. Being gardeners however, we've been this route before. We know that abstinence is impossible. Fragrance is nature's most powerful come-on, a lure no creature can foreswear.

Greeting us at the bottom of the steps is a pungent, spicy scent mixed with camphor. Ahead and to the left against a simmering block wall are 2 yellow-flowered herbs: Wormwood, an ancient vermifuge and narcotic, and Dwarf Feverfew, *Chrysanthemum parthenium* 'Selaginoides', a medicinal of reputable value in fever control. The grey-green, feathery foliage of Wormwood is a stark contrast to the vivid, lime-green oak leaf foliage of its neighbor. Their scents are not unpleasant but a brief encounter is encouraged.

A spicy sweetness in the air seems to come from everywhere and beckons us forward. A tall feathery Tansy with yellow buttons sprinkled all over its top bows to us as we pass and the heat from the sand draws us up a whiff of something waxy, an invigorating odor on a hot summer day. The shorter member of this duo by the stairsteps entertains us with a marbled foliage of creamy white and emerald-green. Our host gently prods it into action with a sandaled foot. A moment later Hawaiian drums throb in our ears and plantations of pineapples ripening in the hot South Pacific sun appear in our mind. Pineapple Mint is true to its namesake.

Moving on, we brush aside a groping branch of Variegated Hops that clings tenaciously to the stair railing. Though not scented, its 12 in. maple-like leaves are smeared with white in fascinating patterns imitating the little pot of Pineapple Mint at our feet.

We stroll past a sentinel Juniper standing guard at the corner of the stairs. At our feet a

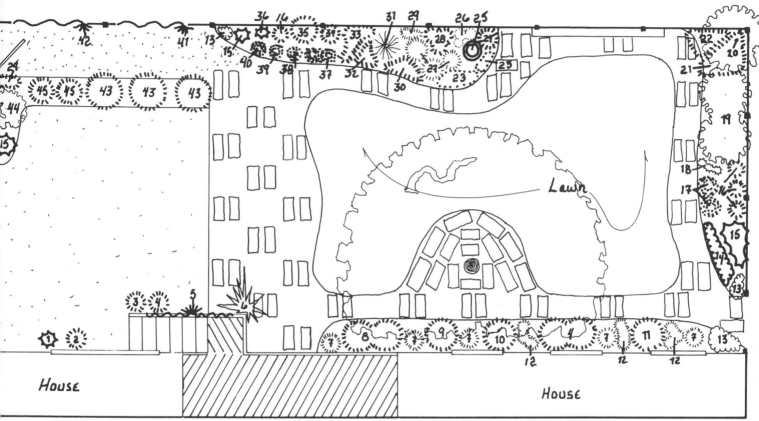

Fig. 6. A Fragrant garden. Dozens of fragrant herbs dangle or creep into the path of passersby giving up their scents for our enjoyment.

KEY

1 Wormwood *Artemisia absinthum*
2 Feverfew *Chrysanthemum parthenium*
3 Tansy *Tanacetum vulgare*
4 Pineapple Mint *Mentha suaveolens*
5 Variegated Hop *Humulus japonicus*
6 *Juniperus communis*
7 Columbine *Aquilegia* sp.
8 Orange Mint *Mentha* × *piperita* var. *citrata*
9 Lime Mint *Mentha* × *piperita* var. *citrata*
10 Black Mint *Mentha* × *piperita* var. *vulgaris*
11 Golden Mint *Mentha* × *gracilis* var. *variegata*
12 Rocambole *Allium sativa* var. *ophioscorodon*
13 Silver Mound *Artemisia lanata*
14 Cr. Red Thyme *Thumus praecox* 'Coccineus'
15 Southernwood *Artemisia abrotanum*
16 White Mugwort *Artemisia lactiflora*
17 Golden Lemon Thyme *Thymus* × *citriodorus* 'Aureus'
18 Dwarf Carnation *Dianthus caryophyllus*
19 Lilac *Syringa vulgaris*
20 Sweet Spire *Itea virginica*
21 Sweet Cicely *Myrrhis odorata*
22 Curly Mint *Mentha aquatica* var. *crispa*
23 Opal Basil *Ocimum basilicum* 'Dark Opal'
24 Lemon Balm *Melissa officinalis*
25 Sweet Bay *Laurus nobilis*
26 Lemon Geranium *Pelargonium melissinum*
27 Peony *Paeonia* spp.
28 *Valeriana officinalis*
29 Foxglove *Digitalis*
30 Lady's Mantle *Alchemilla vulgaris*
31 Blueberry *Vaccinium macrocarpon*
32 Grapefruit Mint *Mentha suaveolens* var.
33 Dwarf Monarda *Monarda didyma* 'Granite Pink'
34 Fernleaf Tansy *Tanacetum vulgare* 'Crispum'
35 Sweet Fennel *Foeniculum vulgare*
36 Roman Wormwood *Artemisia pontica*
37 Wedgewood Thyme *Thymus* 'Wedgewood English'
38 Tuffeted Thyme *Thymus caespititius*
39 Cr. Golden Thyme *Thymus* 'Clear Gold'
40 'Pink Chintz' Thyme *Thymus praecox* ssp. *articus*
41 Arabian Jasmine *Jasminum officinalis*
42 *Jasminum nudiflorum*
43 Lovage *Levisticum officinale*
44 Mock Orange *Philadelphus* sp.
45 Comfrey, Red flr. *Symphytum officinale* 'Coccineum'

cool red brick patio quickly pulls the heat from our soles as we enter the patchy shade of an old man apple. Crossing to the far corner we pass another Juniper sentinel softening the sharp line of a block wall. An arm of the patio extends ahead as a path following the wall leads ever deeper into the shade of the apple tree.

A slender raised bed at our feet is overflowing quite prodigiously with multihued herbs. Our host tells us that many mints reside here mixed incomprehensibly at times. His foot glides through the yellow and green speckled foliage of Ginger Mint and a spicy but still minty aroma evolves in the cool shade. Lacy, light green stems with bobbing daisies poke out here and there, among the mints sometimes as a dense bush, and others as single, thread-thin waifs with a solitary apple-scented flower. The faint apple aroma that comes and goes with the breeze is not from the apples now swelling on the branches above us but from this weedy annual, German Camomile. Little or no movement is needed for Camomile to raise its scent to all the world.

That South Seas aroma reaches us again and nearby is a great green mat of Pineapple Mint, speckled with white as if someone had spilled paint. Quite remarkably several branches of this mint are entirely white. A neighboring, dark green mint is melded subtly with red hues producing a purplish cast from a distance. A swipe of the foot and a delectable minty aroma surrounds us. It is the pure menthol scent Black Mint produces, rarely bitter, spicy or camphoraceous as Spearmint or Peppermint can be, and is highly fragrant even in the shade.

Other mints growing here are Apple Mint, a tall fuzzy leafed mint with fruity overtones. Curly Mint is an ornamental mint with tattered and gnarled leaves that make a colorful bright spot in a partially shaded garden. Horse Mint resembles a wooly, light green spearmint. Spearmint and Peppermint, the most common mints grown, are rather weedy but provide a good mint scent and flavor for little effort.

Appearing as little pools of green molasses, the irresistible Corsican Mint grows here and there self-sown between cracks in the path's bricks. It is a pleasant minty weed that needs no help to spread. We sidestep onto the grass a moment as 3 toddlers on tricycles roar past. The path along the perimeter of the lawn provides an excellent runway for children. The walk was designed with them in mind and adds versatility to a small backyard which serves as an elegant garden, an entertaining arena and a playground. The flowing lines of the warm, rusty red brick hide its utility well.

The last few feet of this mint garden are graced by the most fragrant of all the Mints, English Pennyroyal. Its perky perfume we are told is rarely absent from this end of the garden. Low growing and resilient to traffic, Pennyroyal is allowed to venture onto the walk where it is constantly crushed underfoot, scenting the entire yard on windy days. American Pennyroyal, *Hedeoma pulegioides,* is equally fragrant our host tells us although more upright and bushy in habit. Several plants of it reside across the path. Both are nicknamed Mosquito Plant for their uncanny ability to repel those vicious predators. On hot summer nights a centerpiece for outdoor use must include Pennyroyal to create an effective repellent.

The brick walk divides here, rising gently and entering the kitchen garden ahead, and to the left appearing to descend into a thicket. The thicket is composed of two venerable Lilacs surrounded by other bushes. A fuzzy, green herald immediately ahead on the leading edge of this thicket garden draws our attention. It is a cool, green carpet of Silver Mound, a miniature *Artemisia.* Neat, rounded humps spill casually over the rock ledge taking its shape and scenting the air ever so faintly with a sweet, absinthe scent.

Upon examining it closely we notice another Artemisia close by, Old Man, or Southernwood. In spring the crisp, pine scent of Old Man mingles perfectly with the rich Lilacs and Camomiles. Old Man has been a favorite nosegay for centuries. It is easily cared for and added to every indoor bouquet at our host's dinners.

Another *Artemisia* appearing tall and thin beside its relatives is White Mugwort. Its sweet smelling, yellow-white plume in late summer through autumn is a perfect harbinger of fall for a fragrant garden. Gentle autumn rains by no means spoil its fragrance, often carrying it on misty breezes to where it can be widely appreciated.

A small flowering willow ahead resides in a bed of Sweet Cicely and 'Lime' Mint. 'Lime' Mint has a tart, crisp, citrus note that makes an iced lemonade a special treat.

An inviting bench located at the halfway point around the small garden gives us a moment to rest and enjoy the garden from a sunny perspective. Twining at our backs is Hall's Honeysuckle, *Lonicera japonica,* sporting fragrant pink blooms that last from spring until fall. From below the bench creeps some of the Lime Mint while gobs of apple-scented blossoms of German Camomile peek out in search of sunlight adding to the informal charm.

The color-splashed beds further on attract our attention and we leave the bench to continue our journey. The thought of more new sights and smells piques our interest. Before we reach the raised garden we encounter a tub of Sweet Bay nobly perched in the center of a wide spot in the path. Grown for culinary use this bay is given a spot to bask in the sun.

Approaching the garden a tingling citrus scent greets us. In a large pot is Lemon Verbena emitting a barely perceptible fragrance of grated lemon peel. When touched it literally explodes as if we were squeezing lemons. Nearby, contributing to the lemon-scented air, is a Lemon Balm and a stand of Lemon-Scented Geranium, *Pelargonium limoneum,* with large maple-like leaves. Working together these 3 fragrant herbs yield a pleasant lemon odor recognizable from a distance. Flowing in front of the lemon-scented herbs are *Santolina neapolitana* and Opal Basil for a mellow, silver-blue and purple front border smelling of ginger cakes.

Tucked up against the fence is a low screen of Fragrant Goldenrod, *Solidago odorata.* Though we often speak unkindly of this genus, our host tells us that botanists have found that the Goldenrods do not contribute to the pollen problem. We should be grateful for this because the sweet-scented Goldenrod combines beauty and fragrance in a slender perennial package that never fails to please. From this species an anise essence is obtained, which is also the odor it imparts to the garden here. Others of the genus were once considered as a source of latex rubber. Goldenrod, available in many varieties and cultivars, remains a favorite border and screen plant with showy panicles of lemon-yellow, orange and bronze flowers.

An assortment of Peonies, *Paeonia* sp., join together in providing a crowd of blooms for color and entertainment. Some Peonies are scented: 'Elsa Sags', 'Pink Parfait', 'Vivid Rose', 'Joseph Christie' and 'Kelway's Glorious' for example. Don't think that growing Peonies is out of line in an herb garden. The Peony is one of the oldest herbs. Once used as a medicine, it received its name from the Greek physician to the gods, Paeonia. Even before the Greeks and Romans, who reputedly cultivated hundreds of varieties, they were revered centuries earlier by the Chinese, who grew them in temple gardens. Their attractive foliage provides a medium height background for a selection of Creeping Thymes along the front border. From behind the Peonies spills a dwarf Bee Balm, 'Granite Pink', with pink spidery flowers, and round-leaved or Grapefruit Mint, with large, purplish, fragrant leaves. The wind's invisible hands, as if in possession of a secret formula, are at work gently shaking the proper mixtures of essence from these herbs, rewarding us with a whiff of one of her price-less perfumes.

Rising like a feathery screen at the back of the garden are Garden Heliotrope and Fennel. The former is no longer in full bloom and scenting the entire garden, but the honey and vanilla odor is still unmistakable when we crush a flower. Although the root is a powerful sedative, it is the flowering portion of Garden Heliotrope that is valuable today as a highly fragrant everlasting plume for gardens and dried arrangements. The Fennel is in bloom and we are told that this is its most fragrant period. The anise scent encountered while observing Goldenrod close up is strong enough here to be sensed from a distance. Known as the "candy plant" by our host's children it is kept to the back for its own protection. Its sugar-sweet, anise-flavored leaves and flowers are a delicious breath freshener, a perky treat while gardening or a sweet spice for many delicately flavored dishes. We are told that rice was not a favorite food at our host's table until he began adding several green herbs and the flower umbels of Fennel for sweetness. Leftover rice is a thing of the past.

Fennel's other neighbors are Fernleaf Tansy and a graceful wand of blue-green Meadow Rue, *Thallictrum glaucum,* bearing clusters of musk-scented, yellow flowers that shed their fragrance best during late evening hours. Used here as screens, both make a pleasant contrast to their feathery neighbor.

Primarily for show is a narrow rivulet of red-flowering Yarrow, streaming into a pool of white and pink yarrow. Deep green foliage raises this ruddy sea aloft to ripple in the breeze.

Bent wearily and solemn over its charges before it is a small screen of White Mugwort just behind the Yarrow. Its heavy flower heads are beginning to form their fragrant plumes for fall, drooping over the Yarrow and a compact gold-leaved bush at its feet. This bright patch of yellow and light green is Golden Sage, more compact than Garden Sage and equally provocative in cooking. Beside it is an exquisite Tangerine Southernwood with an orange or lemon twist. A modest, blue-grey puff of *Artemisia lanata* brings this small garden to a neat finish.

Our guide gestures us on. There is more. Immediately ahead is a living screen that separates the sandbox from a pathway. It's a strangely herbed border garden. Among the screen of herbs is one that is quite unique and dominant. The herb is Lovage, a tall, tropical-looking plant with the unmistakable odor of Celery. The jungle-thick Lovage screen, looking like a queue of giant Celery plants, forms a dense barrier to sounds as well as sights.

On our right is a screen of espaliered vines whose flowers are so fragrant we must stop to catch our breath. That scent is familiar. "Jasmine, nature's most fragrant flower. Almost sacred, isn't it?" our guide whispers, referring to the intense feeling this flower's odor arouses. It has also been judged "sensual". If we look closer we can find more than one species joining forces here. Espaliered on the fence are vines of Poet's Jasmine and Winter Jasmine, whose flowers bloom before foliage appears in early spring, and an Arabian Jasmine, the flowers of which are prized for blends with tea, is trained on a trellis from a container.

The afternoon sun baking the damp, wood chip walk has created a hot and steamy air in this fragrant corridor. With the gate closed ahead a mixture of odors cling tenaciously to the air about us. Faintly hidden on the air is a hint of lemons, apples, anise, and a heavy note of Jasmine and gingered Celery. It is a mixture that seems to have been blended together like a recipe for a rare and precious perfume or a great epicurean banquet.

Self-sowing with gay abandon along the path is German Camomile again, its scent commingling and reminding us of spicy apple-butter. Scattered also by their own will and fortune are Coriander, Lemon Balm, and Borage. The scent of Coriander introduces a strange mongrel note in this collection of oversweet fragrances, a note not at all unpleasant. A Mock Orange, *Philadelphus* × *lemoinei,* introduces a lemon fragrance to the garden in very early spring. Our host explains that the Lemon Balm, strategically situated at the base of the gate in the path of the door, almost equals the scent of the Mock Orange whenever the gate is opened.

Staring through the gate dreamily, we can see that our host's garden does not end but becomes a dark, fern-dominated world under a huge walnut where other exciting herbs are surely hidden. This, however, is the end of our stroll through a fragrant garden. We turn and shortcut through the Lovage screen back across the sandbox to the house for the sun is setting and dinner, highlighted by herbs from this very garden, awaits us.

Formal Gardens for Beauty

Formal garden design is never seen anywhere in nature. It is distinct from other landscape forms which take at least some of their cue from the natural world around us. True formal landscapes are a massive undertaking. These are the grand gardens we visit on holidays or associated with a museum, public edifice, or historical monument. These gardens, like that shown in Figure 7, are pieces of art.

The formal landscape is designed to be shared. It is open and inviting, creative, not secretive, and overflowing with little details that beg to be seen, lauded, and loved. Formal designs incorporate round, square, or rectangular beds and may be dotted with ponds or cut by waterways. Intricate topiary, trimmed hedges, vine-smothered arbors, outbuildings for leisure, great urns, exotic herbs, breathtaking beds of a single flower species, elegant lawn furniture, statuary, ponds, palatial staircases, and a liberal application of expansive walks are all a part of formal design. The non-natural aspect is an attractive feature. The ability of a gardener to soften the geometric rigidity with herbs and flowers in all their glory is the crucial path to success.

To venture ahead let us examine the general principles used in any formal design. The first, and most important, is that a pattern must be balanced, whether it is a small decorative plot or an entire landscape. A balanced formal garden does not require geometric symmetry, but such has been the most common method. Asymmetric gardens are becoming popular today, but require considerable knowledge of landscape art.

Second, walkways in the vicinity of "formals" must be wide. Spacious paths give the impression of larger-than-life gardens and are a feature of the landscape to provoke a sense of motion and to open the vista. A path may widen around, pass between, or simply end at one or more formal gardens. However, the garden must be highly visible from the central point, and wide, well directed paths promote this image. (Fig. 8)

Path materials are also important. Solid colors and textures such as concrete, gravel, cobblestone, sawdust, bark or turf do not themselves distract from the panorama of gardens and other features in the landscape. They encourage the eye to keep moving. Brick or stone slab paving set in an unpatterned fashion will be less distracting than in patterns such as herringbone. The latter are intrinsically entertaining and may be used elsewhere, such as an enticing lead-in to a special feature, but never adjacent to a feature. A break in the pattern, such as a 90° rotation, deliberate off-set, different pattern, or a change in paving materials such as from brick to a graveled section bordered by curbs, is used to herald a change in the landscape. It provides a meaningful stopping point for the eye, thereby assisting in discovering a new display—another formal garden—and directing all emphasis there.

Third, water in ponds, streams, or canals are important elements in formal gardens. Shallow ponds striking canal-like into a landscape and bordered by beds of brilliant flowers

Fig. 7. A collection of formal gardens including variations on the maze designed by DeVries in the 16th century for royalty.

and herbs is a Dutch feature, while slender channels of water flowing perpendicularly to a central walk and bordered by elaborate containers of fragrant herbs are a Persian theme. In shallow reflecting ponds water promotes relaxation in any landscape. Unlike inert objects, water, as well as garden plants, appeals to all of our senses, thereby drawing our minds away from the mundane and tedious. Ponds or fountains (Fig. 8) are included as the center of a design or a shallow trough may be featured nearby, in imitation of a medieval dipping well. (Fig. 9) In many regions a pond is a necessity to alter the level of humidity in its vicinity. In dry climates, the humidity allows the gardener to employ otherwise difficult species. A shallow, wide pond is far more effective than a small deep one and should be located in the sun or in the immediate area where it is to furnish humidity.

Fourth, statuary, topiary, and containerized herbs are an integral part of a formal garden. Statues bring emotions in to play with displays of humorous personages, animals in predicaments, frightening beasts whose attacks have been frozen into terrifying poses, or cheerful frolicking creatures from myth or legend. Containers of splendid flowers and strange foliage momentarily draw the viewer's attention from the strict geometry of formal landscapes.

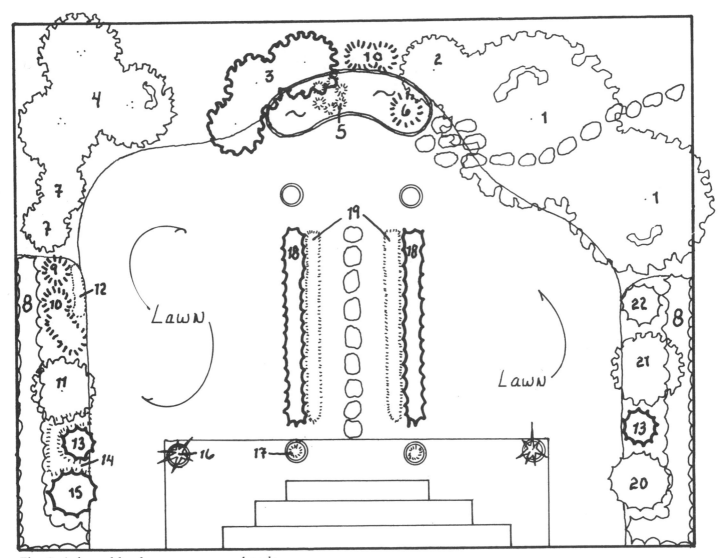

Fig. 8. A formal landscape on a grand scale.
KEY
1 Elm *Ulmus glabra* 'Pendula'
2 Sweet spire *Itea virginica*
3 Witch Hazel *Hamamelis mollis*
4 Birch *Betula pendula*
5 Cattail *Thyphus latifolia*
6 Sweet flag *Acorus calamus*
7 Lilac *Syringa vulgaris*
8 Holly *Ilex aquifolium*
9 Lovage *Levisticum officinale*
10 *Valeriana officinalis*
11 Tamarisk *Tamarix tetranda*
12 'Skeleton-leaf Lemon' Geranium *Pelargonium graveolens*
13 *Santolina neapolitana*
14 Lady's Mantle *Alchemilla* spp.
15 Lavender *Lavandula angustifolia*
16 potted Rosemary (pair) *Rosmarinus* 'Tuscan Blue'
17 potted Jasmine (pair) *Jasminum sambac*
18 Southernwood *Artemisia abrotanum*
19 Saffron/bulbs/Basil
20 *Eleagnus pungens*
21 Japanese apricot *Prunus mume*
22 Oregon Grape *Mahonia aquifolium*

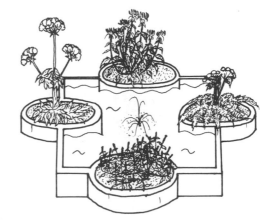

Fig. 9. 16th century formal courtyard pond for residences in hot, dry zones to assist in the cultivation of water loving herbs such as Angelica, Monarda, Sweet Cicely and Mint.

Fascinating works of topiary, including bonsai, espalier and the estrade, are forms of art which stir emotions. Estrade, Figure 10, are standards, a lollipop structure—frivolous entities to amuse visitors. They may also be admired for the craft employed in their making for they require considerable skill to create. They are trained to one or more tiers, each the same or a different shape—spheres, cones, or discs.

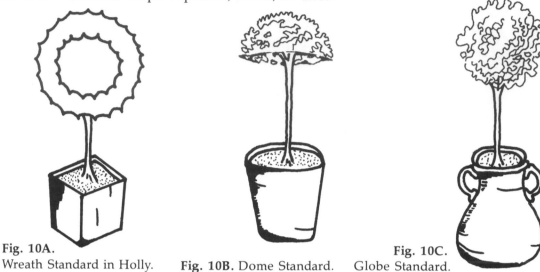

Fig. 10A.
Wreath Standard in Holly.   **Fig. 10B.** Dome Standard.   **Fig. 10C.**
Globe Standard.

Espalier involves the training of shrubs or trees to a shape upon a vertical surface such as trellis or wall. It is the least difficult kind of topiary to exploit. Spirals, sunbursts and candelabra are common espalier designs used. It is often used to train apple and pear trees or to add charm to an otherwise drab fence or garage wall by using a flowering plant in a pleasant design that may repeat an existing pattern in a patio, lawn furniture or the architectural cutwork of the home.

An espaliered fruit plant is healthier and yields considerably more than the natural form. Fewer branches are providing fruit and all are given maximum exposure to sunlight. The design is inherently more open and therefore less prone to the spread of disease. Flowering stone fruits benefit from this technique in wet climates, particularly where an overhang protects them from rainfall.

Bonsai is the most demanding of topiary works and is essentially an art form requiring a great deal of time, effort and creative skill. Bonsai are exhibited alone or in groupings in virtually any setting, whether formal or informal, with the added dimension to a landscape that no other topiary work has—inspiration. Bonsai can be shaped to evoke deep feelings of joy or sadness and can accent other landscape features to bring out hidden forms.

A popular and special form of formal garden is to be found in metropolitan neighborhoods. It is the rooftop garden, composed entirely of container grown plants. Narrow containers 18–24 in. deep, typically of pre-formed concrete or wood planking with plastic liners, may be arranged to accommodate a long walk in the open air high above the bustling world below.

The rooftop container garden is inherently formal because of the rectangular contours of both the building and the containers employed. It is therefore a simple matter to construct a formal garden. Roof gardens are a great asset not only because they create beauty in an otherwise barren environment but also because they yield fresh herbs and vegetables from otherwise wasted space. Metropolitan rooftop gardens place unique demands on the garden concept, the foremost of which is size. Many rooftops provide fewer than 1,000 sq. ft. of space, or an area 33 ft. or less on each side, roughly half the average American front garden

Plate 7

Specimen of 'Camphor' Basil, *O. canum,* in a dooryard garden.

Shining white ground cover of Beach Wormwood in partial shade encircling a clump of Chervil.

The lustrous rich appearance of a 'Cinnamon' Basil goes well in any perennial contemporary feature.

Single specimen of 'Spice' Basil.

'Lettuce Leaf' Basil and Bush Basil—a comparison of the largest and smallest leaved Basils.

A fragrant border in a kitchen garden of 'Dark Opal', Lemon and 'Lettuce Leaf' Basils.

Plate 8

Fragrant herbs awaiting passersby. Several herbs combine here to give an all year display of fragrance and color. From left, Winter Savory, Lady's Mantle and 'Dark Opal' Basil. Peonys, Archangel and *Santolina neapolitana* are background herbs.

A partially closed knot of Sweet Basil, 'Dark Opal' Basil, Chives and Dwarf Feverfew with a frame of carrots as a part of a 17th century kitchen garden replica.

Curly Mint with cheerful dark green ruffles is a choice feature garden Mint, from garden of John Eccles, Winlock, WA.

Stream channel in formal setting with Marsh Marigold, *Caltha palustris,* Sweet Flag and Water Mint in the Cascara Circle of the Medicinal Herb Garden, University of Washington, Seattle, WA.

Pond with Sweet Flag and Water Lily in Garden of Judith Zugish, Marysville, Washington.

A fragrant path between the forested perimeters of a checkerboard garden lined with a fragrant white flowering Rosemary, Medicinal Herb Garden, University of Washington, Seattle, WA.

Plate 9

Golden Lemon Thyme in a perimeter bed with Shasta Daisy, Hyssop and Lemon Balm.

Specimen of Miniature Thyme.

The compact busy nature of Silver Thyme (center) and Lavender Cotton (right) make them invaluable herbs for formal or informal applications.

A mound of 'Broadleaf English' Thyme joins Chives, Sage and Wooly Betony on this raised bed feature. Blue spires of Dwarf Catnip rise in the background.

'Narrow Leaf French' Thyme shares this dry desert site with Spanish Lavender.

Plate 10

Lavender and *Santolina chamaecyparissus* blooming with blue and gold colors in a mixed border on a sloping perimeter of a formal garden at the Medicinal Herb Garden, University of Washington, Seattle, WA.

The marked contrast of a feathery species of Lavender Cotton, *Santolina neapolitana,* and a broad-leaved Lion's Paw or Lady's Mantle, *Alchemilla* sp. makes a splendid feature in this contemporary scene in the gardens of Judith Zugish, Marysville, WA.

A blue green puff of Garden Rue, with a collar of Corsican Mint, joins Creeping Golden Thyme and French Thyme in this evergreen perennial bed.

An ancient mound of Corsican Rue in a square at the Medicinal Herb Garden, University of Washington, Seattle, WA.

Germander blooming in perennial border in garden of Judith Zugish, Marysville, WA.

in suburbia. Other problems to be dealt with include: water cost/supply, wind and air pollution.

One landscaping principle that is difficult to incorporate into rooftop gardens is the tying together of the immediate landscape with features in the distance so that they enhance one another. Architecture is a formal element in such environments. Formality in landscaping, which was once quite commonly related to architecture, may again be the inspiration for a gardener to design a formal garden around the skyline. The raised beds could frame a scene in the distance such as mountains or near or distant skyline. Perhaps a pattern in the fashion of the cutwork parterre could adopt the architecture of an adjacent and dominating building to the garden.

One design that is best expressed is the maze. Figure 11 is such an example. This garden design makes use of far-off vistas of mountains as well as neighboring architecture and yet it captures the true spirit of a maze because it can be seen throughout the year and

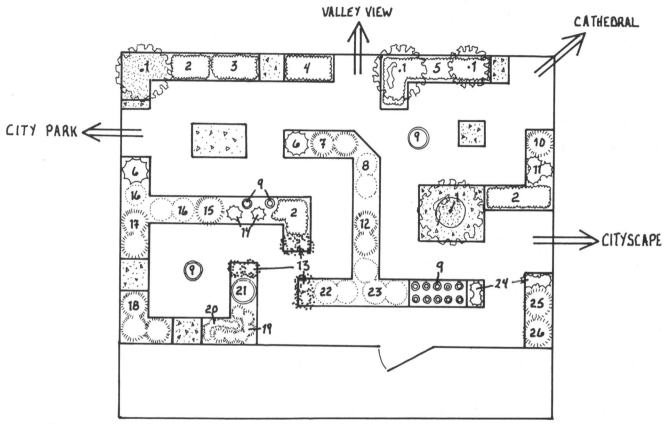

Fig. 11. Metropolitan rooftop maze garden.
KEY
1 Dwarf fruit trees *Malus* sp.
2 Turf Camomile *Chamaemellum nobile* 'Trenague'
3 Caraway Thyme *Thymus herba-barona*
4 Red flowering Thyme *Thymus praecox* 'Coccineus'
5 Sweet Woodruff/Violets
6 Southernwood *Artemisia abrotanum*
7 Peony *Paeonia* spp.
8 Mums
9 potted herbs
10 *Allium karataviense*
11 Winter Savory *Satureja montana*
12 Shasta Daisy *Chrysanthemum maximum*

13 French and Silver Thyme *Thymus* 'Argenteus', *T. vulgaris* 'Narrow Leaf French'
14 Dwarf Sage *Salvia officinalis* 'Nana'
15 Golden Mint *Mentha* × *gracilis* var. *variegata*
16 *Calendula officinalis*
17 Pineapple Mint *Mentha suaveolens*
18 Orange Mint *Mentha* × *piperita* var. *citrata*
19 Chive *Allium schoenoprassum*
20 Dwarf Feverfew *Chrysanthemum parthenium* 'Selaginoides'
21 potted Sweet Bay *Laurus nobilis*
22 Opal Basil *Ocimum basilicum* 'Dark Opal'
23 Sweet Basil *Ocimum basilicum*
24 Azalea
25 'Moonshine' Yarrow *Achillea clypeolata*
26 Painted Daisy *Chrysanthemum coccineum*

incorporates many evergreen plants for winter beauty. Lounge areas for both sun-and-shade-lovers are provided and there is an accent on the more fragrant herbs to counteract the unpleasant, polluted air of the city.

The fifth principle for constructing any formal design is that the formal garden must be isolated within the landscape. It must be surrounded by a barrier which sharply delineates it from its surroundings and restricts entry. It may be either framed so it is visible from without or enclosed for complete privacy. The frame might be wattle, picket, ranch or rail fencing, a low to medium height hedge, or a stone wall that doubles as a sitting bench. It might be enclosed by a board fence, brick wall or a tall trellis clothed in a thicket of vines and espaliered herbs, depending upon the site and the intentions of the gardener.

The enclosed formal garden is refered to as the *Hortus Conclusus,* literally, a contained garden (see Chapter 7). Those of the 12th century are little different from the enclosed patio of today, provided there are herbs and potted plants within (Fig. 12). The smaller formal pleasure gardens originated as extended rooms located within the inner bailey of a castle, the grounds adjacent to the door of a castle keep's bedchamber or hall. The herber and an orchard would surround the keep, but still be within the castle walls, tucked into a part of the outer bailey. Smaller castles with little room for gardens or those situated on unsuitable soils placed the garden a short walk from the main gate and, if possible, visible from a tower window for entertainment, or from the barbicans for protection. These gardens were fenced within wattle, stone, wooden palisades (thick boards nailed side-by-side), or impenetrable shrubbery such as that about which King James I wrote as he gazed from his jail cell window overlooking the garden outside the castle wall:

And Hawthorn hedges knit
That no one, though he were walking by
Might there within scarce anyone espy.

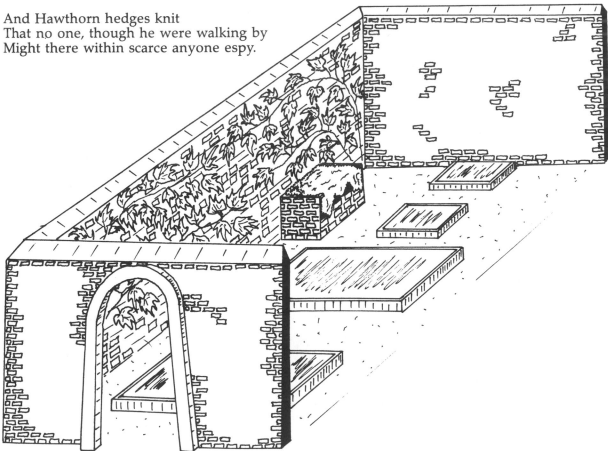

Fig. 12. Hortus Conclusus, looking into the walled herber shown in Fig. 50. An herb garden for the small metropolitan yard.

Near the end of the 19th century, formalism was replaced by the informal and natural look. Small "formals" were relegated to a patch off to the side of the estate, so that lavish and elegant gardens were not forgotten but appreciated on a more modest scale. Three kinds of "formals" were designed for their beauty and incorporated into the landscape. These gardens were the *knot,* the *parterre* and the *maze.* Let's examine each one in more detail.

The *knot* was one of the earliest pleasure gardens. Within a square or rectangular bed, a design was created with herbs and colored earth that resembled a piece of knotted rope. Some examples are shown in Figures 13 through 20. Figure 13 shows one of the most popular designs, originating in the 16th century. It is composed of three separate borders. The garden design in Figure 14 comprised only two interweaving borders. Figure 15 is essentially a single border but quite complicated. The designs in Figures 16 and 17 were popular knots in the American colonies during the late 16th and early 17th centuries. These were the domain of many low-growing beneficial herbs, not necessarily in trimmed borders but rather linear and triangular beds of many varied species. Figures 18 and 19 are examples of modern knots.

Fig. 13. Popular 16th century knot design composed of three borders.

Fig. 14. A simplified version of a multibordered knot from 16th century.

Fig. 15. A single border closed knot design. Interstices are occupied by colored earth for a low border or by flowers if a taller border is used.

Fig. 16. Simple knot from colonial American period.

Fig. 17. Simple knot from colonial American period.

Fig. 18. Contemporary knot for today's gardener. This design can be merged with a sidewalk or patio.

Fig. 19. Contemporary knot.

During the 16th century the knot reached its peak as a popular pleasure garden. Within the raised bed framework a knot could assume an unlimited number of designs. Knots were just as likely to be animal caricatures, the heraldry of a castle's lord (Fig. 20), as religious, mystic or astrological symbols. Whether enjoyed from afar, as an ornamental garden near benches or sitting lawns, or criss-crossed by footpaths, the knot contained both ornamental and beneficial herbs. The "open" knot allows more space for maintaining and harvesting beneficial herbs while the interstices of a "closed" knot were filled with flowers. Virtually any low-growing herb could be worked into the interstices of a knot.

Fig. 20. Heraldry in a knot.

Though there are many ways to approach the design of a knot, several principles are universally observed. First, and most important, the herbs selected should be of markedly different foliage colors to create a strong sense of contrast. Second, all the plants should be about the same height at maturity. Spreading herbs can be corralled but if one herb requires pruning, the others should also be trimmed to maintain a uniform height and appearance. Annuals or perennials can be used, alone or in combination. Tall herbs are generally unsuitable for a knot garden because they will hide a portion of the garden from view or unbalance the design. The knot is intended to be a centerpiece, a feature garden to be strolled about and admired from nearby. Choose herbs that grow less than 24 in. and with a relatively dense habit. Ground covers below 6 in. are best for the interstices or borders surrounding a knot. If a smaller garden is planned, it is important to note that foliage colors produce more appealing and distinct patterns than do flowering plants. Flowers might well be used, however, to fill the interstices of the knot.

Of the perennial herbs, a few should be tried first. Bushy, evergreen candidates, easy to work with and propagate, include Wormwood, Southernwood, Santolina, Germander, Hyssop, Rue, Winter Savory, Thyme and Lavender. The only drawback to evergreen or woody perennials is the difficulty of maintaining a continuous border of 2 dozen or more plants. These herbs might be better grown as closely spaced mounds for easy maintainence and to make replacement of dying plants less tedious.

On the other hand, the best herbaceous perennials include Oregano, the Mints, Chives and Dwarf Feverfew. If an herbaceous perennial garden is desired, two Oreganos will quickly fill the bill. Wild Marjoram, *Origanum vulgare,* with a dark green foliage and Golden Oregano, *O. vulgare* 'Aureum' which has yellow green leaves. Either Apple Mint for a soft green or Orange Mint for a deep purple-green could be used for contrast. The Mints make excellent knot herbs, filling their boxes snugly and providing a tremendous experience for the nose. The variegated Mints are choice for contrast, but solid green colors are necessary for a proper knot.

Starting with annuals is the best way to become familiar with the knot design. Both the plants and the garden are short-lived, allowing for other ideas and designs to follow them. A few of the best herbs for this use are Curly Parsley, Caraway, Sweet Marjoram, German Camomile, Calendula and Basil. They can be accompanied by annual flowering plants, such as Marigolds and Alyssums, or even vegetables such as Carrots, Lettuce, flowering Kale, etc. The Basils are the choice herb with which to experiment. Foliage colors range from dark green in 'Cinnamon' Basil, a range of greens with Sweet Basil and Bush Basil, the light green of Lemon Basil, and the dark purples of Opal and 'Krishna' Basil.

The dimensions of a knot depend upon the plant materials used in it. The more compact herbs and lower-growing ground covers are used in knots as small as 30 sq. ft. Slim, well-trimmed hedges of *Santolina,* Germander, Hyssop or Thyme may be only 6–8 inches in cross-section, or large hedges of Rosemary, Compact Lavender, Bay and Southernwood may be at least 12 in. As a rule of thumb a border should be no wider than one-tenth the shortest dimension of the garden. An 8 in. Thyme hedge will look its best in a small garden of only 30–50 sq. ft., where its leaves and flowers can play an important role. A border of English Lavender, trimmed to 12–24 in., will require a garden that is at least 20–30 ft. on a side.

The interstices of a knot may not only be filled with flowers and ground covers but inert earths or organic materials. It was for the knot and parterre that colored earths were formulated. Intense color is vital to accent the design or balance the color of foliage. Table 5 lists the choices of fill materials that may be used and Table 6, Coloring Agents. Materials such as crushed coal (black), lime (white), or the two combined (blue) provide striking accents for grey foliages, a popular choice for 3 centuries. Crushed brick or tiles (red/yellow), crushed green sand or slate (green/grey or blue/green) all lend character to a design. Organic materials such as sawdust (yellow/red/brown), wood chips (brown), manures (dark brown/black) and even turf (green) are used in gardens with changing designs, thus improving the soil as well as decorating it. Many sizes and colors of crushed rock are available to us today, including cinders (red), lava rock (red/browns/black), gravel (grey), granite (pink or white), quartzite (pink/white) and fabricated concrete mixes of all colors. Pebbles, cobbles, brick, tile, sea shells, boards and even bones have been used as fill.

Table 5
Fill For Knots and Parterres

INORGANIC	ORGANIC
Crushed Rock, gravel	Mulch
Sand	Sawdust
Oyster shell	Woodchips
	Bagged manure

Table 6
Coloring Agents

Black	Crushed coal[1] or charcoal, steer manure[2]
Brown	Wood chips, chicken manure[2]
White	Lime, oyster shell, Dolomite chips, Quartzite, sand
Blue	Lime and charcoal, colored sand
Green	Greensand, grass[3]
Yellow	Crushed brick, sawdust
Red	Crushed brick, sawdust (cedar or redwood)

1. Coal will leave a toxic residue of metals if used regularly
2. Commercially prepared, bagged and pasteurized
3. Use low growing Bentgrass, Fescue, etc.

You will find the knot an immensely gratifying garden. The garden shown in Figure 13 is easy to lay out and simple to plant. It is a basic knot that was popular because of its versatility. In only ten steps, a knot garden like that in Figure 13 can become the center of attraction in your landscape. Table 7 describes the step-by-step construction of this design.

Table 7
Ten Steps To a Knot Garden

STEP 1— Measure off the outside dimensions of garden. All four sides must be equal.

STEP 2— Find center of square (C) and center of each side (#1–4).

STEP 3— Drive stake at each point, 1 through 4, and with stake or trowel tied on the end of string sketch a half circle beginning at each point. Start at a distance (equal to the width of the border desired) from C, the center point.

These lines sketched will be the centerline of one border. Border width should be about 1/10 of the width of the square.

STEP 4— From center point C sketch a circle. The outermost edge (point 5) should equal the distance from the lobe of the first design to the edge of the square.

STEP 5— Measure off border width and sketch inner circle.

STEP 6— Where points 1–4 on edges intercept inner edge of circle will be the four outside corners of the square. Sketch straight lines between intercept points.

STEP 7— Sketch inner border of square according to intended border width.

STEP 8— Identify crossovers.

STEP 9— When planting annual borders, plant seeds in order of germination, longest first, to properly time emergence. Bloom times should also be planned for.

STEP 10— Fill interstices by either coloring the soil surface using one of the recommended soil conditioners, a ground cover or flowers (e.g., Alyssums).

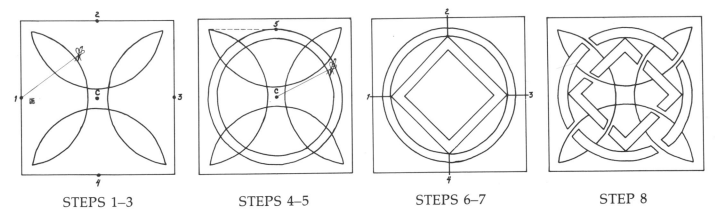

STEPS 1–3   STEPS 4–5   STEPS 6–7   STEP 8

The best method for transferring a complicated design from paper to the ground is probably one you have already encountered while doing cross-word puzzles and scrambled picture games. The picture to be copied is overlaid with a grid of squares. (Fig. 21) The garden plot that will receive the design is also gridded. It is important to remember that the number of squares used on both must be equal though the dimensions will differ. The transfer process is performed by walking from square to square on the garden plot and sketching onto the soil that portion of the design on the picture for the same square. Even the most complicated patterns may be copied with this method.

Fig. 21. Parterre garden design rendered into grid for transfer to garden site. The garden site is gridded in the same fashion and the design traced onto the soil using lime or a trowel.

The flamboyant *parterre* is the most fanciful and intricate garden pattern ever designed. It was evolved to fulfill the wildest dreams of the lovers of formal gardens. Early parterres relied predominantly on colored earths and less on herbs, effectively allowing an increase in the scale of the design with less gardening effort. The parterre, as the name implies, was literally level with the ground and not composed of raised beds, again requiring less gardening effort yet appearing orderly and distinct.

Figures 22 and 23 are examples of a parterre. With the ground already tilled either could be laid out on a weekend. Two alternate designs have been reproduced here to show the versatility. Figure 22 will be set directly into an existing lawn, the paths at 3 ft. wide, easily accommodate a lawnmower. The beds will be filled with numerous flowering and evergreen herbs which may include the ornamental dwarf Catnip, miniature Roses, Feverfew, Camomile, Anise Hyssop, Golden Oregano, Santolina, Rue, English Lavender, 'Rosea' Lavender, Wooly Betony, Monarda and Golden and Dwarf Sage. This is a garden with a blend of colors that are bright and cheerful. It is essentially a garden which does not hug the property line but holds a classical pose in the very center of the lawn.

Fig. 22. Background parterre set directly into the lawn. Paths remain grass.

KEY
1 Golden Sage *Salvia officinalis* 'Icterina'
2 Dwarf Feverfew *Chrysan. parthenium*
3 Lemon Balm *Melissa off.* var. *variegata*
4 Cr. Thyme *Thymus pulegioides*
5 Roses
6 Miniature Roses
7 *Santolina viridis*
8 *Santolina chamaecyparrissus*
9 Lavender *Lavandula angustifolia* 'Hidcote'
10 Bee Balm *Monarda didyma*
11 *Santolina neapolitana*

Fig. 23. Metropolitan courtyard parterre.

KEY
1 *Juniperus communis*
2 Mignonette *Reseda odorata*
3 Opal Basil *Ocimum basilicum* 'Dark Opal'
4 Golden Sage *Salvia officinalis* 'Aurea'
5 Dwarf Sage *Salvia officinalis* 'Nana'
6 Cr. Red Thyme *Thymus praecox* ssp. *articus* 'Coccineus'
7 Dwarf Lavender *Lavandula angustifolia* 'Nana'
8 Variegated Lemon Balm *Melissa officinalis* var. *variegata*
9 White Cr. Thyme 'Foster flower' *Thymus pulegioides*
10 Silver/Golden Lemon Thyme
11 Golden Oregano *Origanum vulgare* 'Aureum'

Figure 23 may be used in a crowded metropolitan neighborhood, where it can become the entire back garden. The scale of the garden is less, 30 x 30 ft. with a surrounding 5 ft. strip of lawn. The beds are 18 in. wide. A rusty red brick has been chosen to match that of the building. The plants chosen are beneficial herbs, including Basil, Oregano, Thyme, Sage and Rosemary, and here and there are patches of ground cover, to allow foot traffic. The central looping border is composed primarily of evergreens for winter beauty. The interconnecting beds are herbaceous perennials and annuals. Four columnar junipers in ornate pots reside in the corners. It is a garden of considerable beauty and benefit for the enlightened metropolitan gardener.

The completed parterre says much about a home owner. It is quite obvious that an appreciation of art is paramount and on a grand scale. But the art must also instruct: that is, teach the viewer about the beauty of two unrelated, but united subjects, geometry and nature. Although the parterre is the medium in which the two so perfectly come together, combining the two is not easy. It is an art.

The parterre was intended to be fairly large, certainly no less than 300–400 sq. ft. The reason was simple—in too small an area a loss of clarity in the design would result. The prime reason for using colored earths was to help refine the image and also decrease the need for maintenance when the garden was boosted to stupendous proportions. Palatial parterres in the 17th and 18th centuries ranged from ¼ acre to several, and quite often, several parterres were interconnected to create one garden feature of immense size.(Fig. 7)

Figure 24 shows a parterre composed of only one plant species, a box hedge, circa 17th century. The English parterre, Figure 25 substituted lawn for earths and the beds were gorged with elegant flowers. Compartmented parterres used geometric subunits that were reversed and connected back-to-back (Fig. 26). Like the links in a chain, these subunits would be used to form intricate patterns from the simple quad to many dozens of units interconnected into an even larger pattern. For the ultrastylish, it became fashionable to own a parterre patterned after embroidery designs or after the architectural scrollwork (cutwork) of their mansions, such as in Figures 25 and 26.

Fig. 24. Single border parterre.

Before choosing herbs for a parterre it is important to determine the background material. Color is applied in the garden just as a painter applies pigments to a canvas to create a painting. The color of the fill is chosen to either contrast or harmonize with the surrounding landscape. As the large size of a parterre is imposing in any landscape, choose the background wisely.

Dark backgrounds will suit light green or grey foliage plants. Black, blue, or chocolate colored earths suggest both an emptiness and vastness that needs to be filled by bright colors such as the yellows of Golden Oregano, Dwarf Feverfew, Golden Creeping and

Fig. 25. English parterre: central oval may be either a bowling green or reflecting pool, paths are grass or Roman Camomile and beds of colorful flowers dazzle the eyes from all around as statuary or topiary grace the circled areas.

Fig. 26. Compartmented and/or Cutwork parterre.

Golden Lemon Thyme, variegated Melissa, and Ginger Mint or the silver-lining herbs, Silver Horehound, Silver Germander, Wooly Lavender, Wooly Betony, Silver or Clary Sage and Silver Thyme.

Brick-red materials add a warmth and depth to a landscape and require the verdant greens of *Santolina viridis,* Myrtle, Germander, Roman Camomile, Curly Parsley, Lemon Verbena, Basil, miniature Roses, Pennyroyal, Holly, and virtually all of the golden variegated varieties and cultivars.

Cooler colors, blue, yellow and white, convey a joyful cordial feeling and are best combined with the fragrant and richly robed herbs such as the scented Geraniums with their fabulous foliage patterns, *Santolina neapolitana,* German Camomile, Silver Germander, Basil, Rue, Dittany, Creeping Red and Wooly Thyme, the dark glossy green Mother-of-Thyme,

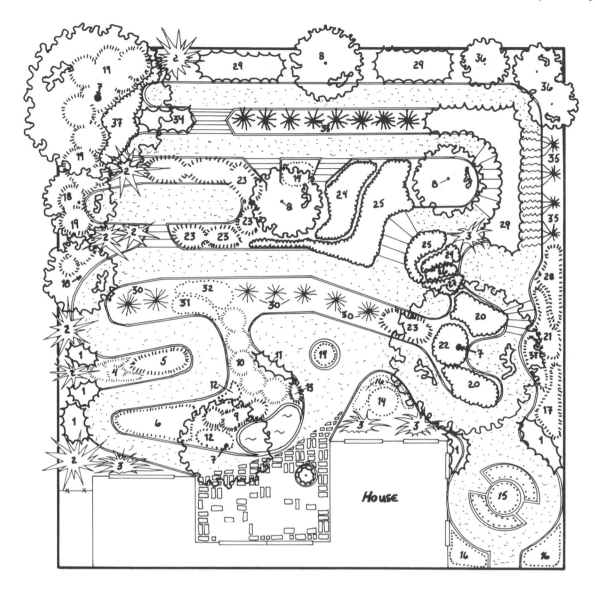

Fig. 27. Maze in informal design on sloping terrain.

KEY

1 Southernwood *Artemisia abrotanum*
2 Mugo Pine *Pinus* spp.
3 Creeping Juniper *Juniperus horizontalis*
4 *Dahlia* selection
5 Valerian *Valeriana officinalis*
6 *Iris* spp.
7 English Walnut *Juglans regia*
8 Apple *Malus* sp.
9 Angelica *Angelica atropurpurea*
10 Peony (selection)
11 Golden Sage *Salvia officinalis* 'Icterina'
12 *Monarda didyma* Bee Balm
13 Golden Oregano *Origanum vulgare* 'Aureum'
14 Calendula *Calendula officinalis*
15 KITCHEN GARDEN
16 annual flowers
17 Meadow Rue *Thalictrum glaucum*
18 Hazelnut *Corylus*
19 Sword Fern *Polystichum* sp.
20 Violets *Viola* spp.

21 Primroses *Primula* spp.
22 Wild Ginger *Asarum hartwegii*
23 Lovage *Levisticum officinale*
24 'White Magic' Thyme *Thumus praecox* ssp. *articus*
25 Cr. Red Thyme *Thymus pulegioides* 'Kermesinus'
26 Golden Thyme *Thymus* 'Clear Gold'
27 Oregano Thyme *Thymus pulegioides* 'Oregano-scented'
28 Fern Leaf Tansy *Tanacetum vulgare* 'Crispum'
29 Lavender *Lavandula angustifolia* 'Hidcote'
30 Roses *Rosa* sp.
31 'Bush' Basil *Ocimum basilicum*
32 Opal Basil *Ocimum basilicum* 'Dark Opal'
33 Blueberry *Vaccinium angustifolium*
34 Azalea *Rhododendron obtusum* 'Coccineum'
35 Grape *Vitus vinifera*
36 Italian Prune *Prunus*
37 Sweet Woodruff *Gallium odorata*

'Pink Chintz' and Caraway Thymes.

The parterre is best planted with hardy evergreen perennials: Lavender, Thyme, Germander, Box, Hyssop, Holly, Yew, Myrtle, Bay, Santolina, Rue and Rosemary. However, in today's bustling world, gardeners do not always stay in one location long enough to enjoy such a laborious design. It is also more satisfying to reap a harvest, if possible, from any garden, be it even the most classical. A parterre using herbaceous perennials and annuals is not at all illogical and may well have been more common than medieval writers would like us to believe. The only rule this is breaking, which must be weighed carefully in designing the garden, is the loss of clarity of the design.

It is vital for the parterre to provide a continual display of flowers or colorful foliages. The beds are generally planted with a homogeneous mixture of evergreen and flowering plants having staggered bloom times. It was popular among the better medieval landscapers to interpose more than one pattern, using each blooming species to create another design. The flowers were arranged in the beds so that they yielded a clearly defined design by themselves alone—a design within a design. The parterre was also used to incorporate into the home site a wooded section of the estate. That is, trees were assembled onto the design in an orderly way. Fruit and nut-bearing trees were used primarily but botanical gardens included every tree possible for the purposes of instruction. With a little planning ingenuity, a home owner can design a parterre around existing trees and shrubs, using them to an advantage.

The *maze,* such as in Figure 7, has enjoyed sporadic popularity throughout the last 3,000 years. This queer, but delightful design was originally developed as a game in commemoration of the fall of Troy (the maze reproduced the convoluted walls of the great fortress). The game was introduced into Europe and Great Britain by the Romans and used as a training arena for mounted knights to hone their riding skills. In medieval times, shepherds and mercenary men-at-arms were fond of maze games and scratched them onto bare soil anywhere.

The maze endured as a feature for entertainment and was a popular festival activity. Rules of the game required a participant to "thread" or "tread the maze" for accuracy and speed. The maze was generally cut from turf with little or no embellishment. Inner borders took on any form, from stone walls to hedges. They were often built without plant materials. Many famous and legendary mazes were constructed of stones or excavated onto flat terrain. Such patterns were equally pleasant to observe in winter and existed as landscape features long after they grew old and useless. Some mazes have existed for centuries.

The maze or labyrinth is described as a convoluted path that utilizes diversions such as cul-de-sacs and circuitous dead ends to tantalize and entertain. A maze may also be a single continuous, albeit tortuous, pathway, inescapable without completing the course, incorporating switchbacks and spirals. Where the former is a challenge, the latter is suspenseful and landscaped more cleverly with containers, statuary and benches.

Although still formal by definition, a maze need not use hundreds of closely clipped hedges and borders, but beds of flowers and herbs paralleling the paths. If the symmetry requirement of a formal maze design is relaxed, as if taking it out of a square frame and letting the pathways fall back again to refill an entire landscape, the path may now be viewed as a meandering wild garden walk, as in Figure 27. The fact that it is a maze will not be revealed immediately, thus adding to the enchantment. Homeowners on steep slopes or forested grounds may consider this scheme. A single path need not hinder the gardener from normal chores. Some stepping stones hidden here and there aid in traversing the yard without having to "thread the maze".

Now let us turn to some of history's most famous formal garden herbs; evergreens such as Germander, Rue, Hyssop, Santolina, Rosemary and Thyme; pond dwellers Angelica and Sweet Flag; and winter-blooming herbs Witch Hazel and Saffron.

Chapter 3 / SECTION 2

Herbs for Formal Gardens

The bush Thymes are veterans of detail design in the formal landscape. They are characterized as small evergreen bushes with spade- or needle-like leaves and cylindrical or pom-pom-shaped flower heads. They grow from 4 to over 16 in. in an erect, mounded habit. The upright growth is an obvious difference from the spreading mat-forming habit of the Creeping Thymes you may also cultivate. They may be trimmed into hedges, grown as solitary mounds, or carefully pruned into shapes or topiary. There are many species and cultivars which are easily confused. It is quite common to receive a cultivar different than what was ordered, particularly if using a common name.

Most of the Thymes conform to an approximate height classification. As an example, 'Narrow Leaf French' Thyme rarely exceeds 16 in. and if healthy, keeps a well mounded shape for 3–5 years. The Bush Thymes in this section are organized by height so that they may be selected for a particular landscape use more easily. Remember, categorizing Thyme by height is not exact because of the polymorphic nature of individual species. The first category includes the dwarf, or low-growing and sprawling Bush Thymes, *T. camphoratus, T. carnosus, T.* 'Argenteus', *T.* 'Wedgewood English', and *T. vulgaris* 'Miniature', which keep a profile of less than 10 in. In the mid-range, between 8–12 in. high, are *T. capitatus, T. × citriodorus,* and *T. hyemalis.* Those Bush Thymes that grow to over 10 in. in the prime of life are *T. mastichina, T.* 'Broadleaf English' and *T. vulgaris.*

The tiniest of all the Bush Thymes is *T. vulgaris* 'Miniature'. It is a delightful cultivar that exactly resembles the species except for its diminutive size. It forms a dense, upright, fastigiate (all branches rise suddenly upward—e.g., the Lombardy Poplar) bush of tiny, dark grey-green leaves harboring the same delicate aroma of common French Thymes. If you do not use much Thyme in the kitchen this is the cultivar to grow.

'Miniature' Thyme is very hardy and holds its shape longer than the larger *T. vulgaris* cultivars. Trim it lightly in the fall to remove any flowers that may have graced the little plant (it generally does not flower). It grows slowly to about 6 in., forming a nice symmetrical bush that requires virtually no maintenance. Specimens of 'Miniature' Thyme are a common substitute for *T. richardii* ssp. *nitidus* and *T. carnosus.*

The rock garden, a dwarf feature in a dooryard or contemporary garden and the formal parterre are the choice sites for 'Miniature' Thyme. Other dwarf or miniature herbs that can accompany it include Dwarf Germander, *Santolina* 'Nana', *Origanum microphyllum*, Curly Parsley, Pygmy Savory, Miniature Roses, Dwarf Sage, Corsican Mint, and two tiny Creeping Thymes 'Languinosus' or 'White Moss'.

Camphor Thyme, *T. camphoratus,* is also a small 4–6 in. bush, with thick, dark green leaves that have a thin, fleecy-white underside. It has not been reported to flower in cultivation. It has a biting, Rosemary-like scent. The oil of Camphor Thyme contains pinene, terpinyl acetate, borneol, and camphene. It is not hardy below 10°F. and must be potted and brought indoors during extended cold spells.

Camphor Thyme resembles *T. zygis* and they are commonly substituted for one another although the latter is much less available. *T. zygis* is a larger, less compact bush with lavender flowers and a stronger thymol scent. It is presently a commercial source of Thyme Oil. Both have a strong fragrance and bitter flavor that is not as appealing as that of French Thyme. Use clippings for strewing and in fragrant bouquets or as an aromatic ornamental in the garden in the same niche as 'Miniature' Thyme.

Another diminutive Thyme often substituted for *T. camphoratus* is *T. carnosus*. 'Miniature' Thyme is also substituted as well. *T. carnosus* is a small 4–6 in. compact bush with dark green leaves that have a thick felty coat on their undersides. It also generally blooms—the flowers are white—unlike either of its substitutes that do not flower. It has a distinct resinous odor and is bitter.

Among the mid-range Bush Thymes is one of the most famous ornamental Thymes, Silver Thyme, *T.* 'Argenteus'. It forms a small dense mound instead of a symmetrical bush. Strong, woody, decumbent branches determine the shape of these mounds and wise pruning can help to shape Silver Thyme into a work of art. Although a single plant will not grow more than 6–8 inches from center, after some time its branches will take root near the tip and the crown will die. It is possible, but infrequent, that healthier clumps will spread 2–3 ft. before the crown dies, leaving many smaller Silver Thymes in a 'fairy ring'. A rocky ground cover will forestall this event.

The leaves of Silver Thyme are olive-green with a cream or yellow-white margin. Their odor is similar to French Thyme but less spicy and often citrus-like. Plants sold as Silver Lemon Thyme are not a distinct cultivar and do tend to lose their lemon scent. Careful propagation is necessary to maintain this emerging cultivar (chemotype). In fall, leaves predominantly at branch tips have a margin of pink or red.

Silver Thyme provides the gardener with a sparkling flat-topped mound that is a charmer in any landscape design. Arrangements with conifers or broadleaf evergreens can be given a boost in character with the glittering accent of Silver Thyme to draw attention. Always use dark ground covers such as fly ash, cinders and crushed lava rock, or basalt chips to bring out the detail in this entertaining herb.

The rock garden is the place to feature it alone or in sparse company with Dittany and *Origanum microphyllum*. But in the perennial bed it is an attractive herb that brightens even the sunniest spots. Although it can grow in partial shade its overall shape and hardiness are superior in full sun.

Since full sun improves its informal habit, use it in informal and wild borders, displaying an irregularly advancing front where the herb will receive no more than a trimming-off of flower stalks at year's end. Silver Thyme is a very beautiful ground cover in contemporary settings that do not cover large areas and has been used as such in formal settings around statues, urns, and sundials, at the center of knots or to fill in large portions of a design ensemble in parterres (i.e. heraldry, non-geometric artwork, etc.). Solid borders or patches of Silver Thyme are excellent for drawing a visitor's attention. Set plants 6–8 in. apart and thin or trim as necessary to prevent criss-crossing branches. Its pink or rose flowers are very petite and in good-sized patches are becoming, especially when they can also contribute their fragrance to the garden. Ornamental herbs that seem to be natural companions to Silver Thyme in a mixed border or perennial bed are *Potentilla, Alchemila alpina* and 'Nutmeg' Scented Geranium.

In the kitchen garden Silver Thyme should be seen cavorting in the strawberry bed, its shiny form poking around in the verdant pasture like a contented Guernsey. Its lack of symmetry is unimportant here and the color contrast is remarkable. If the bed is composed of everbearing varieties the Thyme also assists in pollination.

T. 'Wedgewood English' is a hybrid adorned with a blue-green streak down the center of each dark green leaf. The actual markings are not apparent from even a few feet but the overall color of the herb is shifted to blue-green. It has an agreeable French Thyme aroma. Propagation of branches with crisp or larger markings is advisable.

A mound of 'Wedgewood' Thyme has a habit similar to Silver Thyme, growing 6–10 in. high but spreading much more rapidly, forming a healthy mound to 18 in. wide in a season from a well-rooted clump. It is enhanced by close association with ornamental herbs such as 'Curly Girl' Rue, *Santolina neapolitana* and 'Silver Mound' Artemisia.

The Bush Thyme from which Spanish Origanum Oil is derived is *T. capitatus*, Conehead Thyme or Corido. It grows with a very stiff, upright posture and has showy lavender flowers borne in large globes on 8–10 in. high, thickly foliaged bushes. Corido is the only member of the subgenus of *Thymus*, Coridothymus. Except for the arrangment of flowers, it resembles to some extent the herb Za'atar, *Thymbra spicata* in habit and fragrance. The odor of Corido is distinctly Thyme-like but with a rich camphoraceous note. It is not hardy below 20°F. Corido is a good herb in rockeries and in formal knots and parterres. In the kitchen garden it can be paired with Summer Savory or German Camomile in a border. The flowers, arriving in May, usually last several weeks and will continue to emerge throughout the summer.

Plants sold as *T. hyemalis* or German Winter Thyme are invariably French Thyme or 'Orange Balsam' Thyme. True *T. hyemalis* has smaller leaves than French Thyme and a pink-purple flower. Flannery indicates that neither this species nor *T. adamovicii* are presently in cultivation in North America. The latter is substituted by Winter Savory.

Exceedingly popular are Lemon Thyme, *T.* × *citriodorus*, and its cultivar, Golden Lemon, *T.* × *c.* 'Aureus'. These two could be either a Creeping or Bush Thyme because their habits vary considerably. In general, consistent pruning will control the runaway nature of Lemon and Golden Lemon Thyme and they will form moderately dense mounds from 8–10 in. high.

They are hybrids of garden origin (a cross between *T. vulgaris* and *T. pulegioides*) and contain the chemicals geraniol for a spicyness and geranial and neral for the lemony note. Lemon Thyme is a pleasant, enjoyable hybrid but fails two basic criteria to be a good ornamental herb in the landscape. First, it does not form a compact mound, tending to become scraggly in midsummer. Too much pruning is required to keep it in shape. Second, the Golden Lemon cultivar does not maintain a uniform variegation; many branches are totally green, and the gold color washes out in summer. Propagating only the finest color does not eliminate the reversion back to dark green. Like Silver Thyme, Golden Lemon Thyme will exhibit a dark red margin on leaves near the tip of the branches during late winter months. This color change is uneven; often only a single branch is involved.

The flavor and fragrance of the Lemon Thymes are their only redeeming features. It is an engaging spice that can and should substitute for French Thyme. The camphoraceous note is absent in cooked dishes and a tangy citrus flavor takes over. It is particularly good in rice, potato salad, cheese spread, or salad dressing. Dry Lemon Thyme slowly at low temperature to preserve the lemon scent.

Other than the kitchen garden or dooryard garden confined to a narrow perimeter bed, the Lemon Thymes are useful only as a ground cover of limited size for rocky slopes or rock gardens or perhaps in an arrangement wrapped up in drifts of Creeping Thymes.

Mastic Thyme, *T. mastichina*, is a 10–16 in. shrub that has an atypical Thyme flower. It exhibits a very decorative, fuzzy, white inflorescence. Even on close inspection it is furry to the touch and creamy yellow. It would be more attractive, perhaps spectacular, if it had a flower color other than white, nevertheless it is an ornamental shrub with a pleasing spicy aroma. There is a faint citrus note that is apparently related to its cineole or linalool content. Distinct chemotypes are recognized. Its oil, called Spanish Marjoram Oil, is used in meat sauces and soup mixes. These are the identical uses of Mastic in the kitchen, along with Summer Savory and Sweet Marjoram, all of which influence one another positively. Combine Mastic Thyme with 'Krishna' Basil, Garlic, Black Pepper and Coriander for a superb spicy marinade mix (add to Cream Sherry and a teaspoon of Tarragon vinegar).

T. 'Broadleaf English', or English Thyme, is a shiny, dark green shrub with a very dense, attractive habit. It forms a 12–18 in. mound. Larger specimens have been reported but severe cold weather usually takes its toll on branch ends so that a heavy pruning is required every spring. The better, or more often, 'Broadleaf English' is trimmed the hardier it will be in cold areas.

'Broadleaf English' has a mild Thyme aroma with an herbaceous and spicy note like that of 'Oregano-scented' Thyme. It is not equivalent to French Thyme and in the kitchen it can be used where you would use French Thyme but a new flavor is the result. For heartily spiced sauces, meats, stuffings and dressings, 'Broadleaf English' does not leave a tangy aftertaste and can transform a beef gravy into something new.

A border of 'Broadleaf English' provides a striking green contrast in knots and parterres. Its glabrous (glossy) foliage truly outshines other herbs and is on par with Germander, Box, Myrtle, and Holly as a high gloss border. Light colored ground covers reinforce this effect. White sand, rock chips, or oyster shell are recommended.

A solid, neatly trimmed border is possible in warmer climates. Space plants about 12 in. and be sure to prune them heavily the first 2 years to ensure strong main branches. It is a rapidly growing but short-lived perennial herb, often no more than 5–6 years, before the unkempt, old age look sets in. Then the main branches droop and begin to root as the crown dies. Division is the best method to propagate 'Broadleaf English' Thyme as only female plants are known.

Propagation of Thyme by seed is a difficult matter because many of the choice cultivars do not produce seed true to type. Many bear only female flowers and if viable seed is recovered, it is from cross-pollinization. The cultivar will not win the battle of genetic codes. As a rule-of-thumb, in any cross-pollination the Thyme with the stronger thymol (French Thyme) scent will win. That does not mean all of the seed will be of that species, but likely to be the highest percentage and new cultivars and hybrids are always a possibility. Cuttings are therefore the most effective method of propagating Thyme as it ensures the identity of the herb and selection for superior traits can be done at a faster and more reliable rate.

The last Bush Thyme to be discussed is Garden Thyme, *T. vulgaris,* and its cultivars. Garden Thyme is highly polymorphic, that is showing considerable diversity. Most significant is its chemical diversity, which is evident in the herb's odor and flavor. The species has been divided into many chemical races (chemotypes and chemovars or cultivars) based on this chemistry. There are four chemical races of T. *vulgaris* cultivated by home gardeners: 'Narrow Leaf French' (thymol) with a warm, spicy aroma; 'Orange Balsam' (terpineol) with a fragrance of orange peels; 'Fragrantissimus' (geraniol) has the odor of the Rose Geranium; and 'Bittersweet' (carvacrol) with a Savory or "tar-like" odor. As many as seven distinct chemical races are recognized, although thymol is the main ingredient and is extracted for commercial use in pharmaceutical preparations, perfumes, and flavorings. Thymol is a mildly toxic chemical, and used as an antifungal agent in medicinals. Thymol has been shown to retard the growth of the virulent fungi *Fusarium, Verticillium* and *Botrytis.* This is undoubtedly the factor responsible for the observation that a decoction of French Thyme in water (plus a dollop of dish soap) sprinkled onto a seed flat prevents damp-off.

All of the *T. vulgaris* cultivars are essentially identical. Morphological variants include

Plate 11

The bright orange stigmas of Saffron are one of the world's most costly spices. This patch emerges from a bed of Black Mint that has already been pruned for the winter and mulched.

Masterwort, *Angelica atropurpurea,* in the center of a knot garden.

Looking into the Grey Garden at Fall City Herb Farm.

Sweet Bay sentinel in center of Shakespeare Garden, Fall City Herb Farm.

A fragrant respite in formal style. While the apples are in pre-pink stage Lovage, Sweet Cicely and Sweet Woodruff revel in the warm mid-spring sunshine conjuring their scents to entertain anyone whether seated or passing by. From the gardens of Fall City Herb Farm. (See Chapter 3, A Walk.)

Kitchen Garden replica of 17th century design. Foreground triangle contains Purple Cabbage. Triangle with Calendulas contains French Thyme, Orange Thyme and Sweet marjoram borders. Winter Savory, Borage and Lettuce share a triangle with pole beans in back and a hub of Chives is surrounded with Lemon Balm, Lemon Basil and Sweet Basil.

Plate 12

Formal checkerboard or "squares" arrangement of Medicinal Herb Garden, University of Washington, Seattle, WA.

Checkerboard garden design used extensively in monasteries during the Dark Ages. This four acre retreat is at the University of Washington and contains hundreds of medicinal and ornamental herbs. Reprinted by permission of Eric Hoyte.

Square of a single herb in a formal checkerboard design. Common Giant Fennel, *Ferula communis*. Medicinal Herb Garden, University of Washington, Seattle, WA.

Raised rectangular herb-stuffed bed of dooryard design.

Wild planted triangle of a kitchen garden includes pole beans in center, cucumbers ramble beneath, Southernwood at apex, Italian Parsley and Basil form the borders with self-sown Dill emerging here and there.

A path winds between squares in a formal design that forms a wild corner with tall herbs and small trees as a back border. Herbs in foreground are Sweet Fennel and Prickly Comfrey. Lovage rises behind. Medicinal Herb Garden, University of Washington, Seattle, WA.

Plate 13

A fragrant patch of Chives in a raised bed.

Serpent Garlic or Rocambole shares its fascinating curves within a fragrant bed of Roses in a colorful border. St. Joseph's Church, Chehalis, WA.

Cucumber flavored Salad Burnet snuggles up to a Lady's Mantle in a colorful perennial bed in the garden of Michele Nash, Mercer Island, WA.

Russian Comfrey with an entourage of Chives in a square of a kitchen garden. This Comfrey has smaller, wrinkled leaves and prominent clusters of purple flowers for a more ornamental display than Common Comfrey.

Red flowering Comfrey. Beautiful crimson bells make this variety a valuable informal garden perennial herb.

Plate 14

A dooryard garden containing over one hundred species of herbs.

A low screen of Tansy (right), Wormwood (center) and Honesty.

Nurtured into a formal pose by the gate are two handsome patches of Fernleaf Tansy, each flanked by Chives. Also visible are white-flowering Garlic Chives (center). At Fall City Herb Farm.

Curly Parsley decorating a perimeter bed in dooryard garden.

Arrow-leaved Good King Henry in a perimeter bed displayed with early flowering perennial Primrose and Camas. Pansies and Poppies join the flowery fracas later.

A formal square of blooming Caraway in its second year is displayed at the Medicinal Herb Garden, University of Washington, Seattle, WA.

flat-topped mounds, compact bushes less than 10 in. high, and any combination in between. Leaf size, shape, and color will also vary. Of most importance to gardeners in cold climates is that hardiness will vary as well. It is imperative that gardeners purchase Thyme plants from an outdoor nursery that is located in a climate similar to their own. Care should always be used to propagate hardier cuttings each spring to improve the overall hardiness of the future crop.

'Narrow Leaf French' Thyme is a familiar and legendary herb. This is the French Thyme of culinary, medicinal, and ornamental value even today. Its warm, tangy or spicy aroma is one of the most exciting fragrances in the plant world. It is one of those herbs that embarrasses many a cook who is caught sniffing the spice bottle behind the kitchen door. Imagine now adding to its lingering scent an overtone of oranges or roses. They could be in your garden.

French and 'Orange Balsam' Thyme and less commonly, 'Fragrantissimus' are available from most herb growers. 'Bittersweet' is restricted to private collections. It should become available in the near future. All are available at plant sales sponsored by herb and rare plant or garden clubs.

For all practical purposes, *T. vulgaris* is not a formal border herb. Although it can be neatly trimmed, it has an unfortunate characteristic one would call middle-age spread. Both advanced age (3–6 yrs) and its propensity to survive cold winters at the expense of its crown cause a nice, symmetrical French Thyme to flatten out and eventually lose its central branches.

The death or drooping from old age of one or more plants in formal hedges causes unsightly gaps. Small groups of 3–4 plants nurtured as hedges in the vegetable garden or in containers make easy the task of repairing damage. In the event of diseased plants, remove those plants on either side of the dead one as well. Remove the soil and replace it with fresh. Depending upon the time of year new material is inserted, it will meld completely with the old hedge by fall. In any case, plants to be used as replacements should be root-pruned each spring and replanted to be sure they will survive when needed the most. As long as healthy plants are provided fertilizer (liquid) and sufficient water about ⅓ of the root ball can be removed without the need to prune foliage. In fact most woody herbs do better during and after transplanting if foliage is not pruned. Apparently there is some control of root growth that originates in the juvenile foliage and pruning may actually reduce transplant success. Research indicates that for best results plants should be watered 24 hours before transplanting, and uprooted and moved during the morning hours.

Thymes may be used to create fascinating informal borders that take advantage of a wide range of scents as well as distinct colors of foliage and flowers. Although all are quite fragrant, the Bush Thymes do need some stimulation or a high concentration of plants to be fragrant from afar. Using it as a frame enhances its ability to scent an area. Fragrant beds of Roses, Carnations, and many popular annuals enveloped by an informal or contemporary styled Thyme frame yield a generous amount of perfume at a distance. The Lemon, Orange, and French Thymes and richly scented Roses are excellent companions.

Thyme flowers must not be overlooked. They contribute significantly to the overall Thyme fragrance and color of the garden. Flower characteristics should be part of the original design plan. [Table 8, Flowering Periods for a Selection of Thymes may be used to select species for your Thyme feature in order to yield either a concurrent or continuous display of garden magic.]

It is also important to remember that trimmed plants are more commonly employed because the juvenile foliage has a more pleasant fragrance. One or two trims, once early in the spring and again after flowering is enough to keep Thyme healthy and youthful.

Table 8
Flowering Periods for a Selection of Thymes

THYME	SEASON					
	April	May	June	July	August	

BUSH
Orange Balsam
Silver
French
Mastic
Corido
English
Miniature
Golden Lemon
Wedgewood

CREEPING
Wooly
Peter Davis
Marshall
Caraway
White Magic
Creeping Red
White Moss
Mayfair
Clear Gold
Fosterflower
Oregano-scented
Tuffeted
Pink Chintz

Of major importance to the Thyme grower is the care of the soil. It is one of the few herbs that is truly choosy. In colder climates, frost heave uproots small woody plants like Thyme, leaving the roots high and dry. This stress may cause death and surely encourage disease. In warmer climates, moisture can be fatal if lower branches rest too long on damp soil. Roots from branches that rest on the ground penetrate the soil some distance, anchoring the herb, awaiting the signal to begin a new life, as feeder roots. Excessive moisture here may cause their demise. Both conditions are recognizable when large inner branches wither and die after 2–3 years.

The solution is two-fold. First, Thyme enjoys a sandy or rocky soil, a soil composed of half sand and half garden soil of average richness. An addition of limestone chips or oyster shell is beneficial in areas of highly acidic soils, i.e., areas with high rainfall. Secondly, there must be a layer of inert material on the surface of the soil. A sand layer one inch deep 1) creates a quick drying surface that thwarts disease formation, and 2) inhibits frost action; if the plant is heaved upwards by frost the sand layer will protect the plant from being severely stressed by exposure. This sand layer significantly improves the chances of self-layering branches. Many will automatically root. With a moist sandy layer these branches form healthy root masses that are easily removed without damage and can be planted in the garden where they are to grow, rather than requiring nurturing for a month or more in a rich spot to develop a good root system.

The very nature of a formal or contemporary feature which often uses inert ground covers for balancing and accenting is a boon to the Thymes so they flourish there with little attention. Sand, oyster shell, pea gravel, or finely chipped rock materials are the recommended ground covers with Thyme. Avoid organic mulches, except perhaps in the driest areas. Where an organic soil conditioner is applied, dig it in, then apply to the soil surface an inorganic cover.

The Bush Thymes may be trimmed in spring or after flowering to as much as 50% of their height, or a light pruning amounting to less than 1 in. of material. In the formal setting heavily pruned hedges of Thyme will grow rapidly, requiring a light trim periodically to keep them neat. An informal, untrimmed hedge may only require removal of flower stalks and a light trim in the fall. Heavy pruning should not be done in late summer as insufficient time remains for the plant to put on a healthy protective canopy of evergreen foliage. Not just Thyme, but many woody evergreen herbs require a dense mound of foliage to protect their main branches and crown from extremely cold weather, and particularly from the desiccation of dry winter winds.

The Bush Thymes suggest many exciting possibilities in the formal garden. Their neat mounding and malleable forms are versatile for features commonly using evergreens such as conifers. Their resemblance is worth exploiting in arrangements where the larger conifers are paired with other highly ornamental cultivars and species of the Bush or Creeping Thymes. They are frequently paired with Winter Savory, its variety Pygmy, Dwarf Lavender, Dwarf Sage, Hyssop, the Santolinas and Germanders, Myrtle, Rue, and Miniature Roses. Yet these same combinations can be enjoyed in informal or wild garden rockeries, contemporary features, and in slender sun-baked borders in perennial beds. Other herbs for the miniature border or evergreen/herbaceous perennial bed that combine well with Bush Thymes are Bush Basil, Dwarf Feverfew, American Pennyroyal, *Origanum microphyllum,* 'Krishna' Basil, Chives and other low-growing Alliums, Fringed or Roman Wormwood, Silver Horehound, Indian Borage, or potted, dwarfed topiary and bonsai arrangements.

Some ornamental plants that are choice neighbors for Bush Thymes are *Sedum, Sempervivum,* 'Silver Mound' *Artemisia,* Cactus, Dwarf Snapdragons, Creeping Speedwell, ornamental grasses, Clove Pinks, Lotus, Birdsfoot Violet, and many mounding or tuffeted rockery and alpine plants. Examples of compact features include Golden Lemon Thyme in a sea of all-seasons Crocus for year round color, including clumps of Saffron for winter beauty, or among a field of isolated mounds of Forget Me Not, Lobelia, and Ageratums.

In the kitchen very little Thyme is needed to spice any dish, generally only ¼–½ tsp. of fresh or dried leaves is adequate. This is fortunate since very little is harvested from a single plant each year. One fully grown English Thyme, the largest of all, will yield about ½ c. of dried leaves. The microwave oven is perhaps the easiest method to dry Thyme. Set it on *defrost* and use 4–5, 3 minute bursts or until reasonably dry. If the flowers are included it dilutes the thymol aroma but is pleasant and sweetly aromatic.

Thyme is a spice that is included in a dish to make the nose twitch and the tongue tingle. It's exciting. There is no other word. It is not a spice to use alone so mix it with a sweet herb and a spicy one. Combinations recommended are: Thyme, Sweet Marjoram and Ginger; Thyme, Oregano and Orange Mint; or Thyme, Cumin and Bay. Tomato sauces, rice and gravies benefit from Thyme.

CHEESE SAUCE

1 c. grated cheddar or mozarella cheese	1 tsp. Honey
½ tsp. powdered Thyme	1 Tbsp. Butter
1 tsp. powdered Sweet Marjoram	¼ tsp. Ginger

Melt cheese slowly while stirring in herbs, honey and butter. Serve over your favorite steamed vegetable or biscuits.

An all-time favorite fragrant herb is Rosemary, *Rosmarinus officinalis*. It is one of the herbs most widely used by cooks as well as perfumers and decorators, yet grown in relatively few gardens. The neglect lies in the unwillingness of gardeners to nurture Rosemary in a container, as it is unfortunately a southern-minded herb. It is restricted to about Zone 7 with protection.

Rosemary is an exemplary performer as a fragrant border herb and should occupy a spot near a bench or chairs in a sheltered site in the landscape. It may also be situated adjacent to a patio door or frequently opened window where its luring scent can be appreciated on a hot sultry afternoon from a cool perch indoors. Its fragrance is best when at least four plants are used as a hedge in the landscape.

Many varieties and cultivars are available. From *R. officinalis* var. *officinalis* comes 'Logee Blue', 'Blue Spire' and 'Majorca', while forma *albiflorus* of this variety (often sold as 'Albus') is the only white-flowering Rosemary and one of the hardier forms.

The variety *angustifolius* gives us pine-scented Rosemary and 'Beneden Blue' as a cultivar, both of which are excellent for detailed topiary and bonsai. This variety includes forma *erectus* or upright Rosemary, with a narrow columnar habit suitable for container arrangements and topiary. This forma is frequently sold as 'Jessop's Upright' or 'Pyramidalis'.

The variety *rigidus* supplies the cultivar 'Tuscan Blue', an extremely hardy, handsome and fast growing Rosemary. From this variety comes forma *roseus,* including the delightful pink-flowered cultivars 'Majorca Pink' and 'Pinkie'. Although Rosemary's flowers are not its most spectacular attribute and add little to the overall fragrance, they are nevertheless charming.

Cultivars with an upright habit develop a denser, neater hedge while the open or pendulous forms (including the Prostrate Rosemarys discussed in Chapter 2) are useful for espaliered walls and borders. Any Rosemary may be supported by foundation walls (by wall nails, staples or ties), fences or trellises.

In the formal garden, a hedge of Rosemary is far more appealing when it is allowed to grow with only minimal trimming, providing a large boundary within the landscape. Its pendulous branches, waving dreamily in the breeze, soften the overall rigidity of a geometric design. The dark green Rosemarys are more effective as a background in designs where foliage colors are to be accented. 'Tuscan Blue', and white-flowering have the darkest green leaves.

There is no reason why Rosemary cannot be enjoyed in any ornamental garden: try it trimmed to exacting proportions among other pruned evergreens and conifers in the contemporary landscape; allow it to drape or hover over walks from a perch on a rock wall above; let it stand alone in stark, twisted habit on colored or raked gravels; use it to balance or accent forested backgrounds of Tamaracks, Pines and Firs; provide bold contrast to Bamboo or Rhododendrons; or nurture it into a playful accent in shrubbery borders of Tamarisk, Willow-leaf Pear, Everlasting, Heather and Lavender.

One way to enjoy its flowers is to use it potted or planted among the medicinals in a dooryard garden where the tiny blue flecks emerge continually during the cooler months where they can join a succession of other simple flowered herbs such as yellow-speckled Rue, snow-flecked Creeping Savory, and the blushing pinks of Wooly Betony and *Origanum microphyllum.*

In those regions where Rosemary is a container candidate only, the *standard* should be used in formal settings. Grown like a small tree resembling a lollipop, a single trunk supports a ball of neatly trimmed foliage on top. A Rosemary standard is made by staking a young start and removing lower branches in the fall until the desired trunk height is reached. The more upright forms of Rosemary should be chosen but because the standard may always need a stake for support, they are not mandatory. White-flowering, pine-scented, 'Tuscan blue', Upright and 'Majorca Pink' are good candidates.

When the desired trunk height is reached, branching is then encouraged. Initially, any new branches at that point are pruned back to a few inches to force more branching in order to form a dense cluster atop the trunk. Some lower branches may require tying down to form a more spherical shape if desired. The young standard is pruned heavily the first 2–3 years after the ball is formed on top. Once the desired shape is achieved, only a light trimming is needed to maintain a neat appearance throughout the year. Rosemary standards are choice formal plants, either in decorative pots or planted in the garden for the season, one on either side of a gate or standing as heralds at both ends of long beds of prize flowers.

If Rosemary, or any southern plant, is grown in a northern climate and is to be planted outdoors for the summer, there are a few steps that should be taken to protect them. Near the end of the season, but a safe period before the first frost, plants that are to be brought indoors must be uprooted, root pruned and potted, then left outdoors. As the first frost date approaches, the plant is moved to greenhouse or garage, then, if desired or necessary, weaned to the temperature of the home. Pots should be placed in large drain pans filled with gravel that is kept wet to ease the transition to a new temperature and humidity regimen.

Incana Santolina or Lavender Cotton, *Santolina chamaecyparissus,* is an accent herb used extensively in parterre and knot gardens as a frame or border and as a low hedge-like ground cover. Labeled "Incana" for its soft silvery foliage, it always provides a downy face to the world, while its cousin, *S. viridis,* always appears brilliantly green and shimmering in sunlight. Like Rosemary, Santolina's aroma is reminiscent of pine woods on a hot summer day.

Santolina forms a low hedge, from 8–24 in. depending on species and cultivar, and can be dense enough to support a book and a cup of tea, the ideal fragrant herb to rest and read beside. Excellent for topiary, Santolina borders may also be shaped into wave or zigzag patterns. The smaller compact cultivar, 'Pretty Carrol', may be shaped into nearly spherical bushes, spotlighting an area with fragrant silver balls. A number of cultivars are useful as cottony ground covers that need little maintenance. Trim and neat for accenting sun-drenched steps, patios and formal entrances, the low-growing cultivar 'Nana' is only a few inches high. It spreads slowly but is a tough herb. For less formal borders, Santolina must be allowed to ramble out of the garden onto walks and steps, sidle up a fence, poke through slats, or envelope a cul-de-sac and its reading bench.

Santolina chamaecyparissus can grow to 30 in. and is often used on steep hills or uneven slopes encircling formal designs. Lavender is often mixed into hillsides of Santolina. This combination of purple and gold flowers set off by light green-grey foliages, and announced from a distance by their fragrance, is an unforgettable experience.

S. viridis, the gleaming Green Santolina, should be mixed with its cottony cousins in a 1:3 or 1:4 ratio for contrast. This species should be used among flowering shrubs and evergreens that are in need of a contrasting ground cover. Camelias, bush Honeysuckles, Brooms, Heathers, and Eryngiums are particularly well suited growing on slopes surrounded by a shimmering green expanse of *S. viridis.* Together, they blanket the ground with a gently rolling surface resembling a calm sea. *S. viridis* is a hardy ornamental for austere arrangements in contemporary features accompanied by only creepers such as Sempervivum, Sedum or Thyme and colorful inert ground covers.

The names Incana and Lavender Cotton, by which Santolina is often referred, are old names alluding to the grey fuzzy appearance of *S. chamaecyparissus*—the species name refers to its cypress-like foliage. Perhaps more deserving of either name is *S. neapolitana,* whose white, feathery foliage almost resembles blue-green cotton-wool. *S. neapolitana* grows to 16 in., is less firm in texture and prone to damage, but significantly more ornamental. Display it beside Lady's Mantle, Geum, Coral Bells and the purple foliages of Red Japanese Maple and Opal Basil in informal beds.

As a formal hedge, Santolina requires patience, for it is a slow grower. It needs ample water during the summer and a rich loam to prevent damage from frost action and crown rot in winter. Santolina is not hardy below 0°F. so should be covered with fresh straw, pine boughs, or dry leaves during cold snaps below zero. In the first year, the plants should not be trimmed but allowed to spread. By the second or third year, plants separated by 12–15 in. will have grown together, so shaping and pruning are in order. For a Santolina hedge that has its back to a fence or masonry wall, prune the unseen side to encourage a dense growth of foliage and provide adequate spacing from the wall. The tops should be lightly pruned to keep it advancing with stronger wood and denser habit. In a sprawling informal border, Santolina may be grown with no trimming at all, aside from snipping away dying or damaged branches or flowers when they turn brown in the fall.

Santolina may be used as a repellent in linen closets and as a strewing herb, tossed to the floor to be trampled underfoot. Its pleasant pine scent is particularly useful in washwaters and as air freshening bouquets in the home. Bundles of Santolina, Southernwood, and Pennyroyal branches bound together and hung in doorways will provide a cool, clean odor for several weeks whenever brushed or shaken.

Santolina's curiously serrated foliage dries easily. The dried branches are often sprayed or dyed to use in wreaths. All the Santolinas contribute a late summer treat of countless, yellow, button flowers that bob on slender stems several inches above the foliage. They are in the form of a firm dense "button" that has been popular for decorative uses for many centuries. The Incana Santolinas all produce a yellow to dark yellow "button" that adorns the silvery bushes for up to 3 months, through mid-summer into late fall. The flowers of *S. viridis* are lemon-yellow and flower production is prolific. These larger buttons on long, lax stems are quite showy. Flowers are cut and dried, then painted or left a natural yellow-brown, if picked early, and dark brown or black if left on plants until winter, for use in ornamental arrangements with other dried herbs and flowers.

Hyssop, *Hyssopus officinalis,* has been foremost on the list of strewing herbs since man discovered it. Hyssop, Greek for aromatic, has a sharp camphoraceous fragrance, most pleasant when the herb is kept trimmed. Ever popular for the formal hedge, Hyssop is a versatile herb for minute detail in knot and parterre designs. Long borders with a generous amount of Hyssop become highly fragrant plantings, particularly when allowed to bloom. A mixture of Hyssop and Thyme in a hedge within a tidy knot garden yields a rich and delectable aroma. Excellent combinations include Hyssop and a selection of Thymes such as Moroccan, 'Orange Balsam', Golden Lemon or Silver.

Hyssop's willingness to be pruned down to 6 in. and its hardiness in poor soils make it a choice material for topiary and manicured borders. The small 12–18 in. bushes need continuous trimming, however, or they become unkempt. A variety sometimes called Dwarf Hyssop, is smaller, growing to only 10–12 in., more compact and superior for detail in parterres and knots.

Hyssop may self-sow. Plants from seed bloom by the second year. Cuttings will bloom the same year. The flowers are deep blue, pink and white. The blue flowers are nothing clever and unless Hyssop is grown for culinary uses or as a flowering ornamental, they should be trimmed off for a neater appearance. The pink, 'Rosea', red, 'Rubra' and white, 'Alba' and 'Grandiflora', cultivars are dense and showy, however, and highly recommended. Informal and wild gardens display the white and pink forms best and drifts of all three, within a carpet of flowering annuals, creates a parade of color in summer and a warm evergreen expanse in winter. Golden Hyssop, with golden speckles, is an interesting feature.

Only in the last several centuries has Hyssop been a popular topiary herb. It has been, however, a medicinal plant, a culinary spice, a disinfecting and deodorizing wash water and a strewing herb. The pine fragrance of blue Hyssop is due to the chemical pinene, which is a constituent of, and has an odor resembling, turpentine. There is also a sharp lemony note due to terpenes in young foliage. The young tops and flowers are picked and dried, then sprinkled onto fresh hot bread with sweet butter, on toast with honey, over salads, and for smoking beef or pork on the barbeque. Other varieties and cultivars do not have as remarkable a fragrance as blue Hyssop for most uses.

Southernwood, Old Man, or Lad's Love, *Artemisia abrotanum,* is a popular landscape herb today because it is hardy, has a light green foliage, and a sweet citrus and camphor scent. Southernwood cultivars include 'Tangerine', 'Lemon' and 'Camphor', each alluding to the scent of the foliage. The familiar Wormwood-like fragrance of Southernwood is a result of thujone, but the sweet aromatic notes that are dominant are variously from borneol and camphor (Camphor Southernwood). Also present is the camomile scent of azulene and the floral aroma of farnesol.

A near relative to Wormwood, but with a sweeter fragrance and more finely divided foliage, Southernwood grows in a 3–5 ft. upright mound. In the landscape, its wispy evergreen foliage is a special treat as an excellent light colored background for dark-hued flowers, particularly blues and purples. Because the height of Old Man can be maintained from 18 in. up by pruning, either a middle or low range contrasting border is possible. Southernwood lends itself to further use because it has no soil preferences, therefore, is easily mixed and matched with more temperamental ornamentals.

Southernwood's soft green cast makes it an excellent *transition herb,* used to begin and end plantings, to identify groupings within larger designs, or inserted periodically into borders to provide relief from monotonously long borders of widely mixed species. It is flowerless only in far northern latitudes, otherwise producing a standard artemesia bloom of yellow-green, rayless flowers in late summer that is delightfully fragrant and invaluable for weaving into scented baskets and wreaths.

In mild climates, Southernwood should be pruned heavily 2–3 times a year to encourage new growth and stronger branches. In northern climes, where temperatures fall below 0°F, Southernwood should be pruned to 6–8 in. in late fall. This insures a dormant period. Southernwood allowed to grow through moderate winters may not recover well. from a late winter or early spring cold snap.

Cultivated as a trim hedge in formal gardens, Southernwood should be kept pruned to a dense smooth appearance, which is easily accomplished with constant light top pruning. Figure 8 is an example using Southernwood as a central feature of a simple formal garden. The borders here are pruned to 30 in. and adjoin narrow low borders along the inside edge of the turf runway. Easily sown fragrant annuals, Opal Basil, Sweet Basil, Mignonette and spring and fall bulbs are suggested companions. Large ornate containers with dazzling flower arrangements open and close this feature.

Southernwood can be substituted for conifer evergreens or join them in many arrangements, their fir-like habit pleasing as an accent or contrast. This dual role as evergreen and fragrant ornamental makes it a superb herb for the contemporary landscape. Give it the center stage cast against a weeping Hemlock or dwarf Spruce, an assortment of Creeping Thymes and Birdsfoot or Trailing Violets. For an informal or wild setting let its untrimmed long, pendulous, bottle-brush branches droop onto a surrounding ground cover of Pineapple or Ginger Mint, Lawn Camomile or Dwarf Monarda in partial shade, or in the sun, looking over a miniature look-alike, 'Silver Mound' Artemisia or *Santolina neapolitana.*

Old Man's fragrance has guaranteed it a place in every bouquet and nosegay for centuries. Easily dried, it may be used in fragrant wreaths and bouquets. Old Man is an excellent hot-tub herb and sachet for bathing water, especially when combined with Pineaple Mint and Costmary. Southernwood has been used for thousands of years as a smoking wood for preserving and flavoring meats such as lamb and veal. Branch shavings or trimmings may be mixed with a little grated or dried orange or lemon peel and tossed onto hot coals of a barbeque brazier to add a delicate flavor to anything from veal chops to hamburgers.

Garden Rue, *Ruta graveolens,* may someday prove to be an effective medicine, as it has been touted for over two-thousand years, but its disagreeable taste and foul odor will not endear it to many gardeners. Color and shape are its virtues today. Its diminutive knobby foliage is a charming addition in the garden and in dried arrangements.

Garden Rue, the Herb-of-Grace, has enjoyed a reputation as an analgesic, repellent, counterpoison, ward against witches and evil magic, and an effective repellent of insects. Rue, as a strewing herb or in wash water, thwarts the onslaught of fleas brought into the home by pets. Diluted in water, Rue's odor becomes sweet. This strange chemistry comes about because one of Rue's constituents is methylanthranilate, one of the secret constituents responsible for Jasmine's alluring character. This chemical is detected by our noses even in extremely small concentrations, so while the less pleasing methylnonyl ketone, an almost fishy scented chemical, is diluted out, the rich floral scent of Jasmine flirts with our nose just at the limit of detectability.

Rue is an evergreen perennial best used as a contrasting foliage in a grey garden, or as a medium border behind colorful flowers. *Ruta graveolens* provides a blue-green foliage. The cultivar, 'Curly Girl', has a blue foliage. A variegated form, 'Variegatus', yields a white or yellow or light blue-green, while Fringed Rue, or *Ruta chalapensis,* provides a change in leaf texture, with a teardrop shape instead of round leaf. Graced throughout the summer and fall with dazzling yellow flowers, Rue's ½ in. propellor-like flowers are borne on long cymes, and may be trimmed for a neater appearance.

Growing from 18–36 in., depending on cultivar and species, Rue should be grown in spots protected from heavy rains and wind, which cause its semi-woody branches to droop. Branches can be tethered to one another from within, so as not to be noticeable, to prevent branches from falling to the ground. Although Rue is evergreen, extended sub-zero weather will burn it. It is a very slow-growing herb from seed or cuttings, taking 2 years or more to establish itself. Afterward, it may be heavily trimmed each spring and fall and still return to full height by mid-summer. Branches will become woodier and sturdier if they are left unpruned, but foliage becomes thin. Fall pruning in colder climates and late winter pruning in warm climates is recommended.

As a frame for small gardens, Rue may be pruned to less than 12 in., and as a border for formal landscapes it should be cut back to 6 in. from the ground each spring to encourage regrowth for a denser hedge. Rue is an excellent herb for the bonsai enthusiast. The branches on old, heavily pruned plants become gnarled and thick set, with little knots of misty blue foliage starting up from the oddest places. Small standards of Rue are delicate and pleasing to the eye and often used in parterres with other topiary, mounded or hemispherically trimmed herbs. Rue has also been used to form animals and other caricatures.

Rue's evergreen habit lets it mix with conifers in winter gardens. Winter gardens generally combine evergreen and herbaceous perennials or annuals for a total metamorphosis throughout each season. Evergreens ensure a winter season garden. The bluish hue of Rue is best paired with dark green Salad Burnet and Incana Santolina for a small evergreen contemporary garden. Dwarf Sage, Dwarf Lavender, Germander and Dwarf Myrtle are several companions for Rue in a formal knot or mixed border in an informal landscape. The rugged features of an old Rue, its leaves no longer covering all its branches, makes a beautiful specimen plant in a rock garden or rocky area in any landscape.

Although Germander, *Teucrium chamaedrys*, had been a vital component in electuaries (antidotes), its greatest claim to fame was its rediscovery as the perfect minihedge during the horticultural renaissance in Northern Europe during the 16th and 17th centuries. The search for hardy, slow-growing dwarf or compact evergreens was narrowed to only a few herbs, Rosemary, Lavender, Hyssop, Santolina and Box. When the Germanders were discovered, *T. chamaedrys* and a dwarf form, *T. chamaedrys* v. *prostratus*, half the size of the species, soon became the most popular.

Chamaedrys in Greek means "at the ground", indicating a low-growing or dwarf plant. Its glossy, evergreen leaves and dense habit make it a choice knot herb. It does require mulching in cold climates. A blanket of dry straw and conifer boughs can be used in areas with sub-freezing winds, which tend to desiccate Germander's thick succulent leaves. The Germander hedge has no equal. To some extent its thick, glossy, dark green leaves give it an almost plastic appearance, for a bright and distinct border. It is easily trimmed and propagated and has virtually no pests. Hedges as low as 6 in. are possible, yet even at its fullest height, as much as 24 in., Germander keeps its dense habit. The dwarf form is less manageable because of its procumbent habit, but it too exhibits dense growth for a shiny green mat only a few inches high. Dwarf Germander is not suitable for areas with foot traffic. The best application of Germander is in the mixed evergreen border in formal and informal gardens or with other evergreens in contemporary designs and to brighten a dull lifeless corner with Creeping Red Thyme, *Cerastium tomentosum*, and Roman Camomile.

T. chamaedrys is essentially odorless, on rare occasion being sour or herbaceous smelling. Any scented Germander is likely to be *T. canadense*, American Germander, or Wood Sage, which may become a 3 ft. shrub, and has much larger, light green leaves, with hoary undersides. It, too, may be cultivated at only a fraction of its natural height for a superb hedge. Another fragrant Germander is *T. massiliense*, which grows to 12 in., with showy grey tomentose leaves and pink flowers. The fragrance of both is somewhat floral or vanilla-like, frequently with a sour note.

Other Germanders include *T. pyreniacum*, a flowering ornamental and herbaceous perennial with glabrous, green leaves and flower spikes of white and purple to 8 in. *T. fruiticans*, Tree Germander, is often sold as Silver Germander. It is a large shrub. Its thick green leaves have downy undersides, partially downy above, and very heavily downed stems. The overall appearance is a silvery green compact shrub of sparkling beauty that is further enhanced by large sky-blue flowers with exceptionally long and delicate stamens. *T. flavum* has thick, leathery, green leaves and yellow flowers. It forms an 18–24 in. firm, compact mound when grown in rockeries and on poor sandy or rocky soil. *T. marum*, Cat Thyme, forms a 12 in. dense mound of soft, downy, light blue-green leaves and huge 1–2 in. purple flowers for an extra treat on this very handsome compact Germander. *T. scorodonia*, Wood Sage or Wood Germander, is a hardy, 1 ft. tall rhizomatous shrub with dark green leaves that are rugose (wrinkled and pitted like Garden Sage). Wood Sage bears a profusion of bright yellow flowers with long delicate exerted stamens. Also called Garlic Sage, it has a pleasant camphoraceous odor and has been used as flavoring in ale. *T. polium* has been referred to as Golden Germander because of the thick, golden hairs covering the stems of some plants. It has slim, dark green leaves and white or red flowers. The stem hairs may also be white or light green. From a distance, this Germander takes on a two-tone color from the leaves and the fuzzy golden or white stems. *T. montanum* looks somewhat like a creeping Rosemary. Its 12 in. branches spread laterally over the ground to form a low mat that is moderately effective as a ground cover in high traffic areas. Its best use is in rockeries or along paths bordered by a rock wall, growing where the wall meets the pavement. Its cream colored flowers are not spectacular. *T. aroanium* is similar to *T. montanum*, forming a dense, very desirable ground cover as a procumbent shrub up to 8 in. high, but spreading by tip-rooting. Its dark green leaves have densely wooly undersides and somewhat so above. These tiny hairs capture the dew and give it the shimmering appearance in the morning sun.

Water is an important element in formal gardens and often the main feature. The pond was a vital component of any homesite in the past as a source of irrigation water for gardens. A spring or well was joined with a small dipping pool beside it as either a stone-walled reservoir or a mud-bottomed depression. The latter, called mint pools, were common in monasteries. They were large enough for raising fish as well as many aquatic herbs, the most valuable of which were the Mints; Water Mint, *Mentha aquatica*; Spearmint, *M. spicata*, and others.

Herbs easily cultivated in ponds and streams include *Veronica beccabunga*; Water Eryngo, *Eryngium aquatica*; Water cress, *Nasturtium officinale*; Pond lily, *Nymphaea odorata*; and the Water Lotus, *Nolumbo*. On the banks or in moist soils near seeping pools, many other herbs may be grown. In the shade try Cuckoopint, *Arum maculatum*; Blood Root, *Sanguinaria canadensis*; Columbine, *Aquilegia*; Colt's Foot, *Tussilago farfara*; Goldenseal, *Hydrastis*; Jack-in-the-Pulpit, *Arisaema triphylum*; Lady's Mantle, *Alchemilla*; and the Maidenhair fern, *Adiantum*. In sunny spots grow the Marshmallow, *Althea officinalis*; Asparagus; Dragonwort, *Polygonum bistortoides*; Blazing Star, *Lyatris spicata*; Boneset, *Eupatorium perfoliatum*; Bryony, *Bryonia alba*; Great Burnet, *Sanguisorba*; Dropwort and Meadow sweet, *Filipendula* spp; Nasturtiums, *Tropaeoleum majus*; the Pitcher plants, *Saraccenia*; Pokeweed, *Phytolacca*; Horsetail, *Equisetum*; Cattail, *Thyphus*; and Marsh Marigolds, *Caltha palustris*. Some popular culinary herbs that prefer damp soils near ponds include Lemon Balm, Chervil, Catnip, Burnet, Lovage, Mints, Monarda, Sweet Cicely, Angelica, and Sweet Flag. In this chapter we will discuss the last two, Angelica and Sweet Flag.

Angelica archangelica is a water-loving herbaceous biennial, though often perennial, growing in lush, tropical-looking clumps. With its roots near a plentiful source of water Angelica may be grown in a sunny spot, though it grows best in partial shade in moist soils. In the formal setting, a clump of Angelica should join mahogany or purple flowering Monarda and huge scarlet and yellow poppies near a pond's edge. The same clump will appear less formal when arranged with cattails, yellow iris, and the Marsh Marigold, all with their feet in a few inches of water.

A handsome formal setting for Angelica in the absence of water is a clump of 3–5 plants set in a circle within a surrounding ring of Lavender. In its fall colors, and especially in its waning days during the summer of its second year, Angelica's satiny, yellow leaves are a beautiful and delicate display against the grey-green Lavenders with their deep purple flower spikes. This feature should be one of the four squares of a "quad", a cloister garden arrangement discussed in Chapter 4.

Angelica frequented the ponds of medieval gardens, grown as a ward against evil. "Angelica, that happy counterbane", Du Bartas wrote in 1641, was an invaluable antidote to poisons and magic. A medicinal salve called Eau de Arquebusade, developed in the 16th century, included Angelica tops and seed mixed with Mint, Wormwood, and the oils of Rosemary and Juniper. Friar's Balsam and Balsam Traumatic are two medicinal salves made with Angelica for use as wound antiseptics. The bitter, herbaceous fragrance of Angelica is due in part to phellandrene and archangelicin (an isomer of coumarin).

Other uses of Angelica include candies made by boiling the seeds, roots, and young stems in thick sugar syrup until they become translucent. They are rolled in powdered or colored sugar crystals and stored. The flowering umbels are used in decorations.

Other species of Angelica are found wild in many parts of the northern hemisphere. *A. atropurpurea*, Purple Angelica or Masterwort, has purple-tinged stalks and dark green leaves for a more glamorous look, and *A. sylvestris*, American or Wood Angelica, is a taller species with enormous umbels and is a very hardy perennial. An Asian species, *A.*

polymorpha var. *sinensis,* is a powerful medicinal called Dong Quai and used as a laxative, stimulant and tonic for menstrual cramps.

The biennial nature of Angelica, an *Umbelliferae,* is variable so *A. archangelica* clumps may survive in moderate climates for several years. Removal of umbels improves the chances of survival, but robs the landscape of a very beautiful and delicate globe of seeds from 4–8 in. in diameter. Angelica self-sows readily in moist soils. The seeds, dropped from June to July, will germinate that season and by fall, become a healthy plant. It is recommended that self-sown plants be allowed to remain in a seed bed and transplanted in early spring as the viability of Angelica seed is extremely limited. Fresh frozen seed should be used if at all possible, since spring germination of last year's seed is very poor.

Sweet Flag, *Acorus calamus,* is another herb that is candied. Slices of the peeled spicy root are treated in the same manner as Angelica, providing a gingery treat once called Shaker Candy. The Iris-like leaves smell faintly of lemons and have been a popular strewing herb for centuries, and a refreshing fragrant weaving material for baskets, wreaths and door mats.

Both the leaves and the roots of Sweet Flag contain camphene, pinene, and eugenol, which contribute some of the spicy fragrance. A chemical asarone, also found in the roots of Wild Ginger, gives the sweet, spicy taste so prized in the root of both of these herbs. Extracts containing asarone are called Asarabaca Camphor.

Sweet Flag is different from the Flags of the *Iris* genus in that its flower is a cigar-like object, similar to the Cattail but jutting out from halfway up the plant at an angle like a rude pointing finger. In partial shade *Acorus* will do well in moist garden soil. In the sun, it must have its roots in a shallow pond. *Acorus calamus* includes two forms: a cultivar, 'Variegatus', with yellow-striped leaves, and, *Acorus c.* var. *angustifolius,* with thin, grassy leaves. Another species, *A. gramineus,* or Grassy-leaved Sweet Flag, has three cultivars, a dwarf form, 'Pusillus', which is commonly used in terrariums and only a few inches high, and two white-striped cultivars, 'Alba Variegatus' and 'Variegatus'.

Heralding in the New Year with yellow, orange, purple, and scarlet are two wondrous herbs, the rare and precious Saffron, peeking through a light snow cover, and high above it and us is Witch Hazel. Both are fragrant herbs though their scent is so fleeting one would scarcely notice save for a vast carpet of one and a copse of the other. These two herbs frequent the winter garden, formal or otherwise, joining evergreens and other winter-blooming shrubbery.

Crocus sativus, the Saffron Crocus, is a type of Winter Crocus. Saffron's lily-like flowers of lavender or purple are adorned with striking orange or crimson stigmas that emerge late fall to mid-winter. They vanish after lasting only a day or two, leaving a grassy tuft that remains throughout winter, disappearing just before summer. "Gems and incense bow before them" exclaimed Fortunatus, bishop of Portiers, circa. A.D. 565.

Grown for garden color and fragrance, Saffron is best in a garden where it is planted with an evergreen or other ground cover of 2–4 in. in height. It requires a sandy soil and full sun. Areas partially shaded by deciduous trees in summer may be equally suitable where Saffron may share a spot with Wild Ginger or Violets. In the landscape the rich, herbaceous odor of Saffron, classified as "ambrosaic", can only be sensed from mass plantings within the bounds of a windbreak and adjacent to a sun-warmed path. Such is needed to deflect chilly winter winds that rob the little crocus of its perfume.

In a formal landscape, Saffron is planted in a quantity large enough for its fragrance to be enjoyed. One or two dozen is a good culinary supply, but for perfume, a gardener needs borders 30 ft. or more long and 1 ft. wide, hemmed in by evergreens, such as the inner border along Southernwood in Figure 8. Annual herbs may be grown along the same swath the remainder of the year.

Saffron requires dividing every 3–4 years or blooming will be adversely affected. The plants are lifted in the spring when foliage has died back. The corms are divided, held in a cool dry spot for several weeks, and then replanted. They will bloom again by late fall or mid-winter.

Saffron has been a highly priced commodity for centuries. Though it has lost its appeal of late and Calendula and Safflower petals are substituted for it in commerce, in the past it was protected by rigid laws. Stealing Saffron, a vital export, resulted in death. Early in the 16th century it was spirited away from the Mideast to England by a clever and opportunistic pilgrim. He had hidden a small corm in the hollow handle of his staff. Two centuries of a highly profitable Saffron market followed, with England producing some of the finest Saffron available in Northern Europe.

Rich, golden soups and sunny, yellow breads are the reward for harvesting the bright orange and scarlet stigmas of the Saffron flower. One has to be quick—before rain and wind destroy them. Three stigmas per flower is all the harvester may expect. This is a sufficient amount of Saffron for recipes calling for a yellow hue in foods such as puddings, gravies, cheeses, yogurt and sauces.

The major constituents of Saffron are crocin and picrocrocin, both yellow-red dyes. The term picro means "bitter". The unique spicyness of Saffron is, therefore, best enjoyed by combining it, powdered, with honey, then eaten as a spread or dried and crumbled and used as sunny sprinkles on desserts and salads. Saffron has been employed as a dye for robes, scarves, and other linen. A fragrant, golden ink is easily made by mixing powdered Saffron and egg white.

GOLDEN GARBANZO SOUP

1 can Garbanzo beans
Boullion (chicken) or stock
1 c. chopped ham
1 chopped green pepper
2 Tbsp. butter
½ tsp. Saffron "threads"
2 tsp. Lovage
¼ c. chopped Chives
1 tsp. Fennel
¼ tsp. Savory

Simmer for ½ hour.

—Millie Adams

The other winter-blooming herb, Witch Hazel, *Hamamelis virginiana,* is a large, hardy shrub, growing to 30 ft. in the wild, but cultivars generally grow less than 15–20 ft. in the garden. It is a shade-tolerant shrub, growing best as an understory plant in hardwood copses. The fragrant flowers of Witch Hazel are a rare treat, blooming during the coldest, darkest days of the year, from mid-December to the end of February. The profusion of ragged, strap-shaped, yellow flowers appear to be purposefully decorating a leafless tree. Highly fragrant when in bloom, it is a centerpiece for the winter garden surrounded, perhaps, by a low ground cover of evergreen Wild Ginger, Hellebore, Sweet Woodruff, Saffron, and other fall Crocus, for an open woods effect. A waist-high ground cover of Sword fern, Sweet Cicely, Rhododendrons, and for summer color, Lilies, gives an ancient virgin world atmosphere.

In the formal landscape, Witch Hazel is included in the borders of flowering shrubs and trees. As a large shrub it is on par with many dwarf flowering trees. It is also placed in high visibility locations in groupings, such as the end of a long path against a background of evergreens. Several other species and cultivars are available and superior to American Witch Hazel, *H. virginiana:* Chinese Witch Hazel, *H. mollis,* with bright yellow, highly fragrant flowers whose foliage turns deep yellow in autumn; *H. mollis* 'Pallida', exhibits crowded clusters of ocher-yellow flowers; Japanese Witch Hazel, *H. japonica,* with greenish yellow flowers; *H.* × *intermedia,* 'Arnold's Promise', a cross between *H. mollis* and *H. japonica,* sports 1½ in. dark yellow flowers; the cultivar 'Diana', of the same cross, produces a generous cluster of red flowers from early February on. This cultivar has a yellow and red autumn foliage of exquisite beauty. *H. vernallis* responds to warm spells, blooming much earlier in the South and Pacific Northwest, with light yellow flowers. This species is the smallest of the Witch Hazels, growing to only 6 ft., and useful pruned into a formal hedge or screen. *H. virginiana* is frequently used as the root stock upon which other species are grafted for hardier, fast-growing characteristics.

The bark of, and less often, the leaves, of Witch Hazel are used today medicinally as an astringent for topical relief of inflammation from insect bites, bruises, and muscle ache. One of the active components is gallic acid. Pond's Extract of Witch Hazel is still widely used for minor aches and pains.

Chapter 3 / SECTION 3

A Walk Through a Formal Garden

The garden through which we are going to stroll is formal. Had we never seen a formal garden, the landscape before us would momentarily baffle our senses. (Fig. 28)

Thematic is a safe description of this grand garden. Its formality is based on a geometric design popular several centuries ago. Yet, in some way it still reflects the basic sensibilities of contemporary design. It compartmentalizes the landscape by "functions" and ministers to each with a thematic garden. The theme here is herbs, the place, Fall City Herb Farm. In it is a richly herbed patch divided into a quad. A wide fragrant median of Creeping Thyme separates the halves and allows for better viewing of each quarter. Entertainment may be the rule in contemporary landscaping, the feature garden rendered superficial, but this garden is simply an exciting and extravagant garden adventure. It is, then, undoubtedly formal.

KEY
1 Rosemary *Rosmarinus officinalis* 'Tuscan Blue'
2 Scented Geranium *Pelargonium limoneum*
3 Apple *Malus* sp.
4 Southernwood *Artemisia abrotanum*
5 Fern Leaf Tansy *Tanacetum vulgare* 'Crispum'
6 Valerian *Valeriana officinalis*
7 Lovage *Levisticum officinale*
8 Sweet Cicely *Myrrhis odorata*
9 Sweet Woodruff *Gallium odorata*
10 Red flowering Comfrey *Symphytum officinalis* 'Coccineum'
11 Rose Campion *Dianthus caryophyllus*
12 Wooly Betony *Stachys byzantina*
13 Dwarf Catnip *Nepeta mussinii*
14 Lavender *Lavandula angustifolia*
15 *Santolina chamaecyparissus*
16 *Eryngium* Sea Holly
17 Dwarf Carnation *Dianthus*
18 Yarrow *Achillea clypeolata*
19 Roman Wormwood *Artemisia arborescens*
20 Beach Wormwood *Artemisia stellerana*
21 Dwarf Sage *Salvia officinalis* 'Nana'
22 Silver Sage *Salvia argentea*
23 Bed straw *Gallium verum*
24 St. John's Wort *Hypericum*
25 Safflower *Carthamus tinctorius*
26 *Coreopsis*
27 Woad *Isatis tinctoria*
28 Cornflower *Centaurea cyanus*
29 Dyer's Camomile *Anthemis tinctoria*
30 Lady's Mantle *Alchemilla vulgaris*
31 Saffron *Crocus sativa*
32 White Moss Thyme *Thymus praecox* ssp. *articus* 'White M(
33 Cr. White Thyme *Thymus pulegioides* 'Foster flower'
34 Golden Lemon Thyme *Thymus* × *citriodorus* 'Aureus'
35 Cr. Red Thyme *Thymus pulegioides* 'Kermesinus'
36 Wooly Thyme *Thymus praecox* ssp. *articus* 'Languinosus'
37 French Thyme *Thymus vulgaris*
38 English Thyme *Thymus* 'Broadleaf English'
39 Dill *Anethum graveolens*
40 Summer Savory *Satureja hortensis*
41 Winter Savory *Satureja montana*
42 Sweet Basil *Ocimum basilicum*
43 Coriander *Coriandrum sativum*
44 Sage *Salvia officinalis*
45 Leeks *Allium porrum*
46 Tarragon *Artemisia dracunculus* 'Sativa'
47 Good King Henry *Chenopodium bonus-henricus*
48 Bible Leaf *Balsamita major*
49 Sweet Marjoram *Origanum majorana*
50 Rosemary *Rosmarinus officinalis*
51 Garlic *Allium sativum*
52 Poppies *Papaver orientale*
53 Wormwood *Artemisia absinthum*
54 Calendula *Calendula officinalis*
55 Rue *Ruta graveolens*
56 Lemon Balm *Melissa officinalis*
57 Pansy *Viola tricolor*
58 Sweet Bay *Laurus nobilis*
59 COTTAGE GARDEN, flowers
60 KITCHEN GARDEN, herber

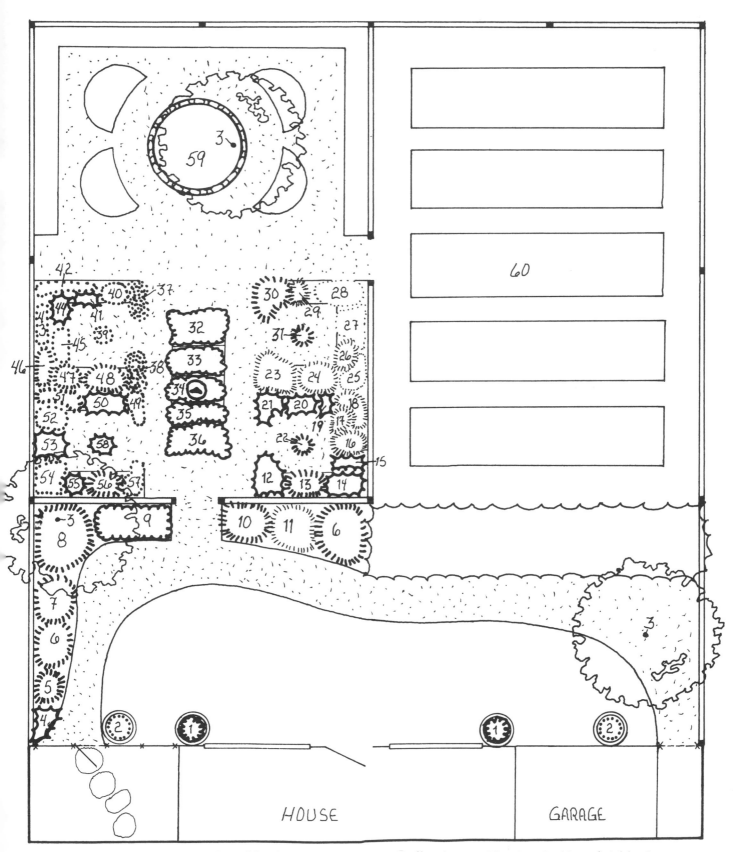

Fig. 28. Today's formal yard landscaped for utility as well as beauty. The Quad of beneficial herbs follows a Walk through a Formal Garden. Adapted from gardens of Fall City Herb Farm, Fall City, WA.

The medieval or monastic formal gardens were not only beneficial but beautiful. Yet they provided something else: instruction. Arrangements of herbs were lessons in art and nature. Some designs reflected botanical compatibilities and plant requirements, others human needs and desires: medicinals, foods, dyes, and scents. The garden we are touring offers five lessons: Grey Herbs, Dye Herbs, Kitchen Herbs, Shakesperean Herbs, and Creeping Thymes.

As we enter the garden the aromas of 2½ score of herbs enrich our understanding of the lives of our ancestors as well as our views of man's most precious plants. Now we are faced with a choice. As we decide which garden is to be our first lesson, we feel as if we are experiencing our birthday or Christmas. We are surrounded by 5 packages, each gaily wrapped with fragrant and colorful foliages, packages of common herbs, in a scheme so intriguing we are helpless to do anything but enter and learn.

Our first choice is the shimmering world of the Grey Garden. It is a monument to nature's unique talent for outfitting her herbs to survive both summer's dog days and the frigid madness of a mountain side. Tiny hairs, the "tomentose" or fuzzy coat that makes leaves grey, forestall the effects of dessication by the vicious claws of either heat or cold. All we care on the other hand is to be allowed to stoop and pet them, to feel their silvery fur. Most impressive is the concierge at the entrance of this garden, the huge and comical Lamb's Ears. By night, they become the downy beds for sprites and faeries. And lo, if you dry enough of them, a fine fragrant pillow stuffing this Wooly Betony will make.

Grey-green mounds of Dwarf Catnip studded with royal blue flowers sprawl beside the Betony. Our inquisitive fingers tell us how soft they are despite their rugose appearance. That fragrance! That is not ordinary Catnip. The strong clove odor is overwhelming and our imagination scrambles to redesign our own garden with a border of this herb.

In the very center of this quarter stands a lone sentinel of Silver Sage, *Salvia argenteus*. Like Clary Sage its mucilaginous seeds are used in eye preparations. Ornamentally, it has an oooh-provoking, silvery-furred rosette of leaves that we gladly fall to our knees before to stroke and fondle.

Like Jekyll and Hyde, a gentlemanly old Lavender, and a gnarled and twisted Incana Santolina stand side-by-side. The pale grey foliage of the latter and the grey-green of the Lavender are an apt backdrop for the purple and blue wands of the fragrant Lavender flowers and the ochre, malodorous buttons of the Santolina. They are inseparable and in many formal gardens their combined ornamental nature is relied upon to create a fragrant and colorful garden hedge.

Tucked between a troupe of Clove Pinks and Gilliflowers, *Dianthus caryophyllus* 'Dwarf' and *D. × allwoodii* (crosses of the old fashioned garden Pinks and perpetual flowering Carnations) are the misty blue and silver flowers of Sea Holly looking like spiral-armed galaxies dashing willy-nilly through the heavens. The Gilliflowers are dazzling neighbors in crimson and hot pink and with a fragrance as thrilling as a spice shop. Hidden behind are the grey, feathered branches from which arise several bright yellow flowers of Yarrow, *Achillea clypeolata*. These laybys for bees shine forth from the background like huge, gold doubloons hidden in this silver-stuffed treasure chest.

Two ornamental Artemisias, Fringed Wormwood and Beach Wormwood, are strange but wonderful tokens of nature's idiosyncratic leaf design. The first are like fern fronds and sea green, the latter dead-ringers for oak leaves of downy white. As we pass out of the Garden of Greys, hundreds of slim grey-green lancettes of Dwarf Sage slash out at our ankles.

On to the Dye Plant Garden. At its gates we are scrutinized by two creeping herbs of totally opposite character. On the right are countless tiny rosettes of Cleavers or Bedstraw— a near relative of Sweet Woodruff. On the left are the scalloped, sea shell-like leaves of Lady's

Plate 15

A dense patch of Wild Marjoram scents this end of the garden, joined by Roman Camomile which grovels at our feet ever desirous of being crushed and smelled.

Tropical Oregano snatches many second glances in this spot sharing the limelight with Incana Santolina and Dwarf Snapdragons.

Indian Borage, *Coleus amboinicus*, (center) is an entertaining herb from the tropics that resembles a thick-leaved Catnip (left-center) but smells exactly like Oregano. Here it is flanked by Greek and Golden Sage.

Bible Leaf (center) has extremely large and fragrant leaves excellent as book marks. Here they drape onto the path where they are likely to be crushed, sending a breath of minty freshness throughout the garden.

Sharing a garden. A frog lounges on a felty Wooly Betony leaf. Creeping Savory lies to the left.

Using an informal perennial border and kitchen garden behind as transition from lawn to forest. Tall herbaceous herbs and vegetables appear to draw neighboring trees into the picture. The garden of Judy Zugish, Marysville, WA.

Plate 18

Petite whorls of Sweet Woodruff create a fascinating shade-tolerant ground cover that is speckled with white flowers throughout the spring. Medicinal Herb Garden, University of Washington, Seattle, WA.

Lemon Balm in informal perennial border in garden of Gail Shilling, Bellevue, WA.

Beautiful scene of Chervil in bloom in spring from a winter planting in formal arrangement at Medicinal Herb Garden, University of Washington, Seattle, WA.

The exquisite coloration of Variegated Lemon Balm makes it a choice ornamental for the informal and contemporary herb garden. From the garden of John Eccles, Winlock, WA. It is shown here in comparison to the species.

A luscious verdant ground cover of Chervil in early summer surrounding a selection of *Monarda*.

Front border of light green Garden Sage is a good contrasting herb to dark evergreen back border ornamentals such as Rhododendrons.

Mantle. Flowers cling to her, like globs of lemon-yellow cotton-candy, spilling their sweet fragrance into the air. Again our minds sketch out a new design for our overburdened garden at home. The Bedstraw, *Gallium tinctorium* and *G. verum*, dyes come in reds and greens and golds while Lady's Mantle provides more verdant greens.

St. John's Wort, *Hypericum*, hidden beneath its yellow flowers, gives the expert dyer greys and golds while *Coreopsis* and Safflower yield yellow-oranges and rusty reds. Safflower, *Carthamus tinctorius*, is also a substitute for Saffron in color, but not in fragrance. A Saffron patch enjoys centerstage, its thin grassy tufts withered and brown this time of year. In late autumn its delicate purple flower will emerge, offering up to man 3 scarlet stigma that not only have been used to dye yellow the robes of kings and the doillied hankies of princesses, but bouillabaisse and breads as well, all with just a hint of ambrosia to entertain the nose.

The blue dye herbs, Woad, *Isatis tinctoria*, and Cornflower, *Centaurea cyanus*, stand back to back and crowd into a clump of Dyers Camomile, *Anthemis tinctoria*, which yields khaki and gold. This thicket of flowers around us in spikes, daisies, and plumes makes us feel as if we've accidentally ventured into a wild garden. Such a profusion of blooms however appears perfectly in place in its quadrant of this formal garden.

As we depart this exotic meadow we must dodge the median of Creeping Thymes. Magenta and rose flowers of 'Kermesinus' and 'Languinosus' grace the far end near the Grey Garden and the whites of 'Fosterflower' and 'White Moss' adorn the plots before us. A glorious frenzied mound of Golden Lemon Thyme encircles a sundial with a colorful lichen integument.

The kitchen Herbs interest us and we gaze fondly at the assemblage before us as if they were all family. French Thyme and 'English Broadleaf' Thyme lounge at the entrance. Good King Henry and Leeks are for pottage. Savory is the bean herb. Basil and Coriander tingle the nose and spice a pasta. Costmary is for the bottom of a cake tin to impart a minty freshness. Fennel is for a tea and condiment, Dill and Tarragon for salad dressings and gravies, and Sage for Thanksgiving dressing or the gamemeat sausages at Christmas. This garden smells like a gourmet's busy kitchen with the ovens abaking, pots aboiling, and chopped fresh greens addressing the air with tangy, herbaceous aromas that make mouths water and tongues tingle in excitement.

Our final adventure is the Shakespeare Garden where we will learn how the Bard used herbs. To him, herbs were for the pen, not the palate.

Decorating the entrance of this idyllic garden is Sweet Marjoram, one of the herbs that was favored for its zesty contribution to the dreadfully dull fare of the day. From this came the Bard's observation that a good woman was the "Sweet Marjoram of the Salad". Yet, if she fit into the class of the most bitter of herbs, Rue, she was "rather, of the Herb-of-Grace".

Rue also came to be used like Rosemary for funerals and fond fare-thee-wells. It was a celebrative herb and hallowed. One could send salutations to the bereaved with a sprig of Rue. So it came to be written, by he who wrote so well,

> "Rue—here shortly shall be seen,
> In the remembrance of a weeping Queen."

For herbs that accompanied memoirs and welcome reminiscences

> "There's Rosemary, that's for remembrance;
> May you, Love, remember;
> And there is Pansies, that's for thoughts."

The pansies scamper near the Lemon Balm in a partially shaded spot. Their confederate colors brighten the garden.

The Sweet Bay in the center patch sings a silent soliloquy warning:

> " 'Tis thought the King dead: [when]
> The Bay trees in our country are all withered."

An awesome thicket of poppies reflecting the colors of the pansies reminds us of this death which, according to the Bard, was "a sleep" that not even the poppy could conceive.

We can't miss the overstuffed patch of golden Calendulas and are reminded that

> "The Marigold that goes to bed with the sun
> With him rises weeping."

Like many daisied flowers, the Calendula draws in its petals at dusk and unfolds them at dawn dripping with dew.

Uncaringly stoic about dew drops or death is Wormwood, its silvered, filligreed leaves fidgeting in the wind. The exceptionally acrid taste of this herb gave reason for the woman scorned to let her rancorus tongue curse,

> "Thou ravisher, thou traitor . . .
> Thy sugar'd tongue to bitter Wormwood taste."

Since all is well that ends well, we'll end with a great dark green gathering of Lemon Balm. The oil of this herb was once so prized it was used to anoint kings. Its true lemon scent and renowned repellent charms encouraged the belief that an ointment of Balm bestowed security, desirability, and authority to a new king. Can you imagine the splendor of such a coronation? Fragrant flower petals flowed like flood waters and court chairs were given to the scour "with the juice of Balm and every precious flower".

The oil of Balm was a powerful talisman.

> "Not all the water in the rough, rude sea
> Can wash the Balm off from an anointed king."

It was unfortunate then that Richard II later lamented upon his regal misfortune, "With mine own tears I washed away my Balm". Tsk, tsk.

It was the formal garden—knot, parterres, and mazes—that inspired Shakespeare to wax so eloquently about the herbs of his day. They were used in a language all their own then, when few could pick up a pen and write a letter. Herbs and flowers were sent instead, symbols of thoughts and intentions, desires and hopes. The language of flowers is a lost art but we can still enjoy the art of the formal garden and admire those herbs that guided the hearts and tongues of romantics and lovers, artisans, philosophers, and bards. Measure for measure, the most sage advice the Bard left us—to improve our delivery when lecturing on herbs—was to

> "Eat no onions nor garlic,
> For we are to utter sweet breath."

Chapter 4 / SECTION 1

The Beneficial Formal Garden

Beauty is not the only reason for designing and planting a formal garden. In the past, gardens that supported a household were constructed using basic geometric patterns, depending upon square or rectangular beds and parallel rows. We know very little of primitive man's first gardens but some archaeological data has revealed that formal, as opposed to wild, patterns were employed, perhaps because of the guarantee that an organized garden would yield more. Food crops were cultivated under less strenuous conditions than ornamentals, given a full sun exposure, ample water and subjected to less competition.

The formal gardens discussed in this chapter are those that were used for the cultivation of beneficial herbs and food crops. The garden design that has re-emerged periodically since the beginning of man's agricultural awareness is the *checkerboard* form, while small cottage yards, whether in town or in farming districts, were suited to the compact *door yard* design. Across many centuries, in colonial stockade and castle keep alike, *kitchen* gardens were used for grains and root crops and *physicks* were employed by physicians.

The design of these gardens was quite subtle when beneficial herbs were placed for show and color and the whole balanced with the home and landscape. Creative use of foliage habits and hues more than flowers was made, but the latter are certainly not avoided. Herbs such as Sage, Thyme, Salad Burnet, Horehound, Caraway, the Savories, Sweet Cicely, Parsley, Calendula, Chervil, Lovage, Cumin and Anise were found in these gardens. Although a pond or water channel was frequently incorporated into these gardens, rarely were artifacts such as statues or ornate urns used, except for the most formal of situations.

The *kitchen garden* included pottage (for soup and stew) herbs, root crops and salad plants, along with a few annual culinary herbs and the major bulk foods such as potatoes, corn and beans. Even in such a utilitarian garden, pleasing designs were commonplace. (Fig. 29) They were patterned on a square format, which was advantageous to the gardener because it simplified maintenance and harvesting. Large squares were generally subdivided by either an X or cross access path, or composed of two or more concentric squares. Today, the kitchen garden has taken on leaner lines and been reduced to the simplest of form. We do not think of our vegetable patch as a garden that is part of the landscape, yet it can be. The delightful formal patterns used in the past can easily become a part of any landscape.

The herbs in these gardens are arranged by height, foliage color and special groupings of the most ornamental varieties. Central patches of each square may display tall ornamental plants; purple or yellow Wax Beans, Cardoon, Asparagus, Corn, Sorghum, Red Orach or fruit trees and trellised vines. The outer border of each square is the domain of the low ornamentals; Strawberries, Gourds, Red Cabbage, Bell and Red Peppers. Perimeter beds, those just inside the fence that surrounds all the squares of the kitchen garden, support vines, espaliered trees, berries or flowering herbs to be used for their fragrance or for dried

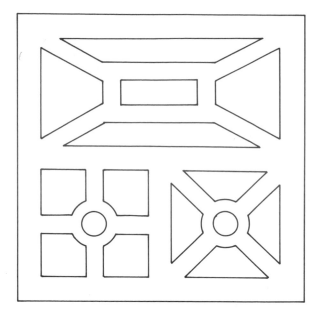

Fig. 29. The kitchen garden. Variations of the Quad from the Dark Ages are efficient and handsome. They were popular during the colonial period in American history.

arrangements, such as Lavender, Yarrow, Monarda, Tansy, Elecampane and Wormwood. Annual herbs are useful as borders. Herbs such as Borage, Coriander, Fennugreek and Calendula are grown for their flowers, which attract pollinators to the garden, while others, such as Dill, Basil and Savory, are grown as companion plants, herbs that protect neighboring garden plants from insect pests.

Perennials are not at all unwelcome in the kitchen garden. One of the advantages of the formal design is that compartmentation allows for differential treatment of plots of herbs. Thus perennial herbs such as Strawberries, caneberries and vines may be tended separately. Certain biennial herbs such as Cardoon, Artichoke and tuber crops like Jerusalem Artichoke, Alliums and Sweet Flag may be grown for their ornamental habits as well.

A garden design that was used extensively by monks was the checkerboard ("squares") pattern, as in Plate 12. Behind massive monastery walls, after the fall of the Roman Empire, the greatest works of herbal medicine were copied and abridged, and all manner of herbs were cultivated with care, keeping herbalism alive during the Dark Ages. Others followed suit during the Medieval centuries, using "squares" to grow herbs vital to life. These gardens were groupings of equidistant square beds, although rectangles were also used. Beds were not raised until after the 9th century, influenced by Charlemagne's successful gardens which employed this new concept. In ornamental use, squares were exhibited in groups of four, called "quads", or within a Hortus Conclusus. The entire garden was framed by a hedge or fence. Turf seats often replaced surrounding hedges, providing a fragrant respite. Quads were generally leisure spots that displayed wild flowers as well as more useful salad and pot herbs. Herbs naturalized into the quads were Lilies, Buttercups, Daisies, Sorrel, Salad Burnet, Camomile, Thyme, Dandelion, Plantain, Strawberry and Violets. When these gardens were allowed to overgrow, they became a "mead", a spot of wildness amidst the rampant formality of the day.

An entire landscape composed of squares, the *checkerboard* design, common in monasteries in the Dark Ages, creates a comfortable setting that encourages a lazy random stroll. It never pressures the viewer. From any point in the garden it is evident that everything is accessible and waiting to be discovered and pondered, not hiding, intending to surprise, as is often the rule in other landscape conceptions. Landscaped in a checkerboard pattern, a garden provides a long, leisurely walk in a small area. Herbs are its essential theme, including those that are valuable only as ornamentals. They too are part of the rich history of this garden form.

Here and there, a square may be paved or spilling over with a low ground cover. Upon it may be an inviting bench, or a clutch of potted houseplants basking in the summer sun. At least one, possibly more squares may be occupied by pools: a shallow one for reflecting a pleasant vista, a deep one for ornamental fish and aquatic herbs. The squares may be large and accommodate many herbs in simple arrangements that accent foliage themes. This is the basic plan of the monastic cloister garden. Or the squares may be small, each containing a single herb. The physician's herber was of this design. (Fig. 31)

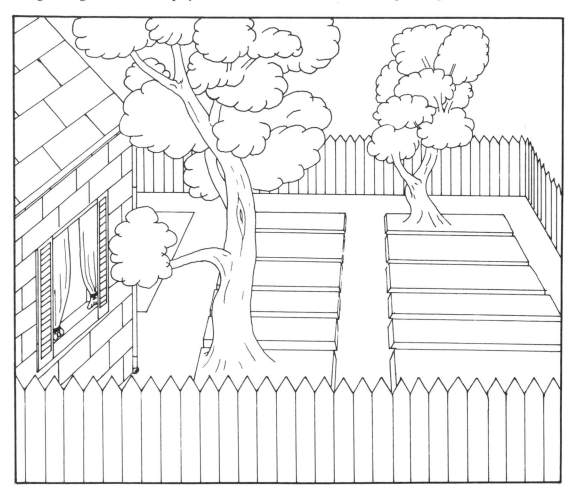

Fig. 31. The physician's herber from the Dark Ages transformed into the average backyard raised bed garden. A small knot or formal sits to the left out of sight.

Physick gardens contained medicinal herbs and used, primarily, the squares format. As early as the 10th century, medicinal herbs and flowers were being separated from other beneficial herbs to facilitate their widely different cultural needs. The advent of ornamentality after the 15th century transformed the physician's herber. One of the most popular designs was the pie or circular shaped herber, that came to be termed a diver. (Fig. 32 and 33). It was used to cultivate diverse species of physick (medicinal) herbs in wedge-shaped beds, each dedicated to a specific cultural regimen. In many instances, over 100 different types of herbs were grown, significantly more than any other garden form. The hub of the diver was typically topiary, a dipping well or fountain, statue or sundial. The diver evolved over the centuries to include slices for other beneficial herbs including dye herbs, culinary and decorative herbs.

Fig. 32. A large diver for cultivation of medicinal or other beneficial herbs in a design popular during the early Medieval period.

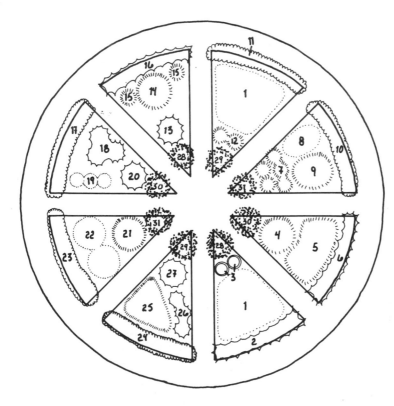

Fig. 33. Small diver for the homesite. It can be laid into a brick or stone patio for a more formal appearance in an informal setting and housing ornamentals and flowers or it can become one of the formals in a kitchen garden in a formal landscape.

KEY
1 German Camomile *Chamomilla recutita*
2 Dwarf Sage *Salvia officinalis* 'Nana'
3 potted Dittany *Origanum dictamnus*
4 Good King Henry *Chenopodium bonus-henricus*
5 Bible Leaf *Balsamita major*
6 Cr. Winter Savory *Satureja pilosa*
7 Chives *Allium schoenoprasum*
8 Calendula *Calendula officinalis*
9 Pineapple Mint *Mentha suavelolens*
10 Cr. Red Thyme *Thymus praecox* 'Coccineus'
11 Cr. Gold Thyme *Thymus* 'Clear Gold'
12 Dwarf Feverfew *Chysanthemum parthenium*
13 Golden Sage *Salvia officinalis* 'Aurea'
14 Yarrow *Achillea* 'Fire King'
15 Curly Parsley *Petroselinum crispum*
16 Dwarf Lavender *Lavandula angustifolia* 'Nana'
17 Roman Camomile *Chamaemellum nobile*
18 Oregano *Origanum vulgare*
19 Sweet Marjoram *Origanum majorana*
20 Salad Burnet *Sanguisorba minor*
21 Saffron *Crocus sativus*
22 Basil *Ocimum basilicum*
23 Caraway Thyme *Thymus herba-barona*
24 Hyssop *Hyssopus officinalis*
25 Black Mint *Mentha* × *piperita var. vulgaris*
26 Golden Oregano *Origanum vulgare* 'Aureum'
27 Southernwood *Artemisia abrotanum*
28 Silver Thyme *Thymus* 'Argenteus'
29 Golden Lemon Thyme *Thymus* × *citriodorus* 'Aureus'
30 Orange Thyme *Thymus vulgaris* 'Orange Balsam'
31 French Thyme *Thymus vulgaris* 'Narrow Leaf French'

The small compact *door yard* garden became the realm of the herbalist. (Fig. 34) Herbal medicine was laced with myth, magic and religion and though often effective, it was actively suppressed by the physicians, who were healers with some academic education in anatomy and basic medical science. During the reign of Henry VIII, herbalists in England were elevated to a status equal to physicians. Their expanding need for medicinals was satisfied by growing their own materials in a personal herber around their dwelling.

The herbalist's garden was small, generally only the front garden of a tiny cottage. Virtually all of the available space was used for cultivating herbs. Vines and espaliered plants covered the perimeter fence as well as the house itself. Just a few steps from the door were living remedies for the treatment of aches and pains of the "Augue" and childbearing, skin care ointments, hair rinses, wound dressings and poultices, potions for depression, cosmetics and secret electuaries for expelling demons, witches and malevolent fairies.

The garden frequently contained rectangular raised beds parallel to one another 2–4 ft. wide, though not so wide they were unmanageable. The raised bed technique was popular for the growing of beneficial herbs because of the ease of amending soils with sand, limestone, compost or any necessary combination that influenced the yield of finicky herbs. Wooden planks and rocks were the most common materials for the supporting sides. Brick and preformed concrete blocks are used today. Wood is not a recommended material because of its cost and short life. Treated wood should never be used in beneficial herb gardens. If wood is truly desired, cedar is the only one recommended. Depending on the height to which the beds are raised they can also double as sitting benches.

Raised beds solved other gardening miseries such as poorly drained or rocky, sandy, organically poor soils. They drain more quickly in spring and after heavy rain or flooding, allowing planting to begin earlier than in ground level gardens. Many more species of plants can be grown in raised beds, particularly those sensitive to poorly drained or acidic conditions.

In the dooryard garden all manner of herbs could be grown as well as the necessary medicinals, including spices, vegetables, fragrant herbs for purifying air or sweetening medicines, and decorative herbs to both cheer the spirits inside the home, or as strips of flowers encircling and enlivening the landscape. Surrounding the garden and home was a waist-high stone, wattle or mud and straw fence. Pathways were constructed of brick, stone or turf and supported many naturalized herbs for a soft and fragrant stroll.

Herbs here were displayed according to their foliage characteristics. Habit and color were used to accent prominent features of herbs that are the most ornamental. Flowering herbs such as Monarda, Calendula, Camomile, Lilies, Poppies, Tansy, Foxglove, White Mugwort, Meadowsweet, Pansies and Yarrow were used to create fascinating patterns of color within beds or as borders along the garden's perimeter.

The checkerboard and door yard designs can become a complete landscape. Into the regular pattern of square and rectangular beds are incorporated shrubbery and trees, shaded fern gardens and even dwarfed specimens for entertainment.

Themes can be woven by the use of limited categories of herbs, such as medicinals, dyes or particular foliage colors or heights. Moods can be controlled by the use of construction materials or the choice of plants. The use of brick or cut stone enhances the formality of a garden, rounded stones, wooden beams and old brick can be used for a rustic appearance, and a modern appearance can be had with the use of preformed concrete "stonework" and paving. The higher a bed is raised the more informal is the feeling it evokes, although it is also possible to invoke a less formal mood with beds that are flush with the paths by encouraging ground covers to spill out of their beds. Include fern and woodsy habitats or thickets of brushy herbs around the perimeter or wild patches by selecting a few squares off in one corner of the landscape to grow tall, flowering herbs and wildflowers through which paths

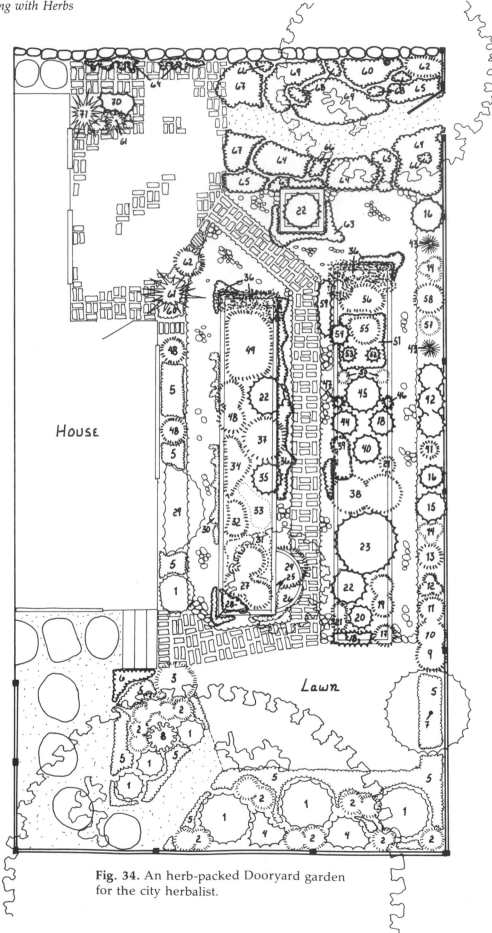

Fig. 34. An herb-packed Dooryard garden
for the city herbalist.

may run entirely hidden.

The kitchen and physick gardens today are essentially "formals" that are incorporated into other landscapes or displayed as featured gardens. Tying other landscape forms together with them requires the "formal" to be transformed by sharing some of the dominant elements featured in the landscape. They can be enclosed, becoming the Hortus Conclusus, so they can exhibit their formality more freely. This device ties it into the whole theme but its strict geometric nature keeps it a disconnected whole, a feature to be investigated and enjoyed.

However the beneficial formal garden is employed, it awakens much interest in visitors and can be an entertaining and educational focal point in any landscape and a mark of pride for the gardener.

KEY

 1 Sword Ferns *Polystichum* spp.
 2 Maidenhair Fern *Adiantum pedatum*
 3 Bladder-Fern *Cystopteris fragilis*
 4 Lenten Rose *Helleborus*
 5 Oxalis and Bleeding Heart
 6 Pineapple Mint *Mentha suaveolens*
 7 Holly *Ilex*
 8 Elderberry *Sambucus*
 9 Fern Leaf Tansy *Tanacetum vulgare* 'Crispum'
10 Yarrow, Red & white *Achillea* cv's
11 Feverfew *Chrysan. parthenium*
12 Yarrow yellow *Achillea* 'Moonshine'
13 Golden Oregano *Origanum vulgare* 'Aureum'
14 Primrose *Primula* spp.
15 Variegated Sage *Salvia officinalis* 'Tricolor'
16 Rue *Ruta graveolens*
17 Basil-Thyme *Acinos arvensis*
18 Roman Camomile *Chamaemellum nobile*
19 Anise-hyssop *Agastache foeniculum*
20 Oregano *Origanum vulgare*
21 Dwarf Catnip *Nepeta mussinii*
22 Sage *Salvia officinalis*
23 Wooly Betony *Stachys byzantina*
24 Sweet Cicely *Myrrhis odorata*
25 Hazelnut *Corylus cornuta*
26 *Ajuga reptans*
27 *Angelica archangelica*
28 Applemint *Mentha* × *vilosa* var.
29 *Rhododendron* 'Jean Marie'
30 Creeping Charlie *Glechoma hederacea*
31 Chervil *Anthriscus cerefolium*
32 Beach Wormwood *Absinthum stellerana*
33 Pansies/Anemonies/Day lily
34 Lime Mint *Mentha* × *piperita* var. *citrata*
35 Greek Sage *Salvia fruticosa*
36 Creep. Golden thyme *Thymus* 'Clear Gold'
37 Bible Leaf *Balsamita major*
38 Cr. Savory *Satureja pilosa*

39 Basil (Cinnamon/Camphor/Thrysiflora)
40 Golden Sage *Salvia officinalis* 'Aurea'
41 Dropwort *Fillipendula vulgaris*
42 Hyssop (red/white/blue) *Hyssopus officinalis*
43 Miniature Roses
44 Lavender Cotton *Santolina chamaecyparissus*
45 Salad Burnet *Sanguisorba minor*
46 Indian Borage *Coleus amboinicus*
47 Tropical Oregano *Poliomintha longiflora*
48 Lemon Balm *Melissa officinalis*
49 Orange Mint *Mentha* × *piperita* var. *citrata*
50 Snapdragons, dwarf *Antirhinum* 'Floral Carpet'
51 Corsican Mint *Mentha requeinii*
52 Dwarf Sage *Salvia officinalis* 'Nana'
53 *Santolina neapolitana*
54 Dwarf Lavender *Lavandula angustifolia* 'Nana Atropurpurea'
55 Saffron *Crocus sativus*
56 Black Mint *Mentha* × *piperita* var. *vulgaris*
57 Shasta Daisy *Chrysanthemum maximum*
58 Good King Henry *Chenopodium bonus-henricus*
59 Cr. Rosemary *Rosmarinus officinalis* var. *prostratus*
60 Violet (wh) *Viola cornuta*
61 Arborvitae *Thuja orientalis*
62 Lovage *Levisticum officinale*
63 Lawn Camomile *Chamaemellum nobile* 'Trenague'
64 Violets/R. Camomile/*Montia*/Sw Woodruff
65 Cr. Thyme, *Thymus pulegioides* 'Foster flower'
66 Florists' Violet *Viola odorata*
67 Cr. Thyme, *Thymus pulegioides* 'Oregano-scented'
68 English Pennyroyal *Mentha pulegium*
69 Sweet Woodruff *Gallium odorata*
70 Southernwood *Artemisia abrotanum*
71 *Juniperus communis*

Chapter 4 / SECTION 2

Herbs for a Kitchen Garden

Each of these four formal gardens could contain every herb known and used. We will limit our discussion here to those herbs that are the most difficult to fit into the landscape. A few are prolific weeds that may become a nuisance. This group includes Comfrey, Tansy, Salad Burnet, and Sorrel. Others tend to be weedy in appearance no matter how much effort is spent in siting and cultivating them—Parsley, Caraway, Summer Savory, and Tarragon. The classical favorites, Calendula, Horehound, and Chives are included here.

Let's discuss the classical herbs first. This group contains Calendula, Chives, and Horehound. They have been used by man for over 3,000 years for both medicinal and culinary uses.

Chives, *Allium schoenoprasum,* has always been an enormously popular herb. It is a member of the Onion family. It grows with a tuft of hollow, grass-like leaves and is commonly used fresh in salads and soups. They are hardy in any soil and relatively pest-free, easily propogated and versatile in culinary use. To harvest, simply cut to 1–2 in. from the ground. Chives can be stored, either dried (in a moderately warm oven, 90–110°F) or as a butter.

CHIVE BUTTER

Add 2 Tbsp. of dried, powdered Chives to ½ c. of Margarine.
Bring to a boil for 3–5 minutes.
Turn into mold and store in refrigerator for up to 6 months.

If filtered, the green-colored margarines make a tasty dip or spread and can be used to baste chicken or as an oil in Chinese stir-fry dishes. The small bulbs harvested in early summer are often pickled and used as a condiment or for a sweet and tart oniony paste for crackers and chips.

Above all, Chive grows well in a container as a house plant during winter months when virtually all edible garden greens are dormant in northerly latitudes. For this reason, they have been a vital dietary complement for many centuries, able to provide necessary vitamins and minerals even in winter.

Chives are another misunderstood fragrant herb that must be grown in large masses to be discovered for what they are, a sweet, floral-scented herb with faint oniony highlights. Very rich, well-drained soils manured heavily 2–3 times per year are important for a full floral scent. Applications of phosphorus or wood ashes after each blooming period will boost subsequent blooming the same season. If calcium is added, it should be in the form of a sulfate, for this Onion prefers an acid soil in which to bloom to its fullest.

Their fragrance can contribute much to tiny scented gardens, their sweetness apparent when they are in bloom. They provide a spot of amusement no matter where they grow as their buoyant balls of lavender fluff bob about gaily on long, sturdy stems. A dozen 6 in. wide clumps will yield a hint of their mouth watering aroma throughout the garden on a rainy day. Chives grow so slowly that frequent uprooting and dividing is not necessary. Give Chives enough room to spread for a few years before dividing and replanting. Clump widths should be 6–9 in. and the distance between clumps from 15–18 in. As the rows broaden with time, the more fragrant the garden becomes.

The sleek vertical lines of a clump of Chives make a notable feature. A 3 year old clump of the North American native Chive, *A. s.* var. *sibiricum* can produce 12–16 in. leaves and scapes from 18–24 in., with flowers up to 2 in. in diameter. They are excellent in the landscape for small-scale vertical balance, such as in a mead or rockery or as a massed planting to balance tall conifers. This reed-like habit also allows them to appear as an expected component of marshes and muddy wallows, down among the Buttercups and Marigolds, so use them in any and every water feature. Here they should join ornamental grasses, Iris, Sweet Flag, and other Alliums.

Established clumps are a bold feature of lavender and dark green. This contrast is responsible for Chives being used more often than any other herb as a transition planting in the informal border or as a fiery burst of color in the contemporary garden. Borders of Chives can be used to form intricate scroll work in formal patterns such as the parterre and maze. They are easily cared for and the twice yearly show of countless, lavender maces jutting from some convoluted design is simply spectacular.

These borders are more entertaining when clumps are spaced rather than planted as a solid border. Varying this sequence,—e.g., 2 closely spaced clumps, then 3, with a double space between each group,—is arresting. The white flowering Garlic Chive, *Allium tuberosum,* and yellow-flowering *A. molly* or *A. flavum* may be substituted in a border for additional color and balance when framing a small circular garden in which fragrant annuals are snugly set. In addition, the white blossoms of Garlic Chives have a spicy or rose-like scent.

A single clump of Chives can be a vital component in a contemporary feature, with ball-shaped Bush Thymes and silvery sea urchin-like Clove Pinks scuttling around and about them. One large clump or several spaced closely for a mass effect, becomes a beacon, drawing the eye back to one point in the garden. At this focal point, they can accent statuary, a dipping well, rock features, or a planter in formal and other designs, or reign over a kitchen garden as its hub. In contemporary and dooryard settings, play them alongside their narrow leaved companions such as Sage, Lavender, Santolina, Bush Thyme, or Savory. Other plants Chives seem to enjoy as companions include the Yucca, Lilies, Snowdrops, Crocus, Salad Burnet, medium-height Yarrows and Veronica Incana.

Some of the hundreds of other members of the Onion family are quite ornamental and valuable as edible herbs. Most are relegated to the kitchen garden. These herbs include Rocambole or Serpent Garlic, Welsh Onions, Leeks, Egyptian Onions, and the Giant Alliums. The early showing Wild Onions grow into long-leaved clumps before most other perennials show and bloom in nodding clusters of white, pink and blue. They are safe for part shade and quite delicious. The larger varieties are all best grown as borders around taller crops such as Corn, Sorghum, Okra, and Pole Beans, or with a low front border of Dill, German Camomile, or Monarda for a surprise. A few of the Alliums, including Serpent Garlic, Elephant Garlic, and Egyptian Onion, have ornamental flowering characteristics that are quite handsome when massed together, forming the hub in a kitchen garden with lower growing herbs and vegetables, or as a feature garden in a contemporary landscape.

The Giant Allium, *Allium gigantium,* is one of the tallest Onions, at 4–5 ft., producing large 6 in. wide fragrant umbels and a fist-sized bulb. Although the fragrance of any Allium is strong and often obnoxious to the uninitiated nose, once in bloom, the Giant Allium's flower's sweet, honey-scent combines with the oniony aroma of the foliage, yielding a fragrance less appreciated than it should be. The lavender to pink globes bobbing about on a breezy day are a comical sight, resembling an alien forest such as described in C. S. Lewis' *Out of the Silent Planet.* "And on the summit, a grove of trees as man had never seen, their smooth columns were taller than a cathedral spire on earth, and at their tops, they grow rather into flower than foliage, large as a summer cloud." Other Giant Alliums which make entertaining garden plants, although not always as fragrant, are *A. flatunence,* light violet, from 3–5 ft., and *A. rotundum,* red-purple, to 3 ft.

Like Chives, these huge bulbs need high nitrogen levels for good growth, finest color, and best flavor. A thick application of manure in the spring and fall and just before flowering is recommended. The Giant Allium forms a modest screen when planted in successive rows. Bulbs should be staggered and set 6–8 in. apart in all directions. 4–5 rows are necessary. The Giant Allium is cultivated for food in Southeast Asia and India. The umbels can be dried to use in striking arrangements.

Another renowned perennial herb is White Horehound, *Marrubium vulgare,* the stuff of cold lozenges and tongue-tingling candies. Although it is a bitter herb (marrub meaning bitter), Horehound has been a favorite cold remedy for centuries. The mucilagenous material contains not only an antibacterial agent but also soothes the throat.

HOREHOUND LOZENGE OR CANDY

Make a decoction of 1 c. of Horehound leaves and ½ c. water.
Filter and add 2 c. sugar, ⅓ c. of honey.
Cook over low heat to 330°F on a candy thermometer.
Pour onto a cookie sheet or into candy molds.
Cut the candy on a cookie sheet when it is still warm.
Roll the pieces in powdered sugar and wrap individually in plastic and store.
For flavors, add ½ c. leaves of desired herb to the decoction or add commercial flavorings after the candy is cooled and just before pouring into the molds.

Horehound masquerades as a hoary (tomentose), round-leaved Mint. It is grey-green or light green and included in gardens for foliage contrast. Silver Horehound, *M. incanum,* has whitened leaves, denser, showy, snow white flower clusters and a more compact habit. Both grow upright like Mint, rising from 12–16 in. Flowers form fuzzy wads at each leaf node and are white and odorless, although quite popular with bees. It spreads quickly unless corralled. It is not a hardy herb, particularly in rich or clay soils, so is best grown in a poor, dry, sandy, or rocky soil. It grows rapidly from seed so may be treated as an annual and cultivated in a kitchen garden or dooryard where a box will confine it. Its fascinating grey, warty foliage may be displayed with patches of dainty flowers such as Dianthus, Camomile, Feverfew, and Phlox, or in a perennial garden as a ground cover alone, or with wildflowers such as the California Poppy, and Toad-flax.

Horehound makes an exceptionally showy border along a dark colored paving or asphalt driveway, thriving in the heat produced by these surfaces. Tall screen plants should be displayed behind it, especially those with spires, such as Delphiniums, Fraxinella, and Lupine. Herbs such as Fern Leaf Tansy and Lovage can be paired behind for contrast, or an *Artemisia* for a ghostly grey border against perhaps a dark stained fence or background of conifers. It also makes a fine ground cover for rocky slopes and poor soil.

The Calendula, or Pot Marigold, *Calendula officinalis* is an ancient flower, once cultivated and worshiped by the Egyptians. It's always there to greet you, displaying its cheerful rays of sunshine every day of the year when you step out into the garden. Its huge, bold green spatula-shaped leaves accent the 1–3 in. yellow, gold, or orange daisies. This little flower has a very special name, Calend, the word from which calendar comes. It was given to the herb for its uncanny habit of sending up a new bloom every month for the entire year. They act as if they were a short-lived perennial, flowering indefinitely wherever and whenever weather permits. The simplest is a small, yellow-orange flower, though many cultivars exist, including bronze and red hues. An annual in Northern climates, the Calendula can handle light frosts and gentle snowfalls. The seeds may be sown where they are to grow. They are fast-growing, very hardy in any soil, and pest-free if kept dry. Overhead watering causes mildew, so for best results, a soaker hose should be used. In the kitchen garden, a hub of Calendulas creates a cheerful, sunny center, attracting bees, therefore, improving pollination and yields from other plants in the garden.

The Calendula is the workhorse of the flowering ornamental herbs. It is used frequently in masses in every landscape form and perfect for a solid color border of exquisite beauty. Its borders are a bit sloppy for formal applications, so if used for such, should be shaped into circular or square patterns centered within a dense border of lower or similar height herbs. Rather large masses are fine in palatial grounds where thick, lush outside borders of Lemon Balm, Rue, or Santolina may be used, but for small garden features the Calendula, growing to 24 in., can be too large. Heavy rain or wind, pummel them to the ground in a nasty mess which still grows and blooms, but in an embarrassing posture. So unless they are grown in full sun and trimmed back when young—they can be pruned at any time—they will need support. They are not at all shy of poor soils. Especially beautiful in the informal and wild landscapes, drifts of Calendulas should be scattered before a verdant background, so as to appear like golden raindrops catching the sun.

Calendula petals contain saponins, chemicals that can both soothe a sore throat or create suds when shaken in water. Saponins are active in forming oil and water emulsions, contributing to the usefulness of Calendula's reputed use as a hair wash and in cooking, to impart smoothness to a soup. The golden petals, which contain significant amounts of vitamin A, may be used to enliven soups, broths, breads, butters, and candies. They are floated on punch or sugared for a treat. Calendula petals are easily dried at a medium temperature, 90–110°F, or they may be preserved in oil. Forgive me, but it does invite a variation on the adage, "One man's soap is another man's soup."

CALENDULA PETALS IN OIL

In a ½ pint jar, add ¼ c. vegetable oil and fill to top with petals, pressing them down regularly into the oil. Add oil to the top. Add 3 thinly sliced garlic cloves and stir.

Seal and keep in the refrigerator. Lasts for 2 weeks. Freeze for longer storage. An ideal method of storage is in an icecube tray. This form is excellent for Chinese stir-fry cuisine, dips, and for salad dressings.

If ice cubes are used, allow at least 24 hours for the mix to cure before transferring it to an icecube tray or the freezer. Separate the cubes and wrap individually in plastic and place in freezer containers. Use 1–2 cubes as necessary in a recipe.

HERB RICE

For each cup of rice, add 1 cube or 2–3 Tbsp. dried Calendula while cooking.

Add flowers of 1 umbel of Fennel (or of Sweet Cicely during early spring) and 1 Tbsp. of whole fresh or dried leaves of Chervil, Sweet Cicely, Tarragon, and Salad Burnet, 4 Tbsp. chopped Chives, 1 tsp. Boullion, (chicken in poultry dishes or beef for beef or pork dishes) and 4 Tbsp. butter or margarine. If an herb butter is used, a Fennel or Chive butter is recommended.

Serve with breast of chicken or beef cubes and for a vegetable, creamed corn or candied pumpkin squares.

This is a meal children will love.

An unusual and indispensible salad herb is Garden Burnet, *Sanguisorba minor*. It has the distinct flavor of cucumbers. *S. minor* ssp. *minor*, or Burnet, is frequently substituted but is nonetheless a valuable cucumber-flavored green herb that, like Salad Burnet, is available to us all year round in a delightful evergreen form. Young leaves picked in spring and fall are more tender and recommended for salad use, while all may be dried for use in cheese dips or cream sauces and soups. During summer months harvest only from first-year plants. Provide them with plenty of moisture in the summer to prevent bitterness.

SALAD BURNET DIP

Use plenty of leaf material for a full cucumber flavor. Be sure leaves are not bitter.

Strip from branches 1 cup of Salad Burnet leaves and chop in blender with a little oil and ¼ clove of Garlic. Fold into sour cream or non-dairy dressing in the amount desired. Allow to stand 4 hours in refrigerator before serving.

Salad Burnet is an evergreen perennial growing in a fascinating rosette pattern like the spokes of a wheel. It resembles a diminutive, dark green, frozen water fountain. The tiny, ½ in. leaves are sharply serrated and arrayed in odd numbers along the branches. It is quite handsome when grown on a layer of white crushed rock with Golden Lemon Thyme, Horehound, and variegated Mints. Its graceful habit is enhanced by combining it in a grey garden or surrounding it by Golden Oregano.

Salad Burnet makes a poor border herb and should be used as a single specimen planting or ground cover. As an annual, Burnet keeps a very low profile, less than 6 in. It can be used to create fascinating spider-like patches in a rock garden or a sparsely planted contemporary feature. As a perennial, Burnet develops an 18–24 in. fountain-like form with long, drooping tentacles tipped with fuzzy, knobby balls. These flowers are small, ½–1 in. capsules that display hundreds of tiny bright red filaments emerging like the many arms of a sea anemone. The flowering stems and fruits are not of exceptional beauty and may be removed to improve the neatness of the herb and to avoid spreading throughout the garden. It will self-sow profusely, spreading rapidly like a weed so needs controlling. Because of its ornamental appearance, however, it is an excellent self-sowing ground cover. As an annual, each plant requires a space about 18 in. in diameter and as a perennial, to 30 in.

An isolated community composed of several Salad Burnet plants in informal, wild or contemporary landscapes is recommended. It should be grown as an annual in a kitchen garden, in rows or as the points of a pentagram, the center of which is filled with Calendula.

Salad Burnet has two larger relatives, Japanese Burnet, *Sanguisorba obtusa,* 12–18 in., and *S. tenuifolia,* 3–4 ft., with larger leaves and fuzzy white, pink or rose, bottle-brush flowers of considerable ornamental value. Their leaves have no culinary use. They are best used sown in a wild landscape with Salad Burnet for size and flower color contrast or alone in a contemporary feature or wild garden.

An herb with a history as a medicinal in the Americas is Great Burnet, *Sanguisorba officinale,* which resembles the Salad Burnet except for its large, 3–5 ft. size. Canadian Burnet, *Sanguisorba canadense,* sports large, 3–4 in., bottle-brush flower spikes which extend out from the plant on 2 foot long stalks bending gracefully towards the ground. All of the Burnets have been used as fodder and medicine for centuries.

Another fodder and medicinal herb, although better known, is Comfrey, *Symphytum officinale.* This herbaceous perennial is a noxious weed so care must be taken to carefully confine a planting to prevent its spread, both by seed and by root pieces, such as when it is transplanted or improperly composted. Broad, 12–18 in. long leaves of Comfrey make it a spectacular plant in any garden, its lush, dark green clumps mimicking lush, tropical undergrowth. The pink, purple, yellow, and red flowers are a favorite of bees. We, too, may enjoy the sugary nectar of Comfrey flowers in salads or as a sweetener in herbal teas and candies.

In the kitchen garden, Comfrey is cultivated in large clumps in the center of the squares. There it will benefit the garden with a flowering display in May and June, and again in the fall, attracting pollinators. Comfrey may also be used as a border if carefully controlled while larger species act as a screen. In unconfined plantings, Comfrey combines well with tall, large-leafed plants such as Poppies, Hollyhocks, Elcampane, Hosta, and Iris.

Comfrey thrives in a moist soil and may be grown in partial shade. A poor, dry soil will help control it. Plantings are improved by a soil covering of crushed rock or bark. To stop Comfrey from spreading below ground, plant it in partially buried barrels or bury 10 in. boards around the plant.

The leaves and roots of Comfrey, or Knitbone, are used medicinally in a poultice (whole leaves applied to sore spot and covered by a warm, moist towel) to cure muscle aches and sprains. The active material is allantoin, which promotes wound healing. Comfrey is useful as a fodder and highly valued as a compost material because of its rapid growth and high mineral content.

In addition to a variegated form of Common Comfrey, *S. officinale* 'Variegatum', with leaves margined in white, red-flowering Comfrey, *S. o.* 'Coccinceum' and Yellow flowering 'Aureum', several other decorative species include: Prickly Comfrey, *Symphytum asperum,* primarily a fodder plant growing to 6 ft. which has flowers that change from rose to blue as they mature; *S.* × *uplandicum,* a cross of Common and Prickly Comfrey, called Russian Comfrey, is more ornamental with heavy flower clusters and also grows to 6 ft. with rose flowers changing to purple.

Another rampantly spreading herb is Garden Tansy, *Tanacetum vulgare.* Tansy is a tall, slim plant with feathery pine green foliage. The oily and herbaceous fragrance of its foliage becomes apparent to passersby, particularly on hot summer afternoons. A clump of Tansy takes little time to develop and needs no care other than occasional staking or tying together of its heavy bright gold button flowers in late summer. (Garden Tansy should not be confused with Tansy Ragwort, *Senecio jacobea,* a toxic weed.) An ornamental cultivar, *T. vulgare* 'Crispum', has fern-like leaves and is usually listed as Fern-leafed Tansy. It is a smaller variety, growing to no more than 3 ft., with the same sunny yellow flowers but a penetrating camphoraceous odor.

Fern-leafed Tansy is definitely more useful as an ornamental herb than the species. It develops a sturdier, denser habit with its dark green, filigreed leaves pointing downward and lying flat against one another. A large clump will stand alone and to some extent it can be molded into shape by pruning and by tying up with twine. The leaves remain on the lower portions of the plant for a very neat, pert appearance.

Tansy's hardiness makes it a choice plant for a screen. As a thick screen, Tansy should, at a minimum, be allowed to spread to a 12 in. wide clump. This provides a moderately dense hedge. The dark green foliage makes an excellent background for medium or low borders of yellow or white flowers. The oily scent of Tansy mixes well with spicy and floral scents of Clove Pinks and Roses. Handsome, fragrant borders can be created with light green or grey fragrant companions such as Wormwood, Carnations, Blue Sage and Valerian.

Tansy achieved a long list of accomplishments during the Dark Ages and for many centuries afterwards. It was an important herb for food during fast days. Tansies, or egg and flower concoctions using Tansy as an ingredient or simply egg and Tansy alone, were valuable foodstuffs for the peasants of medieval Europe. Today its flowers and foliage are valued highly for ornamental use only.

Note: Both Garden Tansy and the previously discussed herb, Comfrey, are no longer recommended as a food because they contain toxic chemicals like those found in Tansy Rag-wort which can seriously harm or kill grazing animals. At present this warning is posted on a guilt by chemical association as no clinical research has been done to support or refute it.

One of the most useful herbs, but which has a weedy appearance, is Parsley, *Petroselinium crispum*. Parsley is one of the most widely used fresh green herbs, as a main course garnish at home, in restaurants, and as bright green flakes in hundreds of prepared foods. Parsley is noted for its high vitamin C content and has been used by man for so many millenia it does not now exist as an uncultivated natural species. Both the root and the leaves are useful in virtually all foods. The fresh greens are used in salads as garnishes in gourmet dishes and as pottage. Easily and rapidly dried by high temperature, 110–140°F, in an oven, Parsley keeps its green color and high mineral and vitamin content for an exceptionally long period. Parsley flakes are also used in soups, potato and egg salads, meats, stews, and vegetable dishes.

Fresh Parsley may be deep fried for a spicy, crunchy treat or as an excellent stir-fry vegetable in Oriental dishes, adding a bright green when pea pods and broccoli are not used or when seasonally unavailable. Crinkly or curly forms, *P. crispum* var. *crispum,* tend to be bitter but a rich soil and ample water will guarantee a refreshing spicy and herbaceous flavor. The spicy notes in Parsley are provided by turpenes and pinene.

Italian Parsley, also called Flat-leafed Parsley, *P. crispum* var. *neapolitanum,* has flat, serrated leaves which are larger and sweeter tasting, much more suitable for pottage or as a green coloring in butter, sauces, and cheeses. It is a tall, rangy herb, not at all suitable to orna-mental use except perhaps in a wild garden, tucked into a screen of Dill and Yarrow, or grown with Lovage and Angelica.

Flat-leafed Parsley is used with butter and cheese to make a peppery, bright green spread for crackers and a hot dip for chips. For a tongue-tingling Parsley dip, combine 1 c. of fresh Parsley leaves, ¼ c. of Lovage leaves, and 1 clove of Garlic, with 1 Tbsp. of Tarragon vinegar in a blender. Fold into sour cream or non-dairy dressing. The dip may be used imme-diately but best flavor is achieved after standing several hours or overnight.

For fresh herbs, cut plants as near the ground as possible, removing only as many stems as needed. Plants trimmed heavily in mid-summer will regrow by late fall for a second crop. In warmer climates, Parsley will grow throughout the year and go to seed the following summer. For culinary purposes, only the first year growth is used. Seed from one plant is

Plate 19

A colorful feature and transition herb is Golden Sage. Here it shares a slender evergreen perennial bed with Rue, Caraway Thyme (blooming), German Camomile and a backborder of Garden Sage and Oregano (right).

Variegated Sage adorned in cream and pink creating a colorful feature in this dooryard perimeter bed along with a pink flowering Lavender (right), Oregano, Scarlet Poppy and a clump of red flowering Florist's Violet.

Informal garden of red-hued herbs including Za'atar, *Thymbra spicata*, (center) with a coat of pink flowers, Melon Sage, *Salvia dorisiana*, with crimson trumpets and a Gilliflower or Dwarf Carnation. Creeping Red Thyme and pink flowered Lime Mint reside at opposite ends of this feature just out of sight.

Mound of Red Sage in garden of John Eccles, Winlock, WA.

Silver Sage with chalk-white flowers at Medicinal Herb Garden, University of Washington, Seattle, WA.

Plate 20

Informal landscape. Home and gardens of Michele Nash, Mercer Island, WA.

A fragrant seat by one of three Rosemarys which play an important role in tying together the separate parts of this contemporary landscape. From the gardens of Angelo Pellegrini, Seattle, WA.

A border of Golden Oregano, Chives and Silver Thyme. On the patio Creeping Thymes cascade over the walls. Garden of Michele Nash, Mercer Island, WA.

A garden on fire with red-orange Calendulas, Dahlias, Roses and Nasturtiums. Calendulas form the theme in all the interconnected gardens on this homesite in Chehalis, WA.

Small island garden dividing lawn area from kitchen garden at home of Judith Zugish, Marysville, WA.

Plate 21

A patch of early spring color juts into the path. Sweet Cicely and *Ajuga* (bottom) contrast each other in color and texture.

Mound at one side of street entrance that is colorful and fragrant using 'Hidcote' Lavender, Wooly Betony and sunny Toadflax.

Austere perennial feature fingering into a backyard, includes neatly clipped hedges of French Thyme, Chives, Oregano, Calendula and Garden Sage. Color and vertical contrast is provided by Rose Campion and Daisies. It is an excellent example of an edible landscape from the gardens of Gail Shilling, Bellevue, WA.

Isolated entrance feature with Golden Sage, Lavender, fruit tree, Curly Parsley as a ground cover and evergreens at home of Michele Nash, Mercer Island, WA.

Edible landscape. Perennial bed with Garden Sage, Giant Alliums, Garlic, Strawberries as a ground cover, Rhubarb, fruit trees and many ornamentals in garden of Michele Nash, Mercer Island, WA.

Incana Santolina growing merrily among the Strawberries in an edible landscape by Michele Nash, Mercer Island, WA.

Plate 22

Costmary with a profusion of little daisies in mid-June. This species is also known as the Camphor Plant because of its strong camphor odor.

Hops as a ground cover.

Young Variegated Hop clinging to a rock wall.

The stately flowering portion of Common Giant Fennel, an imposing herb in any garden feature. The Marshmallow, *Althea officinalis*, shares this square at the University of Washington, Medicinal Herb Garden, Seattle, WA.

French Cardoon feature in formal square at Medicinal Herb Garden, University of Washington, Seattle, WA.

Bee Balm, *Monarda didyma* 'Cambridge Scarlet', in formal feature at University of Washington, Medicinal Herb Garden, Seattle, WA.

more than sufficient for the home. A variety, Turnip-rooted Parsley, *P. c.* var. *tuberosum,* is grown for its large edible roots.

Japanese Parsley, *Cryptotaenia japonica,* is an *Umbelliferae* resembling Italian Parsley. It is, however, lower in stature with a more pleasing taste and aroma that is popular in salads and Oriental cuisine. It grows well in partial shade but is best grown as an annual in the kitchen garden. As a perennial herb it grows to 18–24 in. in a slowly spreading clump. Honewort, *C. canadensis,* is a North American species often substituted.

As landscape ornamentals the curly forms of Parsley are choice. They make dense, 12–14 in. wide borders from 8 to 14 in. high in a number of green, dark green, and red hued varieties. When closely packed, they will merge to form a neat and admirable border. A high contrast planting of Curly Parsley may be used in formal arrangements to encircle specimen plants. In centuries past, Parsley was used to form the intricate scrollwork in knot gardens or parterres. Grown as an annual, little effort is needed to maintain it as a border. Single plants of Curly Parsley make a fine addition in a mixed border and may be used as transition plants for the beginning and ending of borders of flowering companions or interspersed in a long border in repeated fashion to break monotony and introduce motion. Today, the curly varieties are used as a border in informal and kitchen gardens and as isolated clumps of bold green contrast to greys in contemporary features.

It is important to remember that Curly Parsley purchased from a garden center may be last year's crop. In that case, as a biennial herb, it will not form a pleasant ornamental bush but a twiggy, thin form that will soon go to seed and die. Plant all Parsley from seed for guaranteed results. Parsley is not an ornamental herb in its second year and is less useful for culinary purposes as well.

Parsley is an extremely hardy herb, relatively pest-free and easily propogated by seed. It has been said that Parsley is slow to germinate but with the advent of good potting soils and hotbeds, fresh seeds that have been pre-soaked 24 hours will germinate in 7–21 days. Parsley seed fertility declines rapidly so use it fresh, no more than one year old. Purchased seed requires 3–4 weeks to germinate and longer as the seeds age. Sow all borders where they are to grow.

French Sorrel, *Rumex scutatus,* is strictly a kitchen garden herb used as a companion to corn, grains and tall vegetables. Its succulent leaves are used as Spinach in soups and as a boiled vegetable. It is highly valuable for both its mineral and vitamin content in early spring well before other pot herbs are available. Several culinary varieties are available so gardeners are advised to try more than one. Sorrel will spread if allowed to go to seed; cultivate only one or two plants for seed production. It requires full sun and a rich, moist garden soil. The useful life of a Sorrel patch is from 6–10 years.

French Sorrel may be used in large arrangements as a self-sowing ground cover that is hardy and quick to spread. Its 12 in. bold green to yellow-green growth is a fine accent for large grey herbs and around dark evergreen shrubs. Sorrels have been used in knot gardens as borders and in parterres to fill large areas.

Common Garden Sorrel, *Rumex acetosa,* is a perennial broad-leafed plant growing to 24 in. with reproductive spikes to 3 ft. The green leaves are arrow-shaped and from 4–6 in. long. 'Bellville' is a prominent and tasty cultivar. French Sorrel, *R. scutatus,* is a smaller species from 12–18 in. with arrow-shaped leaves but of a more oval form and better flavor. Other species include common weeds: Patience Dock, or Spinach Dock, *R. patientia,* growing to 6 ft., with 12 in. leaves; Red Sorrel or Sheep Sorrel, *R. acetosella,* a low, 6–12 in. rampantly spreading, but edible weed, with reddish flower spikes; and *R. crispus,* Curly Dock, which is used medicinally.

Looking considerably like a creeping form of Sorrel is Good King Henry, *Chenopodium bonus henricus,* an old-fashioned pot herb. In fact, the similarity, most noticeable in their inflorescence, reveals their distant relationship. Its dark green, arrow-shaped leaves are quite tasty and an excellent Spinach substitute in a hardy perennial package. This member of the goosefoot family has more ornamental potential in the garden than its annual relatives Lamb's Quarters, *C. album,* and Strawberry Blite, *C. capitatum.* Its low height, 6–12 in., and moderate spreading rate make it a useful front border herb in a mixed arrangement accompanying dark green or ruby-stained lettuce and chard or with Silver Sage and Meadow Clary for a wild ornamental effect. A grouping of Good King Henry with low Alliums or other herbs and ornamental plants with a strong vertical habit in a small area give the most pleasing arrangement.

Caraway, *Carum carvi,* is a weedy carrot-like biennial. In the first year, Caraway may be used as a low, 8–12 in. border. Its feathery, pine green foliage is excellent in salads and soups, having a discernible anise scent and flavor. Young, 2–4 in. seedlings may be eaten whole in salads and soups. The roots of first year plants are sweet and tasty either raw in salads or steamed. In stir-fry recipes the finger-thick roots of older plants add a crunchy sweetness which may substitute for water chestnuts. The second year, Caraway will grow rapidly to 2–3 ft., its insignificant white-flowered umbels developing (by early June) the popular Caraway seeds, used in bakery goods, sausages, and cheeses.

If a small row or plot is planted for its greens the first year, Caraway may be transplanted to another location such as a kitchen garden or wild garden for seed production, which is quite unornamental. Caraway seed must be allowed to ripen on the plants, which require tying or support. The tiny, brown seeds, borne Dill-like, are sweet and have a strong Anise flavor, much prized by gardeners, for it is easier to grow Caraway, a biennial that is hardy in cold climates, than Anise, the seeds of which may not even ripen. Predominant fragrant constituents in Caraway are carvone, carvacrol, cuminal, and limonene, the same chemicals found in Cumin and Coriander. Caraway seed is a complementary spice to Coriander, Cumin and Ginger and not as widely used in meat dishes as it should be. Crush it to release its essence. To fully enjoy the flavor of Caraway seed, use it in Chili or spaghetti sauce, with meat balls in a rich Basil sauce or with honey and Lovage on baked chicken.

MEAT BALLS

3 pounds ground beef	1 Tbsp. Lovage
2 pounds pork sausage	2 Tbsp. Caraway seed, crushed
1 c. oatmeal	1 Tbsp. Oregano
2 eggs	1 tsp. Savory
2 Tbsp. sugar	1 tsp. Basil

Combine ingredients. Make into 60 balls. Bake in oven at 350°F for 45 minutes. Place in a sauce and simmer for two hours.

TOMATO SAUCE

3 cans tomato sauce	1 Tbsp. Lovage
2 Tbsp. Caraway seed, crushed	1 Tbsp. Oregano
1 tsp. Coriander seed, crushed	1 tsp. Fennel
1 tsp. Basil	

Combine the ingredients and simmer for one hour, then add precooked meat balls. Add ½ c. brown sugar 45 minutes before serving.

For a pasta dish without tomato sauce, drench noodles in Lemon Basil butter and sprinkle with fresh, chopped Chives, Fennel, and Lovage leaves and serve with hot meat balls.

Caraway is easily dried by hanging the plants upside down in a paper bag to dry, The seeds are shaken loose and stored in airtight jars. They retain their flavor for several years. To hasten ripening and protect the seed heads from dust, paper bags may be tied over the plants in the garden. Any seeds that fall off early will be trapped in the bag. After no more than 1–2 weeks, the tops are cut and bags inverted and hung in a dry location for storage. There is an annual form of caraway that is grown commercially. It is planted in early spring and harvested in late fall. Another variety of Caraway is grown for its plump, tender Anise and Carrot flavored root.

As with all *Umbelliferae* mentioned in this text, the umbel from which the Caraway seeds are removed is valuable in decorative arrangements and may be used to make an ornamental ball resembling a sea urchin. To design a *gossamer sphere:* 1. Remove all seeds from the umbel gently so as to leave the fine hairs on the tips of the branchlets, or, 2. Trim all umbel branchlets to 1–2 in. by folding together and pruning. 3. Attach fishing line to the head of a pin and insert into the end of one branch. 4. Bend the tip of the pin to secure. 5. To the stems of each new umbel added use a dab of glue on stems in the center and connect the branchlets like the spokes of a wheel. 6. When complete, coat the hub with extra glue and spray the sphere with a paint fixative, spray paint or lacquer.

Summer Savory, *Satureja hortensis*, is a delightfully fragrant herb. It is also an unsavory, weedy looking thing and although Winter Savory, *Satureja montana,* its relative, is a great herb for borders in neat trimmed lines, Summer Savory, an annual, is best used in a kitchen garden or wild garden and grown for its culinary virtues.

Due to its lax habit and spindly growth, it is best suited to mass plantings in the wild garden, protected from foot traffic, but nevertheless bisected by paths, where its rich, spicy, camphoraceous scent may be relished and its tiny, fragrant, pink flowers appreciated. Or plant this thin little waif as a low border herb in the dooryard or kitchen garden where it will droop over a path, ever ready to emit its rich aroma when brushed.

Under the best of conditions, Summer Savory forms a 12–16 in. dark green or black stained bush. Its meager habit makes it hard to find it a home in the ornamental landscape. To keep their bush forms sturdy, plants must be allowed adequate light and ample space or they become spindly and will topple in the first heavy rain. It must be cultivated in full sun and rich soil. A patch of Summer Savory 30–50 sq. ft. will scent an entire garden.

The culinary value of Summer Savory exceeds that of its relative, Winter Savory. Unless it is grown separately in a vegetable or culinary herb garden where whole plants are harvested and dried, clippings may be taken from an ornamental garden any time through bloom. Summer Savory has a mellow camphoraceous aroma composed of thymol and carvacrol, a scent reminiscent of Oregano Thyme. It is excellent in hardy potato or meat soups, bean stews, chili, egg and cheese omelets, sausage and tangy sauces for the barbeque or broiler. Poultry and lamb may be smoked to a sharp, sausage-like flavor with 2–3 c. of Savory spilled onto the hot coals then covered to allow meat to smoke for 30 minutes.

CHILI BEANS

4 quarts water

Add: 4 c. pinto beans   2 Tbsp. chili
      6 large tomatoes   1 Tbsp. Lovage
      1 large green pepper   4 Cloves of Garlic
      1 tsp. beef bouillon   1 tsp. Fennel seed
      2 Tbsp. Chive butter   ½ tsp. Ginger
      2 Tbsp. Summer Savory   ½ c. maple syrup

Simmmer 3–4 hours until beans are cooked but firm.

Tarragon's weediness has been forgiven for centuries. It's an herb no gourmet would be without and so it is grown, groomed and harvested no matter if it does try to fall all over the ground and screw itself into a tangled web both above and below the ground. The entanglement of roots is the source of its ancient name, Dracunculus, for the serpentine mess that must be lifted and divided before it constricts itself. Its Hyssop-like leaves are nothing to look at but once dried have a flavor and fragrance that simply cannot be described. Sweet, cool and ethereal come close, without resorting to a comparison with another herb, the most common of which is Licorice.

This 2–3 ft., herbaceous ragamuffin must be grown where it can be staked to prevent it from touching the earth. It needs a spacious plot of top quality soil that is half sand or otherwise very well drained. Oyster shell and bonemeal are recommended as well as a good organic fertilizer in early spring and again in mid-summer. A fall mulch is not necessary and on poor soils will only accelerate decay. An annual lifting and root pruning is advisable in heavy soils.

About one cup of dried leaves is possible from an average Tarragon plant. It dries quickly, 2–3 hours at low temperature and in only a few minutes in a microwave. Tarragon is very different fresh and dried. The biting, anesthetic activity of fresh Tarragon, due perhaps to methoxycinnaminaldehyde, rapidly loses ground to ocimene, myrcene, methylchavicol and phellandrene as it dries. Tarragon sweetens a vinegar and performs a vital service for Tartar Sauce as we know it and is "one of the perfumery of spicy furniture of our sallots" as Sir John Evelyn noted in 1693. Fresh, dried, as a vinegar or wine, Tarragon adds a different flavor in each case to a dish. Its special virtue must be taken advantage of. Use it in a Sweet Rice recipe or with buttered vegetables such as carrots, coles and baked or candied squash. A butter of Tarragon is very strange and delicate, superb for a basted bird or for buttered noodles with bits of mild pork sausage. German potato salad demands a Tarragon vinegar and a tart mayonnaise sandwich spread is made with it and a pinch of dried Lovage and Thyme.

There are two types of Tarragon: Russian Tarragon, *Artemisia dracunculus,* and the popular and almost legendary French Tarragon, *A. d.* 'Sativa'. The former is nice but not the real thing. The Russian form can be grown from seed, and although it is hardier it is exceptionally weedy and does not have the bite and heady aroma so cherished in the French. French Tarragon can only be propagated by root divisions or cuttings.

Confine French Tarragon to the kitchen garden. Experiment with it elsewhere. It may join in an herbaceous perennial bed but keep it far to the back and never near the dripline of trees. Under an eve in partial shade is a possibility but expect a smaller harvest. Give it a long border in the kitchen garden, at least 4 plants, and allow it to neighbor with a perennial border of Gooseberry or Blueberry behind it and Strawberry before it. Every year divide and root prune ¼ of your plants to freshen them.

Chapter 4 / SECTION 3

A Walk Through a Formal Dooryard Garden

Touring a dooryard garden is a romantic experience. It conjures visions of storybook scenes. Before us is a quaint homestead, its eaves and gingerbread cloaked in gnarled vines, its dooryard garden thick with simples. (Fig. 34) Through squinted eyes we can almost see Hansel and Gretel frolicking among the herbs and spices that are used by the Wicked Witch for all her cakes and candies. Her medicinal and magical herbs for aches and incantations are there, portents of the awesome power of the one who wields them well. The landscape's medieval marks, formality and herbalism, remind us of castles and queens, kings and conquests. Here we will find all manner of healing herbs.

Before us is an old wooden gate, buttressed by thorny twisting briars. Beyond is an imposing garden, at first glance wild and free, but on closer inspection there is a suggestion of some power at work, cordoning these herbs into an unnatural, but handsome habitat for edification and introspection. No one comes to greet us; perhaps that is best. We were told that all the herbs were labeled. We were also told that in this tiny garden, 20 × 40 ft. are 140 different species, varieties, and cultivars of herbs. We enter and find ourselves on a cobblestone path, with herbs spilling and writhing from every nook and cranny available.

A grinning black grimalkin, eyeing us contemptuously from her perch on a honeysuckled porch rail, eerily reminds us of the old woman we spoke to on that very spot a week ago. She informed us that from this garden she could extract all she would need for "sauces and seasonings, syrups, scents and pretty condiments, bugbane and air freshener, robegarde and dye, for salves and syrupy simples, an herb for everything from childbirth to extreme unction." In a sense a dooryard garden is a little like visiting your pharmacist, grocery and health food store all at the same time.

There seems to be no beginning and certainly no end before us. The best place to start is with our nose. We sense a multitude of herbaceous odors but one or two nearby are minty and fresh. Since it had rained only an hour before, the scents of Mint, Camomile, Sage, and Lemon Verbena have taken wings about us. The purple leaves of Black mint emit a fragrance of mouthwatering menthol that summons visions of gum and penny candy while its neighbor, Pygmy Savory, exudes a rich camphoraceous aroma. It is flanked on either side by an equally fragrant but reclusive species of the same genus, Creeping Savory, that swarms over the side to the cobblestones below. Reaching out from its station on the cobblestone walk to catch hold of the Savory is pine-scented Rosemary. In late summer, the slender branches of both entwine while displaying their Sunday best, sapphire blue and pink-white flowers.

Now a strong apple-scent finds its way to our nose. We look down to discover we have trod upon some Roman Camomile. Draped to the stony path below, it waves its feathery tendrils and tiny, white daisies deliberately in our path. Bumping or stepping on it brings the scent of hot apple-cider to our nose. We back away, believing we have hurt it, but remember the saying "Like a Camomile bed, the more it is trodden, the more it will spread". Its neighbor is a dark green mound of Basil Thyme, which boasts a minty, Thymish scent and hosts of pink flowers, growing from long, drooping flower stalks like many rows of little bells.

A delicate wooly grey Greek Sage rests comfortably in a raised bed nearby. Anemones and Creeping Thymes share its box. This Sage has an ornamental character that resembles Horehound, with fuzzy, warped leaves and a stance that reminds us of their close alliance with the Mint family. Either Greek Sage or Blue Sage may be combined as a powder with Caraway Thyme, Rosemary, Mint, and baking soda for a tongue-tingling herbal tooth cleanser.

Sliding between the box and two long, parallel, raised beds we see the countless herbs that we were promised would be here. Hollow cylinders of drain tile provide support for the raised beds as well as a secure home for precious specimens or rampant spreaders. Many contain creeping herbs such as a Golden Thyme with a 2 in. high habit and light green leaves. There is Wild Thyme, *Thymus pulegioides*, with tiny, dark green leaves spreading in a ½ in. thick mat; Caraway Thyme, *T. herba-barona*; a Thyme called Brittanicus, *T. praecox*; and Red-flowering Thyme, *T. praecox* ssp. *arcticus* 'Coccineus', with tiny, dark green, needle-like leaves. Draping over the edge to the cobbles below are Creeping Savory, Roman Camomile, and *Ajuga*. These low mats are for sitting, a modest, but fragrant padding, in a fashion that has not been common for nearly 500 years.

The beds around us contain splendid colors. Snapdragons peek out from just about anywhere, without rhyme or reason, adding charm and color to nonflowering ornamental herbs such as a globe of Lavender Cotton, Bible Leaf, with spade-sized leaves, a dense bush of Golden Lemon Thyme, a patch of fragrant Eau de Cologne or Orange Mint, and spidery mounds of Creeping Savory. Crimson and gold Nasturtium flowers peek from among Mint and Angelica. Perky white and lime-green clusters of Dwarf Feverfews dot the landscape, accenting patches of Lemon Balm, Peppermint, Applemint, Oregano, and Sweet Cicely.

Snug within the confines of the boxes are all kinds of Sages and Basils. Most striking are the sky-blue flowers of Blue Sage, which are born in Monarda-like whorls, one above the other. It has blunt, spatula-shaped leaves with a refreshing lemony tang and is one of the most beautiful Sages. A cheery, yellow Golden Sage shares a cramped site with a Lemon Catnip and the most diminutive member of this genus, a Dwarf Sage, Dwarf Lavender, Pink Hyssop, and *Santolina* 'Nana', emerge from an emerald carpet of Corsican Mint. A hedge of Chives impedes the progress of this tiny creeping Mint on one side and a bumbling, fountain-like Burnet spreads its cucumber-flavored foliage in its path on the other.

The exceedingly long and slender rugose leaves of Mealy Cup Sage, *Salvia farinacea*, reach out from under two tall, spade-leafed, ornamental *Salvia*, *S. guarantica* and *S. mexicana*, while the wispy branches of Bog Sage, *S. uliginosa* confront them all, dangling over and through the patch willy-nilly. Below is the creeping, Lobelia-like form of Canyon Sage, *Salvia lycoides*, with tiny blue flowers. In late fall they produce a dramatic display with enormous plumes and spikes of blue and purple as well as serving up a fall treat of nectar to hummingbirds and bees.

Two long rows on either side of the middle of the box house a vast assortment of Oreganos, for color and charm and culinary delight. White and pink flowers strike out in graceful arcs from emerald, pine, and grey-green Marjoram foliages. On closer inspection we find Italian and Greek Oregano, Sweet Marjoram, and Pot Marjoram. A single plant of any is enough for a year's supply in any gourmet's kitchen. The cast includes Russian Oregano with dark green leaves, red-stained stems, and a surplus of pink powderballs and *Origanum microphyllum,* with dazzling, neon-pink flowers decorating what appears to be a miniature Money Plant whose silver baubles are actually leaves no bigger than an "O". The luxuriant frosted form of Cretan Dittany graces a small, cedar pot nestled in a grove of bushy 'Spice' Basil while a clump of Golden Oregano tries to outdo its neighbor, Golden Sage, a few feet away. A sample of each of the Oreganos reveals that their aroma is as different and as delicate as rare French perfumes.

Adding to the confusion are two odd herbs that reside in small clay pots sunk into the warm soil. Strange, succulent leaves on one and thick, rubbery leaves on the other remind us of tropicals. A sample under the nose tells us they are both Oregano, not Oregano by botanical nomenclature, but chemical. Because of their carvacol content these two herbs, Indian Borage, *Coleus amboinicus* and *Poliomintha longiflora,* are grown and used in Zone 9 to the tropics as Oregano substitutes. Both are beautiful and exotic herbs for the ornamental garden.

The far end of the box is overstuffed with a grey conglomeration of Lamb's Ears and Garden Sage. Called Lamb's Ears because of their soft, furry texture and size, the leaves are sweet, smell faintly of apples and are used in medicinal teas for soothing sore throats. This duo of Betony and Sage displays blushing pink and ice blue flowers for 3 months throughout summer, attracting every flying creature known. "On new moon nights, other flying things may come", warns our host who has been stalking us for several minutes. "Ye should pluck this" she says, swooping down with one hand to find a sprig of Rosemary. "Wave it about thee, so, then never you mind, they'll flee any of Mary's yarbs they will." Mary's herbs are numerous here; Pot Marigolds, Rosemary, Costmary, etc., and reputed to turn away evil spirits.

Colorful red blooms and a spicy scent nearby lead us to a Rose Geranium intertwined in the branches of the Sage and Betony. Blue, clove-scented flowers draw our attention as well, down to where the frogs and the snails creep. Clumps of grey-green Dwarf Catnip send wispy branches into the moist comfort of the Sage but grow more thickly toward the edge of the box, their lake-blue flowers cascading down in a continual show throughout the summer and into fall. Wild and free at the end of the box is a thick patch of Organy or Wild Marjoram. Its tall pink and white plumes of everlasting, fragrant flowers decorate this end of the bed.

The opposite bed sits in partial to full shade. In it dwell the sleepers, herbs that excel in the early spring or late fall, when the trees do not hide them from the sun. A triumvirate of Angelica, rising magestically over a ground cover of Applemint and seedling Chervil, dresses one end of this garden. A mat of purple and mocha *Ajuga* glides out from under the Angelica as well and down and around the trunk of a small Hazelnut, where a handsome, pea-green patch of Sweet Cicely governs. In early spring this scene is flecked with *Crocus, Eranthis,* and *Hyacinth.* A frail waif of Red Fennel pokes its sheepish head skyward, trying to eke out a living in this shady neighborhood. Its attempts to withdraw fail, thanks to its dashing rust-red appearance. Spilling out into the open, the dainty, filigreed leaves of the tender Chervil encounter an orgy of colors: here golden Calendulas, hot pink Nepetella and magenta and yellow Snapdragons fight for the sunlight with sky-blue, purple, and gold Heartsease Pansies.

As though planted for comic relief, a patch of Bible Leaf, with huge heavenward-pointed leaves appears indignant at the unabashed display of color around them. Those near the edge of the bed have given up hope and fall limp over the brink where they are sacrificed underfoot, releasing a wonderful minty aroma. Bible Leaf, placed here to balance the Lamb's Ears across the path, is combined with its neighbor, Orange Mint, for a tangy tea to clear the head. Hiding behind is Lemon Balm, a great, dark green mound with citronella-scented leaves of rugose character. An effective bugbane (insect repellent) when rubbed on the skin, Lemon Balm also provides a lemon twist for teas and tarts, potpourries, and herb pillows. Yet another citrus scent catches our attention here. A large patch of Orange Mint with purple-marked foliage resembles the odor of an overripe orange rind, at once sweet and bitter. It is a perky flavoring with honey in a strong black tea, or with honey, Camomile and roasted Chickory. The more familiar foliage of Peppermint shows itself, confined in a cylinder for a tidy appearance and to control spreading. The strong menthol flavor of this Mint can effectively numb the mouth and gums and its refined oil functions as an oral anesthetic today.

Our host beckons us to sit and rest beside her a moment upon a fragrant seat of Creeping Golden Thyme. Her ancient but sturdy hand plucks a cat-faced Pansy with whiskers of white and yellow. She kisses it fondly and begins her monologue on the healing value of the herbs around us.

"The Violets, they be for the bowels and scurvy, Angelica for the airs and innards. For blood pressure there be Chervil and Parsley. For the gout, Pennyroyal and Betony. Use Camomile and Sage for the cleaning of hair, and Cleavers and Comfrey for the skin. For bruises bathe with Thyme, for pains 'tis best to use a poultice of Witch Hazel. Horehound's to soothe the throat, and Fennel to stay the appetite. There is Milfoil for sores of the mouth and Mint for toothache, a Lavender bath for calming muscles, Valerian to calm the nerves, and Dill to lull thee to sleep. Here too be Wormwood, a scourge to vexing serpents, Boneset for breaks, Betony for wounds, and Mallows for birthing."

A clump of Lovage, lush and caressable, lounges in the shade before us. Creeping Charlie creeps about our heels, hugging the base of our herb seat, its oval leaves buoyed up on tiny stems complementing the cobblestones above which they seem to float. Here and there Violets and isolated shocks of flowerless Lawn Camomile extrude themselves from between the cobbles, while far to the other side of the yard is an entire mead composed of Violets and Camomile. There they join Creeping Thyme, Anemones, Wild Ginger, English Pennyroyal, Miner's Lettuce, and Mallows. On the opposite side of the yard is a forest of large Swordfern, Christmas Rose, Wood Sorrel, Elderberry, Lungwort, Solomon Seal, Jack-in-the-pulpit, Wild Strawberry, and Trilliums, all of which dwell in the dark shade of Old Man Walnut.

A perimeter bed along the fence is occupied by an odd assortment of ornamental herbs. Curly Parsley, its crisp green leaves gnarled into infinity, is a perky counterpart to a patch of arrow-leafed Good King Henry, *Chenopodium bonus-henricus.* Miniature Roses and ruby-red rag Poppies decorate this bed of dwarf and diminutive herbs, including Rue, Golden Lemon Thyme, Silver Thyme, red, white, and blue Hyssop in trim 10 in. tussocks, blue-bearded *Salvia viridis*, Dwarf Feverfew, Dropwort, 'Opal' Basil, 'Bush' Basil, Variegated Sage, Ariculas, with exotically fragrant yellow bells, and a youthful pink 'Rosea' Lavender snuggling up to an elderly Dwarf Lavender. The herbs rise in height as the bed confronts the forest beneath the Walnut. 'Moonshine' and 'Fireking' Yarrow, and a double-flowered Feverfew press against a screen of Tansy that abuts a Wormwood-collared American Holly.

This dooryard garden is a wondrous place to think, a place to ponder the histories of the great Herbalists of centuries past and examine their herbs, and a place to be alone, with the hummingbirds and goldfinches, flickers and robins, squirrels, moles, mice, frogs, snakes, snails, ladybugs, and damselflies. They, too, find it their dooryard garden.

Chapter 5 / SECTION 1

Informal Landscape

The dawning of informal gardens in the 18th century was a reaction to the extreme formalism of the preceding landscaping tradition. Formal gardens had been appreciated for their beauty and craftsmanship. They were an art form whose reign endured throughout the Middle Ages and the Renaissance, influenced more by the simpering minions of the courts than the gardeners who often deplored the contrived and unnatural creations dictated by courtly convention and fashion. Dynastic rivalry, self-indulgence, the desire to be considered fashionable and correct all fueled the self-appointed arbiters of taste, who seem to be able to fasten on the arts and cultural patterns in every era, including our own, ultimately drove formal garden design to the insufferable and unpalatable. Coupled with other historical developments a new view of nature and man emerged, which was reflected in the naturalistic garden.

The naturalistic mood was created with casual arrangements of trees and plants in their natural form, set around a centerpiece of lawn. The softening of formal lines required the substitution of flowering shrubs and small trees for squared hedges. The vertical lines of stately, towering topiary shifted to the use of large trees and tall perennials and herbs. Woodlands were substituted for the surrounding impenetrable border. Perennial flower beds evolved into features that melded meadows (the lawn) with forests (the woodland), flowing in a sinuous rather than straight, rigid geometric line. Impromptu rock outcroppings and restful meads of naturalized wildflowers provided subtle, earthy cues about the intended naturalness of this landscape. Foundation plantings arising from the house stretched into and blended with the landscape to endow the home with a sense of peaceful isolation.

Serenity is the word that best defines the mood of the informal landscape. Its casual style and quiescent atmosphere were favored by the ambitious, for it is a landscape that is designed to entertain during those cherished moments of relaxation away from the challenging undertakings of a hard-driving, commercial civilization.

We will deal with the use of herbs in five basic and distinct environs of the informal landscape: 1) woodlands, 2) borders of herbaceous perennials, 3) the lawn and mead, 4) rock gardens, and 5) foundation plantings.

Woodlands as the background make an informal landscape impressive, not the expansive lawn. Rising stark and magestic just out of reach beyond borders of dazzling shrubs and perennials, a forest or woodland is where visitors begin their survey. The massed vertical lines of trees immediately steal their attention, while individual groupings sustain the pleasure of viewing and stimulate curiosity and interest in examining the landscape more closely. Although a single tree dominates its immediate environment, all the trees within a design must be composed so that the garden and residence are brought together, balanced and accented one by the other.

A good rule of thumb in selecting trees is that their eventual size should be no higher than the shortest width of the property. Slender, high-story evergreens toward the back of the wooded area give an impression of an endless forest. Deciduous trees set well apart provide filtered shade, essential for many woodland wildflowers and ground covers. Native species should be included for their hardiness and to repeat natural patterns of growth seen in the vicinity.

Vital to a natural appearance is an understory of shade-tolerant species of trees, shrubs, and herbaceous perennial herbs with distinctive foliage and flowers. Shrubs should fill the boundary between woodland and meadow for a smooth transition to the lawn. This thickened perimeter of the wooded area reinforces the image of dense forest. Small properties, forced to rely on only one or a handful of trees, particularly require perennial borders and flowering shrubs to create the sense of a woodland setting. Metropolitan lots can often take advantage of tree scenes beyond the property line. Tying them into the view as if no boundary exists gives the impression of a forest without.

A few valuable shade-tolerant trees include: the American pawpaw (*Asimina triloba*), which bears an edible, banana-flavored fruit; the *Styrax japonica,* a fragrant summer flowering tree which is the source of Storax, a vital component in incense; the graceful and fragrant flowering Willow, *Itea virginica;* some flowering plums; and the Wild Cherry. The Hazelnut, *Corylus* spp., is shade-tolerant with beautiful fall color and a late winter display of plump yellow catkins, as is the flowering May Tree, or Hawthorne, *Crataegus* spp., an old favorite of the Druids, who surrounded their dwellings with barriers of it, which they called the "haege thorn", a hedge of thorns. Flowering Dogwoods, *Cornus* spp., Persimmon, Holly, American Beech, and California Bay are other suggestions. Visit an arboretum to acquaint yourself with the true form and habit of trees suitable as understory trees in your region.

Some useful understory shrubs include: Witch Hazel, *Hamamelis* spp., which are discussed in Chapter 3; *Skimmia,* or Mountain Ash, with exceptional fall colors and berry clusters; the fragrant winter and early spring blooming *Viburnum fragrans,* and the ever-green summer-blooming *V. davidii;* or the summer-blooming Blueberry and Whortleberry, *Vaccinium* spp., with gold and crimson fall colors, complemented by a prolific yield of edible berries. Understory shrubs for dry, rocky woodlands include Snowberry or Coralberry, *Symphoricarpos* spp. and Fragrant Sumac, *Rhus aromatica,* and for wet or boggy regions the evergreen Oregon Grape, *Mahonia* spp. and Huckleberry, *Vaccinium ovatum.*

As the woodlands open to fields and meadows, wide borders of tall herbs and low shrubs thrive in this cool, damp, and protected site along the forest front. The microclimate of constant humidity and moderated temperatures encourages the development of these thickly foliaged bands, made up of a variety of herbaceous perennials which, with their large leaves and dense habits, intercept all the sun they can to form thick screens. Their foliage disappears in winter, providing an unobstructed view into the woodlands, where wildflowers, bulbs, and colorful, clambering ground covers abound.

Herbaceous perennials commonly used in a similarly designed landscape are those that are noted for their sudden spring beauty and their self-maintaining habits. Densely planted borders of herbaceous perennials inhibit the spread of weeds since established beds emerge early in spring and proceed quickly to a dense covering. Progressive seasonal display is necessary and may well include drifts of Tansy, Peonies, Mugwort, Fennel, Yarrow, Valerian, Sweet Cicely, Chrysanthemums, Lovage, Angelica, Poppies, and Monardas. Few annuals are employed unless they may be seeded directly and ignored thereafter. The self-sowing annuals include German Camomile, Borage, Calendula, Dill, and Coriander.

Ornamentally foliaged herbs such as Lemon Balm, Horehound, and other genera in the Mint family, such as Dead Nettle, *Lamium,* and Archangel, *Lamiastrum,* as well as the Mints

Fig. 35. The essence of a mountain meadow with sharply focused ridges penetrating a sloping lawn surrounded by sparse but colorful shrubby vegetation.

KEY

1 Douglas Fir *Psuedotsuga menziesii*
2 Roman Camomile *Chamaemellum nobile*
3 German Camomile *Chamomilla recutita*
4 *Valeriana officinalis*
5 *Angelica atropurpurea*
6 Lovage *Levisticum officinale*
7 Azalea

8 *Lamium* 'Silver Beacon'
9 Fragrant Sumac *Rhus aromaticus*
10 Tree Roses
11 Blueberry *Vaccinium ovatum*
12 Red flowering Thyme *Thymus pulegioides* 'Kermesinus'
13 Pink Chintz/Caraway Thyme *Thymus praecox, T. herba-barona*
14 Wildflowers (Campanula/Camas etc.)

themselves, are delightful herbs despite their modest floral displays. Even relatively drab herbs, such as the salad herbs, may be used to good effect. Carrots, Sorrel, Rocket, Good King Henry, Chervil, Spinach, Skirrets, and Parsley are examples. Candidates for borders that twist in and out of the sunshine are such shade-tolerant herbs as Lovage, Angelica, Fennel, White Mugwort, Sweet Cicely, Tansy, and Monarda.

In the informal landscape an imitation of this natural border, suggesting a succession from meadow to forest, is attained using wide perennial beds situated between a centerpiece of lawn and the forest background. Borders should be as wide as possible: at a minimum no less than 2 ft., to which an additional 1–2 ft. for every 10 ft. of open lawn should be added.

The decorative curves of an informal boundary need not be laid out as a series of gentle arcs but should be laid out in keeping with the natural scene intended. A garden designed to recall a steep mountainous landscape will have a few slim conifers penetrating the property in long, narrow, parallel processions representing the steep slopes that end abruptly in alpine meadows. In this case, herbaceous borders are narrow and filled with many flowering species of low to medium height herbs and a few tall plants. See Figure 35. Marshy meadows have gently rounded boundaries and wide swaths of a very wide selection of herbaceous species, as in Figure 36, while relatively flat forests on prairie margins may be replicated by an isolated tree around which flows a narrow strip of lawn wedged between deciduous woodlands. Here the dense herbaceous foreground is composed of relatively few species, as in Figure 37.

A multitude of landscaping possibilities can be found in nature. Use holidays to pursue and appraise them for inspiration and models. Make your summer excursions an investigation in which the flora and georgraphy of the area visited is pursued as conscientiously as are your recreational activities. In lieu of visiting, careful reading of pictorial texts of geographical regions of the world are useful, as are maps and books on geography.

As borders winnow around the edge of the yard, abrupt changes in foliage patterns may occur, particularly between special features. The task of blending becomes a challenge. Blending involves the use of *transition plantings* that form a smooth bond between widely different plant habits and textures. The transition plants used may be of an entirely different genus or simply a different form of the same species. The latter choice tends to accentuate the novelty of the featured forms and gives a sense of movement to the border.

Where paths move into the woodland, the informal border should present an open, uncluttered appearance deriving from a ground cover or low-creeping or mat-forming herb (Fig. 38). The ground cover will follow the path into the woods so should be chosen to thrive in full sun as well as partial shade. This effect is reminiscent of an animal trail. Deer, etc. commonly browse at the edges of a forest. Wherever a path leads out of the forest, the vegetation is heavily browsed. The junction is marked by stunted trees and densely foliaged ground covers. Light penetrates further inward here because the tall screening plants have been eaten so ground covers eventually spread into the forest along the path.

One of the most vital features of an informal landscape is the lawn. It recalls a meadow. Lying comfortably beyond the forest's edge it suggests both seclusion and security, the demesne of deer and elk. Uncluttered and unadorned by ornamentation, a well-mown lawn is a relaxing scene, satisfying from every point of view. Owing to the amenable color green, the informal lawn is in essence a major transitional planting drawing the entire landscape together around it. It is a special design domain suggesting relaxation and contemplation, where viewing is the primary concern.

The lawn must not be thrown into confusion by criss-crossing paths, statuary, furniture, or potted plants. It is a gently sloping or rolling surface that may, on large grounds,

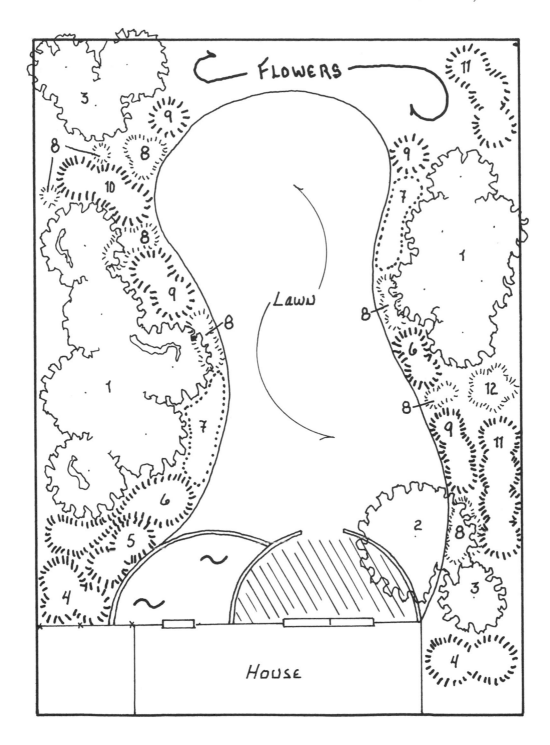

Fig. 36. The temperate meadow thick with small deciduous trees and flowery herbaceous plants.

KEY

1 Hoary Alder *Alnus rugosa*
2 Quaking Aspen *Populus tremuloides*
3 Hawthorne *Crataegus* sp.
4 Bee Balm *Monarda didyma*
5 *Angelica atropurpurea*
6 Golden Mint *Mentha* × *gracilis* var. *variegata*
7 *Calendula officinalis*
8 Tree Roses
9 Lemon Balm *Melissa officinalis*
10 *Valeriana officinalis*
11 Lovage *Levisticum officinale*
12 Violets *Viola* spp.

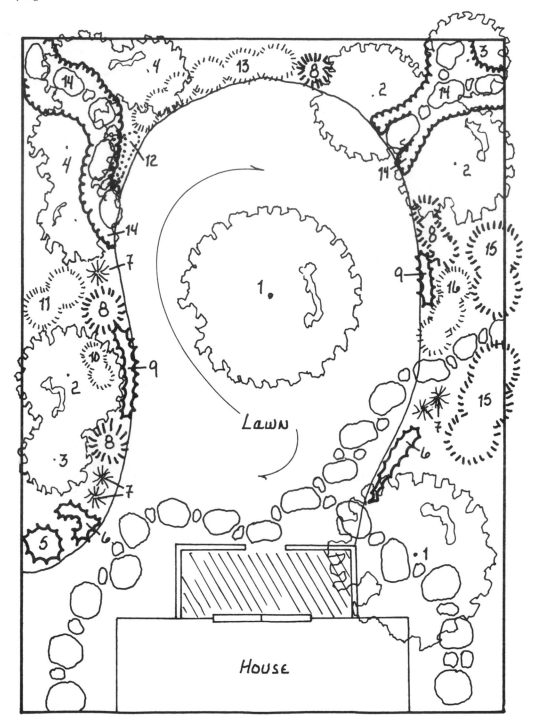

Fig. 37. The prairie meadow with large lawn, central tree and crowded perimeter with well spaced trees and a wide variety of plants crowded into every cranny.

KEY

1 White Oak *Quercus alba*
2 Sugar Maple *Acer saccharum*
3 Hawthorne (white) *Crataegus* sp.
4 Hawthorne (red) *Crataegus* sp.
5 Lavender *Lavandula angustifolia*
6 Golden Sage *Salvia officinale* 'Aurea'
7 Fragrant Sumac *Rhus aromatica*
8 *Valeriana officinalis*
9 Dwarf Sage *Salvia officinalis* 'Nana'
10 Primroses *Primula* spp.
11 *Astilbe* spp.
12 German Camomile *Chamomilla recutita*
13 Lupine/Nigella
14 Sweet Woodruff *Gallium odorata*
15 Lovage *Levisticum officinale*
16 Meadow Clary/Clary Sage *Salvia pratensis, S. sclarea*

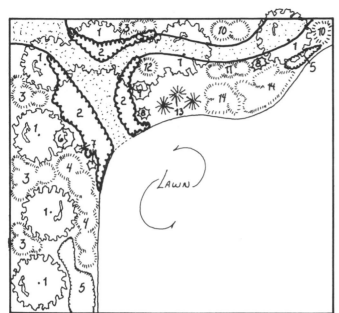

Fig. 38. Deertrail effect on pathway
at its junction from meadow into a forest.

KEY
1 Fl Cherry *Prunus*
2 Roman Camomile *Chamaemellum nobile*
3 Ornamental Grass
4 Peony *Paeonia* spp.
5 Lamium 'Silver Beacon'
6 Southernwood *Artemisia abrotanum*
7 'Silver Mound' *Artemisia frigida*
8 *Santolina neapolitana*
9 Lavender *Lavandula angustifolia*
10 *Valeriana officinalis*
11 Elecampane *Inula helenium*
12 Sweet Cicely *Myrrhis odorata*
13 Roses
14 Perennial flowers

include mounds bedecked with naturalized bulbs and wildflowers. Along its perimeter, near walks or the tree line, where perennial beds are absent, naturalized plants may again be used as transitional plantings to draw attention to and enhance the notion of a succession of plant forms, from the simple blade of grass to the lofty tree.

On larger home sites the landscape can be partitioned into two parts: One the lawn; the other a flowery mead. The mead is a region where low grasses, wildflowers, and herbs comprise the lawn. Shade-tolerant herbs used in naturalized meads include Sweet Woodruff, Variegated Creeping Charlie, Primroses, *Oxalis*, Wintergreen, Roman Camomile, *Ajuga*, English Pennyroyal, Violet, Yerba Buena, Corsican Mint and Wild Ginger. Herbs for sunny meads include Yarrow, Creeping Yarrow, Creeping Savory, Roman Camomile, English Daisy, Creeping Thyme, and Wooly Betony. Held under control by intense competition, even some weeds can be tolerated in such sanctuaries: Dandelions, Mallows, Creeping Charlie, Speedwell, Dead Nettle, and Miner's Lettuce.

The mead is a quiet zone composed to remove one's thoughts from the present and project oneself into a setting where flowers flow ankle deep around an ancient sitting bench. Quiet zones hidden among the trees, barren of all but ground covers, are designed to evoke the feeling of a timeless void within a vast forest.

The mead need not share its domain with turf grasses. A mixed ground cover devoid of grass has much to recommend it. In this case, adjoining turf should be discouraged from encroaching by installing a boundary; e.g., a path, a raised stone outcropping, a low fence or hedge, etc.

The informal landscape makes great demands of the plantings around the home itself. Foundation plantings must be congruous with the casual, unstructured nature of the informal grounds. Some suggestions: 1) vines, which cloak the home in green, thereby blending the contrasting structure with the natural world; 2) low contrast shrubbery placed in disconnected clumps about entrance walks or flowing away from the corners of the home at an angle, Figure 39; and 3) trees, planted as a small copse to one side of, but connected to the house, Figure 41.

Homes once displayed a foundation garden called the "goose foot", comprising a group of a few to several raised beds projected at angles away from one side of the house.

Fig. 39. Melding home with perimeter border using a foundation bed and island of low growing evergreen or shrubby herbs.

KEY
 1 'Silver Beacon' *Lamium*
 2 Wooly Betony *Stachys byzantina*
 3 'Long Leaf Gray' *Thymus*
 4 'Linear Leaf Lilac' *Thymus*
 5 Dwarf Sage *Salvia officinalis* 'Nana'
 6 Lavender *Lavandula angustifolia* 'Hidcote'
 7 Dwarf Lavender *Lavandula angustifolia* 'Nana Atropurpurea'
 8 *Juniper horizontalis*

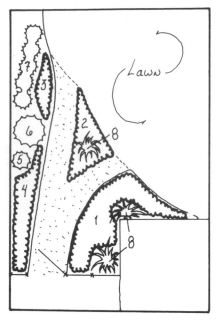

Fig. 40 A & B. Examples of the Goosefoot. Originally an informal design for melding the homesite with an informal landscape it evolved into a formal with the geometric rigidity shown here and contained beneficial herbs.

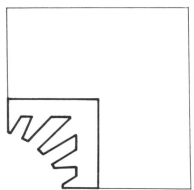

The outside beds were half the length of those between, giving the impression of a goose's webbed foot. (Figures 40 A & B). In fact, the design represented, in miniature, the forest as it advances into a meadow. It functioned as a mirror image of the wooded grounds at the periphery of the landscape, drawing the home and landscape together (Figure 41). The "goose foot" often replaced the knot as a "formal" garden, and was planted in beneficial herbs.

    The rock garden came into its own with the advent of informal landscaping. The unstructured appearance of a rock outcrop appealed to gardeners who wanted their informal gardens to exhibit more rugged natural settings. Borders were cut into hillsides to yield solid rock faces or mounds were thrown up over rock debris and dilapidated brick or stone walls. Forested sites were scoured down to bedrock and streams diverted or formed from springs to cascade through new rocky beds. If at all possible, waterfalls were constructed. A quiet pool and trickling rivulet tucked within the woodland setting helped to isolate the scene in the imagination. Its solemn singsong sounds accompanied by the rustling of trees and the chattering of birds helped deaden urban noise.

    Small clumping, mounding, or mat-forming herbs are chosen and planted as features along rocky crags. Dwarf and alpine Saxicoles, plants that thrive in rocky soil, are commonly used. Herbs such as *Alchemilla alpina,* Pygmy Savory, Creeping Savory, Winter

Plate 23

A wild walk with flowers and herbs on both sides including Garden Sage, Thyme and Rosemary. Calamint issues from the cracks in the path for a minty treat in the garden of Angelo Pellegrini, Seattle, WA.

Anise-Hyssop, a wild patch in a kitchen garden at home of Judith Zugish, Marysville, WA.

A truly wild display in a corner of a horse arena including the three common adventitious herbs found in the wild, Catnip, Feverfew and German Camomile. Home of Judith Zugish, Marysville, WA.

Walk leading from porch through wild yard where many species of Violets, Creeping Thymes and Camomiles share their niche with wild things such as Mallows and Miner's Lettuce. English Pennyroyal creeps out of the garden between bricks yielding mint-scented airs whenever stepped upon.

Plate 24

Drifts of French Thyme (right) and Wooly Thyme (left) among Iris on a sloping perimeter bed at the Medicinal Herb Garden, University of Washington, Seattle, WA.

Even in partial shade Borage performs mightily as a wild herb.

The magnificent Elecampane with sunny, spidery flowers on 6 ft. plants in the garden of Mary Medalia, Seattle, WA.

'Coronation Gold' Yarrow rises magestically in the same border as Elecampane. An assortment of gold-hued herbs dress this slim entrance-way border in the garden of Mary Medalia, Seattle, WA.

Lady's Mantle in bloom spilling her fragrant yellow cottony flowers at our feet.

An intimate relationship between Black Cumin, Lupine, Feverfew and other herbs and ornamentals graces this wild patch.

Fig. 41. The true informal Goosefoot. A large foundation planting with a small grove of trees and dense herbaceous cover for melding the home with the surrounding informal landscape.

KEY
 1 Grey Birch *Betula populifolia*
 2 Golden Creeping Thyme *Thymus* 'Clear Gold'
 3 *Juniperus horizontalis*
 4 Southernwood *Artemisia abrotanum*
 5 Foxglove *Digitalis* spp.
 6 Elecampane *Inula helenium*
 7 *Valeriana officinalis*
 8 Sweet Cicely *Myrrhis odorata*
 9 Coral Bells *Heuchera sanguinea*
10 Lemon Balm *Melissa officinalis*

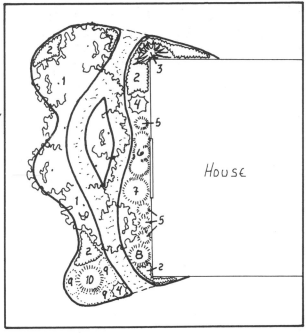

Savory, *Santolina* 'Nana', Dwarf Lavender, Violets, Corsican Mint, Thyme, Dwarf Feverfew, German and Roman Camomile, English Daisy, Saffron, Hyssop, and Wooly Betony are some of the obvious choices.

Ground covers are an essential element in any informal landscape. They are used to meld the subunits of the landscape. The use of ground covers softens junctions and boundary lines of paths by providing a uniform background. Ground covers displaying a marked color or foliage difference are chosen to accent featured plants. They can be used to veil a sunny knoll in somber hues or radiate a spectrum of color in gloomy recesses. In the contemporary landscape the ground cover becomes a feature itself with ornamental foliages and flowers exhibited along a hillside or path.

A mingling of various ground covers should be treated like any other mixed perennial planting, with forethought as to the overall texture. In expansive arrangements of many ground covers it is recommended that they be unified using "drifts". A drift is a clump of identical plants arranged in a variety of shapes that are combined with other groupings or drifts of other plants. Upon viewing a garden with drifts, the eye, seeing the undulating shapes, responds to the notion of movement. A collection of drifts is appealing to the eye because of the sense of motion.

A ground cover is also used to mask unwanted sections of the landscape with a uniform texture. A rocky or uneven terrain can be transformed by the gentle touch of a ground cover into a rolling sea of green. Cloaked in creeping herbs such as Hops, Wooly Betony, Roman Camomile, Creeping Germander, Creeping Rosemary, or Thyme, an area of poor soil becomes an asset instead of an eyesore in the landscape.

The herbs we will examine in detail in this chapter are all either shade-tolerant or shade-loving plants. For the most part, they are vital herbs for the preparation of elegant cuisine. Those that like total shade, at most a filtered shade (a site of shifting light intensity beneath the trees where neither sun nor shade dominates for more than an hour at a time), are Sweet Woodruff, Wintergreen, and Wild Ginger. Others grow preferentially in partial shade (part of the day in shade and part in sun): Sweet Cicely, Violet, and Chervil. Still others require a sunny environment but will tolerate some shade during the day: Lemon Balm, Oregano, Catnip, and Sage.

Chapter 5 / SECTION 2

Herbs for an Informal Garden

The hardiest, most easily cared for of the popular herbs is Oregano. It is an excellent ornamental herb with many applications, from thick borders and fluffy mounds to a dense ground cover of dark green or golden yellow, for steps and walks, creeping along low retaining walls, or tucked between the stones in rock walls. Oreganos thrive in sun-baked nooks and crannies, spreading quickly. The flower has a sweet, desirable floral scent and the delicious scent of its foliage reminds one of rich dishes of spaghetti or the stuffing in hot plump game hens.

The Oreganos are a confusing genus, with many common names for each species and some species quite variable in size, leaf shape, and flower color. The genus *Origanum* contains herbs that are called both Marjoram and/or Oregano. The major species available include Sweet Marjoram, *O. majorana;* Pot Marjoram or Rigani, *O. onites;* Wild Marjoram or Oregano, *O. vulgare* ssp. *vulgare;* Italian Oregano, *O. v.* ssp. *hirtum;* Russian Oregano, *O. v.* ssp. *gracile;* Golden Oregano, *O. v.* 'Aureum' and 'Golden Creeping'; Hop Marjoram or Dittany of Crete, *O. dictamnus;* and *O. microphyllum.*

The showiest of all Oreganos, excellent for both ornamental and culinary needs are Dittany, *O. dictamnus;* Wild Marjoram, *O. vulgare;* and *O. microphyllum.* They have larger flower clusters, often larger corollas, and longer blooming periods.

Except for *Origanum vulgare* the members of this genus should be considered tender perennials and either mulched heavily or brought indoors for the winter. During winter indoors, they should be kept dry, watering infrequently, and placed in a sunny, but cool location. An alkaline soil is necessary for the Oreganos to flourish, as they are susceptible to wilt in acid soils. They will grow in a poor soil as well as a rich loam, but it should be sandy for a dry root zone. The Oreganos also need organic fertilizer or they become bitter and herbaceous. Chemical fertilizer will cause both lax spindly foliage and poor fragrance for their oils are not properly stored when growing too rapidly, resulting in poorer keeping quality of the dried product.

The stronger Oreganos of *O. vulgare* contain carvacrol and thymol as the main aromatic ingredients, as well as linalyl acetate for a sweet note. Sweet Marjoram, Dittany, and Italian Oregano contain significant amounts of geraniol, eugenol, and a unique selection of the sharp, sweetly ethereal turpenes for a pleasantly floral scent.

All of the Oreganos are equally useful as a culinary spice. It is fortunate that the flavorful and fragrant virtues of all the Oreganos are reasonably equal because incorrect substitution occurs regularly when ordering any of the Oreganos, whether as seed or live plants. The finest are Italian Oregano, Dittany, and Sweet Marjoram. Wild Marjoram has a strong thymol aroma, at times medicinal. Greek and Italian are chemovars and vary only in that Italian is sweetly scented, but the robust Greek Oregano aroma is a pleasant one, nonetheless.

The fuzzy, grey, oval leaves of Hop Marjoram or Dittany makes it a dainty addition among bold green compact herbs in an informal border or contemporary perennial bed. Its bright pink flowers are ½ in. long and nearly everlasting, contrasting with their grey foliage. The name Hop Marjoram is derived from the Hop flower likeness of its flower head, which of course means very little to most people today. If we were to be a bit imaginative we could better describe them as miniature cabbages with tiny pink flowers poking out from among the leaves.

Dittany forms a small 12 in. compact plant whose showy nature is accentuated in a rock garden in any landscape or as a small grouping, accompanied by dark green or yellow-green ground cover such as Creeping Golden Thyme, 'White Moss' Thyme, Corsican Mint, or Caraway Thyme for added aroma. From a distance the blooms of Dittany are difficult to see so the grey, wooly foliage is the feature that is visible and must be planned around. Dittany should be planted no closer than 12 in. to prevent damp conditions from killing leaves. In wet climates, damp soil is best controlled by a sand layer or other inert ground cover. Plants kept in pots should be cut back in late spring or when transplanted to the garden to assure healthy, strong wood for a bushier habit.

The hybrid, *O. × hybridum*, a cross of *O. dictamnus* and *O. siphylem*, is a hardier, Dittany-like herb except that the flower stems are less showy and prone to be floppy. Branches, too, tend to be lax, but in close groupings their appearance is similar. *O. microphyllum* is another Dittany-like Oregano, with tiny, 1/16–1/8 in. ovalish leaves that are grey-green, but not fuzzy. This Oregano has pink, Dittany-like flowers and splendid foliage, making it a delightful herb for contrast in a Thyme rockery or among dwarf herbs and orna-mentals.

Less showy, but an excellent ground cover in a perennial garden are the various subspecies of *O. vulgare*. The flowers are spectacular, especially their fragrance, so a large area of at least 30–50 sq. ft. should be planted to enjoy them. The flowers vary from white to red-purple. A subspecies with purple stems and bracts called Russian Oregano, *O. v.* ssp. *gracile,* is more ornamental and has a deep green foliage for a bold appearance. Its fragrance is similar to Italian Oregano except for a sharp tangy note. All the subspecies of *O. vulgare* form a copious mound in 2–3 years. A single full grown plant will produce more material for culinary use than anyone could ever use. For borders, they should be spaced 12–18 in. apart in full sun. First year cuttings should be pruned to encourage bushier growth. Flower stalks should be pruned in late summer. They dry easily and are everlasting.

As a winter ground cover, some subspecies of *O. vulgare* spread in dark green or golden mats up to 2 in. high and can be planted close so there is no semblance of single plants. Flower production is less rubust, but a dense and beautiful ground cover is created. Thin clumps to 24 in. on center to produce heavy flower harvests. Italian Oregano develops a more bush-like habit significantly more useful in arrangements and decoratively as bonsai, although it may be decidious in Zones 6 and 7, the limit of its range. *O. vulgare* subspecies *vulgare, gracile* and *viride* usually remain evergreen, even through subzero weather. Cold winds are a significant factor in placing Oregano in the garden. In extremely cold climates it should be given a sheltered position, along a fence or protected by an evergreen hedge. Full sun is required to produce the best fragrance from foliage or flowers, but all will grow well in partial shade that receives afternoon sun.

The foliages of two cultivars, *O. v.* 'Aureum' and 'Golden Creeping' have a yellow tint. The latter has a lower growing habit and is superb as a bright, colorful ground cover. Both are good border and pathway herbs where a bright color is needed to liven the scene and they are most beautiful along red brick walks or raining down terraces of dark stone. Both grow well in partial shade.

Pot Marjoram, *O. onites,* resembling Sweet Marjoram, is more strongly flavored and hardier, though it must still be considered a tender perennial in Zone 7. The seed from packets labelled Pot Marjoram are commonly Sweet Marjoram or a hybrid *O. majoricum*, and purchased plants of Wild Marjoram are often *O. onites*.

As a culinary flavor and fragrance plant, Oregano is more widely used around the world than any other herb. It has many forms, and not everyone employs herbs from the Oregano genus for the uses previously discussed. Other herbs that are commonly substituted are Za'atar, *Thymbra spicata*; Indian Borage or Spanish Thyme, *Coleus amboinicus*; Puerto Rican Oregano, *Poliomintha longiflora*; and Mexican Oregano, *Lippia graveolens*. There are oregano-scented herbs represented by the Thyme genus, as in *T. pulegioides* 'Oregano-scented' and Corido, *T. capitatus*; several species of Lippia and Lantana; a species of American Pennyroyal *Hedeoma floribundum*; *Monarda citriodora* var. *austromontana*; and many others. Plants that contain the chemical carvacrol yield the fragrance of Oregano but not entirely the same flavor or keeping quality. *Lippia graveolens* does not have the best oregano scent, being more herbaceous. *Thymbra spicata* has a strong camphoraceous note, excellent storage life, and is in fact a common constituent of the spice Oregano we buy at the grocery store. Oregano Thyme dries well and can be made sweeter by including its flowers, but in either case its storage life is shorter than true Oregano. The thick fleshy leaves of *Coleus amboinicus* are difficult and time consuming to dry. It gives off a pleasantly sweet oregano scent but does not retain this scent for long in storage. These herbs are all for southern gardens or containers and can be remarkably entertaining in any feature.

As a culinary spice Oregano is a facilitator, capable of enhancing the fragrance and flavors of other herbs. The large variety of terpenes in the essential oils of both the Oregano and Marjoram are available to give a boost to concentrations of such chemicals also found in many herbs that are culinary companions to Oregano: Cardamom, Basil, Thyme, Savory, Coriander, Caraway, Cumin, and Ginger. These herbs combine well in tomato sauces, thick soups, gravies, and beef stews. The sweet or floral constituents of Oregano or Marjoram enhance the flavor of herbs such as Ginger, Coriander, Dill, Caraway, Bay, Monarda, Rose, Blue Sage, Lemon Thyme, and Lemon or 'Spice' Basil. Combinations of these herbs are used in salad dressings, stuffings, veal and lamb stew, gravies, and thin broth soups.

An excellent recipe for Oregano is a *GIBLET STEW.*

Braise 1–2 pounds of chicken gizzards (whole) in 3 Tbsp. Basil butter. Add 1 c. stock or boullion and the following ingredients:

¼ c. Sherry	1 Tbsp. Oregano
2 garlic cloves	1 tsp. Chives
1 Tbsp. Lovage	1 tsp. Fennel

Combine the ingredients and simmer for 3 hours until the juices are browning, then add 1 c. water, reheat to boil, and serve as a soup with noodles.

A delicious *POTATO PATTY* is made with Sweet Marjoram.

Grate 4–6 potatoes. Add the following ingredients:

4 Tbsp. Calendula	1 tsp. Thyme
2 Tbsp. Sweet Marjoram	1 tsp. Lovage
1 Tbsp. Fennel	1 tsp. salt

Butter a baking pan or grill and form patties to ⅜ in. thickness. Cook at 425° for 20–25 minutes.

Another recipe for Sweet Marjoram is *SALMON CROQUETTES.* The ingredients include:

2–3 pounds canned or precooked Salmon	1 Tbsp. Fennel
3–4 medium mashed (chunky) potatoes	1 Tbsp. Lovage
3–4 carrots, mashed	1 Tbsp. Chives
2 eggs	1 Tbsp. Caraway seed, (crushed)
3 Tbsp. Sweet Marjoram	1 Tbsp. sugar

Mix all ingredients. Roll into 1 in. balls and flour with a mixture of ¾ c. barley or rye flour, 2 Tbsp. sugar, 1 tsp. salt, 1 Tbsp. Chinese Five Spice.

Deep fry for 3–5 minutes. Serve hot with fresh fruit and a salad.

Catnip, *Nepeta cataria,* famous for its erotic effect on cats, is an easily cultivated ornamental herb. All the Catnips are herbaceous perennials, hardy and eager to spread willy-nilly unless corraled. Best used as ground covers or thick drifts in perennial borders, Catnip's grey-green to green, serrated foliage becomes dense when plants are nipped regularly throughout the growing season. Catnip has a dainty, lavender to pink-spotted flower that is quite pretty, though so small that it is virtually invisible in a richly herbed garden.

Catnip's herbaceous, faintly citrus or "musty mint" scent is not as universally pleasing to people as it is to cats. The chemical attractant responsible has been aptly named, nepetalactone, and much research is underway concerning it. Citral, carvacrol and geraniol contribute a spiciness to its odor. A medicinal tea is brewed with Catnip that is sweet and peppery, used for the relief of sore throat or to ease the burning, scratching feeling of an insect bite. It is also reputed to make one sleepy. The chemical nepetalactone is similar to the active principle in Valerian which can promote sleep. It is best mixed with Camomile, which is also an anodyne, or pain reliever, and with Caraway seed as a flavor enhancer.

Two dwarf forms are available that provide a colorful flower display for an ornamental landscape effect. *N. mussinii,* often called Persian Catnip, rarely grows more than 12–14 in. high. *N. X faassenii,* which cannot produce fertile seed, grows 18–24 in. high. Both have a profusion of purple or deep blue flowers than remain for a long period. They are as hardy as the species, but superior as a ground cover and border herb. The flowers are prominent due to the smaller leaf size and 6 in. long spikes, thick with flowers. The foliage of both smell strongly of cloves and the flowers like cinnamon.

Lemon Catnip, *N. cataria* var. *citriodora,* has a pleasant lemon fragrance and is certainly a good substitute for the species in a medicinal tea. However, no research has indicated whether this variety can indeed be substituted for the species as a medicinal plant. It is a far more pleasantly scented Catnip for a fragrant patch in full sun or partial shade.

Any soil will suffice for Catnip. Tall, large-leafed plants will develop in manured garden soil, with a more pleasant citrus odor—rich soils generally tend to bring out the sweeter aspects and scents of herbs. The cultivars of catnip smell strongly no matter where they reside. Poor soils are equally suitable and it is just this soil type that they were intended to adorn. The flowering of the cultivars changes little with the addition of either manure or chemical fertilizer and they will grow well under alkaline conditions. They are herbaceous, although in protected spots an early frost will not hurt them. In late spring or early summer plants should be pruned to a uniform shape, whether that is a flat top in a closely spaced ground cover area or a hemisphere for individual plants, to encourage a dense growth and improve fragrance.

Catnip combines well with Monarda, Anise Hyssop or Korean Mint, Pineapple Sage, Feverfew, and Horehound in a small area for an enjoyable garden feature with bold colors.

Dwarf Catnips are quite frequently used with evergreens as an entrance theme or as colorful borders for long driveways against a background of darker evergreens.

Sweet Cicely, *Myrrhis odorata*, could very well be called the Licorice plant, for its flavor and scent are identical and as satisfying as commercial Licorice from the root of *Glycyrrhiza*. The ferny fronds of Sweet Cicely are a welcome sight in early spring. It has only a 2–3 month resting period, from November to February, depending on the extent to which the ground is frozen, but it often emerges in mid-February and lasts until Christmas. In cold regions, it will not usually emerge until the ground is thawed, in early to mid-spring. Sweet Cicely's sweet smelling flowers, ofttimes blooming through a light cover of snow, are a delicious treat for visitors strolling through the garden. The seeds ripen nearly 3 months later. They turn from green to shiny black, although they may be picked earlier to improve the appearance of the planting. If the seed is to be used in floral arrangements leave it on the plant to ripen to a hard ebony form that is quite handsome. A highly fragrant oil is pressed from the ripe seeds and was used as furniture polish in the 18th and 19th centuries to protect wood and to provide a licorice-scented finish. The oil that is expressed may be mixed with any paste wax for easier, more even application.

The light green, fern-like branches of Sweet Cicely are a delightful addition in the shady parts of the garden. It will spread slowly by reseeding and prefers a moist spot in the drip-line of trees or around ponds, even in full sun. It usually grows from 12–16 in. and can be used as an accent for tall or ungainly herbs such as Lovage, Angelica, and dwarf fruit trees or shrubs. A ground cover of Sweet Cicely and Turk's Cap Lilies spilling out of the shade under a group of hemlocks or evergreen oaks appears as a primeval forest, untouched and uncluttered by civilization. In isolated clumps it may be surrounded by a low ground cover such as Creeping Charlie, *Ajuga*, Sweet Woodruff, or *Oxalis*, and low-growing wildflowers in a small feature garden where it could be enjoyed for itself.

Sweet Cicely is a good ground cover, following paths into and out of the woodland, as it is tolerant of full and part shade, or full sun if provided with enough water. It is easily propagated by root divisions and seed, however the seed must be sown fresh and in late summer, or from fresh frozen seed in early spring, germinating in about 2 months. Sweet Cicely is not too picky about soils provided there is ample moisture. However, organic soils, such as leaf mold, encourage it to spread faster and self-sown seeds germinate better.

The flavor and scent of Sweet Cicely is probably composed of Anise-like constituents such as fenchone and anethole, common among many of the *Umbelliferae*. As a culinary spice it imparts more fragrance to a dish than flavor unless it is cooked for only a short period or used as a garnish in hot stir-fry or vegetable dishes. Experiment with Sweet Cicely in the kitchen. Use it with cooked vegetables such as carrots, sweet potatoes, rutabaga, and kohlrabi. For Sweet Carrots, slice or dice 3–4 c. of carrots and just cover with water. Add 1 Tbsp. Sweet Cicely, 1 tsp. Sweet Marjoram, ¼ tsp. salt, and 1 Tbsp. honey and cook to desired tenderness.

A delicious Oyster Stew is made with Sweet Cicely. The ingredient list includes:

OYSTER STEW

1 c. water plus chicken boullion	1 Tbsp. Sweet Cicely
3 Tbsp. butter	2 Tbsp. Calendula
1 Tbsp. Chive butter	1 tsp. Basil
1 Tbsp. honey	1 tsp. Lovage
¼ c. Sherry	½ tsp. Oregano

Combine the ingredients and simmer for 10 minutes, then add 3 sliced tomatoes, simmer for 10 minutes more, then add 1 green pepper, diced, and 1–2 pounds oysters. Simmer for 8–10 minutes after bringing it to a boil. Serve with crackers.

In woodland settings and in long perennial borders, Violets, *Viola* spp., are a choice border or ground cover. As a border, they spread only diffidently onto adjacent lawns, choosing rather to droop lazily over the edges, creating an appealing transition, not marred by a trench or small vertical guard placed to prevent the grass from moving into the garden. *Viola odorata,* often called the Florist's Violet, has a fragrance that can only be appreciated in large areas; at least 100 sq. ft. is required. Filtered shade within woodlands is a prime location for a fragrant patch. Plants should be spaced 8–10 in. They will grow to form 12 in. clumps with 2 in. flowers on stems from 6–10 in. long. The large leaves of *Viola odorata* combine well in mixed plantings with Wild Ginger, Wintergreen, Anemones and an occasional Jack-in-the-pulpit.

The Violet should be present in drifts of at least one dozen clumps. Overrunning by other plants should be controlled. In the wild, Violets are generally found in large masses where they are in control, holding other plants at bay because of their thick canopy of foliage that inhibits invaders from below by denying them light. Healthy Violet masses will stay weed-free. Bare patches due to dying or pest-riddled plants are quickly filled by small, slow-growing, self-sown plants that were hiding below in the darkness.

Small clumps of Violets do well on very steep, shady banks where they mix with small ferns and mosses. Some of the native species of *Viola* are very easily naturalized into the cracks of stone paths and are very hardy and pestfree, providing many different colors of flowers, from white to yellow, blue, and grey. Two species provide very ornamental foliage, the Lance-leaf Violet, *Viola lanceolata,* which has long, narrow leaves, and *Viola pedata,* the Bird's Foot Violet, whose leaves extend out like the fingers of a hand. The latter is one of the Violets that will grow in full sun in a rockery and blooms very early in the spring.

The Violet is an excellent salad herb because it is an early spring plant that is high in vitamin C. Use it sparingly however as both the flower and the foliage are good laxatives. The Violet scent in the flowers consists of two chemicals, ionone and irone (both of which occur in the root of the Florentine Iris, or Orris Root, the source of a perfume fixative).

A relative of Summer Savory and a fine ground cover is the herb Yerba Buena, *Satureja douglasii.* Its fragance is fleeting, most noticeable on a hot summer afternoon, but as a shade tolerant ground cover it is excellent. Growing from 2–4 in. it is a camphoraceous and fruity or Mint-scented creeper that needs a rich woodland setting and filtered sunlight for best appearance. It makes a fine tea.

Lemon Balm, *Melissa officinalis,* is a favorite garden herb because of its lemony scent and flavor and its hardy, no-nonsense growth habit. Lemon Balm contains two lemon-scented chemicals, citral and citronellal. The latter is an effective insect repellent when brushed on the skin. The tea of Lemon Balm is a fair representation of lemon and is best used to improve real lemonade or substitute for a lemon twist in a cup of green or a good Jasmine tea.

The light green to green foliage of Lemon Balm varies with the amount of sun; the shadier the site, the lighter the green. However, a good iron-rich fertilizer will reverse this fading. Lemon Balm looks its best only when a healthy green. A variety sold as Variegated Balm or Golden Balm is available and quite attractive for borders along hot, sunny paths or around a partially shaded patio.

Lemon Balm will grow in all soils, in full sun or shade, but it does prefer a moist environment. It will reseed itself and naturalize in lawns. In an herbaceous border it will form slowly-advancing clumps 12–14 in. high. In partial shade it should be trimmed back in early summer to 8–10 in. or less to force it to branch and thicken. Clumps 2–4 years old exhibit the best ornamental form. It may be useful to cultivate it in a separate garden for transplanting to the feature site in fall for a more impressive display. Older clumps forming woody centers that are sparsely foliaged should be divided and replanted.

In the full sun, this bush-like neatness is perfect with evergreen features in perennial beds, as a trim border in formal or informal gardens, or as a featured planting in single ornamental clumps, contrasted with dark green background foliage or variegated ground covers such as the spicy-scented Creeping Charlie, *Glechoma hederaceae* var. *variegata,* in partial shade, or Creeping Golden Thyme in the sun. It arrives early in the spring to add a new dimension to a feature garden when joined by Dittany and Golden Oregano in a conifer arrangement or surrounded by a field of white Violets and spring bulbs.

Lemon Balm is not an easy herb to dry and should be dried slowly at a low temperature. In most cases, air or microwave drying is recommended. The latter will preserve the green foliage color better. It may be used as a strewing herb, in a bouquet as an insect repellent, or made into a syrup or powdered and used in puddings and other sweet desserts. The name, Melissa, means bee, stemming from its use in attracting bees to hives and its use as a honey plant.

In northerly latitudes an herb called Wild Ginger, genus *Asarum,* grows in the wilder parts of woodlands. It is unrelated to the tropical Ginger, *Zingiber.* Like true Ginger, however, Wild Ginger roots are the source of a tangy, spicy flavoring for candies, spice cakes, and some meat dishes. Dried roots are powdered and used as a substitute for true Ginger. Wild Ginger is a moist woods dweller that creeps along the ground, sending up an occasional heart-shaped glossy green leaf. Its purple and brown flowers are almost never seen, for they hide under the forest litter where they are pollinated by browsing beetles.

A number of species exist; some are evergreen and a few are variegated. The largest is a deciduous species, *A. canadense,* with 3–6 in. wide glossy green leaves that stand up on 10 in. high stems. Two evergreen species, *A. europeum* and *A. caudatum,* have 3–5 in. leaves and stand up to 6 in. high. Two species with light green mottling of the leaves are *A. virginicum* and *A. shuttleworthii.* They bloom late spring to early summer and have 1–3 in. leaves, up to 8 in. high. The most ornamental Wild Ginger is *A. hartwegii* that has white-mottled, 3–5 in. leaves on stems up to 8 in. high.

Wild Ginger is a superb ground cover in full or partially shaded areas with rich moist soils. Moisture is imperative and a thick cover of leaf litter or mulch is necessary for it to thrive and spread. It grows slowly but is very hardy. Rocky, shaded areas that have been amended with pockets of peat moss, leaf mulch, or rich loam are excellent. With time, a dense dark green cover is formed.

The informal landscape offers many sites where Wild Ginger may frolic with Anemones, Violets, and native forest wildflowers. A lone clump of fern looming from behind an aging statue or handsome tree trunk is brought into focus and subdued by a rich carpet of Wild Ginger surrounding the scene. The quiet zone nestled in a small woody setting is best carpeted with Wild Ginger. The shifting shadows of surrounding trees provide enough shade to keep the leaves from burning, but enough sun to guarantee a gorgeous, emerald ground cover.

The roots of Wild Ginger are harvested in early spring, dried, and stored whole. They are easily candied but are usually ground, powdered, or peeled into shavings for use in cooking. In general, a greater quantity is required when Wild Ginger is substituted for commercial Ginger. Meat dishes can be vastly improved with the liberal use of Ginger root.

BEEF CUBES

2 lbs. beef cubes braised in 3 Tbsp. Fennel butter	1 Tbsp. Lovage
1 c. stock	1 tsp. Basil
½ c. Sherry	1 Bay leaf
6, 2″ pieces of Wild Ginger root (or 1 tsp. Ginger)	1 tsp. Sweet Cicely

Simmer until juices brown (approx. 2 hrs.) then add ½ c. water, 3 Tbsp. honey, and ½ c. Sherry and simmer for 1 hour. Serve over rice.

The Teaberry, or Wintergreen, *Gaultheria procumbens,* is another forest dweller with shiny, dark green leaves. It resembles strawberry to some extent but with leathery, bristled leaves. Small, urn-shaped, white flowers bowing bell-like beneath the canopy of leaves become bright, orange-red berries in the fall. The berries have the unmistakable odor and taste of the oil of Wintergreen. It contains the compound methyl salicylate, which is a form of the analgesic, aspirin, used for topical pain relief from the itch of insect bites and minor muscle aches.

Wintergreen is relatively slow growing, prefers a moist, acid soil composed of considerable leaf litter or peat moss, and will tolerate a sandy soil. It will, however, grow in regular garden soil, but much more slowly and may not be as hardy. The foliage may exhibit a slight reddish color in some soils. It combines well with the beautiful Bunch Berry, *Cornus canadense,* and Wild Ginger. Because it does not grow over 8 in. high it should be combined with slow-growing, ground-hugging herbs that are not invasive.

A related species, *Gaultheria hispidula,* the Creeping Snow Berry, grows to only 2–3 in. high in moist, acid soils. It is even slower-growing and has a white fruit. Both are very hardy herbs, evergreen through the coldest of winters, and have been used to reclaim strip-mined land.

A medicinal tea made from Teaberry is just that, medicinal in odor and flavor. The leaves are fermented for 24–36 hours in canning jars by pouring boiling water over a jar filled with leaves. The liquid is then strained and diluted as needed. (Fermentation allows an enzyme to free the active chemical, methyl salicylate, thus imparting both the analgesic and Wintergreen fragrance to the mixture. This fragrance is in the native state, and the berries do occasionally taste medicinal.)

Sweet Woodruff, *Galium odorata,* with its zillions of glossy, green whorls, is a pleasant smelling herb and a hardy ground cover. This distant relative of Cleavers and Bedstraw is an old ale herb, with the fragrance, when dried, of new mown hay. The chemical responsible is coumarin, which is characterized by a sweet, herbaceous aroma. Although Sweet Woodruff can be used in herbal teas to enhance the aroma it is not recommended because it has very powerful blood thinning properties that can be dangerous. Use it as a strewing herb and in dried arrangements for ornamentation with a summertime fragrance. It is also used as a fixative in potpourri and perfume.

May wine could not be what it is without Sweet Woodruff, nor should any evergreen forested landscape be without it. The glossy, green leaves, resembling the spokes of a bicycle wheel, are a curious sight. Nodding in the breeze beneath the boughs of conifers, Woodruff's whorls bear an uncanny resemblance to the lofty trees above. This complementary texture and its preference for dark, dry woods and acid soil make Woodruff one of the choicest ground covers among conifers and a perfect contrast beneath large Rhododendrons in an evergreen woodland.

Woodruff spreads rapidly in moist, friable soils, even into the dense shade. In early spring a patch of flowering Woodruff is adorned with countless, tiny, white flowers which last for about a month. Woodruff is a fragile herb and cannot handle foot traffic. Paths can be worn into a patch, however, Woodruff constantly clamoring into the open space, its journey repeatedly foreshortened by the treading of feet. A natural effect is created in a wooded site in this way. An imitation of a deer trail can be created by using ferns and low shade-tolerant underbrush placed along the path at corners and junctions with Woodruff filling the spaces between.

Because it is a shade-loving herb it is suited to forested homesites where a green lawn is desired but grasses are not successful. Prepare the soil as you would for a lawn and plant rooted cuttings 12 in. on center. Keep it moist until plants show healthy signs of spreading then fertilize 2–3 times per year. Iron should be used to maintain a rich dark green.

Wildflowers and bulbs do not balk at this benign ground cover so stock it with many resplendent varieties. Woodruff's dark green compliments light hues and is especially companionable with rayed flowers, shaggy petalled flowers, herbs with clusters of small flowers borne in umbels, or herbs with broad spathes such as Jack-in-the-Pulpit and Skunk Cabbage. It can also share a wooded site with culinary herbs such as Sweet Cicely, Lovage, Wild Ginger, Roman Camomile, Chervil, English Pennyroyal, and Saffron.

Sweet Woodruff is one of the more ornamental ground covers for a contemporary landscape. Its leaf whorls can be cleverly repeated in building architecture, such as octagonal or spoked clerestory windows and transoms, or in yard furniture, patio designs, and fences that employ, for example, a wheel pattern or fleur-de-lis.

An interesting and remarkably practical use for Sweet Woodruff is soaking up automotive oil resulting from spills or leakage in the garage. Traditionally, straw or lawn grass is used, but Sweet Woodruff soaks up the oil just as effectively but with a fresh hayfield fragrance that overpowers the oily odor.

Chervil *Anthriscus cerefolium,* one of the "fine herbs", is a highly fragrant, annual *Umbelliferae.* The leaves, seeds, and roots of Chervil all taste and smell of Licorice, resulting from the fenchone and anethole content. Green seeds are used as condiments or as a sweetener in candy, cakes, and pastries. The unripe seeds straight from the garden are one of nature's most exquisite condiments and are a complement to the already legendary flavor of Chervil foliage.

A shady spot is required to fully enjoy the licorice fragrance of Chervil. Damp forest litter such as the rich soils of Hemlock, Fir, and Oak leaf mulches are best and here healthy stands will reseed themselves. It is important to cover at least 100 sq. ft. with Chervil alone to be able to enjoy its scent. A patch grown only for seed measuring 3 × 3 ft. should produce enough seed to cover 100 sq. ft. Chervil should be sown evenly over the area and not be vital for early summer appearances when it bolts to seed. The fine, white mist of tiny flowers is priceless and only enjoyed in mass plantings.

Chervil's bright foliage is a welcome shade of green, and best used in filtered sun in a wooded recess. A setting of ferns, Hellebore and *Oxalis,* in a wooded stretch, seeded generously with Chervil and criss-crossed by wood-chip foot paths, is an enchanting forest. Shafts of sunlight flashing here and there glint off the glossy Chervil leaves, suggesting the flitting activity of wood fairies. In the forest setting, Chervil is a good ground cover around and under a closely planted grouping of ferns or large evergreen shrubs such as Rhododendrons.

Chervil may be grown nestled under other herbs such as Angelica or Fennel. It does not combine well with dense, evergreen ground covers such as the Violas due to poor germination and pests hidden under their leaves. Thin ground covers are recommended, such as Tea Berry or Strawberry. Its fall color makes it valuable for replacing waning annuals in early autumn or in herbaceous beds to fill in for winter-slumbering herbs such as Mints, Monarda, and Wood Sorrel.

Chervil has a short growing season, although both a spring and fall planting is possible in most climates. A spring planting will go to seed by summer. For this reason, Chervil must be joined with other ground covers or considerable background foliage. Exposure that is part shade early in the season and stands in considerable sun by mid-summer, such as on the northwest side of the home, is best. When ripening in full sun the stems darken as they age in the hot summer sun, eventually turning a russet or a purple color and very attractive for dried arrangements. In late fall, Chervil is best planted in full sun exposures or among deciduous woods where fall and winter sunlight can penetrate to keep green plants nourished and the ground warm. As long as the surface of the ground does not freeze solid, Chervil will survive a winter. Chervil is frost-hardy and may grow through cold snaps as low as 0°F. This statement is conditional, for it depends upon the gardener's willingness to propagate plants using seed from preceding years. Many of the *Umbelliferae* are frost-tolerant but gain considerable hardiness if the seed is saved from year to year rather than purchased.

Although Chervil will grow to 18 in., in the process of setting seed it generally maintains a low profile, from 6–10 in. Young plants of Chervil should be harvested regularly to keep them small and producing new growth, which is the only fresh foliage that should be used. Older leaves become bitter quickly, particularly in sunny locations. Chervil is a very sweet herb and should be added to salads fresh and is a must as a sweetener in rice puddings or soups and as a garnish on potatoes and vegetable dishes. A sweet garnish of fresh Chervil sprinkled on vegetable dishes and potato or egg salads adds flavor and fragrance rarely experienced even in the finest restaurants. Vegetables are pleasantly flavored when cooked with Chervil. The following Sweet Carrot and Chicken recipes are excellent dishes to discover the power of Chervil.

SWEET CARROTS

3 c. sliced carrots
1 tsp. Sweet Marjoram
2 Tbsp. fresh chopped Chervil
1 Tbsp. honey
¼ tsp. salt
2 Tbsp. butter

Boil in enough water to cover until desired firmness is reached.

CHICKEN BREAST

1 chicken breast, boned
¼ c. broth
1 Tbsp. Sherry or white wine
1 clove Garlic
½ tsp. Lovage
3 Tbsp. Chervil, chopped
½ thinly sliced green pepper

In baking pan add chicken, broth, wine, and garlic. Sprinkle with herbs and arrange green pepper diagonally over chicken. Cover. Bake at 325° for 45 minutes. Serve with fresh fruit and garlic toast.

Two unrelated herbs, American Sweet Cicely or Sweet Chervil, *Osmorhiza* ssp., and Tuberous Chervil, *Chaerophyllum bulbosum,* are often confused with Chervil. The root of the latter is a popular sweet vegetable in Europe.

Garden Sage, *Salvia officinalis,* is undoubtedly one of the most widely grown herbs, not for its culinary use, which is of course part of the attraction, but more for its ability to grow well anywhere. Although Sage is hardier when grown in a rocky alkaline soil, it satisfies millions of gardeners by growing wherever it is planted.

Garden Sage displays three distinct phases each year. In the first, it is a fast growing perennial that may be treated as a deciduous plant in the colder climates, therefore becoming part of the perennial herbaceous border. In early spring, it adds grey or silver-green foliage to the scene.

Secondly, its mid-summer display of blue flowers are a special treat for both the gardener and hummingbirds. Rising half again the height of the plant, the flower stalks bear a dense coat of large, blue flowers and either purple or light green bracts. As the flowers fade, the bracts often give a second display for a month or more, with reddish purple stalks now providing the color.

The evergreen nature of Sage is its third feature that can be enjoyed far into the winter season in warmer climates. Sage will keep its leaves through severe frosts but at the expense of its vigor the following spring. When snow cover stays it is time to prune the Sage, both to protect the branches from snow breakage, so inviting disease, and from desiccating winds that kill young branches, often splitting them, thus tearing into healthy wood below, and again, possibly introducing decay and disease.

The light, grey-green, rugose (pitted and bumpy) leaves of Sage are enjoyably fuzzy and highly fragrant. It is an aroma that constantly brings to mind a fine sausage or turkey dressing. Sage inspires many visitors because it is so rewarding to rub the velvety leaves between the fingers, releasing its aroma to the air. It is an herb which provides instant gratifaction and wonderful memories.

The strong scented chemical in Sage, thujone, is also present in the *Artemisia* such as Sage Brush, and can delay the putrefaction of meat. Thus, plants containing it are used to spice prepared meats in the form we call sausage. Garden Sage, however, also contains some pleasantly scented chemicals such as eucalyptol and borneol for a pure camphoraceous odor, and pinene for a tangy note. It also contains uracilic acid, also found in the waxy coating on apples, that displays some antibacterial activity.

Because Sage is a borderline evergreen in cold climates, it may require cutting back in fall. Strong main branches must be nurtured so the plants are not killed by sub-zero weather. A plant cut back for the first 3 years to 6–8 in. in fall will last many years if it is continually pruned in the same fashion. It will better tolerate partial shade if pruned this way. In warmer climates, flower stalks should be removed as they wane near the end of the summer. Avoid the crew-cut; instead cut them back at least two leaf nodes from the flowering portion of the stem in order to stimulate new growth and to encourage further flowering the remainder of the year. Prune again in the spring to whatever height is desired.

Sage's claim to fame as an ornamental herb is also due to its grey color, which remains relatively constant throughout the year. As a grey herb it is used to brighten up a dark, drab corner in the midst of evergreen conifers, add sparkle to a semi-shady niche overgrown with blue and gold annuals and wildflowers, or as the centerpiece of a grey garden. Historically, grey gardens were composed of the herbs Sage, Lavender, Wormwood, Incana Santolina, Horehound, and Dittany. Many more possibilities have been amassed to our greater benefit: Wooly Lavender; Wooly Betony; Curry Plant; Silver Sage; Beach, Fringed and Roman Wormwood and many more *Artemisia*; 'Silver Beacon' Lamium; *Origanum microphyllum*; Silver Thyme; and Cardoon. Other grey-foliaged ornamentals used today include Everlasting, *Helichrysum lanatum*; *Veronica incana*; *Senecio* 'White Diamond'; Carnations; Wormseed, *Artemisia maritima*; *Cineraria maritima*; New Zealand Mountain Daisy, *Celmisia spectabilis*; and *Anthemis cupaniana*.

Sage blends well with other large-leaved or tall mat-forming herbs such as Costmary, Lamium, Wooly Betony, and Lady's Mantle. Its flowers add special charm among these lesser beauties yet their fragrances contribute equally to scent the air, yielding mixtures of camphor and mint, lemon, apple, or spice. It is a tough herb that should be located on well travelled paths where passersby will come into contact with its foliage. Highly fragrant ground covers scooting out from around it and under the feet add to the effect. Creeping

Thyme, Corsican Mint, and Lawn Camomile are preferred.

For borders of Sage set plants 24 in. apart. Sage is an open, airy herb in any case and closer spacing down to 18 in. will not significantly thicken a border but rather confound the herb's ability to get sufficient light and nutrients to stay healthy. The informal border is recommended. Dead plants are easily replaced and only a fall pruning is necessary. Keep borders under 24 in. wide. Unfettered, Sage will grow to 36 in. or more but tends to suffer during cold winters and in damp conditions. The shorter, pruned hedge develops stronger wood and denser habit for better winter protection and remains more manageable.

Because of its numerous cultivars, Garden Sage can fulfill many dreams of the rockery enthusiast, providing grey and gold, lavender, and magenta, white and sundry greens; something for every spot. A pocket of sandy chalky soil is heaven for Sage and it will look its best when only a few large gnarled old branches emerge from a warty stump to droop lackadaisically into the path of pedestrians. Whenever it is brushed or jostled it releases its delicious odor for us inspiring dreams of plump, hot sausages.

For a strange, but simple ornamental grey garden in the contemporary landscape, use a centerpiece of a single Cardoon, several Garden Sage flowing away in a teardrop shape from it, and a surrounding cover of Snow-in-summer, *Cerastium tomentosum*. In the perennial border use it as a transition plant and match it up with Scarlet Bee Balm or Crimson Geraniums and thick-set clumps of Shasta Daisy and white Alpine Poppies. In the fragrant garden, a massive planting about a reading bench can refresh the air and clear the harried mind, preparing it for deeper concentration.

Garden Sage is sometimes sold as Dalmation Sage, but this label refers more to a spice mixture imported from the Dalmation coast of Yugoslavia and Albania than it does to *S. officinalis*. The spice contains a combination of Garden and Greek Sage and hybrids in between. Garden Sage has numerous ornamental cultivars, and other Sages of the *Salvia* genus offer extensive variations so let us discuss them individually beginning with the cultivars of Garden Sage.

Dwarf Sage is a cultivar of Garden Sage which makes a snappy border on hot exposed banks or driveways. Rarely growing more than 10 in. high, it has a small, narrow leaf with a grey-green color, essentially a miniature of the species, but tends to pale after blooming before the new growth in late summer. Dwarf Sage is the recommended variety for planters and arrangements of live herbs often used in the kitchen and to adorn the porch, where they are easily accessible. It is a slow-growing, undemanding herb with a true Sage flavor and aroma, often superior during late summer.

Another fine container variety is Golden Sage which is available in two cultivars, *S. officinalis* 'Aureus' and 'Icterina'. Because they are slower growing they do not outgrow other plants in a small arrangement. They have a slight citrus scent if grown in well-limed soils and are fine culinary substitutes for the species. 'Icterina' is variegated—yellow or gold margin and wide green veins—and forms a low 14–18 in. dense mound that is a pastel yellow-green from a distance. 'Aureus' is an unvariegated form with entirely yellow leaves. 'Icterina' is one of the hardiest of the Garden Sages, remaining evergreen in areas to −10°F. The dense habit is a major factor in its survival.

Golden Sage is understandably the most popular cultivar of Garden Sage. It can put a touch of warmth into any garden, particularly in a wintry scene with dark green, evergreen Azaleas blooming in early and late winter, or with grey herbs having colorful flowers such as *Santolina neapolitana; Anthemis cupaniana;* or the Newfoundland Mountain Daisy, *Celmisia spectabilis*. The gold foliage goes well with purple or red hued herbs such as 'Opal' or 'Krishna' Basil or complementing a crimson Blueberry in the fall.

Variegated Sage, or Tricolor Sage, *S. o.* 'Tricolor', a fascinating, scintillatingly patterned Sage, with dabs of cream, pinegreen, and purple, and Red Sage, *S. o.*

'Purpurascens', with entirely red-purple leaves, are both lanky, weak herbs that must either be grown in a poor, chalky, dry soil in full sun or be constantly nipped in the bud to force them to bush. It is unlikely that either will winter over unless so treated, but they are alluring ornamentals, particularly in evergreen settings, with Thymes and/or conifers. They quickly develop root rot in areas other than those with dry, chalky soil. A mixture of oyster shell or dolomite chips and sand should be added to an equal amount of soil, thereby giving them the medium required. They are best combined with other drought-and alkaline-tolerant herbs such as Dwarf Lavender, Creeping Rosemary, Dittany, Savory, and Thyme. Variegated Sage is best displayed against a dark green background provided either by conifers or broadleafed evergreens. Red Sage can be cradled in a recurved border of Italian Oregano or flanked by Golden Oregano for added color. Red Sage is recommended as contrast in grey gardens or among light colored foliages. Both are suitable alternates for Garden Sage in the kitchen.

Greek Sage, *S. fruticosa,* has wide, blunt, fuzzy leaves with a wavy margin and a pair of small lateral lobes snuggled up to the base of the larger terminal leaf, forming an arrowhead shape. Its flowers are pale lilac and arrive in late spring and continue all summer. This species constitutes more than half of the Sage purchased as a spice because of its exceptional Sage flavor and fragrance. There are a few subspecies, and crosses of Greek and Garden Sage are common. In growth and habit treat it like a Garden Sage but remember that it is not hardy below 20°F and must be brought indoors—where it is a delightfully fragrant plant throughout the winter—or kept in a cold frame or greenhouse and pruned regularly.

Blue Sage, *S. clevelandii,* very closely resembles Garden Sage in overall shape and habit, but its flower is exceptionally beautiful. Twinned China-blue flowers are borne in large, 2 in., Monarda-like whorls on long stems. They are a special treat for hummingbirds, as are all Sage flowers. They are an exotic addition in any garden and can be easily combined in perennial beds with Daisies and Monardas. Its slim, lanceolate leaves mix with many smaller leaved ornamentals as well.

Although it may be used wherever you would place Garden Sage in the landscape, it is not hardy below 10°F, so should be potted in the fall and brought in for a stint out of the weather. While Garden Sage can easily flourish in partial shade, Blue Sage must grow in full sun for fullest blooming. It may grow larger than Garden Sage, however it should be kept pruned to a more compact size; 18–24 in. is recommended for improved flowering and better winter protection when it can remain outside. This small size also facilitates transplanting to a pot for wintering over in a greenhouse or the home.

The 2–3 in. long, ¼–½ in. wide, butter knife-shaped leaves of Blue Sage have a very strong and pleasant citrus aroma. It is a more pleasant, less camphoraceous species that is superior to Garden Sage for stuffings and potato salad or beans. It has a lasting, lemony scent and flavor that can appreciably transform the common Sage-spiced dish into a special treat.

Clary, *S. sclarea,* and Silver Sage, *S. argentea,* are biennial herbs that provide two shows for the price of one. For their first year their unique foliage is attractive by itself. Silver Sage has thick, downy leaves that rest on the ground and appear to be encased in spider webs. These fascinating hoary rosettes can dot a perennial bed among non-invasive ground covers or grace a potted arrangement with 'Opal' Basal and Variegated Lemon Balm. The following spring an 18 in. branched spike of white flowers adorns the little, fuzzy, mother plant. Clary, on the other hand, forms a modest pile of large, delightfully fragrant, grey leaves—excellent contrast in any perennial bed and a fabulous contemporary feature herb. In the second year it rockets forth with a tall spike of blue flowers. Clary has a variety, *S. s.* var. turkestaniana , with a prolific display of pinkish white flowers. If you want to entertain your palate, or have brave guests, two enjoyable uses of Clary leaves include hiding them whole inside pancakes or substituting them for cabbage leaves and stuffing with mildly spiced pork or veal.

Pineapple Sage, *S. elegans,* is true to its name in flavor and fragrance and is definitely an elegant herb in the ornamental garden. Its large, dark green leaves are a perfect background for its scarlet flowers. Pineapple Sage must be pruned to force it to bush or it will shoot straight up 3 ft. or more. In the latter habit it is used in the informal landscape as a tall screen or back border and allowed to shoot up with Tansy, Yarrow, and numerous other ornamental *Salvias* for late summer color. Or it may be pruned to a 12–18 in. bush, joining German Camomile, Golden Oregano, and 'Opal' Basil for a remarkably colorful, fragrant, and beneficial feature garden in the contemporary landscape. It is not hardy below 30°F.

Meadow Sage, *S. pratensis,* has a habit similar to Silver Sage but with large, green, ground-hugging leaves. Its leaves were once used in ales and as a pot herb. Dozens of flower spikes, decorated in violet or navy blue, writhe, like the many serpents on Medusa's head, above this tough little perennial Sage. Use it, as its name suggests, in wild garden meadows among other low-growing herbs with strong vertical habits. Let it surround taller herbs, its many purple arms begging at the feet of a mixed feature of White Mugwort and Valerian, or waving in triumph while surrounding a centerpiece of 'Coronation Gold' Yarrow and Elecampane.

There are countless other ornamental Sages, any of which have beautiful flowers or fragrant foliage, or both, including the crimson flowering fruit-scented Sage, *Salvia dorisiana;* Texas Sage, *S. coccinea,* which also has a fruity-scented foliage and a quick, annual habit; or the blue or purple flowering *S. guarantica, S. mexicana,* Bog Sage, *S. uliginosa,* and Canyon Sage, *S. lycoides.* Virtually none of these are hardy below 30°F and many succumb to temperatures around 36–38°. Treat them as annuals. They are fast-growing and many are prolific fall-blooming ornamentals, each possessed of its own virtue that must be experimented with to be appreciated fully.

Chapter 5 / SECTION 3

A Walk
Through an Informal Garden

The postman told me that it was far easier to get to the house I was seeking by water than by land. (Fig. 42) It is also true that the best way to enjoy an informal garden is to approach it in an informal way. With this advice to guide us, we will now stop paddling our canoe and let it glide up onto the lawn, not up to the boat dock, for as I said, we will arrive informally and disembark on the lawn to refresh ourselves in the cool shade of a willow tree.

A mystical kingdom looms before us, rising up into the mist that seems to have snagged itself on the trees farther up the slope. A modern-day castle, a masterpiece of wood and glass hiding among the trees, peers down tolerantly at us through all its windows, silently mindful of our approach. Flowery mats of Thymes and Sedums spill across the hillside. The faint, woodsy aromas of turpentine and spice exite our nostrils. A silver lining of red, ripe Roses across the top suggest to us that the summit is not far off and perchance we will find our way up there later.

The lawn beneath our feet is soft and firm, like green suede cloth pulled taut over a drum. Our footfalls make no sound as we move to the center of the yard. From here, it is less than a few paces in any direction to the surrounding flower beds. As gardeners, we may reflect on how much an informal garden is an arena, where as victors in our struggle to conquer we stand in the center of our creation and watch nature shift and vie for space in the grandstands around us.

This is a somber crowd we are gazing upon, a group of no nonsense plants that provide the patron with more than a pretty face, a kingdom of mystical herbs that even the burden of centuries of toil could not weaken. Marching upslope along the pathway leading to the house is a column of culinary herbs. A bright bundle of Golden Oregano is a fitting standard bearer followed by a clump of Silver Thyme, a silver epaulet on every leaf. Coming behind, tall and proud, are Chives, with great, shocking purple maces held high. A dark green swath of Caraway Thyme, trying hard to keep up, is prodded from behind by a hundred silvery lance-leaves of a Dwarf Sage. Bringing up the rear in an uncontrolled cabaret are the white and purple blossoms of 'White Moss' and Wooly Thymes swarming over the ground. A few overzealous strands plunge over the escarpment to the patio below.

Majestic evergreen shrubs and dwarf conifers hug the escarpment as well. They appear to be stalking the hillside, their mantis-like forms crouching behind their downslope prey. Their prey includes an Old Man, *Artemisia abrotanum,* or two, hardy evergreen com-

Fig. 42. Informal landscape. Gardens of Michele Nash, Mercer Island, WA.

KEY
1 Cr. Thyme *Thymus pulegio*   'Foster Flower'
2 'Silver King' *Artemisia ludoviciana* var.
3 Dwarf Feverfew *Chrysanthemum parthenium* 'Selaginoides'
4 Barberry *Berberis thunbergii* 'Atropurpurea Nana'
5 *Sedum* spp.
6 Wooly Thyme *Thymus praecox* ssp. *articus* 'Languinosus'
7 *Fushia magellanica* Evergreen Fuschia
8 Kurume Azalea
9 Dwarf Mugo Pine *Pinus* spp.
10 *Tsuga mertensia*
11 Sweet Cicely *Myrrhis odorata*
12 Wood Sorrel *Oxalis acetosella*
13 Violets *Viola cornuta*
14 Cr. Red Thyme *Thymus praecox* ssp. *articus* 'Coccineus'
15 Caraway Thyme *Thymus herba-barona*
16 Chive *Allium schoenoprasum*
17 Silver Thyme *Thymus* 'Argenteus'
18 Golden Oregano *Origanum vulgare* 'Aureum'
19 Dwarf Sage *Salvia officinalis* 'Nana'
20 Weeping Hemlock *Tsuga* spp.
21 *Euonymous*
22 Golden Lemon Thyme *Thymus* × *citriodorus* 'Aureus'
23 Southernwood *Artemisia abrotanum*
24 *Viburnum fragrans*
25 'White Moss' Thyme *Thymus praecox* ssp. *articus*
26 Sweet Woodruff *Gallium odorata*
27 Strawberry *Fragaria* sp.
28 Weeping Willow *Salix babylonica*
29 Red Leaf Maple *Acer palmatum* 'Atropurpurea'
30 *Santolina viridis*
31 Azalea
32 *Heuchera sanguinea*
33 *Armeria maratima*
34 San Jose Juniper
35 Painted Daisy *Chrysanthemum coccineum*
36 Violets/Wild Ginger
37 Elecampane *Inula helenium*
38 Sword Fern *Polystichum* spp.
39 Primrose *Primula* spp.
40 *Ajuga*
41 *Primula aricula*
42 *Eremurius*
43 Ornamental Grass *Festuca ovina* 'Glauca'
44 Black Hellebore *Helleborus niger*
45 *Iris* spp.
46 Variegated Flowering Dogwood *Cornus florida* 'Welchii'
47 Peppermint *Mentha* × *piperita*
48 Corsican Hellebore *Helleborus corsicus*
49 Basil-Thyme *Acinos arvensis*
50 Golden Mint *Mentha* × *gracilis* var *variegata*
51 Roses
52 Oregon Grape

petitors with rapidly growing branches that resemble bottle-brushes emerging wrong side out of a bucket.

Immediately before us, shades of red and yellow clamber around like a challenging army preparing for a charge uphill. Their handsome prince in purple robes, an *Acer palmatum* 'Atropupureum', perched by the patio, directs his armies and confers with his generals: a ghostly tuft of *Festuca ovina*, a gold baubled, silver-chested Incana Santolina and an elegant crimson braided Coral Bell, *Heuchera sanguinea*. Scattered camps of Wild Marjoram, with flowering Mother-of-Thyme and other exotic Creeping Golden and 'Tuffeted' Thymes join the ornamental evergreens adorning this garden.

A great finger of forest swoops down to the far right. Swarms of Evening Primroses, *Oenothera tetragona*, Swordferns, and fragrant Ariculas decorate the forest front. Here an inviting Ajuga-cloaked path, its entrance marked by a clump of maroon *Aremuria*, disappears into a dense tangle of Pfitzers and Primroses. Nearby, pink everlasting bouquets of Golden Oregano and the yellow and violet flowers of Oregon Grape and Barrenwort, *Epimedium grandiflorum*, dance around a boulder under the watchful eyes of a pink-flowering Dogwood. Some Basil Thyme, a youthful pair of glossy-leaved Corsican Hellebore, *Helleborus corsica*, and a soft golden yellow Ginger Mint, all dew-covered and sleepy-eyed, reside in the shade of the boathouse.

In the left-hand garden are a few familiar herbs; Wild Thyme, Wooly Thyme and Lemon Thyme, creeping wildly in unrestricted glee with their neighbors, a clump of Chives, a petite mound of Dwarf Feverfew, a back border of Strawflowers, *Helichrysum bracteatum*, and espaliered Pyracantha.

Near the patio is a young Willow, *Salix babylonica*, with Sweet Cicely, Violets and purple-eyed *Oxalis* flourishing in the filtered shade beneath its lazy branches. Two exotic ornamentals also decorate this spot: an evergreen Kurume Azalea, 'Hi No Mayo', and a splendid, hardy *Fuschia magelanica* spreading to form a small hedge.

What lies beyond? What is above the trees? After ascending the slope up to the ridge of Roses we saw from below, we can see that alongside the house is a forest path, dense with undergrowth; shade tolerant shrubs, ferns, Sweet Woodruff, Violets and Wild Ginger reign here with countless wildlings lifting their haughty flowered heads through the forest litter.

Our journey is cut short however. Alas, viewing the grand gardens above will not be an opportunity we will get today, for the guard has picked up our scent. With the baying of Brindle behind us, we scamper back to our canoe, grab up a paddle, and push off. As we drift away, the magical kingdom melts into the mist and vanishes.

Chapter 6 / SECTION 1

The Contemporary Landspace

The contemporary landscape could be described as an artist's impressionistic interpretation of a formal garden. Both employ geometric patterns to compartmentalize the homesite into separate gardens and separate functions. Each compartment, whether for lounging, play, entertaining, or dining, is a distinct element in the landscape highlighted by a small feature garden. This is analogous to the formal landscape, with parterres in one place, a fountain and pool in another, and an enclosed courtyard nestled against the home.

The contemporary landscape is intended to be visually nondemanding. While formal gardens are strict geometric puzzles, and plant materials are grown to perform according to the design, the contemporary design organizes natural features and plant forms into an uncomplicated relationship. It exhibits the least textural contrast of any design style, very few species are displayed and one species is used repetitively to form the theme.

In the formal landscape, visitors are aware that it is the gardens they have come to enjoy, other pursuits aside. Not so in the contemporary landscape. The various divisions are designed to encompass functions that are active, being centered around recreation, rather than passive, such as the solely ornamental parterres and fountains. The extensive use of inert ground covers in lieu of turf throughout the landscape makes it a foregone conclusion that the contemporary homesite is definitely intended for one or more nonviewing functions.

The entertaining or eyecatching aspect of a contemporary feature is that it is oriented either asymmetrically within a compartment and/or as a simple, asymmetrical design. (Figs. 43 and 44) Asymmetry and simplicity are vital, asymmetry for visual interest and simplicity to maintain a subdued presence. Because the feature is not located in the center or all the way around the edge of the space provided, it is understood to be an accent only.

Much of the asymmetry in a contemporary landscape is kept in balance by large areas of bark, mulch, or gravel used for ornamental purposes. Methods of controlling horizontal balance include the introduction of wide paths, the use of curving or angular lines and striking repetitive patterns, and broad, stone-paved patios and courtyards. Vertical components are satisfied by a few trees or small clumps of tall ornamental herbs. Emphasis is placed on their unique stature and branching habits, not exlusively on foliage characteristics, although showy autumn colors are desired.

A multitude of inert and organic materials are available to provide the balance for asymmetry in the contemporary landscape. They should be chosen according to their task: coarse fill for paths and balancing blocks of broad-leafed and robust herbs; fine, earthy mulches for a warm, moody or expressive garden blanket; colored fill for small, visually intense features; sand for visual stability in well harmonized arrangements; and pea gravel for a monotonous background where the barest hint of life is desired.

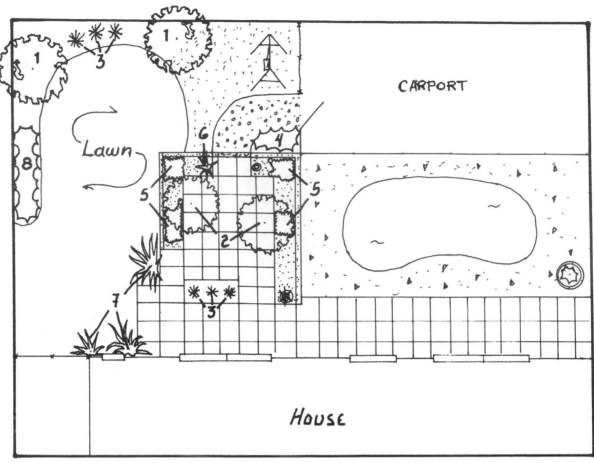

Fig. 43. Spanish style landscape shows the details of contemporary design; compartmentation, assymetry and minimal use of vegetation.

KEY
1 Dwarf Apple *Malus*
2 Pear *Pyrus communis*
3 Roses
4 Southernwood *Artemisia abrotanum*

5 Cr. Thyme, Caraway/'Pink Chintz' *Thymus herba-barona, T. praecox ssp. articus* cv.
6 *Yucca gloriosa*
7 Pftzer 'Aurea' *Juniperus × media*
8 *Eleagnus pungens*

Fig. 44. Looking into the courtyard of Fig. 43 we can see the simplicity and naturalness that converts a geometric pattern into contemporary styling.

The inert category includes rock (from sizes as small as sand to boulders), brick, concrete, and cinders or flyash. The advantage of inert materials is their longevity and cleanliness. A gravel path may last decades if weeds are controlled. The types of rocks used are numerous but include basalt, limestone, granite, quartzite (crystal rock), shale, and sandstone. Other inert materials of local origin may include beach sand (with shells), beach shells, oyster shells, pumice, travertine (hot springs rock formations of unusual character), and volcanic ash.

Organic materials include mulches (leaves, grass, hay, pine needles, manure, compost, and recycled wastes), lumber products (planks, posts, railroad ties), and wood by-products (sawdust, wood chips, bark). Organic and wood by-products mulches are generally used in herbaceous beds, doubling as soil improvers. Well composted vegetable material is the best mulch while bagged manure is a close second, although not as economical. Wood chips, bark, and nut shell wastes are generally spread over polyethylene when used on paths or in feature gardens to inhibit decay. Rounds, the butt end of a log removed before milling, and posts or ties cut in sections make long-lived paths with a woodsy or rustic appearance. Some composts include mushroom culture media and municipal sewage or land fill materials of organic nature that have been specifically composted for sale. Recycled organic wastes include nut shells, beer hops, beet and corn silage, or other vegetable waste from processing plants and sediments from clarifying or sedimentation ponds (pollution control devices in the food industry).

Grass, whether it be Kentucky Blue, Zoysia or Pachysandra, is an important living ground cover for its color contrast, balancing effect and influence on the microclimate of a homesite. Other ground covers are handsome, ornamental or perhaps more clever, but grass can cool a garden in the summer, warm it on cool evenings, control humidity and hold down dust in a way that no non-living ground cover can. Don't ignore it because it doesn't sound like a clever idea. Use it to lessen the burden of maintaining a large area where existing ground covers are simply not up to your expectations. Consider using grass for paths. A path carpeted with a cool spongy grass is kind to the weary-footed and ornamental in a landscape with little or no lawn.

Let's examine some popular garden uses and the gardens that accompany them.

In the contemporary landscape, the kitchen garden is displayed as mounds with herbs planted in a series of arcs, concentric circles (maze-like) or as part of the entire landscape. This latter design features herbs and food plants as ornamental borders and specimens in what is called an edible landscape. Many vegetable crops can be used ornamentally in herbaceous perennial beds. Borders may be composed of Carrots, Curly Parsley, Lettuce (dozens of shapes, sizes, and hues exist, the most ornamental being the old European varieties variegated with purple, red, and dark green), Salad Burnet, Beets, Spinach, and the highly ornamental Kohlrabi and Kales. Screens of Peas, Pole Beans, espaliered Tomatoes, Corn, Red Orach, and Sorghum (an excellent wild bird seed) are productive and entertaining. Isolated features of Purple Cabbage, Brussel Sprouts, Asparagus, Artichoke, Cardoon, and the Purple Okra, with huge, yellow flowers are exciting additions to any landscape. Ground covers include potatoes or the pot herbs, Good King Henry and the ornamental, but edible Strawberry Blite, *Chenopodium capitatum,* which resembles Lamb's Quarters but with a blushing pink sheen on new leaves and a deep red spike of seeds in fall (a treat for many meadow birds), or the Squashes with all manner of fascinating edible gourds. A number of cultivated grains can be displayed in controlled clumps, to add character to the edible landscape, in addition to supplying bird seed for a family pet or wild birds. The most ornamental include Bearded Wheat, *Triticum aestivum;* Barley, both 6- *Hordeum vulgare* and 2-row *H. distichon;* Oats, *Avena sativa;* Millet, *Panicum miliaceum;* and Sorghum.

The putting green (Fig. 45) is formed by a small, oval section of turf (Bent Grass cut to ⅛th in. with a reel mower) forming a flattened mound surrounded by sand pits and evergreen shrubbery. Immediately edging the green is a ground cover of low contrast Wooly Thyme that flows naturally down the sandy slopes of the sand pits, in which are featured a stately Yucca and several barrel-chested Bush Thymes. Around the periphery are Incana Santolina and Lavender, forming a fragrant hedge.

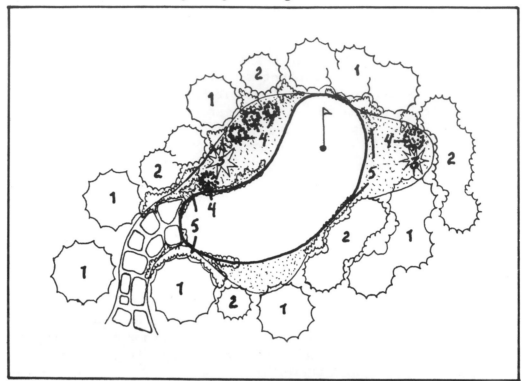

Fig. 45. Compartmentation for recreational endeavors allows the isolated garden, such as this golf green to become part of the landscape in much the same way the parterre does in a formal landscape.

KEY
1 Lavender *Lavandula angustifolia*
2 *Santolina chaemecyparrissus*
3 *Yucca gloriossa*

4 Silver Thyme *Thymus* 'Argenteus'
5 Cr. Red Thyme *Thymus praecox* ssp. *articus* 'Coccineus'

A clover leaf outdoor entertainment or meeting area (Fig. 46) for business-at-home, uses a warm, red or toasty, yellow-brown, brick patio, partitioned by slender austere beds. A rich, natural mulch with deep, earthy tones and odors helps emphasize the garden's simplicity. It is a garden that can't get in the way of mingling crowds. Creepers and evergreens are used because of their crisp, no nonsense appearance. A slope is generated by mounding a 3 ft. berm the north side. A hollow formed around the trees gives the impression of a deep forest, and while the partitions on the north side are mounded to 12 in. in the center to suggest ridges, the south side is mounded to 6 in. or less so the effect of a slope is more pronounced. The pond and lush foliage of the water feature create a limited but none-the-less relaxing scene.

A small circular concrete pad at the side of a garage becomes a fenced basketball court (Fig. 47). One tall Arizona Cypress and low Junipers, that can take the thump of a ricocheting ball, are blended here with a silver carpet of Wooly Betony for a rough, tough garden needing virtually no maintenance. As Wooly Betony creeps onto the pavement and paths it naturalizes the atmosphere of this recreational space. Hops or any other espaliered

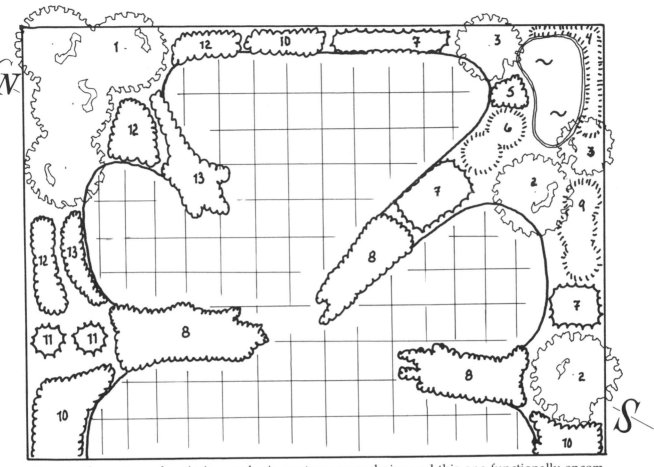

Fig. 46. The patterned patio is popular in contemporary design and this one functionally encompasses a major portion of the homesite.
KEY
 1 Grey Birch *Betula populifolia*
 2 Dwarf Apple *Malus* spp.
 3 *Viburnum fragrans*
 4 Coyote Mint *Monardella villosa*
 5 Golden Lemon Thyme *Thymus citriodora* 'Aureus'
 6 *Angelica archangelica*
 7 Wooly Betony *Stachys byzantina*
 8 Wooly Thyme *Thymus praecox* ssp. *articus* 'Languinosus'
 9 Lovage *Levisticum officinale*
10 Silver Thyme *Thymus* 'Argentea'
11 Greek Sage *Salvia fruticosa*
12 Oregano Thyme *Thymus pulegioides* 'Oregano-scented'
13 Red Flowering Thyme *Thymus pulegioides* 'Kermesinus'

Fig. 47. The basketball court landscaped to be fit and frugal is increasingly popular for recreationally active families.
KEY
 1 Wooly Betony *Stachys byzantina*
 2 Lavender *Lavandula angustifolia* 'Rosea'
 3 Arizona Cypress *Cupressus glabra* 'Glauca'
 4 Cr. Juniper *Juniperus horizontalis*
 5 Serbian Spruce *Picea omorika*

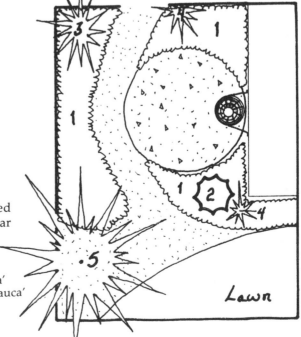

ornamental planted along the cinder block wall reduces both the glare and the air temperature.

Hops, low creeping Junipers, Red Japanese Maple, and Creeping Thyme create a grand entrance theme for a small front yard (Fig. 48). A few large clumps of basalt loom like denizens of the deep, lurking in the dark green sea of Hops. Variegated Hops provide a lightening effect, imitating frothy waveforms wherever necessary. The walkway of sandstone with paving blocks set well apart and separated by oyster shells and sand, gives the impression of a beach. Swaths of colorful green Thymes creep over this sandy beach or peek from soil pockets in the rocks like seaweeds.

Do not forget that one of the attributes homeowners must consider when designing a garden is minimal care. Because the contemporary landscape uses fewer plant materials and fewer species but more inert ground covers in wide open areas it requires much less effort to maintain than any other landscape, leaving more time for recreation and relaxation.

Herbs ideal for the contemporary landscape include ground covers of Costmary, Wooly Betony and Hops, magnificently flowered towers of Monarda, *Agastache*, and Cardoon, and the majestic, exotic herbs Sweet Bay, Lemon Verbena and Giant Fennel.

Fig. 48. A metropolitan homesite may be small but can be converted by a ground cover of Hops and a few evergreens to a comfortable and clever landscape.

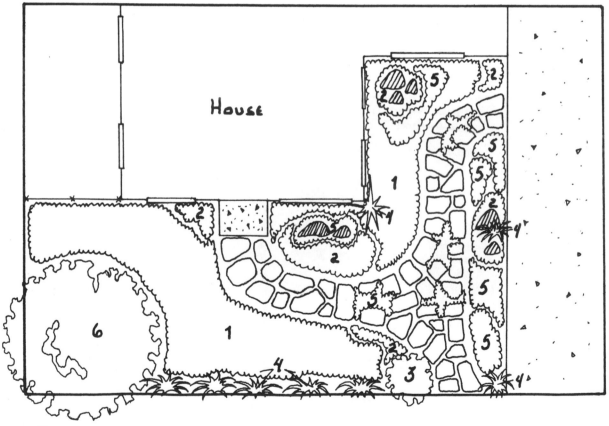

KEY
1 Hop *Humulus lupulus*
2 Variegated Hop *Humulus japonica* var. *variegata*
3 Red Leaf Maple *Acer palmatum* 'Atropurpurea'
4 Creeping Juniper *Juniperus horizontalis*
5 Cr. Golden Thyme *Thymus* 'Clear Gold'
6 Maple *Acer saccharum*

Chapter 6 / SECTION 2

Herbs for a Contemporary Landscape

A luscious, green carpet of Costmary, *Balsamita major,* capping a sunny mound near a hot patio is an attractive and irresistible minty treat within the contemporary landscape. There are two forms: Camphor Plant and Bible Leaf. Camphor Plant has silver-grey to grey-green leaves and a strong camphor aroma closely resembling Wormwood. Its taste is extremely bitter. It forms a low growing mound 12–18 in. high and in mid-summer is covered in tiny white daisies. Bible Leaf is a tastier culinary version of Costmary. It has satiny green leaves with a refreshing minty fragrance and taste. There is still some bitterness, but in a tangy salad with vinegar and oil dressing it is unnoticeable. This form grows to 30 in. and has tiny, yellow-green button flowers in late summer. While Camphor Plant is a shimmering ornamental and covered in swarms of daisies, Bible Leaf's flower stalks if left unchecked are weedy and unnecessary. They should be removed to bolster the growth of large handsome specimens of leaves which may grow to be 12 in. long and 3 in. wide. It is this habit that is pleasing to the eye in an arrangement and most certainly a centerpiece for much conversation.

Costmary is a quick-spreading, herbaceous perennial that is very hardy. It emerges in spring and grows rapidly into a green carpet. Leaves that hang into paths release their minty aroma when brushed. Costmary cannot be tread upon; the succulent leaves are damaged easily. Young leaves point skyward, but eventually bend earthward as they mature, whereupon they overlap each other, completely blanketing the ground and virtually excluding all light beneath, eliminating weeding.

Bible Leaf, once known as Alecost, was a prominent bitter flavoring for ales in the Middle Ages, and a popular nosegay herb because of its fragrant ornamental leaf. The keeping quality of its perky, minty scent made it a good book marker. The name Bible Leaf evolved from its use in Bibles to mask their musty odor. Costmary also provided a refreshing whiff during overly long sermons.

The large decorative leaves of Costmary are attractive in small contemporary arrangements with Garden Sage and purple-tinged Mints. Their combination of aromas is a bonus. In partial shade, a clump of Costmary surrounded by Lemon and Nutmeg Scented Geraniums and an edible ground cover of Nasturtiums is a colorful ornamental feature for the herbaceous perennial garden.

Costmary should be a neighbor to only large-leafed plants as it will obscure the beauty of the mini-leafed plants such as Thyme, Savory or Rosemary. Accent the Costmary feature with fragrant herbs and colorful flowers instead. Examples for contemporary features include Borage, a few dark red Himalayan Poppies surrounded by a carpet of California Poppies, or a patch of Costmary, Wooly Betony and Golden Sage, is a joyous mixture. Other large-leafed, herbaceous perennials that go well with Costmary are Elecampane and Comfrey.

The fragrant leaves of Costmary can be dried in either a flower press or between the pages of a book. The book should be placed flat in a dry location and other books or some heavy object placed on top. Glossy pages should be avoided as they absorb moisture too slowly and leaves may discolor. After 1 week the leaves should be turned over or moved and pressed again for another week. They may be used in arrangements or as fragrant book marks. A musty old book is given a refreshing lift by pressing several Costmary leaves between its pages. This procedure is not recommended for valuable texts since some warping of the pages may occur.

Costmary can be used in a fresh green salad or a combination shredded cabbage and flavored gelatin salad. In the same fashion as Bay, Costmary can be added as a whole leaf covering a baking fish, in beans or some cream sauces and placed on the bottom of a cake tin to impart a minty freshness to white cake.

Wooly Betony, *Stachys byzantina,* is a strangely lovely herb, valuable for its relentless but alluring habit of carpeting the ground with a great grey mat of fuzzy "Lamb's Ears". The common name, Lamb's Ears, aptly describes the large, 3–6 in. long, 2 in. wide, and ⅛ in. thick, densely wooly leaves. Its shimmering, silver flower spikes are flecked with pink blooms for up to 2 months, all the while attracting billions of bees and hummingbirds.

Wooly Betony is little used other than an ornamental, but its faint apple scent and flavor make it a pleasant and attractive salad herb or sweetener in a tea. The sweetness is due to betonicine, a chemical also found in Yarrow. Wooly Betony is not cultivated as a medicinal source of betonicine. The species, Betony, *Stachys officinalis,* is cultivated for medicinal purposes. It has an attractive flower spike and large green leaves. Of great repute, and valued above most, if not all, other herbs as a healing herb, Betony lost favor quickly in the last century. Betony, from the Celtic meaning a "head herb", makes a flavorful tea taken to alleviate headache or migraine. It has also been used as an astringent in minor cuts, thus its name, Woundwort.

Wooly Betony provides a bright, dense ground cover in poor soils or on rocky slopes. It will spread quickly. For large areas in a rocky feature, it is a splendid herb to take up space, demanding little, including water. An established clump of Wooly Betony is drought resistant. It is an attractive herb which should be planted where it is highly visible so that frequent visitations to it by hummingbirds may be enjoyed. In the past, Wooly Betony was allowed to sprout between the paving stones, much like a weed, and enjoyed by sitting around or over it. It is an excellent foundation planting, in full sun or partial shade and will draw attention to a dark colored home or provide contrast for arborvitae and broadleaf evergreens that surround a home or parade along the driveway.

Wooly Betony is very hardy and evergreen to about Zone 5. It does not handle foot traffic well, but if it borders a pathway, as from a patio door to poolside, or down steps to a parking area, it should be allowed to amble where it sees fit. It will attempt to venture onto the path. To keep it neat remove any crushed leaves and branches. It will try again, and again, and again. Few other flowers compete successfully with Wooly Betony since it overtakes any open space quite rapidly. Fast-growing, self-sowing annual wildflowers such as California Poppy, Toadflax, etc. are beautiful with Wooly Betony. If the garden becomes clogged with the herb, remove a square foot of Wooly Betony here and there and reseed the wildflower.

As a clump of Wooly Betony ages it tends to produce fewer and fewer flower stalks from the center—analogous to a fairy ring, the flowering part is always on the outside edge of the circle—so it may not be appealing to a gardener. The flowering stalks form on new stems as they advance. To produce flowering throughout the patch, it must be thinned. Completely remove portions down to bare earth to allow new branches to advance into the open spaces. The best way to maintain a Wooly Betony patch is to remove the flowering branches all the way back to their roots, pulling with them some of the lateral shoots to provide enough open space for regrowth in the spring. There is a flowerless cultivar, 'Silver Carpet', which grows more slowly, forming a tight rosette of silver wooly leaves that can be used for sparkling accents in herbaceous perennial gardens or in rockeries.

Wooly Betony is primarily used in dried arrangements where its silver-wooly appearance is much appreciated. The leaves are easily dried at high temperature and a whole branch can be dried and hung for use later, snapping the leaves off as they are needed. Dried and pulverized Wooly Betony is used to add some sweetness to orange-spiced and Camomile teas.

The Hop, *Humulus lupulus,* is a rather gregarious vine that always wants to grow into or around another plant, shrub, or tree, rather than on a fence, where we would like it. Unlike the grape, which uses its coiling tendrils to anchor itself, the Hop is extremely sticky, due to tiny hairy hooks that cling tenaciously to anything from tree bark to concrete.

The Hop is famous for its major role in bringing medieval ale manufacturing out of the doldrums. Hops were originally used to leaven and improve bread. Because of its powerful antibacterial activity (the chemical humulon is responsible) bread was better and stayed fresh longer. Frequently, bread was used to initiate fermentation in alcohol. When it was discovered that Hop-leavened bread could significantly increase the alcohol content of a fermented beverage the hop beer industry was born. Two chemicals provide a spicy note—farnescene and myrcene.

In the garden today, the Hop is an unbeatable ground cover. One seed planted in late spring will eventually cover about 50 sq. ft. The Hop should also be grown and featured alone as a climbing plant. It will easily scale anything in its path, although a bare concrete wall is somewhat of a barrier. In the rockery, control it by planting only enough plants to cover a designated area in a single year. Although it generally branches, it should be forced to do so with a machete or pruning shears. Poor soil will slow its growth, but essentially it is a superb ground cover for areas such as this, where a low cover is needed quickly. In the contemporary landscape, the Hop is a good ground cover for service areas to beautify a refuse can collection, coal bin, wood shed, a fence around a well house, along an entrance walk, or for a garden without grass. Although it does not handle foot traffic it grows quickly enough to regrow after minor damage from an occasional stroll through a patch. For the landscape without a lawn, the Hop has advantages that no inert fill such as bark or rock can match—reducing heat buildup around the home. A living ground cover reduces the air temperature 10°F or more, as compared to soil or most inorganic ornamental materials.

In Northerly latitudes it is often grown as an annual although plants can live and produce hops (the female flowers) for up to 10 yrs. The species *H. lupulus* is the most hardy and is an herbaceous perennial to about Zone 5. An extraordinary species, Variegated Hop, *H. japonica* var. *variegata* has enormous, maple-like leaves to 10 in. wide that are lime-green splashed with white. No two are alike.

Hop tea is an effective medicinal treatment for sore throats and by virtue of its antibiotic activity can cure Strep throat. It is generally combined with other throat remedies and strongly flavored since it has an astringent and strongly bitter taste.

Hop vines are often woven into arrangements. Their white, fluffy, cone-shaped flowers and fan-like leaves are an interesting counterpart to solid forms such as Cattail and Teasel. The variegated variety provides more contrast since its flowers are often pink and its vine red, not to mention the spatter-painted leaves, for the ultimate in a contrasting effect. They are easy to grow and have few pests.

There is a strange, but entertaining genus of the *Umbelliferae* family, *Ferula*. Of most interest are Common Giant Fennel, *Ferula communis,* and Asafetida, *Ferula assa-foetida.* "Giant" is certainly apropos since they both resemble a 12–15 ft. Fennel plant. The stalk, like Bamboo, may be over 2 in. in diameter. As such, they are definitely eye-catching, if not imposing herbs. These herbaceous perennials grow much less gargantuan as annuals, forming handsome dark green bushes early in the spring, resembling huge, glossy green piles of fishing line. Their foliage has a pleasant Dill/Fennel odor.

Asafetida is used medicinally and in the kitchen. When the plant is 2–3 years old the flowering stalk is cut off at the ground in early summer. The sap emerging from the stump is collected, dried, and rolled into balls. It has a spicy, garlic and vanilla odor and among other uses, is incorporated into Worcestershire sauce. This sap contains disulfides with pesticidal properties. It has been used to repel garden varmints such as rabbits and deer, and is used by veterinarians to prevent bandage chewing.

In the contemporary landscape, let Giant Fennel be itself, perhaps encircled by another tall herb such as the Marshmallow, *Althea officinalis,* Hollyhocks, Lupines, Delphiniums, Yucca or ornamental grasses.

Cardoon, *Cynara cardunculus,* is a relative of the Artichoke, *C. scolymus.* Both belong to the thistle family although Cardoon is one of the largest and certainly the most ornamental of all, growing into a silvery, fern-like plant, with leaf stalks 2–4 ft. long. The upper part of the stalk is thick and fans out, resembling a large, grey Dandelion leaf. The leaf margins of French Cardoon have tiny, ½–1 in. needles that are wicked looking. The spineless form is more popular in the kitchen garden for obvious reasons.

Cardoon's satiny, silver-blue, thistle-like leaves make a choice contrast in contemporary gardens, growing with Himalayan Poppies, Kniphofia, and surrounded by a carpet of 6–10 in. wildflowers. It can also be used as a major vertical component in an arrangement of low rotund evergreens, neatly trimmed for maximum contrast. A procession of 'Moonshine' or 'Fireking' Yarrow and 'Opal' Basil winnowing in and out among the plants adds color and charm.

Used ornamentally in the kitchen garden, a group of Cardoon should be the central feature, surrounded by purple cabbage and peppers. In either a kitchen or contemporary landscape, Cardoon is a fascinating screen which combines well with tall-spiked flowers, particularly Clary and Delphiniums. Ornamental plants with large, dark green leaves make a striking contrast with the large, silvery leaves of Cardoon. In any garden where Cardoon will be used as a screen it should be accompanied by Fennel and purple Okra for an extremely entertaining and beneficial border.

When grown as a culinary staple, Cardoon is treated like Celery; that is bound and wrapped with black plastic or burlap to blanch stems for better flavor and crispness. It should be planted in rills, or shallow troughs, for more efficient watering and to assist in banking earth up around the main stalk as it grows. Its large, purple flowers are displayed in a hair-raising shock of petals atop a globe-shaped bud. The buds resemble, and are eaten like, an Artichoke. The Artichoke is essentially a step beyond Cardoon in that most of the herb's vegetative production, and hence the culinary attraction, has been confined to the bud. It is also a unique and handsome herb for the contemporary kitchen garden. Cardoon requires full sun and a rich loam for the finest flavor, but it will grow virtually anywhere there is sufficient moisture. Poor soils or limited water reduce its normal 5–6 ft. height to 3–4.

For wild gardens, Cardoon's erect silvery stature is a bold vertical component in a setting with Tansy, Lupine, Poppies, Valerian and Yarrow.

The Monardas are an enjoyable and rewarding ornamental genus of herbs. Their variously scented foliage and brightly colored, spider-like flowers are two excellent reasons for growing this handsome native American herb. The *Monarda* genus encompasses such delightful herbs as Lemon Mint, Oswego Tea, Horse Mint, Mountain Balm, Wild Bergamot and Bee Balm. The herb sold as Mountain Mint is not *Monarda* but from the closely related genus, *Monardella*.

The major species of concern is *M. didyma,* Oswego Tea or Bee Balm. This herb was originally popular among early American colonists as a tea substitute. The leaves are often wilted and fermented for varying periods before being brewed as a hot beverage. There are at least a dozen cultivars in various hues of red, including 'Cambridge Scarlet', 'Violet Queen', 'Salmonea', 'Mahogany', 'Alba' and a dwarf form, 'Granite Pink' growing to only 10 in. Many of the cultivars available may belong to *M. × media* which is a hybrid of *M. clinopodia, M. didyma* and *M. fistulosa.* The hybridization has been only to the benefit of gardeners. Monarda is one of the most ravishingly beautiful flowers in the herb world.

The flowers of *M. didyma* are about 2, but often 3, in. wide in rich, moist soils and sunny spots. It grows to 4 ft. in a nettle-like fashion. Its 4 in. long, serrated leaves are pleasantly aromatic; a mixture of herbaceous, spicy and camphoraceous scents. Its fragrance and flavor is the result of the chemicals thymol (of which *Monarda didyma* is a commercial source) and the oregano-scented carvacrol. Its spicy notes come from eucalyptol and cymene. Frequently a small flower appears out of the top of the one below. Such is the habit of many herbs of the Mint family—repeated vertilicasters—but not with the show of these uninhibited, crimson spiders, one atop the other.

The tea of this herb is mildly stimulating. For a hot beverage it should be mixed with some Lemon Balm or Camomile. Honey should not be used as a sweetener as it spoils the mild flavor of the tea, particularly the apple aroma of Camomile.

The Monardas may be cut back early to force a low, bushy growth. Every three to four years they must be divided and replanted. No shade and plenty of water are required for the best and most fragrant flowering. The better the quality of the flower, the more useful as a coloring agent, both in culinary applications and in cosmetics. Popular with American Indians, Bee Balm was highly regarded as a cosmetic herb, the flowers used on the face and skin as a rubefacient. The leaves were woven as bracelets and worn on the arms and legs, symbolic of age and status as well as in a practical fashion as a deodorant. From the diary of John McCowan comes this description of his meeting in 1872 with an Indian brave. "A handsome brave came first, with the painted tin horse hanging down from his neck to his naked bronze breast, skunk fur around his ankles, hawk's feathers on his head, and a great bunch of sweet smelling Monarda on one arm to set him off the more." The Blackfeet called this flower "Young Man".

Wild Bergamot, *M. fistulosa,* resembles Bee Balm in most respects, but its leaves are often hairy and the flower is usually lavender. *M. fistulosa* f. *albescens* has a white flower and a variety, *M. f.* var. *menthefolia,* spicy scented leaves.

Dotted Mint or Horse Mint, *M. punctata,* is shorter, growing to 3 feet, and much branched. Its repeated vertilicasters have led to a less frequently used common name, Twin Flower, recalling the superimposition of 2 or more spidery flowers arising one out of the other, much as in *M. didyma,* though more regular. They are small, 1¼ in. yellow flowers spotted with purple. Horse Mint is a hardy species, tolerant of dry, sandy soils.

A species sold as Lemon Mint is really Western Balm, *Monardella odoratissima.* Both are named for their strong citrus scents. Western Balm, or Mountain Mint, is an 18–24 in. perennial forming a densely branching mound of small, slightly pubescent leaves and large 2 in. rose flowers. It is a very hardy Western U.S. native. Its small, 18 in. compact habit makes it an especially ornamental Monarda in herbaceous perennial borders. The leaves are strongly aromatic and make a good, citrus-flavored tea. Lemon Mint is more properly the annual, often biennial, *Monarda citriodora,* with pink flowers spotted purple. It is rarely available, Western Balm being substituted, which has a more ornamental value in any case.

The genus *Monardella* contains another ornamental species that is often offered as *Monarda*. Coyote Mint, *M. villosa*, is an 18 in. hardy perennial with a decumbent habit, akin to the creeping Thymes. The stems hug the ground, rising only at the tips. It forms a dense ground cover displaying many small 1 in. rose-purple flowers throughout the summer into fall. It is also a Western U.S. native.

In the contemporary garden, the taller Monardas are excellent for features or borders in partial shade. They are enhanced by a ground cover of Columbine, Primroses, Sweet Cicely and small ferns. Also in the contemporary setting make a small corner garden featuring Monarda, Elecampane and a front border of German Camomile backed by tall spiked flowers such as white Delphiniums or Hollyhocks.

The Giant Hyssops, *Agastache* spp., are an enjoyable group of herbs from the Mint family. They all closely resemble the Mints, with an especially ornamental, fragrant flower spike and aromatic leaves that give off a minty or spicy and herbaceous odor. Pulegone and menthone are two mint-scented chemicals common in the Giant Hyssops. They make fine teas and good ornamental herbs in herbaceous perennial borders.

Korean Mint, or Wrinkled Giant Hyssop, *A. rugosa*, and Anise-Hyssop, *A. foeniculum*, are the most ornamental and fragrant. Anise Hyssop, also called Blue Giant Hyssop, has an exceptionally fragrant foliage and can be distinguished from substitutions based on that characteristic. Substitutions include the common native American species Purple Giant Hyssop, *A. scrophulariifolia* and Nettle-Leaf Giant Hyssop, *A. urticifolia*.

In the landscape the *Agastache* should be clumped in small groups of 3–6 plants. Do not surround them with tall materials that will hide their handsome shape. Well-spaced plants spread outward to 18 in. and become relatively dense, particularly if pruned in early summer. A 3–4 in. pink or purple spike graces the plant for 2 months or more to make a remarkable display. The flower spike is dense and firm and keeps its color and fragrance on drying.

Combine *Agastache* with light green or grey herbs such as ground covers of Wooly Betony, Santolina, yellow-green Junipers, Silver Thyme or Wooly Lavender. An enticing display for a small garden might include 2 clumps, each containing 5 plants of Korean Mint, 1 of Shasta Daisy, 3 Dwarf Feverfew, and a smattering of deep blue Pansies. The gaily blooming patch is a spot of summer color year after year.

Full sun and rich soil are required for best flavor and fragrance, but *Agastache* will grow in any soil and in partial shade. They are a favorite plant of the bees and hummingbirds. A few species of Giant Hyssop are grown commercially to produce honey. These include *A. mexicana*, or Mexican Giant Hyssop, to 2 ft. with showy red flowers, and *A. cana*, Mosquito Plant, with large pink flowers that bloom for a long period of time.

A popular herb that must be grown in containers throughout most of the northern latitudes is Sweet Bay, *Laurus nobilis*. Sweet Bay is most widely cultivated for its culinary value. Although Bay is a tree, it may grow as a multi-branched shrub, especially if it has been frozen back once or twice. Temperatures below 28°F will damage youthful growth, but only extended freezing of the ground will kill it. As a potted herb the bushy habit is considerably more ornamental and provides more leaf area than otherwise possible. The sweet, spicy notes so cherished are captured only by a mid-to-late-summer harvest when the levels of Bay's aromatic chemicals are peaking.

Sweet Bay leaves are thick and tough and can take considerable abuse in high traffic areas where its fragrant pine-green leaves may flaunt themselves on paths and porches near sitting benches. It was once a popular topiary medium because of its quick regrowth and dense habit after pruning. The species is often called Grecian Laurel, but the two other types of Bay are atypical and more ornamental. A sweet and exceptionally fragrant Sweet Bay is the forma *angustifolius* or narrow-leaved Bay. The forma *crispa* has crinkled leaves which are large and dark green and have an undulating margin for an entertaining appearance. The narrow-leaved form is hardier and significantly more valuable in the kitchen.

In the contemporary landscape, Sweet Bay may be planted out in the garden for the summer and then repotted in late summer, to be brought indoors for the winter. If care is taken to assure its survival each fall it makes a beautiful, brilliant green standard. When trimmed, Sweet Bay should be joined with other low-growing trimmed herbs such as Thyme, Germander and Santolina in a very small garden. Sweet Bay is often trimmed as a formal hedge in southerly climates and can become a large tree from 20–40 ft.

Sweet Bay is a popular aromatic herb used as part of a fragrant wreath or Yule log for the fireplace. The soothing, spicy aroma of Bay, composed of eucalyptol, eugenol and methylchavicol, permeates the room. Bay is also used as a flavoring, particularly in meat dishes and commercially in baked goods. The berries are edible and quite sweet and are used to flavor soft drinks; however, it rarely flowers or sets fruit in northerly climates.

A culinary substitute for Sweet Bay is Oregon Myrtle or California Laurel, *Umbellularia californica* (not to be confused with *Myrica californica*, California Wax Myrtle). It is a handsome, slow-growing, broad-leaved evergreen tree. In the landscape it takes on a shrubbery form with a summer treat of white flowers. The leaf is several times the size of Sweet Bay and is of a stronger, more camphoraceous aroma. California Laurel is used in dishes exactly as the legendary Sweet Bay but sparingly as it is stronger. The berries have a bitter, minty taste when green and in fact contain a fair amount of menthol. The chemical umbellulone gives the foliage its strong camphoraceous note.

Lemon Verbena, *Aloysia triphylla,* is another herb that should be grown in a tub or ornamental container in cold climates and brought indoors for the winter. It is valued for its pleasant lemon fragrance and profusion of lemon scented flowers. It is truly a wondrous herb. Its fresh lemon scent is so pure the tongue is deceived into a sensation of tartness. In a tea its lemony contribution is welcome and possibly superior to lemon juice due to the absence of acidity. Lemon Verbena does not discolor a black tea as does lemon juice, and yet adds a strong lemon flavor and aroma. The chemical contributions from its oil to flavor and scent include citral, myrcene and citronellal.

Lemon Verbena leaves should be dried carefully. They rapidly lose their fragrance if dried quickly and with much heat. It is best to freeze them to retain the natural flavor. They can be preserved for a short time in sugar or an alcohol solution for culinary uses and in almond oil, wax or lard for cosmetic applications, simply to add a pleasant lemon fragrance to products. As it is essentially an evergreen in tropical climates it can be enjoyed year-round if nurtured in a greenhouse during the winter. To maintain it through northern winters it must be grown in a greenhouse at 55–60°F. Water, fertilizer and misting should be continued frequently. At mid-point of winter prune to 6–8 in. and decrease maintenance until early spring. Cuttings are taken from spring growth and can put on 18–24 in. of growth in one season, so prune repeatedly for a dense vigorous habit that is more useful in an ornamental garden.

There are a number of useful species in the *Lippia* genus which are related to Lemon Verbena and are categorically called the Verbenas: Licorice Verbena, *L. alba,* is a glossy green, anise- and vanilla-scented herb; Mexican Oregano, *L. graveolens* and *L. origanoides,* both strongly scented by the chemical carvacrol; Sweet Herb, *L. dulcis,* an exceedingly sweet herb popular for centuries in Central America; and dozens of others with fragrant leaves and decorative flowers from cream to purple. They will not generally survive a cold snap below 30°F but are easily planted back into the garden each spring after being sheltered indoors for the winter. They are all shrubs, and should be pruned heavily before being brought indoors and kept dry through the winter. Some may be deciduous.

In the contemporary landscape, the Verbenas may be used as a fragrant centerpiece in a small garden with other fragrant plants, particularly the Scented Geraniums, Basils and Sages, for a delightfully fragrant garden. Keep them accessible for caressing in areas where entertaining or a considerable amount of foot traffic occurs and wandering hands are commonplace. In southerly climates it may attain 8–10 ft. though it is best to trim it into a 3–4 ft. hedge surrounding patios and along entrance walks or as a centerpiece in a courtyard near a doorway or sitting area.

The flower of Lemon Verbena is cream-colored and deliciously fragrant, unequalled for adding both sweetness and lemon tang in a good orange pekoe tea. Other Verbenas have lavender flowers with exotic sweet and spicy scents. Their secret is not preservable except by freezing so enjoy their simple beauty.

Note: Many tropical plants have not undergone the scrutiny of Old World herbs and have been less clearly defined. Presently, Lemon Verbena is most often classified as being within the *Aloysia* genus. Older references place it in the *Lippia* genus. *Lippia alba* and *L. origanoides* have also been classified within the *Lantana* genus, a group of popular and highly fragrant houseplants.

Chapter 6 / SECTION 3

A Walk Through a Contemporary Garden

The contemporary landscape we will visit belongs to a large family. (Fig. 49) The yard is designed to meet a variety of expectations. An enormous sandbox provides the 3–12 year old crowd with ample entertainment: enough sand for the largest castles possible, a swing set, picnic table and tether ball pad. The lawn is petite, just right for the teenagers to soak up the sun and mowed close enough for Dad to get in his putting practice. The brick patio is spacious and partly covered. It plays a role in entertaining not only friends but also business associates. The greenhouse is Mom's, and off-limits to all but her garden club cohorts. The kitchen garden is a conspiracy, a vegetable patch turned entertainer, with color and texture and charm all its own. This landscape paints a significant contemporary picture.

We enter this contemporary domain by the side entrance passing through a side yard that has been designed as a miniature basketball court (See Fig. 47). The ground cover is exclusively Wooly Betony. A few conifers and a large sweet-smelling Lavender imbues this site with a rugged, wild feeling.

The great, grey, board gate opens and a peaceful land lays beyond. Through the branches of a dwarf apple tree we can see a most beautiful kitchen garden. A hedge of golden down catches our eye in an instant. This telltale sign of fall is a back border of Asparagus which has turned and its autumn color is a dazzling backdrop to knobby-kneed Brussel Sprouts and a few remaining Artichokes with their delicious tophats gone to fluff. Parchment brown shocks of corn, countless scarlet fingers of Cayennes hanging from frost blackened bushes, and swollen purple cabbages also decorate this garden, a feature garden of vegetables.

As we move into the yard over a sun-warmed ground cover of red-brown bark, pastel-green clumps of fresh herbs are evident beneath each of the fruit trees. Like one another, yet not, they are Sweet Cicely and Chervil, and likely they will remain green for weeks to come, succumbing only to heavy snow. Their anise foliage provides sweetness in a long list of dishes that can be enjoyed almost all year.

The feathery, bronze figure of a clump of Red Fennel can be seen hiding behind the tree. Our host tells us that in summer it is only the centerpiece for a trio of purple herbs, which included to its left a circle of Purple Okra, which grew to almost 7 ft. and aside from lemon-yellow trumpets their enormous 6–8 in. pods are a special treat in Gumbos. On the right was a double row of Opal Basil bordering the lawn releasing a clove and citrus fragrance on hot afternoons.

Across the lawn is a vermillion hedge of autumn-dressed Blueberries jutting out

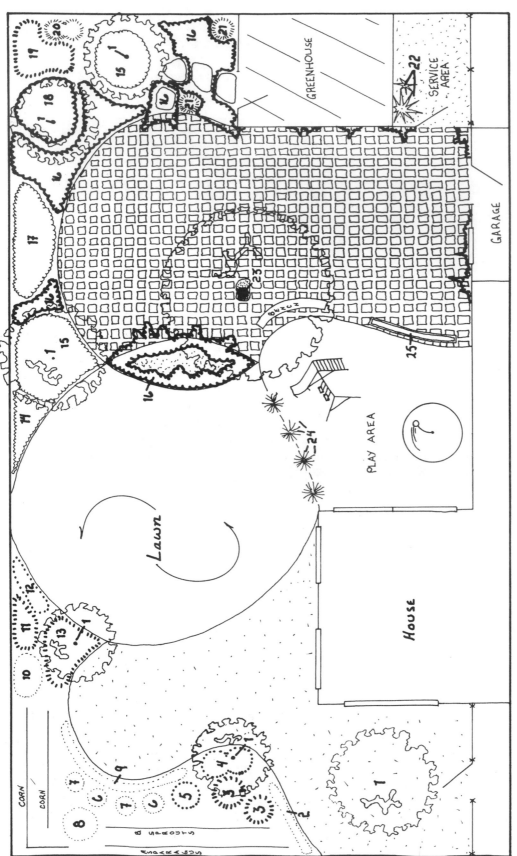

Fig. 49. The contemporary homesite—a valuable recreational facility that fulfills the basic needs of all the family members in many ways. Coordinating these needs into a landscape can be a challenge.

KEY
1 Dwarf Apple *Malus*
2 Ruby Chard
3 Lovage *Levisticum officinale*
4 Chervil *Anthriscus cerefolium*
5 *Calendula officinale*
6 Red Cabbage *Brassica oleracea* var. *rubra*
7 Red Pepper *Capsicum*
8 Scarlet Runner Beans *Phaseolus* spp.

9 Lettuce *Lactuea* spp.
10 Purple Okra
11 Red Fennel *Foeniculum vulgare* 'Rubrum'
12 Opal Basil *Ocimum basilicum* 'Dark Opal'
13 Sweet Cicely *Myrrhis odorata*
14 Hops, Variegated *Humulus japonica* var.
15 Wild Ginger *Asarum hartwegii*
16 Caraway Thyme *Thymus herba-barona*
17 Strawberry *Fragaria* spp.

18 Violets *Viola* spp.
19 Pineapple Mint *Mentha suaveolens*
20 Shasta Daisy *Chrysanthemum maximum*
21 Ornamental Grass *Festuca ovina*
22 Arborvitae *Thuya occidentalis*
23 Japanese Walnut *Juglans seiboldiana*
24 Blueberry *Vaccinium corymbosum*
25 planter, annuals

from the corner of the house to intercept an amber-yellow Walnut that is just now shedding its spiny capsules of sweetmeats. The chocolate-brown paving of the patio is such a complementary color it is evident it was chosen to emphasize the autumn colors around us.

Creeping Golden Thyme, its minute pine-green foliage with swatches of rich yellow, decorates the entrance way to this entertainment area. Bright red berries of espaliered Pyracanthas, scarlet and white berries of Wintergreen, juicy, blood-red fruits of everbearing Strawberries all combine in a small but breathtaking scene.

The enormous white-stained, maple-like leaves of a Variegated Hops run along the fence in the recesses behind the trees, while cream-spotted patches of Pineapple Mint frolic at its feet. A few white and gold Violets, Anemones and other fall flowers poke their shy heads skyward under the cover of the dwarf apples.

Creeping Thymes and Creme-de-Menthe Mint scamper everywhere on this patio unfettered by a gardener's demands and seemingly unaffected by feet. Their verdant hues are a vivid, provocative contrast to the chocolate brick beneath them.

A wafer-thin veil of dark green creeping Thyme has overflowed some stepping stones, revealing little of the path to the greenhouse. It is enough however to lure anyone along. On this cold autumn afternoon, spying on the herbs within is not possible as the panes are fogged with condensation. Our host glides up beside us and between nervous glances over his shoulder he draws the door ajar for us to see inside. A fragrant rush of humid air tickles our chilly nose and recipes dash through our minds as we take tally of the herbs within: Sweet Basil, Marjoram, Parsley and Summer Savory revel in beds, their feet warmed by cables of heat. So too are Rosemary, Lemon Verbena, Blue Sage and two exotic Lavenders, French and Spanish, lounging in cedar tubs awaiting their cues to entertain guests either in the house or on the patio when weather permits. Other ornamentals and houseplants share the confines of this small but ample greenhouse.

As we depart it is evident again from a single glance across the yard that fall is not forgotten in this landscape and indeed it is plainly part of the scheme. What of the other seasons? Perhaps we will return in the spring to see for ourselves what is revealed.

Chapter 7 / SECTION 1

The Wild Landscape

In late spring or early summer, millions of pilgrims venture to the mountains and secluded valleys of the wilderness to witness one of nature's greatest wonders—wildflowers. In an endless procession, these insignificant herbs emerge and bloom in boundless profusion, to the awe and delight of everyone. Rare is the heart without envy for, as any homeowner or gardener knows, wildflowers are fickle worts, bowing to no man's fancy.

The wild garden, one with an endless display of flowers and gay foliages throughout most of the growing season, is the most difficult landscape to design and maintain. This is so because the natural forces that govern where and how plants grow are complex. In our tiny little lots, the power of these laws suddenly become evident. What we desire and can offer is all too frequently incompatible with natural rules.

The solution is for the gardener to be more thoroughly knowledgeable of the needs and niches of hundreds of plants. These are not herbs to be sown and abandoned to the unnatural circumstances surrounding man's houses. Because the garden is by no means a natural thing, it is not uncommon for Mother Nature's laws to be carelessly avoided or misapplied. Limitations of space, moisture levels, soil constituents, light exposures, the length of the annual growth cycle, temperature, winds, and on and on must be fine-tuned to prevent death. In most cases, we can circumvent disaster through knowledge and with extended care. Because the wild garden is a rapidly evolving, highly competitive and complex community with which to work, this care cannot be remedial or after the fact, but rather academic and preventative. Our understanding and knowledge must be deep and broad enough that we are capable of seeing the trouble spots where nature's power diminishes our vision of wilderness.

To provide a starting point let us think of a natural garden, one that is designed according to the principles of permaculture. Here, many of the plants and their relationships in the landscape are indigenous or adventitious. They have grown so long in the area to become naturalized. This strong, natural component in the design is appealing because there is no sudden boundary separating the garden and the home in it from the real world. But this does not suggest simply letting the wild things at the margins in and leaving them alone. This is after all a human habitation and must be organized—designed—with the needs, wishes, and hopes of its inhabitants in mind. So selection of plants and their placement relative to one another requires the intervention of the inhabitant's mind and hand. From this intervention unique elements can be incorporated to create garden features.

On the other hand, a wild garden is an imaginary meadow, a richly robed reproduction of a refuge found once in a wilderness far, far away, living now in the mind of the gardener.

In essence, the wild garden takes its cues from the informal landscape. The mead and quiet zones within the forest and its deep herbaceous borders are excerpted from the informal picture and are drawn with a new and different emphasis into a setting where they are dominant features. Naturalized wildflowers, bulbs, and herbs dominate the landscape. The forest is only suggested and lawns are limited to scattered patches of ornamental grass or herb-choked stone walks.

The wild landscape becomes an enchanted mead suitable for inner reflection and a serene abode not found in other landscape forms. Sitting on a tuffet among waist or shoulder high flowers banishes all thoughts of the corporeal world from the mind. Amidst a thicket of flowers, extravagant alien colors, and all fashion of flowers and foliages, we can expect to meet, if not come to terms with, life's underlying meaning. This is a place where we are at ease, entering into conversation with ourselves and with nature.

Many centuries ago, cloistered monks used this same garden, dedicated to silence and prayer. If this garden was large it was called a "Field of Paradise", if it was small, the "Hortus Conclusus", a minute garden designed expressly as the place for meditation. (Fig. 50)

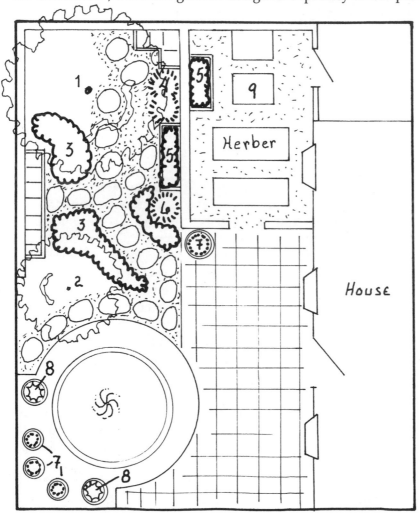

KEY
1 Elm *Ulmus*
2 Golden Rain Tree *Laburnum anagyroides*
3 Violets *Viola* spp.
4 Valerian *Valeriana officinalis*
5 Caraway Thyme *Thymus herba-barona*
6 Variegated Lemon Balm *Melissa officinalis* var. *variegata*
7 potted fragrant annuals
8 Rosemary standard *Rosmarinus officinalis*
9 Herber

Fig. 50. For the metropolitan garden two ancient wild designs hark from the Dark Ages. The enclosed garden filled with flowering plants galore is the Hortus Conclusus (see Fig. 12) and the open garden drawing nigh to the patio contains many wildflowers and bulbs and is called the Field of Paradise. Both follow in the monastic tradition, the former a place of solitude where the flowers for the altar and celebrations were cultivated and the latter a place for tranquil strolling or lounging.

Encompassed by trellises of twining espaliered herbs such as Blackberry, Rose, Grape, Honeysuckle, Hop, and Jasmine, the Hortus Conclusus was a secluded spot from which the herbs and flowers necessary for altar decorations and celebrations were derived. Indeed a celebration is the perfect description of a wild garden.

So how do we create this unworldly world? The natural laws must not be flagrantly violated. When we do break them, two forces must intervene to keep chaos at bay: knowledge that we have broken the law, and therefore, what we must do to compensate, and physical effort.

To understand wild garden design we must first understand the wilderness environments where wildflowers are the predominant flora: temperate and alpine meadows and forest glades.

The temperate meadow (Fig. 51) is home to the robust herbaceous perennials of tall

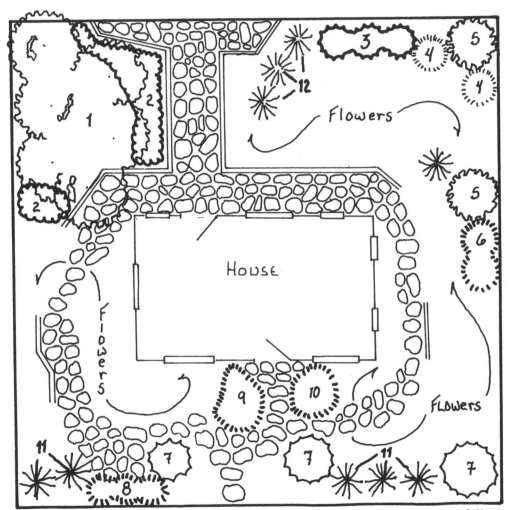

Fig. 51. The temperate meadow is an exciting medium for the wild landscape full of herbaceous perennials of tall rangy or spreading habits and small trees and shrubs. The semi-walkway and wall are reminiscent of aged paths, conveying timelessness yet contributing to the form of the design.

KEY 1 Chinquapin *Castanea pumila*
2 Violets, Primroses
3 Sage *Salvia officinalis*
4 Maltese Cross *Lychnis chalcedonica*
5 *Viburnum fragrans*
6 *Valeriana officinalis*
7 Oregon Grape *Mahonia aquifolium*
8 Lovage *Levisticum officinale*
9 Orange Mint *Mentha* × *piperita* var. *citrata*
10 Black Mint *Mentha* × *piperita* var. *vulgaris*
11 Roses
12 Buckthorn *Ceanothus americanus*

dense habit. Evergreens are not uncommon here. Because water and nutrients are not limited, many species can compete even though patterns change from year to year as one species overtakes another. Red, yellow, and white are the predominant colors and daisies, plumes and spikes, are the more common flower arrays. The temperate meadow requires a sloping or uneven terrain. It may be divided by a stream either real or abstract as in a dry bed. A pond or rock outcrop provides the basis for a feature garden and widely different plant types.

The alpine meadow (Fig. 53) should feature a limited number of dwarf or low plants, to 12 in., scattered in equally distributed groupings with taller, medium height evergreens as the background. On mountain slopes, evergreens act as microclimate modifiers, abating winds and therefore, the chill factor; they hold top soil and therefore, moisture. They must be the background from which the meadow originates and flows into the homesite. Rocks are common, either as outcrops, protruding abruptly from the ground, with little or no soil at the sides to cover or soften their strong vertical lines, or as stone fields, rocks littered over the surface in a random, runaway fashion. Alpine gardens may contain grasses or none at all, being defined instead by scree, loose rock chips in irregular heaps, characteristic of landslide materials. They are often terraced on steep slopes or narrow valleys and littered with mounds of large rocks.

Woodland wildflowers are the embodiment of the Sylvans, legendary beings of enchanted forests. Flower-filled glades are transformed into a grand arena of sprightly music and dance at the touch of the waxing moon on a clear night. Mists and underbrush, of course, prevent our viewing these events. We can prepare for it by sowing an assortment of sylvan seeds; herbs such as Violets, Wood Sorrel, Camomile, Pansies, Creeping Thyme, Corsican Mint, Saffron, and Dwarf Monarda, and weeds such as Miner's Lettuce, Foamflower, Mallows, Solomon Seal, Buttercup, Blazing Star, Anemone, and wildflowers by the hundreds.

Sylvan wildflowers should be ankle or knee deep, and as thickly set as possible. Deciduous or evergreen backgrounds of small trees and shrubbery (copse) or a thicket of medium-sized trees (spinney) are recommended. Some flowers must overflow into the forest and the garden should be interrupted by a stream bed, whether real or false, which doubles as the site of a pathway. For the most part, sylvan flowers are shade tolerant and enjoy the filtered shade beneath widely spaced deciduous trees. Herbs and wildflowers able to grow in partial shade to full sun may be used as long as sufficient sunlight is made available. Because the garden itself can be perceived as an open and gloriously sunny glade, surrounded on the periphery by trees, plants requiring full sun can be enjoyed. (Fig. 52). Rich soils and moisture make the woodland meadow a thriving world for every imaginable wildflower.

There are four features to consider in designing a wild garden: rocks, trees, water, and topography. Rocks are used to break monotony, add feature gardens, or provide access, such as with a path. They may be a memory of more than a score of geologic features, scree, outcrops, tallus, glacial deposits, or man-made features such as walls, cairns, and ruins. Trees provide balance, shade, and perspective; i.e., making a scene appear closer at hand or farther away than it actually is. Water is soothing and imparts peacefulness but provides humidity, water for irrigation, and in the case of a stream bed an access route. Topography is the lay of the land: rolling, steep, rugged, or flat.

The meadow is a rapidly evolving environment that is home to many kinds of flowers, vines, dwarf trees, shrubs, and grasses. It is a total picture we wish to design, not just put in plants. Many evergreen shrubs are unsurpassed for year-round beauty, such as Azaleas and Oregon Grape. Small ornamental trees, including Mountain Ash and Conifers, are useful. Vines such as Jasmine and Grape are easily naturalized over exposed rocks and

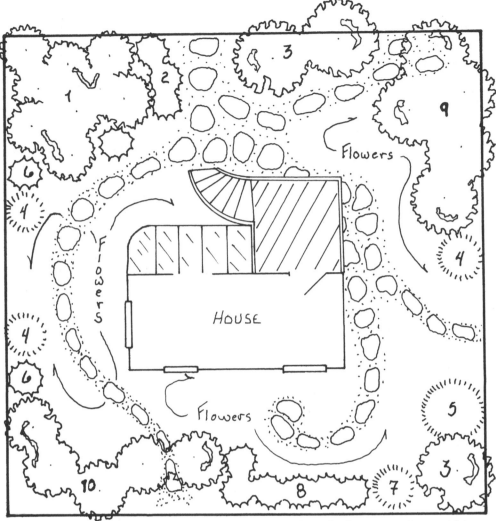

Fig. 52. The open glade, fashioned after the sun drenched retreats deep within a forest, is seemingly surrounded by small trees and large shrubs, in a sense isolated. A drybed path provides accesss and contributes to the natural artistry of the landscape but is far from lifcless and home to creeping herbs and clumps of ornamental grasses.

KEY
1 Mtn. Ash *Sorbus sargentiana*
2 Southernwood *Artemisia abrotanum*
3 Flowering Cherry *Prunus triloba* 'Flore pleno'
4 *Valeriana officinalis*
5 Bee Balm *Monarda didyma*
6 Variegated Holly *Ilex aquifolium* 'Golden Queen'
7 Meadow Rue *Thallictum aquilegifolium*
8 'Puget Blue' Buckthorn *Ceanothus imperssus*
9 *Viburnum fragrans*
10 Lilacs *Syringa vulgaris*

along walls where naturally occuring weeds such as Bryony, Morning Glory, or brambles thrive. And finally, grasses. Most of what we see immediately is grass, Field Grass or Canary Grass and countless others that compete vigorously for limited space. Ornamental grasses must be substituted in our gardens. Their visual effect far surpasses ordinary grass and the challenge of incessant weeding is less likely to become a torture so we can more enjoy the product of our toil. Grasses do not produce more seed than any other plant but they are remarkably fertile and grow rapidly to maturity, so choose the most ornamental: Fescue, *Phalaris*, Zebra Grass, Quaking Grass, Cloud Grass, etc. Many are useful decorative materials and provide winter forage for birds. A well-balanced wild garden will preferentially draw meadow birds to it because familiar foods are available. In the garden a variety of grasses and herbs with large and small seeds will attract more species of birds than an excess of any one type. Determine your local species of birds and plant to their needs if you wish to attract them.

Both perennial and annual herbs are found in meadows. Most early spring flowers are perennials while a large number of the summer-blooming plants are annuals, which continue to germinate until the first frost. Herbs blooming in the late summer or early fall, surviving the frosts and even gentle snowfalls, are predominantly perennials.

All of these assembled plants provide a plethora of textures and habits but they do not appear in nature in a random fashion, growing whenever their seed is given life, nor should they in our gardens. Each plant species occupies a specific "niche". In ecological terms, a "niche" can be defined as the role played by a specific plant type within its immediate surroundings. Tall herbs tend to accumulate more tall species around them because they deprive lower plants of sunlight. Only a tall herb can successfully compete. Evergreen shrubs are dense so they can keep other species from invading their territory. They tend to produce rounded mounds in regions of poor soil where only grasses or low herbs will grow. However, they are usually shade-tolerant so during their life any tall herbs or small trees successfully maturing beside them will not severely stress them. Meadow trees are fast growing, able to survive some shade during early years, when they might be overtaken by tall herbs, and many are able to produce their own nitrogen. Surround the garden with these and the meadow's edge is complete.

The textures created by these natural processes are fairly consistent over a period of time. We will find in any meadow an overall smooth appearance that flows gently into taller and taller herbs as well established clumps survive and push outward. There is little abruptness on a meadow. Tall plants should not jut unceremoniously from a low ground cover. Smooth transitions are important in the wild garden to accentuate contrasting colors and foliage textures.

The last matter of concern in the wild garden design is the manner in which plants propagate. The first realization that species of plants grew in drifts was derived from extensive studies of the natural meadow environment. Be sure to apply this principle to the arrangement of wildflowers. The drift emphasizes a downhill procession in the wild garden. It also recalls the directional dispersal of the plant type. Plant communities can move slowly, as old plants die, younger ones further ahead continue on while adjacent species move in. Thus the colony progresses, albeit slowly and erratically. For the same reason, a species will not always be spread uniformly throughout a meadow and will succeed better as a clump than as a lone plant. Meadow flowers are invariably found as clumps of a few to hundreds of the same species. How many clumps and where is governed by environmental restrictions—i.e., soil type, moisture or acidity—and is up to the gardener.

It is important to remember that water in the wild garden will imply to the well travelled visitor tall herbs and dense thickets. Meadow streams are rarely unobstructed unless soil is virtually absent, or the stream is intermittent so life cannot survive the summer months. A stream bed in a wild garden must reflect this natural pattern. If it is to be used as a dry bed, a path and access way, it must be inhabited by low, hardy and possibly evergreen herbs. With water available, taller herbs will need to be nurtured there or nature will do it for you.

A number of tall and ungainly herbs are suited to the wild landscape. The majority are annuals. Three, Dill, Anise, and Cumin, are *Umbiliferae,* members of the Dill Family. Three others, Borage, Sesame, and Fennugreek are popular for their use as sprouts. The perennials include Mugwort, Elecampane, and Yarrow, three very decorative herbs. Another perennial, Lovage, has been a pot herb, valuable since antiquity. In one fashion or another, these herbs reveal themselves most satisfactorily in the wild garden.

KEY

1 Oregano Thyme *Thymus pulegioides* 'Oregano-scented'
2 Cr. Red Thyme *Thymus pulegioides* 'Kermesinus'
3 'White Magic' Thyme *Thymus pulegioides*
4 Dwarf Lavender *Lavandula angustifolia* 'Nana Atropurpurea'
5 Compact Lavender *Lavandula angustifolia* 'Compact'
6 *Santolina* 'Nana'
7 *Santolina neapolitana*
8 Heather *Erica* spp.
9 Silver/French/Gold Lemon Thyme
10 *Juniper horizontalis*
11 Redwood *Sequoia semperviren*
12 Azalea/Oregon Grape
13 Rhododendron
14 Primroses *Primula* spp.
15 Black Hellebore *Helleborus niger*
16 Violets/Creeping Charlie
17 Wild Ginger *Asarum canadense*
18 Pearlwort *Sagina procumbens*
19 Lady's Mantle *Alchemilla* spp.
20 Golden Oregano *Origanum vulgare* 'Aureum'
21 Corsican Mint *Mentha requeinii*
22 Golden Lemon Thyme *Thymus × citriodorus* 'Aureus'
23 Chive *Allium schoenoprasum*
24 Dwarf Sage *Salvia officinalis* 'Nana'
25 Golden Sage *Salvia officinalis* 'Aurea'
26 *Alliums*
27 'Rosea' Lavender *Lavandula angustifolia*
28 *Hyssopus officinalis*
29 Cr. Winter Savory *Satureja pilosa*
30 Lawn Camomile *Chamaemellum nobile* 'Trenague'
31 Daisy Garden
32 Avens/Pansies/Eng. Daisy/Coral Bells
33 Lupine/Alliums/Campanula
34 CA poppy/Alliums/Wildflowers
35 Chinese Lantern/Lupine/Nigella
36 Lupine/Foxglove/Everlasting

Fig. 53. The wild alpine retreat, like Fig. 35, is a stark contrast of basic elements. A few large trees and ravines of exposed rock shape the design. Tuffeted, mounded and creeping herbs and low evergreen shrubbery dominate the site for year round entertainment. Rivulets of flowers splash into every nook and cranny for that wild tousled look.

Chapter 7 / SECTION 2

Herbs for the Wild Landscape

The most commonly cultivated herb of the *Umbelliferae* is the family's namesake, Dill, *Anethum graveolens.* This rapidly growing, self-sowing annual is popular in the kitchen garden, where its use for pickling and seasoning is paramount. Yet beyond its utilitarian value, Dill's pungent, spicy aroma is a delightful addition in the wild garden to the many floral and aromatic scents that abound there. Dill provides a dilute pervasive odor that accentuates other spicy aromas from herbs such as Rosemary, Southernwood, Basil, Roses, Sweet Peas, and Mints. Many late-flowering fragrant annuals and perennial ornamentals are highlighted by the catchy familiar scent of dill. If a small patch is planted, it makes enough of a come-on to attract attention without spoiling the overall fragrance or the view.

In enriched garden soils with plenty of moisture, Dill rises from 3–5 ft., producing large fragrant umbels bearing the seeds that are vital components in pickling recipes. Under poor conditions, Dill should not be expected to exceed 12–18 in., and if planted late, bolts to seed, producing little foliage. The deep blue-green of Dill's feathery foliage is attractive in groupings of light green or silver foliaged plants.

In the wild garden, Dill should be composed into long sinuous drifts that wind among many isolated clumps of Day Lily, Yarrow, Artemisias, German Camomile and Poppies. Add as many tall ornamental fragrant flowers such as Carnations and Roses as needed, where their scents will collide in a pleasant fashion. On a hot summer day, or after a rainstorm, the refreshing pungency of Dill's familiar pickle aroma becomes a prevalent scent in the garden.

More than one type of Dill is available. Garden Dill, *Anethum graveolens,* is often sold in a reputedly dwarf form, which rarely performs as such in good gardens. This variety variously sold as 'Bouquet' or Dwarf still grows to 3 ft. under excellent circumstances. If a dwarf is desired, mid-summer sowing of seed will suffice to reduce the height of Dill. Indian Dill, *A. sowa,* is often desired for its more fragrant foliage and larger seeds. Both will self-sow with little assistance and may cross-pollinate with a few other *Umbelliferae,* occasionally losing both the fine fragrance and flavor. Wild, self-sown Dill is not always as flavorful as it is fit, therefore, save seed only from plants grown in ideal conditions, where cross species pollination does not occur. Dill, Fennel, Queen Anne's Lace, and other *Umbelliferae* all bloom about the same time and may potentially cross, with adverse results.

Dill is, of course, most popular in the kitchen garden. It may be grown as a tall back-border or screen or as a tall massed planting of at least 6–12 plants. It should be grown only in full sun in the best soils. In a dooryard garden or a garden used to cultivate herbs for ornamental purposes, Dill can be grown with Yarrow, Tansy, and Feverfew in a perimeter bed.

The foliage of Dill is excellent in soups and salads. Fresh green seed is also used. The sharp, concentrated Dill flavor needs getting used to, so seeds should be used sparingly. The name, Dilla, is from the old Norse, "to lull", and the seed is used in a nerve-calming tea famous as a sleepy-time drink for children. The seeds themselves may be used and mixed into a soft candy or peanut butter, or given in a spoonful of corn or maple syrup. Dillweed, as the foliage is called, is used in cooking fish and poultry, particularly in stuffings and sauces. For a tangy dip:

TANGY DIP

½ c. Dill weed
¼ clove Garlic (crushed)
1 Tbsp Lemon Basil butter
6–8 oz. sour cream or non-dairy
   dressing

Combine herbs and puree in blender, then fold into dressing. Allow 2–3 hours before using.

The lower leaves of Anise, *Pimpinella anisum,* like Coriander, are fanlike while the upper ones are divided and feathery. But while Coriander releases its fragrance from only a gentle touch, Anise is a treat only for the tongue. In full bloom, a large patch carries only a faint suggestion of its delicate flavor so cherished in cookies, cakes, and candies. The Anise cookie is a traditional favorite Christmas season gift, as is the liqueur, Anisette.

Anise is a quick-growing annual which has a longer ripening period than other *Umbelliferae* and requires hot weather to produce an abundance of seed. It grows from 12–18 in. high, although in northerly latitudes, when sown from seed, it rarely grows over 12 in. The plants are not sturdy and are susceptible to wind and heavy damage from rain.

In the wild garden, Anise should be tucked away in a thick drift between other herbs for protection. It can be used as a border and should be planted with a 6–8 in. spacing between plants to ensure a dense, uniform appearance. A kitchen garden is probably the best home for Anise, as it requires a very high quality soil and much care for weeding and protection from wind and rain.

The entire Anise plant is edible. The roots may be chopped into salads and vegetable dishes. The leaves are used fresh in rice and stir-fry cuisine and recommended in green salads and potato salads. The seeds may be eaten as a condiment before or after dinner or used in potato or lettuce salads, puddings, and desserts. Crushed green or dried seeds are extracted in any liqueur to add flavor. The strong extract is called Anisette and is added to other drinks or used over crushed ice or ice cream.

CHICKEN ORIENTAL

1 Tbsp. sesame oil

Add: 1 crushed Garlic clove
   1 Tbsp. crushed Anise seed

Fry thin strips from chicken breast and add:

1 Tbsp. Sherry
Sliced green and red peppers
Mushrooms
Slices of Caraway or Lovage root
1 tsp. Lovage
1 Tbsp. fresh chopped Parsley

Simmer ingredients to desired tenderness and serve with hot rice.

Anise seeds are equally enjoyable green (unripened) and may be harvested and frozen for future use. In short-season climates, it is difficult to thoroughly ripen Anise. Seeded directly into the garden it requires 4 or more months to ripen. In warm climates, rain just as the seeds ripen will ruin them. The green seeds and flowering tops and leaves are parts of the Anise plant that the grower of Anise should learn to use in cooking. They can be dropped into a sugar syrup and crystallized, made into sticks or patties, and then chocolate-covered.

Cumin, *Cuminum cyminum,* finds itself at home in a wild garden. Resembling Dill but growing only 12–18 in., it has white or pink flowers with a spicy odor to the foliage. Its spicy seed is cherished for taco and curry spice and is used in Central American and Indian cuisine.

As a culinary spice, Cumin imparts more odor than taste. The pungent camphoraceous odors of pinene, cymene, and dipentene are mellowed by heavy, spicy aromas of anisealdehyde and cuminal, which can create a sensation of taste from a deep whiff. These penetrating odors are allies to those of Chili powder, Coriander, Black Pepper, and Ginger, which are frequently combined in recipes because of their synergistic effect. Adding Fennugreek and Turmeric, we have the basic ingredients of curry powder. Children will love this recipe for a sweet taco meat that uses no sugar.

SWEET TACO MEAT

2 pounds hamburger
1 6 ounce can tomato paste
1 tsp. beef boullion
1 Tbsp. Cumin
1 Tbsp. Sweet Marjoram
1 Tbsp. Sweet Cicely
1 chopped green pepper
1 tsp. Lovage
6 cloves Garlic

Cumin is an expensive spice and is worth cultivating properly. It is grown as an annual and like Anise, requires a long, hot summer for ripening. It should be broadcast in thick rows or in drifts like Dill. It likes to be transplanted or sown into warm, 70°F soil. If started indoors, use a larger pot than for Dill as its longer growing season is often a result of an inadequate root system, the result of growing in a cool climate. Irrigating with water which has been held in containers will benefit since tap water can be 20 to 30°F below air/soil temperatures, essentially slowing the growth of Cumin. A row or patch of Cumin containing one dozen plants will yield, under good circumstances, more than enough seed. Less than 1 tsp. of seed is called for in most instances and a single plant will produce about 2 Tbsp. of seed. Unripened seed of Cumin often tastes like Caraway seed.

Black Cumin, *Nigella sativa,* or *Bunium persicum,* are spicy seeds used like Cumin. They have a sharp, peppery taste and odor with a hint of orange rind. The former is also called Roman Coriander or Black Caraway. Its seeds were once used as a condiment like Fennel and Caraway seed. Curries and hot, spicy S.E. Asian cuisine still employ this spice and its relative, Love-in-a-Mist, *N. damascena,* which has become an ornamental border flower. Experiment with this spice in taco meat, sparingly in stir-fry dishes or in a zippy vinegar and oil dressing with White Pepper, Garlic and Sweet Marjoram.

The seed pods of *Nigella* are prized for their unique and attractive nature, valuable in dried arrangements. They resemble a golden rosehip entwined or suspended within a collar of looped threads. Both are easily cultivated annuals suitable for informal or wild garden borders or preferably, mass plantings in sunny areas. Love-in-a-Mist, also called Wild Fennel, has several colorful cultivars.

Another herb rarely grown in the home garden today is Fennugreek, *Trigonella foenum-graecum*. Quite common in health food stores or on nutrition counters in grocery stores, Fennugreek seed is a popular sprout herb with a pleasant, nutty or maple-like odor. Next to Poppy seed, Fennugreek has one of the highest nutrient levels of all the cultivated herbs and figures into many balanced diets and herbal treatments.

The most precious gift of this herb is only seen in the wild garden, its profusion of extremely fragrant, Sweet Pea-like flowers. This semi-bushy leguminous herb with clover-like leaves will grow from 12–18 in. tall and produce long, slim pods with flat seeds. It is easy to grow in moist fertile soils and germinates in 5–7 days. It will reseed with some success from late plantings and can be sown very early in the spring, from April to mid-July but grows poorly on wet soils. It is a good cover crop (green manure) if enough seed is available. Because it is leguminous, it will not rob the soil of nitrogen. It is often grown with silage to act as an insect repellent in the dried hay.

Young leaves of Fennugreek can be eaten in salads but tend to be bitter and, therefore, are included in soup and stews. Fennugreek seed may be used like sesame seed on breads and in rolls or as sprouts in salads or in oriental stir-fry cuisine. An imitation maple syrup is made from the oil of Fennugreek seed. Recent medical research has found that Fennugreek is an excellent biological source of diosgenin, a precursor of progesterone, a sex hormone used extensively in the treatment of menstrual problems. Its primary medicinal use has been in poultices and salves because of its mucilaginous nature and the detergent (antibiotic) properties of its saponins.

The large, pink flowers of Sesame, *Sesamum orientale*, with their long blooming periods, are this herb's main value to the gardener in most climates. If plants are hot-house grown and set out in mid-April or early May in Zones 7–10, Sesame will produce seed by late August or mid-September. Heat is imperative and like Cumin, Sesame should be irrigated with warm water in cool climates for best results. The 3 ft. tall, unbranched plants of Sesame begin blooming after 1–2 months and continue blooming higher up the plant as it grows and adds height. Seeds form on the lower portion and must be harvested before frost or rain is imminent. A small harvest can usually be expected. The legendary phrase "Open Sesame" is perhaps derived from the habit of the Sesame seed to open explosively, throwing seeds in every direction. Sesame has such an extended ripening period, however, it may never produce seed in northern climates so this occurrence is rarely observed. Sesame seeds are a major southern European agricultural crop, harvested for use as flour, cooking oil, and heating oil. Animal fodder is recovered as a by-product of the sesame oil industry.

Halva is a sweet condiment made from the Sesame seed and honey. By adding seeds of Caraway, Anise, Fennel, or Sweet Cicely, an Anise or Licorice flavor is imparted to the Halva.

HALVA

3 c. Sesame seeds
¼ c. Anise seed or 1 tsp. extract
1 tsp. Sesame oil
½ c. honey
1 Tbsp. Almond extract

Blend into a paste and refrigerate

In the wild garden, Sesame's long pink flowers are bright, cheerful, and endearing. Crowded clumps or drifts of Sesame with plants separated by 6–10 in. are recommended. It makes an excellent background plant. The large green leaves and attractive, unbranched stalks are a useful vertical component in garden design. It combines well with Mugwort and Borage for a garden full of autumn colors. An ornamental grass such as Quaking Grass surrounding a clump of Sesame provides fall contrast that is pleasing visually for the tan rattles of the grass that huddle around the blooming Sesame, and acoustically from hundreds of tiny quaking castanets.

Borage, *Borago officinalis,* is a mighty herb from its beginning as a large seed and seedling to a dense tower of prickly stems and leaves that spread 3 ft. in all directions on massive succulent branches. Huge, bristled leaves like plate-armour hang down defying anyone to trespass or reach in and pluck it from the earth. A few may be allergic to these bristles, but for all they are quite nettlesome in any case and ofttimes remain behind in the hand. As bristly as they are, these huge leaves are nutritionally valuable pottage, cooked and eaten like spinach. Generally, the tender leaves of young plants not yet in flower are utilized.

The most relished use of Borage, however, is in its seedling stage. Plucked from loose, fertile soil, deeply sown seeds will provide long, crisp, juicy stems. These sprouts and the newly opened leaves, are virtually indistinguishable from the taste and texture of cucumbers. Plants that matured in vegetable gardens provide ample self-sown seed in the spring for sprouts. As the soil warms, the sprouts come up from ever deeper levels in the soil. There never seems to be an end to them. They will continue to emerge well into summer. They should not be treated as an uninvited guest but edible weeds, plucked regularly for salads, soups, and dips. They should be picked before the secondary leaves have developed significantly but older sprouts in very fertile circumstances are equally tasty. Sprouts last 3–4 days held in a wet towel at 45°F. Add ¼ c. of sprouts per person to a hot stir-fry dish as it is served or as a side dish with hot buttered mushrooms and green peppers for a unique taste of cucumber in a combination not otherwise possible.

The flowers, too, are a culinary treat. Plucked by pulling on the hub of the flower, the little, blue star can be dipped in egg-white and then sugar for a sparkling decoration on cakes and cookies, or eaten as a condiment or in place of sugar cubes for sweetening beverages. Borage's flowers are frequently used to decorate a huge bowl of punch, their starry, sky-blue shapes floating daintily on flavored, sparkling waters. Borage reputedly brings happiness and courage to everyone and is a grand herb for use as confetti at weddings.

Borage can become a very large plant, with prickly leaves 12 in. long and massive stems to 2 in. in diameter—a gargantuan herb guarding its flock of delft-blue flowers. These humble little blue stars, with faces forever gazing down, are the plant's only redeeming feature in the landscape. They should never be taken too seriously, however. The sky-blue haze they impart to a hedge of Borage is soothing to the eye and the buzzing of the unbelievable number of bees further accentuates the tranquilizing affect. Because of its masses of nectar-rich flowers, Borage has been called the "bee plant". Its deep root is a boon to gardeners used effectively in the poorest soils to break up clay or hard pan. It is rampantly self-sowing but does not germinate in cold soil, although raised beds or cold frames may encourage sprouting earlier in the spring. Borage is a hardy annual which can be sprouted indoors, hardened off, and planted in the garden well before the last frost in early spring. Plants grown in full sun and well-drained soil can withstand several degrees of frost. Hardy plants self-sown for many years can produce offspring hardy to 20°F in wet climates. Dampness and moisture facilitate cold hardiness, because water on leaves insulates them from cold snaps.

In the wild garden, Borage is best used as a background herb blended with other large-leaved herbs such as Comfrey, Elecampane, White Mugwort, or Calendula. The kitchen garden is undoubtedly the home of Borage but it is equally admirable in a wild or informal garden, used in sentry-like positions, at corners, the top of a mound, the center of a colorful patch of wildflowers, or at the very edge of a forest, where it may self-sow its way slowly into the forest over the years.

A misty hedge or screen placed well back in a wild or informal garden can be made using Borage, White Mugwort, Sweet Fennel, and Yarrow. This gives a grey-green background throughout the year and a late summer through fall display of colors; the white of Mugwort, the blue of Borage, and red, yellow, or white of Yarrow.

In the kitchen garden, Borage is a companion to vegetables that are dependent upon bees for pollination. Use it as a central theme in a square divided four ways, with each plot containing Bush Beans, Squash, Tomatoes, and Peppers. Purple Cabbages, Chives, or flowering Kales in blues and lavenders set all around a clump of Borage is also pleasing to the eye. A tight ring of Pepper plants with bright green and red fruits contrasting with the hazy blue flowers of Borage they encircle is an attractive display.

Of the four perennials discussed in this chapter, Lovage, Mugwort, Elecampane, and Yarrow, Lovage, or the Maggi plant, *Levistium officinale,* is the least showy. Being of the Dill family, its flowers, born in umbels, are not spectacular and should be discouraged, as they rob the herb of vigor during long, dry summers. It is, however, a hardy, herbaceous perennial resembling Celery in habit and flavor. The leaves are used rather than the stems which, like Bamboo, are hollow and stringy. Although Lovage prefers wet, clay soil it will thrive in any moist soil from full sun to full shade. Minus its ungainly flowering umbels it is a handsome, tropical looking herb that has some landscape value.

In the wild garden, Lovage provides a dense screen or background for low flowering perennials and annuals. Emerging early in the spring, it brings life and color to the garden long before other ornamental perennials. In either the wild or informal landscape, Lovage does well as an understory herb along woodsy walks that wander in and out of sun and shadow. Its lush growth suggests a tropical origin and enhances such a vision in a water feature, along with Angelica, ornamental grasses, and Bamboo.

For a contemporary feature, enjoin the odd charms of Lovage, variegated Comfrey, Elecampane, and Monarda. This garden can be in the shade a few hours of the day if necessary, or in full sun if plenty of moisture is provided. Red or yellow flowering Comfrey can be substituted for variegated Comfrey. In the contemporary landscape, Lovage is an excellent herbaceous hedge.

In most any garden, Lovage is best used as a screen, along open borders. A mature, healthy clump of Lovage produces a 4–6 ft. barrier that fully obscures sights and muffles sounds. It may be cut back to the ground at any time to clear the way for other flowering ornamentals nearby and will emerge again as healthy and dense as before. It is a pleasant privacy screen for secluded informal walks or cul-de-sacs.

The hardiness of Lovage is one of its virtues, growing in any zone and any soil. Under excellent conditions, Zones 7–10, its flower stalks will climb to 10 ft. The large, celery-like leaves emit a refreshing, but sharp herbaceous aroma on hot days, or whenever brushed. If allowed to bloom, the tiny, inconspicuous yellow-white flowers smell sweetly floral, reminiscent of honeysuckle. As the seeds swell and ripen, they become more decorative, eventually turn a toasty hue and are a favorite of many wild birds. Those that fall to the ground germinate readily in 14–21 days to produce a healthy plant by fall. Lovage seed, as in many *Umbelliferae,* is extremely short-lived. It is recommended that it be frozen for use for the following year. Since Lovage is easily divided as it matures, it is seldom necessary to collect the seed. A portion of the root may be severed from a clump and planted in a cool moist spot to produce a more robust plant more rapidly than from seed.

As a mature plant, a Lovage clump will yield about 30–40 spears, like Asparagus.

These spears are a nutritious, early spring vegetable and partly responsible for Lovage being an invaluable herb for several millenia. Although relatively uncommon in gardens today, Lovage was well known to the Greeks and brought to Northern Europe and England with the Roman armies. It is cultivated today as a commercial crop for the manufacture of tobaccos and perfumes.

LOVAGE SPEARS

Harvest 6 spears per person, 4 in. long
Sprinkle with lemon juice and ¼ c. chopped Chervil or Sweet
Cicely (early spring herbs)
Steam and serve as a vegetable, or in a sauce of Romano or Mozarella cheese
to which has been added Thyme and 2 Tbsp. of Sherry

Lovage seeds are certainly useful in cooking and impart the same flavor as the foliage. They require long, low heat cooking times for tenderizing and will add a sharp, tangy taste when crushed in the mouth. They can be ground to a flour as needed after the ripened seeds have been dried and stored. Because of the prolific production of seed, Lovage flour can be a useful food source during winter to complement wheat and other flours in biscuits and rolls.

The root of Lovage may be washed and peeled down to the pith, which is a soft, white, spongy material that can be steamed or deep-fried and eaten as a vegetable side dish, used cooked or raw in salads, or in stir-fry dishes. An aromatic oil is extracted from the root, used in perfumes and beverages. The pith can also be candied. As young plants, leaf stalks can be blanched by shielding them from the sun with a burlap cover. This should be done only with early spring foliage, as older foliage becomes stringy.

The leaves of Lovage have a tangy or peppery Celery-like flavor, which once used, is never left out of a recipe again. Soups, rice, potato and egg salad, seafood, meat stews, tomato sauce, and chili dishes are vastly improved with the liberal addition of dried Lovage. The high vitamin and mineral value of Lovage can be tapped in this flavorful way. The leaves are easily dried at high temperature, 140°F or air-dried by hanging and storing in paper bags in a dry, cool, storage room. Both the green color and the flavor are retained on drying.

LOVAGE SOUP

1 c. of chicken broth per person
¼ c. of chopped onion per cup of
    broth
¼ c. chopped fresh Lovage
1 diced carrot

1 Tbsp. Calendula
¼ tsp. Oregano
1 tsp. Parsley
¼ tsp. Basil

The exquisite spidery flowers of Elecampane, *Inula helenium,* are reason enough to include it in every garden. This herbaceous perennial produces several blooms or one large bloom if all the competing buds are pruned off. Its 3–4 in., yellow hued flowers gently swaying atop a 6 ft. stem are as ornamental as any popular show flower such as Dahlias or Chrysanthemums. Flowers can be as wide as 5–6 in. while the herb itself may grow to 10 ft. and produce enormous leaves 6–8 in. wide and 24 in. long—a truly gigantic herb in the average garden setting. In poor soil or partial shade, Elecampane grows only 2–5 ft. high with leaves up to 18 in. long.

Ornamental effect is best exploited as a small feature in a contemporary landscape with 1–2 clumps of Shasta Daisy, Rudbekia, and a ground cover of Costmary, bordered by English Daisies. This arrangement provides a procession of Daisy-like flowers from early spring through fall.

In the wild landscape, the huge, yellow daisy of Elecampane, carried aloft throughout July and August, is best joined by Yarrow combined with a carpet of California Poppies, Marguerites, Narcissus and Calendulas for a sunny garden from the last frost to the first. If several Elecampanes are grouped together they should be spaced 2–3 ft. and should not be grown within a ground cover unless it is non-invasive and not a climber. Violets, Creeping Charlie, Sweet Woodruff, Yerba Buena, and Corsican Mint are recommended for partial shade with Sword Fern and Solomon's Seal.

The imposing form of Elecampane is a valuable vertical component in herbaceous perennial borders. This function is best employed in a wild garden containing few shrubs or trees. In such a garden a sizeable clump of Elecampane will create a focal point in the back of the garden. Rising magestically out of a crowd of Bee Balm, Chrysanthemums, and Dahlias, the impression of a hill can be created,—the rising herbs' heights drawing the eye upward as if such a mound actually existed.

The young leaves of Elecampane have been used as a pot herb although the camphor-scented root is the most desirable product. Crisp, fresh slices are used in salads, deep-fried, or boiled and mashed like potatoes. The starch in Elecampane does not create problems for diabetics and has been powdered and used as a sweetener in bread and tea.

Will the real Mugwort please stand up? There are three herbs from the genus *Artemisia* referred to as Mugwort; Common Mugwort, *Artemisia vulgaris;* White Mugwort, *A. lactiflora;* and Western Mugwort, *A. ludoviciana.*

Common Mugwort, *Artemisia vulgaris,* is a ghastly weed. It is, however, a nutritional pot herb with a mild herbaceous scent and flavor, not at all unpleasant or camphoraceous, like many Artemisias, though not nearly as pleasant as Tarragon, *A. dracunculus.* Common Mugwort is distinguished by dark green leaves with downy, white undersides and a purple-striped stem. It is grown strictly in the kitchen garden as a pot herb. Common Mugwort has little ornamental value, even in a wild garden, and can be a serious problem if allowed to go to seed or its perennial roots to become established.

White Mugwort, *A. lactiflora,* from China, is a smaller species than Common Mugwort but similar in appearance except that it does not have stripes on the stem nor white undersides on its leaves. Also called Ghost Wormwood, it is cultivated as a fragrant ornamental. The fragrance of its foliage is similar to Common Mugwort but harbors a bitterness when eaten. The flower's fragrance is reminiscent of Camomile and Southernwood.

White Mugwort is a semi-hardy perennial that requires full sun and a fertile soil for best production of flower blooms. The blooms develop in late summer and last into the fall months. They are usually cut just after opening and dried for use in dried arrangements for their everlasting color and fragrance.

A White Mugwort screen, planted to provide a barrier at the edge of a wild or informal garden, succeeds well. On misty mornings in late summer and far into the fall months, its appearance suggests a band of ghosts sneaking along the back of the bed, their huge, white heads hung secretively down. As easy to grow as any Artemisia, it rises gracefully from 3–6 ft. and long into fall is topped with dense, creamy white blooms. For a screen, it should be planted in full sun and the plants set in 2–3 rows, 18 in. apart with plants set 18–24 in. apart. Its plain green exterior and simple Eiffel Tower-shape are enhanced by low spreading companions with bright flowers and foliage such as Dwarf Monarda or a clump of ornamental Sage such as *Salvia viridis* or *Salvia dorisiana.* In a contemporary garden White Mugwort should be featured with pink and white Poppies and surrounded by a selection of ornamental Thymes, in particular Moroccan and Peter Davis.

Western Mugwort, *A. ludoviciana,* is a native North American herb. A handsome, silver-leaved, Wormwood-like herb, it is used only as an ornamental. It is a hardy, evergreen perennial, available in garden centers. A cultivar, 'Silver King', *A. ludoviciana* var. *albula,* is more commonly cultivated and grows from 2–4 ft. in dry soils in full sun.

Yarrow, *Achillea millefolium,* is the common weed, Milfoil. It is a beautiful perennial in the wild or informal garden. Various flower colors and degrees of filigreed foliage make it a versatile herb in the ornamental garden. The flowers and foliage are excellent for dried arrangements. It is commonly grown as a valuable addition to the mead and used medicinally as an astringent for the cessation of bleeding or soothing the pain of a small cut or toothache.

There are Yarrows from 2 in. to 6 ft. tall, all with tiny, ¼ in. flowers that form flat heads (corymbs) from the size of a quarter to a dinnerplate. Most of the Yarrows do not produce a prominent odor, though a few, under some circumstances, have a spicy aroma similar to Camomile. In fact, the same chemicals present in Camomile, azulene and chamazulene, are also found in Yarrow. *A. moschata* and *millefolium* also contain a small amount of eucalyptol for a camphoraceous note and the sweetener, betonicine. The tea of Yarrow, once a treatment for bleeding ulcers and toothache, is not at all unpleasant, if the herb is grown in fertile soil, full sun, and very young leaves are harvested in early spring. Known by many native peoples as the "wound herb", Yarrow was given the genus name *Achillea* because it was believed that Achilles first employed this herb to heal his soldiers. It can also be used for an astringent in a rinse for oily skin.

Yarrow, or Thousand Leaf, is an herb with a thousand names as well. It is an ancient plant brought in on the hooves of cattle that were driven into Europe from Central Asia by primitive man. Its use in staunching the flow of blood both internally and externally has earned it many handles on the battlefield, including Knight's Milfoil and Soldier's Wort, and to the cabinet maker, Carpenter's Weed. Its popularity in magic potions won it the name Devil's Nettle, its flavor, Old Man's Pepper, and in brewing a heady ale, Field Hops.

All of the Yarrow species are hardy, rewarding herbs, each with just the right character for a particular occasion. *A. millefolium* can be both a 2 ft. column of dark green capped with white or an exceptionally hardy, dark green lawn in poor, dry soil where grass will not grow. For that reason, it is one of the finest mead herbs, planted in those spots where traffic is heaviest and soil is poor. It must have a well drained location and can be mowed from ¾–1 ½ in.

Common Yarrow, *A. millefolium,* represents the white, red, or pink forms of Yarrow. 'Fireking' and 'Cerise Queen' are cultivar names with *rubra* and *rosea* as varieties. Their foliage is dark green, exceptionally filigreed and most grow from 18 in.–3 ft.

A. filipendulina and some crosses of that species and *A. clypeolata* (*A. taygeta*) are the yellow-hued Yarrows; the 4–6 ft. 'Coronation Gold', the diminutive 18 in. 'Moonshine', and giant flowered 'Gold Plate' with flowers as wide as 8–10 in. *A. clypeolata* has charming soft grey leaves, perfect in a grey garden, and grows to only 18 in. with 2 in. wide, lemon-yellow flowers.

A. tomentosa and *A. chrysocoma,* the creeping Yarrows, are mead herbs forming low-growing mats from 2 in. for *A. t.* 'Nana', up to 6–8 in. for other species and varieties.

As single plants or in large drifts, Yarrow is a natural wild or informal garden herb. Its value is in its ability to provide vertical balance in a colorful and simple way. The small yellow flowers of 'Moonshine' emerging crisply erect from a patch of dainty Sweet Cicely in semi-shade provide a bold and attractive asymmetry for a sylvan glade or contemporary feature. Other tall herbs such as Teasel, *Eryngium* and Cattail are often found in gardens with Yarrows cultivated both for their decorative uses and vertical contrast. In the kitchen garden, tall, slim

Yarrows join Sunflowers and Jerusalem Artichokes in sunny central patches.

Contemporary gardens have not seen much use of Yarrow due to its rangy habits. Two exceptions are the red, and diminutive white Yarrows such as *A. ptarmica* 'The Pearl', tucked into a mixed ground cover of Wormwood or Western Mugwort and Horehound or Santolina for a contemporary feature that appears cool and composed. Tall, yellow 'Gold Plate' Yarrow can be featured with Elecampane in a closeknit patch offset in a field of orange and white Poppies.

Long, solid color borders of Yarrow are a fashionable use of this flower in formal gardens, while mixed borders in informal gardens combine 2 or more species of Yarrow and Valerian, Foxglove, Fern-leaf Tansy, White Mugwort, or Elecampane. Their hardy, profusely blooming nature has given them a reputation as trustworthy, colorful border plants. There are many flower colors to choose from: light yellow to white to cream, dark yellow, orange, pink, and red. Yarrow is also at home as a tall border or screen along the back of a bed, its foliage providing a dark green background for light colored flowers or ornamental foliages.

Chapter 7 / SECTION 3

A Walk Through a Wild Garden

Tucked among the Redwoods up a coastal draw somewhere along the endless warm Pacific beach was Wildhaven. (Fig. 53) I came upon it a while back but never drew a map. A few steps hidden by scrub and a name carved into driftwood were sufficient to suggest more. Searching again with a more serious eye I could see Heathers and Thymes wrestling above on the brink of a ledge, each trying to force the weaker over. My nose was quick to ascertain what other pleasures grew up there: Sage, Lavender, Savory and Camomiles in great swatches no doubt. So with the breeze off the land and the ebbing ocean at my back I bravely ascended the steps which wound steeply upward out of the sight of the ever-curious sea.

The first dozen or so steps were obviously flotsam, lashed together with ship's chain and anchored in concrete. Apparently the sea plays roughly even this far above the berm. A mixed hedge of Dwarf Lavender and Heather scampers along the path beside me. On one side the border becomes a wall that rises steeply, inviting the Lavender to drape down from several feet above. Dew and perfume drip from thousands of deep blue magic wands.

On the other side the landscape dips back toward the sea. Creeping Thymes charge out from the edge of the path, plying their way across the landscape and eventually piling up in frothing fury before a border of silver-grey *Santolina* 'Nana' and *S. neapolitana,* which slow, but do not stay, the advancing Thyme. A pinch of the white flowered Thyme tells my nose it is the lemon-scented 'White Magic' and a pinch of the other reminds me of 'Oregano-scented' Thyme, one of my favorites.

The Heathers and Thymes I saw from the beach play beyond in the far garden, the two separated by a wide swath of fist-sized river rock. Silver, French and Golden Lemon Thymes battle it out with a dozen red-haired Heathers while a girdle of golden Alyssums hold fast the inside edge, keeping them from invading the rocky access area.

Reposing beneath a heavy load of flowered sod and staring sullenly upon this landscape is an earth home. A decorative wreath adorns the door. Peeking through a window to see if anyone responds to my knocking, I see a wealth of wreaths, swags and dried arrangements laying about inside. The owner is apparently an artist of sorts, herbs and dried plants her medium.

A rocky path leading to the right around the house and upslope passes a large patch of Azaleas that engulfs the side yard, diverting traffic down into the Heather and Thyme or up into a shady nook Lounging in the shade of a Redwood are Black Hellebore, *Helleborus niger;* Wild Ginger; and thousands of Violets. This, rich dark green carpet is all aglitter from a few filtered sunbeams. Wedged between two islands of Corsican Hellebore is a bed of Primroses robed in elegant habiliments of gold and crimson and royal blue. Invading from above is a sheet of Violas and Variegated Creeping Charlie, *Glechoma hederacea* var. *variegata.*

The rocky path winds around to a patio in the backyard that opens up and up and up. I can just see the tops of two parallel ridges that have entered this property. They have been flattened to make room for scores of Azaleas and some Oregon Grape. Between the ridges is a stone-filled gully that allows access to the rich beds on their flanks. These beds have become the home of many perennials, evergreens and wonderous little alpines. Heathers and Campanulas are a strong theme, while herbs such as Pygmy Savory, Dwarf and Golden Sage, Bush and Creeping Thymes, neatly trimmed Lavender and Red and White 'Grandiflora' Hyssop fill in between banks of ornamental ground covers. The fragrance of a few want to lull me into an effortless sleep: Lady's Mantle shaking her huge yellow plumes at my feet filling the air with a floral-scented magic potion; Corsican Mint cavorting between the gully stones sending waves of menthol upward; 'White Moss' Thyme giving up its crisp thymol aroma; and little raggedy-mop tufts of Creeping Savory are making me hungry with the aroma of smoked meats at Christmas.

These beds are host to innumerable sorts of ornamental herbs and alpine plants. I can see Mountain Avens, *Geum montana;* Soapwort, *Saponaria ocymoides;* Tomentil, *Potentilla arbuscula* and *P. nepalensis* with yellow and scarlet flowers; Fairy Thimbles, *Campanula pusilla,* scattered everywhere; and strings of yellow Alliums, *Allium flavum,* like the colored beads of a necklace, striking across the wash again and again, vanishing near the top in an orange-red sea of California Poppies, *Eschscholzia californica.* Dwarf Sage and Dwarf Lavender are accompanied by a few Bluebells, *Campanula carpatica;* a white muffler of Snow-in-Summer, *Cerastium tomentosum;* and Spiderwort, *Tradescantia virginiana.*

A broad elevated bed in the center of the landscape boasts a dozen or more annual herbs and ornamentals, undoubtedly used for the dried arrangements I saw through the window. There are slender drifts of fire-orange *Lupine;* Love-in-a-Mist, *Nigella damascena;* Chinese Lanterns, *Physalis alkekengi;* and Honesty, *Lunaria biennis.* They are joined by herbs such as Coriander, Cinnamon Basil, Summer Savory and Dill for a banquet of fragrances, and more Bluebells and California Poppies for exotic color.

The ridge tops are swarming with knee-high Azaleas all dressed in their Sunday finery, blossom prints of pink, snow white, vermillion and royal purple. The gentle arms of three matronly Redwoods hover lovingly over these little mountain children and offer soothing contrast to the stark rocky earth that is the common ground in this landscape. Though harsh, this rocky expanse is not sterile but teaming with minute things: quick clumps of blue-fingered *Campanula zoysii;* luscious patches of Corsican Mint; paper-thin mats of red and pink flowering Creeping Thyme; and a clump of Heather with a collar of Lawn Camomile.

Rounding the back of the home, the rocky path is carpeted in Pearlwort, *Sagina subulata.* The yard slopes steeply back to the beach. A small grey garden clings to the front corner of the house affording the inhabitants a scene of uncluttered beauty through two windows that face the garden. From inside only a flowered meadow, a stately Redwood and the distant sea can be seen. Within the ring of Lavender are Painted Daisies, *Pyrethrum rosea; Gazanias* in bold golden sunset colors; cloud-white New Zealand Mountain Daisies, *Celmisia coriacea;* and sky-blue Mountain Knapweed, *Centaurea montana* joining in a scene of artistic design. Dozens of dwarven Canterbury Bells, *Campanula medium* 'Dwarf', dance among the daisies, and the silvery, pink-speckled spikes of Wooly Betony jut upward from everywhere inside, trying to outdo the blue splendor of the highly ornamental ring of 'Twickle Purple' Lavender.

A duo of Heather and sitting stones in the middle of the wasteland beyond the grey garden is an inviting reststop from which to admire this wilderness retreat. True, it is only a suggestion of wilderness. It is an imaginary world created by the wild imagination of its designer. It is fitting it should be neighbor only to a Redwood forest and the sea.

APPENDICES

APPENDIX I

Physical Characteristics of Ornamental Herbs & Herb Culture

KEY

BOTANICAL NAME:	the binomial used is the one that is most commonly accepted today.
LIFE CYCLE	A = annual B = biennial D = deciduous E = evergreen H = herbaccous P = perennial S = semi
NATURAL HEIGHT	because plant materials come from sources world wide, there is a significant variation in the height of a species; many species themselves are polymorphic as well and vary considerably.
HABIT	UP, *upright,* inverted pyramid, tall and thin BU, *bushy,* implies a spherical or hemispherical shape MAT, *mat-forming,* implies a spreading herb (mint-like) or a creeper that will continue to spread unless corralled. SHB, *shrub,* like bushy, but grows from a main stem and does not root along branches to any great degree. CL, *clumping,* very slowly spreading herbs (chive-like) that form dense central patches with time. TR, *tree* VN, *vine*
FOLIAGE	TEXTURES: thin, dense, coarse, fine and feathery (as seen from a distance of several feet. COLOR: GN=green, DGN-dark green, BGN-blue green, YGN=yellow green, GY=grey, PUR=purple (or red stained on dark green), YonGN=variegated.

BLOSSOM	SEASON: W=winter, SP=spring, SM=summer, F=fall. COLOR: BLU=blue, R=red, PUR=purple, LAV=lavender, RO=rose, Y=yellow, PK=pink, W=white, BRN=brown, GN=green, O=orange, CRM=cream, MAG=magenta. *showy flowers.
SUN EXPOSURE	FS=full sun, PS=part sun, SH=shade.
GERMINATION	d=days, wk=weeks, yr=years (seed germination data is provided as a *range* because seed can be very old, thus lengthening germination, and many plants do vary considerably depending upon the ripening conditions). Brackets [] indicate rooting period for cuttings.
PROPAGATION	S=seeds, SS=self sows, D=root or crown division, L=layering, C=cutting, B=bulb, BLT=bulblet.
SOIL MOISTURE	WD-well drained (the most common, implies good drainage and is used when no other specific soil moisture level is recommended) M=moist AQ=aquatic (which includes all soils in and around a pond) DR=drought resistant.
SOIL TYPE	G=garden (herb is not choosy), R=rich, S=sandy, L=limed, A=strongly acid
PESTS	The few pests noted here are derived from texts on commercial culture of ornamentals, not word of mouth. Unless otherwise noted, pests listed under the first entry in each genus may be considered common to the entire genus. The following is a guide that provides the cure for what ails your herb, as noted in the tables or as you may have discovered. Be absolutely sure of the pest first or the cure will be wasted and useless.

STERILIZE SOIL:	root rot, crown gall, stem rot, crown rot, nematodes
REMOVE & DESTROY LEAVES:	leaf spot
DESTROY PLANTS:	crown gall, stem rot, smut, virus, stalk borer, wilt, rust
DORMANT OIL/LIME SULFUR:	leaf gall aphid, scale
WETTABLE SULFUR:	powdery mildew, blight
BORDEAUX:	anthracnose, severe leaf spot, blight
LYE SOAP:	aphids
MALATHION:	white fly, severe scale, psyllids

ZONES	Like other characteristics of herbs the zone in which they can survive is quite variable. Herbs may be purchased from many zones where they have been acclimatized, and do better or worse as the case may be in your garden. I advise you to experiment and talk with gardeners in your immediate area to find out what they can grow— get a cutting from them, if at all possible. This is very important in cold climates.

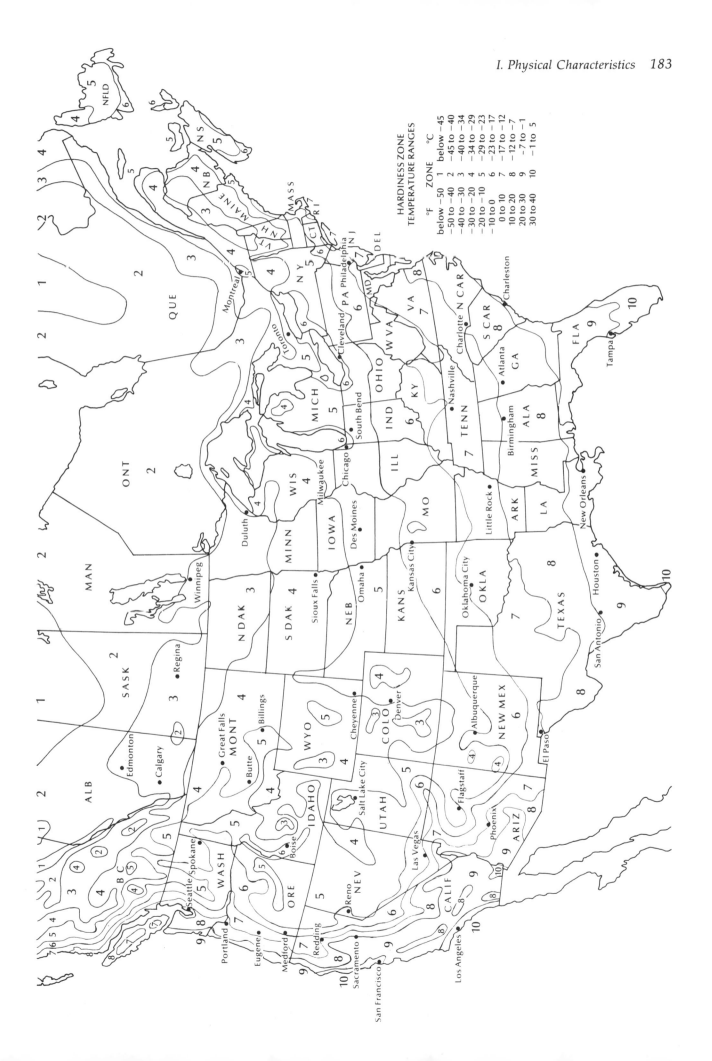

HARDINESS ZONE
TEMPERATURE RANGES

°F	ZONE	°C
below −50	1	below −45
−50 to −40	2	−45 to −40
−40 to −30	3	−40 to −34
−30 to −20	4	−34 to −29
−20 to −10	5	−29 to −23
−10 to 0	6	−23 to −17
0 to 10	7	−17 to −12
10 to 20	8	−12 to −7
20 to 30	9	−7 to −1
30 to 40	10	−1 to 5

BOTANICAL NAME	LIFE CYCLE	HEIGHT	HABIT	FOLIAGE TEXTURE	FOLIAGE COLOR	BLOSSOM SEASON	BLOSSOM COLOR	SUN	PROPAGATION	GERMINATION	SOIL MOISTURE	SOIL TYPE	PESTS INSECTS	PESTS DISEASE	ZONE
Achillea clypeolata Yarrow	HP	12"	CL	fine/dense	GY	SM	Y*	FS	D		WD	G			
A. filipendulina Yarrow	HP	1–1½'	CL	fine/dense	GYGN	SM	Y*	FS	D		WD	G		rust	4–9
A. millefolium Yarrow	HP	2–3'	UP	fine/dense	DGN	SM	W/R/PK*	FS	D/S	4–6wk	DR	G		crown gall stem rot	2–10
A. tomentosa 'Nana' Creeping Yarrow	HP	2–4"	MAT	fine/dense	DGN	SM	Y	FS-PS	D/L	[8wk]	WD	S			6–9
Acinos arvensis Basil-Thyme	HP	10–16"	CL	coarse/dense	DGN	SM	PK	FS	S/C/D		M	G		rust leaf spot	3–10
Acorus calamus Sweet Flag	HP	3–6'	UP	grassy/thin	GN	SM	BRN	FS-PS	D		AQ	R			3–9
A. gramineus Grass-leaved Sweet Flag	HP	18"	UP	grassy/thin	GN	SM	BRN	PS	D		AQ	R			5–10
Agastache cana Mosquito Plant	HP	18–30"	UP	coarse/thin	DGN	SM	RED*	FS	S/D		WD	G			6–10
A. foeniculum Anise Hyssop	HP	2–4'	UP	coarse/thin	DGN	SM	BLU*	FS	S/D	1–2wk	WD	G			4–9
A. rugosa Korean Mint	HP	2–3'	UP	coarse/thin	DGN	SM	PUR	FS	S/D/C	1–2wk	WD	G		mildew, rust leaf spot	6–9
A. scrophulariifolia Purple Giant Hyssop	HP	2–4'	UP	coarse/thin	DGN	SM	ROSE	FS	S/D		WD	G			4–9
Alchemilla vulgaris Lady's Mantle	HP	12–18"	MAT	coarse/dense	LGN	SM	Y*	FS-PS	C/D/S	3–4wk	WD	G			3–8
Allium ascalonicum Shallot	A	12"	CL	grassy/thin	DGN	SM		FS	B		WD	R		mildew root rot	A
A. flavum	HP	10–15"	CL	grassy/thin	DGN	SM	Y*	FS	D/S	3–4wk	WD	R			4–9
A. giganteum	HP	4–5'	UP	coarse/thin	DGN	SM	ROSE*	FS	D/S	4–8wk	WD	R			6–10

Garlic				thin										root rot	
A. s. var. ophioscorodon Rocambole	A/P	12"	UP	grassy/thin	GN	SM		FS	B/BLT		WD	R		mildew root rot	3–9
A. schoenoprasum Chive	HP	10–18"	CL	grassy/thin	DGN	SP/F	ROSE*	FS-PS	D/S	2–4wk	M	R		white mold	3–10
A. s. var. sibirica	HP	18–24"	UP	grassy/thin	DGN	SP/F	ROSE	FS-PS	D/S	2–3wk	WD	G			2–9
A. tuberosum Garlic Chive	HP	1–2'	CL	grassy/thin	DGN	SM	W*	FS	D/S	2–4wk	WD	R			3–10
Aloysia triphylla Lemon Verbena	D/EP	3–6'	SHB	fine/thin	GN	SM	W	FS	C/L/S	[6wk]	WD	R		leaf spot crown gall	8–10
Althea officinalis Marshmallow	HP/B	2–3'	UP	coarse/thin	GN	SM	PK/W*	FS	S/SS	2–3wk	WD	G		rust anthracnose	2–10
Anethum graveolens Dill	A	3–5'	UP	feathery/thin	DGN	SM	Y	FS	S/SS	2–3wk	WD	G		leaf spot	A
A. sowa Indian Dill	A	3–5'	UP	feathery/thin	DGN	SM	Y	FS	S/SS	2–3wk	WD	G		virus	A
Angelica archangelica Angelica	HB	3–5'	UP	coarse/thin	GN	SP	GN-W*	PS	S,SS	2–4wk	M-W	R	leaf miner	leaf spot	2–10
A. atropurpurea Masterwort	HB	4–6'	UP	coarse/thin	GN-PR	SP	GN*	FS-PS	S,SS	2–4wk	M-W	R		rust	3–9
A. sylvestris Wood Angelica	HB/P	4–6'	UP	coarse/thin	GN	SP	GN*	FS-PS	S,SS	2–4wk	M-W	R		rust	2–10
Anthriscus cerefolium Chervil	A	1–2'	UP	fine/thin	GN	SM	W	PS-SH	S/SS	1–2wk	M	R	leaf miner		2–9
Artemisia abrotanum Southernwood	EP	3–5'	BU	feathery/dense	LGN	SM	Y	FS	C/L		WD	G		root rot	4–9
A. absinthum Wormwood	EP	1–3'	BU	fine/dense	GYGN	SM	Y	FS-PS	L/D/S	4–6wk	DR	G		rust	4–9
A. arborescens	EP	2–3'	BU	fine/dense	GY	SM	BRN	FS	C/L		WD	G			4–9
A. dracunculus Russian Tarragon	HP	2–3'	UP	fine/thin	GN	SM	Y	FS-PS	S/D	3–4wk	M	R,S		root rot	4–8
A. dracunculus 'Sativa' French Tarragon	HP	3–5'	UP	fine/thin	DGN	SM	Y	FS	D/C	[10wk]	M	RS		root rot	6–8
A. frigida 'Silver Mound'	HP	8–12"	MAT	feathery/dense	GY	SM	Y	FS	D		WD	S		crown rot	3–9

BOTANICAL NAME	LIFE CYCLE	HEIGHT	HABIT	FOLIAGE TEXTURE	FOLIAGE COLOR	BLOSSOM SEASON	BLOSSOM COLOR	SUN	PROPAGATION	GERMINATION	SOIL MOISTURE	SOIL TYPE	INSECTS	DISEASE	ZONE
A. lactiflora White Mugwort	HP	3–5'	UP	fine/dense	DGN	F	Y-W*	FS	D/S		WD	R	slug	mildew root rot	7–10
A. lanata Silver Mound	HP	6–8"	MAT	feathery/dense	GY	SM	Y	FS	D		WD	S		crown rot	3–9
A. ludoviciana Western Mugwort	EP	2–3'	UP	fine/thin	GY	SM	Y	FS	D		DR	G			4–9
A. l. var. albula 'Silver King'	EP	1–2'	UP	fine/dense	GY	SM	Y	FS	D/L		WD	G			5–9
A. pontica Roman Wormwood	SEP	2–3'	BU	feathery/dense	GYGN	SM	Y	FS	C/L/S	[8wk]	WD	G		root rot	6–10
A. stellerana Beach Wormwood	DP	12–18"	MAT	coarse/dense	GY	SM	Y	FS-PS	L/C	[6wk]	DR	S		white mold	3–9
A. vulgaris Common Mugwort	HP	4–6'	UP	fine/thin	DGN	SM	R-BRN	FS	S/D	2–3wk	DR	G			2–10
Asarum canadense Wild Ginger	EP	8–12"	MAT	coarse/dense	DGN	SP	PUR-BRN	SH	D		M	RA		leaf spot	5–8
A. europeum Wild Ginger	EP	4–6"	MAT	coarse/dense	DGN	SP	BRN	SH	D		M	RA			6–8
A. hartwegii Wild Ginger	EP	4–8"	MAT	coarse/dense	Won DGN	SP	PUR-BRN	SH	D		M	RA			6–8
A. virginicum Wild Ginger	EP	6–8"	MAT	coarse/dense	LGNon DGN	SP-SM	PUR	SH	D		M	RA		rust	4–8
Borago officinalis Borage	A	2–3'	BU	coarse/dense	DGN	S-F	BLU	FS-PS	S/SS	5–7d	DR	G		leaf spot	ALL
Calendula officinalis Calendula	A	1–2'	UP	coarse/dense	GN	SP-F	Y/O*	FS	S/SS	5–7d	DR	GL	cab. looper	virus	ALL
Calamintha nepeta Calamint	HP	12–18"	MAT	coarse/thin	GN	SM	PK	FS-PS	S/L/C		M	R			4–9
Chamomilla recutita German Camomile	A	15"	BU	fine/dense	LGN	SP-F	W*	FS-PS	S/SS	2–3wk	DR	G		mildew rust	ALL
Carum carvi	HP	2–3'	UP	feathery/	GN	SP	W	FS	S	2–3wk	M	R		stem rot	3–9

C. n. cv. Rayless Chamomile	SEP	4–6″	MAT	feathery/thin	LGN	SM	Y(rayless)	PS	D/S	5–10d	M	R		7–10
C. n. 'Trenague' Lawn Camomile	EP	1–3″	MAT	feathery/dense	LGN	None	—	FS-PS	D		M	R		6–10
Chenopodium bonus henricus Good King Henry	HP	12–16″	MAT	coarse/dense	DGN	SM	BRN	FS	S/D	2–3wk	WD	R	leaf spot	3–9
Chrysanthemum balsamita Camphor Plant	HP	18″	MAT	coarse/dense	GY	SP	W*	FS-PS	D/L	[8wk]	M	G · slug		3–10
Balsamita major Costmary	HP	1–3′	MAT	coarse/dense	GN	SM	Y-GN	PS	D		M	R · slug	leaf spot	3–10
Chrysanthemum parthenium 'Selaginoides' Dwarf feverfew	HP	10–12″	BU	coarse/dense	YGN	SM-F	W*	FS-PS	S/D	1–2wk	WD	G	mildew	4–9
C. p. 'DoubleBonnet'	HP	18–24″	BU	coarse/dense	YGN	SM-F	W*	FS	S/D	1–2wk	WD	G		4–9
Coleus amboinicus Indian Borage	EP	1–3′	UP	coarse/thin	GN	SM	LAV*	FS	C	[6wk]	M	R		9–10
Coriandrum sativum Coriander	A	2–3′	UP	fine/thin	DGN	SM	W-PK	FS	S/SS	1–2wk	WD	R		4–10
Crocus sativus Saffron	HP	12–16″	CL	grassy/thin	DGN	W	PUR*	FS-PS	B/S	8–10wk	WD	SL	dry rot	7–10
Cryptotaenia japonica Japanese Parsley	HP	18″	UP	coarse/thin	GN	SM	YGN	PS	S	2–6wk	M	R		2–9
Cuminum cyminum Cumin	A	12″	UP	fine/thin	DGN	SM	PK	FS	S	1–2wk	WD	R		6–10
Cynara cardunculus Cardoon	HB	3–6′	UP	coarse/thin	GY	SM	ROSE*	FS	S	1–3wk	M	R	crown rot, leaf spot	4–10
Ferula assa-foetida Asafetida	HP	6–12′	CL	feathery/dense	DGN	SM	Y	FS	S/D		M	R		8–10
F. communis Giant Fennel	HP	5–10′	CL	feathery/dense	DGN	SM	Y	FS	S/D		M	R		8–10
Filipendula ulmaria Meadowsweet	HP	2–4′	UP	coarse/thin	DGN	SM	Y-W*	FS-PS	S/D		M	R	mildew, rust	2–9
F. vulgaris Dropwort	HP	1–2′	CL	fine/thin	DGN	SM	W-CRM	FS	S/D		M	R		2–9

BOTANICAL NAME	LIFE CYCLE	HEIGHT	HABIT	FOLIAGE TEXTURE	FOLIAGE COLOR	BLOSSOM SEASON	BLOSSOM COLOR	SUN	PROPAGATION	GERMINATION	SOIL MOISTURE	SOIL TYPE	PESTS INSECTS	PESTS DISEASE	ZONE
Foeniculum vulgare ssp. vulgare var. azoricum Finocchio	A	2–3'	UP	feathery/thin	DGN	SM	Y	FS	S	3–6wk	M	R			2–10
F̄. v. ssp. v. var. dulce Sweet Fennel	HP	3–6'	UP	feathery/thin	DGN	S-F	Y	FS-PS	S/SS	2–4wk	M	R	aphid	stem rot	3–9
F. v. ssp. v. 'Rubrum' Bronze Fennel	HP	3–4'	UP	feathery/thin	RED-GN	S-F	Y	FS	S/SS	1–2wk	M	R	aphid		3–9
Galium odorata Sweet Woodruff	HP	4–8"	MAT	fine/dense	DGN	SP	W	PS-SH	S/D/L	2mo.	M	RA		leaf spot rust, mildew	3–9
Glechoma hederaceae Creeping Charlie	HP	2–8"	MAT	feathery/dense	DGN	SM	Y	PS-SH	S/D		M	RA		mildew	7–10
G. h. var. variegata	HP	2–6"	MAT	coarse/dense	Won DGN	SP-SM	BLU	PS-SH	D		M	R		mildew	2–9
Gaultheria hispidula Creeping Snowberry	SEP	2–3"	MAT	coarse/thin	DGN	SP	W	SH	D/L		WD	RA		leaf spot	4–9
G. procumbens Wintergreen	EP	4–6"	MAT	coarse/thin	DGN	SM-F	W/PK	SH	D/L		WD	RA		leaf spot	4–9
Hamamelis japonica Japanese Witch Hazel	DP	20'	SHB	coarse/thin	DGN	W-SP	Y*	PS-SH	C/G		WD	R		mildew	4–9
H. mollis Chinese Witch Hazel	DP	20'	SHB	coarse/thin	DGN	W-SP	Y-O*	PS-SH	C/G		WD	R			3–9
H. vernalis	DP	6'	SHB	coarse/dense	DGN	SP	Y*	PS-SH	S/C		M	R			4–9
H. virginiana Witch Hazel	DP	15'	SHB	coarse/thin	DGN	W	Y*	PS-SH	C/S	2yr	M	R	leaf gall aphid	leaf spot	2–9
Hedeoma pulegioides American Pennyroyal	A	10–16"	BU	fine/thin	GN	SM	BLU	FS	S/C		M	R			4–9
Helichrysum italicum Curry plant	EP	1–2'	BU	fine/thin	GY	SM	Y	FS	S/C	[6wk]	WD	SL			6–10
	HP	12'	VN	coarse	DGN	F	GN	FS	S	1–2wk	WD	G		mildew	5–10

Plant	Type	Height	Habit	Texture/Density	Foliage	Leaf	Flower	Light	Soil	Propagation	Water	Hardiness	Pests	Disease	Zone
Hyssopus officinalis Hyssop	EP	8–16"	BU	fine/dense	DGN	SM	B/W/PK	FS	S/C	1–3wk	WD	G		nematode	2–10
Inula helenium Elecampane	HP	4–6'	UP	coarse/thin	DGN	SM	Y*	FS-PS	S/D	6–8wk	M	R		mildew	2–10
Jasminum humile	EP	20'	SHB	coarse/thin	GN	F	Y	FS	C		WD	R		leaf spot	5–10
J. officinalis Poet's Jasmine	DP	30'	VN	fine/dense	DGN	SM-F	W	FS-PS	C		WD	R	scale	blossom blight	5–10
J. sambac Arabian Jasmine	EP	15'	VN	coarse/thin	GN	SP-F	W*	FS	C	[10wk]	WD	R			7–10
Laurus nobilis Sweet Bay	EP	40'	TR	coarse/dense	DGN	SM	Y	PS	C	[16wk]	WD	R	psyllid	leaf spot	8–10
Lavandula angustifolia ssp. *angustifolia* English Lavender	EP	3–5'	SHB	fine/dense	GYGN	SM	LAV*	FS	S/C/L	2–3wk	DR	S		root rot nematode	2–10
L. a. ssp. *a.* 'Munstead' 'Hidcote' 'Mitcham Gray'	EP	1½–2'	SHB	fine/dense	GYGN	SM	PUR*/PK	FS	C/L		DR	S			3–10
L. a. ssp. *a.* 'Nana Atropurpurea' 'Nana Alba'	EP	12–18"	SHB	fine/dense	GYGN	SM	PUR/W	FS	C/L		DR	S			3–10
L. a. ssp. *a* 'Compacta' 'Twickle Purple' 'Irene Doyle'	EP	2–3'	SHB	fine/dense	GYGN	SM	LAV	FS	C/L	[8wk]	DR	S			3–10
L. dentata French Lavender	EP	2–4'	SHB	fine/thin	GY	SM-F	LAV	FS	C		WD	S			8–10
L. latifolia Spike Lavender	EP	3–4'	SHB	fine/dense	GYGN	SM	PUR	FS	C/L		DR	S			4–10
L. lanata Wooly Lavender	EP	2–3'	SHB	fine/dense	W	SM	PUR	FS	C/L		WD	S			8–10
L. multifida Fringed Lavender	EP	2–3'	SHB feathery/dense	GYGN	SM-F	PUR	FS	S/C		WD	S				8–10
L. stoechas Spanish Lavender	EP	3–5'	SHB	fine/dense	GYGN	SM-F	PUR*	FS	S/C/L	3–4wk	DR	S			7–10
L. viridis	EP	2–3'	SHB	fine/dense	GYGN	SM	Y	FS	C		WD	S			8–10

BOTANICAL NAME	LIFE CYCLE	HEIGHT	HABIT	FOLIAGE TEXTURE	FOLIAGE COLOR	BLOSSOM SEASON	BLOSSOM COLOR	SUN	PROPAGATION	GERMINATION	SOIL MOISTURE	SOIL TYPE	PESTS INSECTS	PESTS DISEASE	ZONE
L. × *intermedia* Lavandin	P	3–4'	SHB	fine/dense	GYGN	SM	LAV	FS	C/L		WD	S			ALL
Levisticum officinale Loveage	HP	4–6'	CL	coarse/dense	GN	SM	Y	FS-SH	S/D	2–3wk	M	R	leaf miner	crown rot	9–10
Lippia alba Licorice Verbena	EP	2–4'	SHB	coarse/thin	DGN	SM	W	FS	C/L	[6wk]	WD	R			9–10
L. graveolens Mexican Oregano	EP	4–6'	SHB	coarse/thin	DGN	SM	CRM	FS	C/L		WD	R			7–10
Marrubium vulgare Horehound	EP	1–2'	MAT	coarse/thin	GY	SM	W	FS	S/C	2–3wk	WD	S			2–9
Melissa officinalis Lemon Balm	HP	18–30"	BU	coarse/dense	GN	SM	W	FS-SH	S/D/C	2–3wk	M	R	cutworm		
M. o. var. *variegata* Variegated Balm	HP	12–18"	BU	coarse/dense	YonGn	SM	W	FS	C/D	[4wk]	M	R			2–9
Mentha aquatica Water Mint	HP	1–2'	MAT	coarse/dense	DGN	SM	ROS	FS-PS	D/C/S	[4wk]	M-AQ	R		mildew wilt	
M. cervina Holt's Pennyroyal	HP	2–3"	MAT	fine/thin	GN	SM	BLU	FS	S/D/C		WD	G			
M. × *gracilis* var. *variegata* Ginger Mint	HP	12–16"	MAT	coarse/dense	YonGN	SM	PK	FS	C/D	[4wk]	M	R			4–9
M. × *piperita* Peppermint	HP	2–3'	MAT	coarse/dense	GN	SM	LAV	FS-PS	C/D/S	3–4wk	M	R		anthracnose wilt	2–9
M. × *p.* var. *citrata* Orange Mint	HP	16–18"	MAT	coarse/dense	P-DGN	SM	LAV	FS-PS	S/D/C		M	R			4–9
M. × *p.* var. *piperita,* 'Mitcham'	HP	1–2'	MAT	coarse/dense	DGN	SM	ROS	FS-PS	D/C		M	R		rust resistant	4–9
M. × *p.* var. *vulgaris* Black Mint	HP	1–2'	MAT	coarse/dense	PUR	SM	LAV	FS-PS	C/D	[4wk]	M	R		rust resistant	4–9
M. pulegium English Pennyroyal	EP	1–2'	MAT	coarse/dense	GN	SM	PK*	FS-SH	S,SS/D		M	G			6–10
M. pulegium var	HP	2–3'	MAT	coarse/...	LGN	SM		FS-PS	D/C		M	G			6–10

Plant	Type	Height	Habit	Texture	Color	Form	Flower	Light	Propagation	Time	Moisture	R/G/S	Pest	Disease	Zone
M. spicata Spearmint	HP	1–2'	MAT	coarse/thin	GN	SM	LAV	FS-PS	S/C/D	[4wk]	M	R		rust	2–9
M. suaveolens **Pineapple Mint**	HP	18"	MAT	coarse/dense	WonLGN	SM	W	FS	C/D	[6wk]	M	R			3–9
M. s. var. Round-leaved Mint	HP	1–2'	MAT	coarse/dense	DGN	SM	LAV	PS-SH	C/D/C		M	R		rust, mildew	2–9
M. × *villosa* var. Applemint	HP	2–3'	MAT	coarse/thin	LGN	SM	W/PK	FS-SH	S/D/C		M	G			3–9
Monarda didyma Bee Balm	HP	3–4'	UP	coarse/thin	DGN	SM	R/W/PK*	FS-PS	S/C/D	2–6wk	M	R	stalk-borer	crown rot	2–9
M. d. 'Granite Pink' Dwarf Monarda	HP	10–12"	MAT	coarse/dense	DGN	SM	PK*	PS	S/C/D	1–4wk	M	R		leaf spot, rust	2–9
M. fistulosa Wild Bergamot	HP	3–4'	UP	coarse/thin	DGN	SM	ROS/LAV*	FS-PS	S/D/C	2–6wk	M	R		mildew, wilt	3–9
M. punctata Dotted Mint	HP	18"	BU	coarse/dense	GN	SM	Y	FS	S/D	4–6wk	D	S			3–9
Monardella odoratissima Western Balm	HP	18–24"	CL	coarse/thin	GN	SM-F	ROS*	FS-PS	D/S		WD	R			2–9
M. villosa Coyote Mint	HP	12–18"	MAT	coarse/dense	DGN	SM-F	ROS*	FS-PS	D/S	1–2wk	WD	R			2–9
Myrrhis odorata Sweet Cicely	HP	18–24"	CL	feathery/dense	LGN	SP	W*	PS-SH	S/D	2–3m	M	R			2–9
Nepeta cataria Catnip	HP	2–4'	UP	coarse/thin	GYGN	SM	W/PK	FS-PS	S/C/D	1–3wk	WD	G		leaf spot	2–9
N. c. 'Citriodora' Lemon Catnip	HP	2–3'	UP	coarse/thin	GYGN	SM	W/PK	FS	C/D	[6wk]	WD	R			6–9
N. × *faassenii* Catmint	HP	1–2'	MAT	coarse/dense	GY	SM	VIO*	FS-PS	C/D	[8wk]	WD	G			2–9
N. mussinii Dwarf Catnip	HP	12"	MAT	coarse/dense	GYGN	SM	BLU*	FS	S/D	1–2wk	WD	G			2–9
Ocimum americanum Lemon Basil	A	12"	BU	fine/thin	LGN	SM	W	FS	S	1–2wk	WD	R			9–10
O. basilicum Sweet Basil	A	1–2'	BU	coarse/dense	GN	SM	W	FS	S	5–7d	WD	R	beetles		9–10
O. b. 'Bush'	A/SP	12"	BU	fine/dense	LGN	SM	W	FS	S/C	1–2wk	WD	G			9–10

BOTANICAL NAME	LIFE CYCLE	HEIGHT	HABIT	FOLIAGE TEXTURE	FOLIAGE COLOR	BLOSSOM SEASON	BLOSSOM COLOR	SUN	PROPAGATION	GERMINATION	SOIL MOISTURE	SOIL TYPE	PESTS INSECTS	PESTS DISEASE	ZONE
O. b. 'Dark Opal'	A	18"	BU	coarse/dense	PUR	SM	PK*	FS	S/C	5–7d	WD	G			9–10
O. b. 'Thyrsiflora'	A/SP	12"	BU	coarse/dense	PUR-GN	SM	PK*	FS	S/C	1–2wk	WD	G			9–10
O. canum Hoary Basil	A/SP	2–3'	UP	coarse/thin	DGN	SM	W	FS	S/C	2–3wk	WD	R			9–10
O. kilimandscharicum Camphor Basil	A/SP	2–4'	UP	coarse/thin	GN	SM	W	FS	S/C/L	2–3wk	WD	G			9–10
O. sanctum 'Sri' Holy Basil	A/SP	1–2'	UP	coarse/thin	GN	SM	W	FS	S/C/L	1–4wk	WD	G			9–10
O. s. 'Krishna' Purple Holy Basil	A/SP	1–2'	UP	coarse/thin	PUR	SM	PK	FS	S/C/L	1–4wk	WD	R			9–10
O. 'Spice' Spice Basil	A	15"	BU	coarse/dense	PONGN	SM	PK	FS	S/C	5–7d	WD	R			9–10
Origanum dictamnus Dittany of Crete	EP	8–12"	BU	coarse/dense	GY	SM	PK*	PS	C/D	[4wk]	WD	SL			9–10
O. × *hybridum* Dittany	EP	12–18"	BU	coarse/thin	GY	SM	PK	FS	C/L		WD	SL			8–10
O. majorana Sweet Marjoram	A/SP	12–18"	MAT	coarse/dense	GYGN	SM	W	FS	S/D/L	1–2wk	WD	R			8–10
O. microphyllum	EP	12–18"	BU	fine/dense	GY	SM	PK*	FS	S/D/L	[4wk]	WD	S			7–10
O. onites Pot Marjoram	A/SP	1–2'	MAT	coarse/thin	GYGN	SM	W	FS	S/D		WD	G			7–10
O. vulgare ssp. *vulgare* Oregano	EP	18–24"	MAT	coarse/dense	DGN	SM	W/PUR	FS	D/C/S	1–2wk	WD	GL			6–10
O. v. ssp. *gracile* Russian Oregano	EP	18–24"	MAT	coarse/dense	PURGN	SM	PK*	FS	S/D/L	2–4wk	WD	G			4–10
O. v. ssp. *hirtum* Italian Oregano	SEP	18–24"	BU	coarse/dense	LGN	SM	W	FS	C/D	[6wk]	WD	GL			8–10
O. v. 'Aureum' Golden Oregano	EP	12–18"	MAT	coarse/dense	YGN	SM	W	FS	D/L		WD	G			6–10

Plant	Type	Height	Habit	Texture	Foliage Color	Flower Size	Flower Color	Light	Soil	Propagation	Moisture		Pests	Diseases	Zones
Perovskia atriplicifolia Russian Sage	EP	2–4'	BU	fine/thin	GYGN	SM-F	BLU	FS	S/C		WD	G			5–9
Petroselinum crispum var. *crispum* Curly Parsley	HB	12–18"	BU	coarse/dense	GN	SM	YGN	FS	S,SS	1–2wk	WD	G		leaf spot stem rot	2–10
P. c. var. *neapolitanum* Italian Parsley	HB	2–3'	UP	coarse/thin	GN	SM	YGN	FS	S,SS	1–2wk	WD	R	leaf miner	leaf spot	2–10
Phlomis fruticosa Jerusalem Sage	EP	2–4'	BU	coarse/dense	GYGN	SM	Y*	FS	S/D		WD	GL			6–10
Pimpinella anisum Anise	A	12–18"	BU	fine/dense	DGN	SM	W	FS	S	1–2wk	WD	R			5–10
Reseda officinalis Mignonette	A/B	1–2'	CL	coarse/thin	GN	SP-F	Y*	FS	S	5–10d	WD	R		leaf spot	3–9
Rosmarinus officinalis var. *officinalis* Rosemary	EP	4–6'	BU	fine/dense	DGN	SP-F	BLU/W	FS	S/C/L	4–6wk	WD	GL		root rot	8–10
R. o. var. *angustifolius* Upright Rosemary	EP	3–4'	BU	fine/dense	DGN	SM	BLU	FS	C/L	[10wk]	WD	S			8–10
R. o. var. *prostratus* Creeping Rosemary	EP	12–18"	MAT	fine/dense	DGN	SM-F	BLU	FS	C/L	[12wk]	WD	SL			7–10
R. o. var. *rigidus* 'Tuscan Blue' 'Majorca Pink'	EP	3–4'	BU	fine/dense	DGN	SM	BLU	FS	C/L	[12wk]	WD	GL			8–10
Rumex acetosa Garden Sorrel	HB	2–3'	CL	coarse/dense	GN	SM	BRN	FS	S,SS	1–2wk	M	R			3–9
R. scutatus French Sorrel	HB	12–18"	CL	coarse/dense	GN	SM	BRN	FS	S,SS	1–2wk	M	R		leaf spot rust	3–9
Ruta chalapensis Fringed Rue	SEP	2–3'		fine/dense	BGN	SM	Y	FS	S/C/L	4–6wk	WD	GL			7–10
R. graveolens Rue	SEP	1–2'	BU	fine/dense	BGN	SM	Y*	FS-PS	S/C/L	4–6wk	WD	GL			6–10
R. g. 'Curly Girl'	SEP	12–18"	BU	fine/dense	BGY	SM	Y	FS	C/L	[12wk]	WD	GL			6–10
R. g. var. *variegata*	SEP	1–2'	BU	fine/dense	WonBGY	SM	Y	FS	C/L	[15wk]	WD	GL			7–10
Salvia argentea Silver Sage	B/HP	3–6"/18"	CL	coarse/thin	GY	SP	W	FS	S/SS	5–10d	WD	GS	stalk borer	stem rot	7–10

BOTANICAL NAME	LIFE CYCLE	HEIGHT	HABIT	FOLIAGE TEXTURE	FOLIAGE COLOR	BLOSSOM SEASON	BLOSSOM COLOR	SUN	PROPAGATION	GERMINATION	SOIL MOISTURE	SOIL TYPE	PESTS INSECTS	PESTS DISEASE	ZONE
S. clevelandii Blue Sage	EP	3–5'	BU	coarse/thin	GYGN	SM	BLU*	FS	C/L	[8wk]	WD	GL			8–10
S. dorisiana	EP	2–3'	BU	coarse/dense	LGN	SM-F	R*	FS	C/L/D	[6wk]	WD	RL			7–10
S. elegans Pineapple Sage	EP	3–5'	UP	coarse/thin	DGN	SM-F	R*	FS	C/L		WD	RL			8–10
S. fruticosa Greek Sage	EP	2–3'	BU	coarse/thin	GY	SM	LILAC	FS	C/L/S	2–3wk	WD	GL			8–10
S. officinalis Garden Sage	EP	2–3'	BU	coarse/thin	GYGN	SM	BLU*	FS-PS	S/L/C	1–2wk	WD	GL	stalk borer	stem rot rust	3–9
S. o. 'Aurea' Golden Sage	EP	12–18"	BU	coarse/dense	YGN	—	—	FS	C/L	[12wk]	WD	GL			2–10
S. o. 'Icterina' Golden sage	EP	12–18"	BU	coarse/dense	YonGN	—	—	FS	C/L	8wk	WD	GL			4–10
S. o. 'Nana' Dwarf Sage	EP	12"	BU	coarse/dense	GYGN	SM	BLU*	FS-PS	C/L	[8wk]	WD	GL		rust	4–10
S. o. 'Purpurascens' Red Sage	EP	12–18"	BU	coarse/thin	PUR	—	—	FS	C/L	[10wk]	WD	GL			8–10
S. o. 'Tricolor' Variegated Sage	EP	12–18"	BU	coarse/thin	W&P on DGN	—	—	FS	C/L	[6wk]	WD	GL			8–10
S. pratensis Meadow Clary	EP	1–3'	CL	coarse/thin	DGN	SM	PUR	FS	S,SS	1–2wk	WD	R			4–10
S. scalarea Clary	HB	2–5'	UP	coarse/thin	GY	SM	W/PK	FS-PS	S,SS		WD	GL			6–9
S. uliginosa Bog Sage	EP	3–4'	UP	coarse/thin	GN	SM-F	BLU*	FS	C/D		WD	GL			7–10
S. viridis Annual Clary	A	12–18"	CL	coarse/dense	VIO/PK ON DGN	SM	PUR/PK*	FS	S/SS	1–2wk	WD	GS			4–10
Sanguisorba canadense Great Burnet	HP	2–4'	CL	coarse/thin	DGN	SM	W	FS	S/D	2–4wk	WD	G			2–8
S. obtusum	HP	1–2'	CL	coarse/	DGN	SM	PK*	FS	S/D	2–4wk	M	G			4–8

Name														Pests/Disease	Zone
Santolina chamaecyparissus Lavender cotton	EP	1–3'	SHB	fine/ dense	GY	SM	Y*	FS-PS	C/L	[12wk]	M	S	crown rot	6–10
S. c. 'Nana' Dwarf Santolina	EP	8–12"	MAT	fine/ dense	GY	SM	Y*	FS	C/L	[12wk]	M	S		6–10
S. neapolitana Fringed Santolina	EP	12–18"	SHB	fine/ dense	GY	SM	Y*	FS-PS	C/L	[10wk]	M	S		7–10
S. virens Green Santolina	EP	18–24"	SHB	fine/ dense	GN	SM	Y*	FS	C/L	[8wk]	M	S		3–9
Satureja douglasii Yerba Buena	HP	1–3"	MAT	coarse/ dense	DGN	SP/F	W/PUR	PS-SH	S/L		M	RA		7–9
S. hortensis Summer Savory	A	12–18"	BU	fine/ thin	DGN	SM	PK	FS	S	1–2wk	WD	R		ALL
S. montana Winter Savory	EP	6–16"	BU	fine/ dense	DGN	SM	W/PK	FS	S/C/L	3–4wk	WD	G	mildew	4–9
S. m. ssp. pygmaea Pygmy Savory	EP	6–8"	BU	fine/ dense	DGN	SM	W	FS	C/L	[6wk]	WD	G		4–9
S. pilosa Creeping Savory	DP	4–10"	MAT	fine/ thin	DGN	SM	W	FS	S/L/C	2–3wk	WD	S		6–9
Sesamum indicum Sesame	A	3–4'	UP	coarse/ thin	GN	SM-F	W/R*	FS	S	1–2wk	WD	R	leaf spot	4–10
Solidago odorata Fragrant Goldenrod	HP	2–4'	CL	coarse/ dense	GN	SM-F	Y	FS	S/D		DR	GS	leaf spot, rust, mildew	4–9
Stachys byzantina Wooly Betony	EP	12–18"	MAT	coarse/ dense	GY	SM	PK/RO	FS-PS	S,SS/L	1–2wk	DR	G		3–9
S. b. 'Silver Carpet'	EP	6"	CL	coarse/ dense	GY	—	—	FS-PS	D		WD	G		4–9
S. officinalis Betony	HP	2–3'	UP	coarse/ thin	GN	SP	ROSE*	FS	S	1–2wk	WD	G	leaf spot mildew	3–9
Symphytum officinale Comfrey	HP	3–5'	CL	coarse/ dense	DGN	SM	LAV/R/Y	FS-SH	S/D	1–2wk	M	G	leaf spot	2–10
S. × *uplandicum* Russian Comfrey	HP	3–6'	CL	coarse/ dense	DGN	SM	RO/PUR	FS	S/D	1–2wk	M	G		2–10
Tanacetum vulgare Garden Tansy	HP	3–5'	CL	feathery/ dense	DGN	SM	Y*	FS-PS	S,SS/D	3–4wk	WD	G		2–9
T. v. 'Crispum' Fern Leaf Tansy	HP	3–4'	CL	feathery/ dense	DGN	SM	Y*	FS	S/D	3–4wk	WD	G		2–9

BOTANICAL NAME	LIFE CYCLE	HEIGHT	HABIT	FOLIAGE TEXTURE	FOLIAGE COLOR	BLOSSOM SEASON	BLOSSOM COLOR	SUN	PROPAGATION	GERMINATION	SOIL MOISTURE	SOIL TYPE	INSECTS	DISEASE	ZONE
Teucrium chamaedrys Germander	EP	1–2'	SHB	fine/dense	DGN	SM	ROSE	FS	S/C/L	[12wk]	WD	G		rust	2–9
T. c. 'Prostratum' Creeping Germander	EP	6–8"	MAT	fine/dense	DGN	SM	ROSE	FS	C/L	[12wk]	WD	G			4–9
T. fruticans Silver Germander	EP	18–24"	SHB	fine/dense	GY	SM	BLU*	FS	C/L		WD	G			8–10
T. marum Cat Thyme	EP	12–18"	SHB	fine/dense	GY	SM	PK*	FS	S/C		WD	G			4–9
T. scorodonia Wood Sage	EP	8–10"	SHB	fine/dense	DGN	SM	Y	FS	S/C		WD	G			4–9
Thymbra spicata Za'atar	EP	12–16"	BU	fine/dense	DGN	SM	PK*	FS	S/C		WD	G			8–10
Thymus 'Argenteus' Silver Thyme	EP	8–10"	SHB	fine/dense	Won DGN	SM	PK	FS	C/L		WD	SL			4–9
T. 'Broadleaf English' English Thyme	EP	1–2'	SHB	fine/dense	DGN	SM	ROSE	FS	C/L		WD	S			5–9
T. brousonetti Moroccan Thyme	EP	10–12"	SHB	fine/thin	GN	SP-SM	PK*	FS	C/L		WD	S		root rot	8–10
T. caespititius 'Tuffet' Tuffeted Thyme	EP	to 3"	CL	fine/dense	LGN	SM	ROSE	FS	S/D/L		WD	S			4–10
T. camphoratus Camphor Thyme	EP	4–6"	SHB	fine/dense	DGN	SM	ROSE	FS	C		WD	S	mealy bug		9–10
T. capitatus Corido	EP	8–10"	SHB	fine/dense	DGN	SP-S	LAV	FS	S/C		WD	SL	mealy bug	root rot	8–10
T. carnosus	EP	4–6"	SHB	fine/thin	DGN	SM	W	FS	S/C		WD	S			9–10
T. × citriodorus 'Aureus' Golden Lemon Thyme	EP	8–12"	SHB	fine/thin	YonDGN	SP-SM	PK	FS	C	[6wk]	WD	SL			6–10
T. 'Clear Gold' Transparent Thyme	EP	8–10"	MAT	fine/thin	YGN	SM	LAV	FS-PS	C/L		WD	S		root rot	6–10

Thyme

T. herba-barona Caraway Thyme	EP	1–4″	MAT fine/dense	DGN	SM	ROSE	FS	S/C/L	[9wk]	WD	S		3–9
T. leucotrichus Peter Davis Thyme	EP	3–4″	MAT fine/thin	GYGN	SP	ROSE*	FS	C/L		WD	S		6–10
T. 'Linear Leaf Lilac' Marshall Thyme	EP	3–8″	MAT fine/dense	GYGN	SM	LAV*	FS	C/L	[12wk]	WD	S		4–10
T. 'Long Leaf Gray'	EP	3–6″	MAT fine/thin	GYGN	SP-S	LAV*	FS	C/L		WD	S		3–9
T. mastichina Mastic Thyme	EP	10–16″	SHB fine/dense	GYGN	SP-S	W	FS	S/C/L		WD	S		8–10
T. praecox ssp. *arcticus* Wild Thyme	EP	2–4″	MAT fine/dense	DGN	SM	PUR	FS	S/L/C	4–6wk	WD	SL		1–9
T. p. 'Coccineus' Crimson Thyme	EP	1–3″	MAT fine/dense	DGN	SM	R*	FS	S/L/C	[9wk]	WD	S		4–9
T. p. 'Languinosus' Wooly Thyme	EP	to 1″	MAT fine/dense	GY	SM	ROSE	FS	L/C	[9wk]	WD	SL		2–9
T. p. 'Mayfair'	EP	to 1″	MAT fine/dense	YonDGN	SM	ROSE	FS	L/D	[6wk]	WD	SL		4–9
T. p. 'Pink Chintz'	EP	to 1″	MAT fine/dense	YonDGN	SM	ROSE	FS	L/D	[6wk]	WD	SL		2–9
T. p. 'White Moss'	EP	to ½″	MAT fine/dense	GN	SM	W	FS	L/D	[6wk]	WD	SL		2–9
T. pulegioides Mother-of-Thyme	EP	4–10″	MAT fine/thin	DGN	SM	LAV	FS-PS	S/L/C	3–4wk	WD	C	cut worm root rot	6–10
T. p. 'Fosterflower' Creeping White Thyme	EP	4–6″	MAT fine/thin	DGN	SM	W	FS-PS	L/C	[4wk]	WD	S	cut worm	6–10
T. p. 'Gold Dust' Creeping Gold Thyme	EP	8–10″	MAT fine/thin	YonDGN	SM	ROSE	FS	C/L		WD	W	root rot	7–10
T. p. 'Kermesinus' Creeping Red Thyme	EP	6–8″	MAT fine/thin	DGN	SM	MAG*	FS	C/L		WD	S		6–10
T. p. 'Oregano-scented' Oregano Thyme	EP	6–10″	MAT fine/dense	DGN	SM	LAV*	FS-PS	L/C	[4wk]	WD	S	cut worm	6–10

BOTANICAL NAME	LIFE CYCLE	HEIGHT	HABIT	FOLIAGE TEXTURE	FOLIAGE COLOR	BLOSSOM SEASON	BLOSSOM COLOR	SUN	PROPAGATION	GERMINATION	SOIL MOISTURE	SOIL TYPE	PESTS INSECTS	PESTS DISEASE	ZONE
T. vulgaris French Thyme 'Orange Balsam' 'Fragrantissimus'	EP	12–18"	SHB	fine/dense	DGN	SM	W/PK	FS	S,SS/C/L	4–6wk	DR	SL			2–9
T. v. 'Miniature' Dwarf Thyme	EP	4–6"	SHB	fine/dense	GYGN	—	—	FS	C	[10wk]	WD	SL			4–9
T. 'Wedgewood'	EP	4–6"	MAT	fine/dense	BGN	SM	W	FS	C/L	[6wk]	WD	S			4–10
T. zygis	EP	6–8"	SHB	fine/thin	DGN	SM	LAV	FS	S/C		WD	S			6–10
Trigonella foenum-graecum Fennugreek	A	18–30"	UP	fine/thin	DGN	SM	W/PK	FS	S	5–10d	M	R			3–9
Valeriana officinalis Valerian	HP	3–6'	UP	fine/thin	DGN	SP-SM	W/PK	PS	S/D		M	R		crown rot rust	2–9
Viola odorata Florist's Violet	HP	4–8"	CL	coarse/dense	DGN	SP-SM	PUR/W/R*	SH-PS	S,SS/D	1–2wk	M	RA	cut worm slug	crown rot root rot	4–9
V. canadensis	HP	8–10"	CL	coarse/dense	DGN	SP-SM	W*	PS-SH	S,SS/D	5–10d	M	RA	cut worm	rust leaf spot	2–9
V. lanceolata Lance-leaf Violet	HP	6–10"	CL	coarse/thin	DGN	SP-SM	W*	PS	S,SS/D		AQ	RS			4–9
V. pedata Bird's-foot Violet	HP	4–6"	CL	fine/dense	DGN	SP	PUR/LAV*	FS-PS	S/D	1–2wk	WD	GS			2–9
V. tricolor Pansy	HP	6–10"	CL	coarse/dense	DGN	SP-F	PUR/Y	FS-PS	S/SS	5–10d	WD	G	slug cutworm		4–9

Landscape Uses & Herbal Uses of Ornamental Herbs

HERB COMMON NAME	Scent	Bee Herb	Flowers	Bonsai	Shade	Ground Cover	Hedge	Screen	Border	Potted	Rockery	Pond	Tea	Salad	Spice	Smoking	Pottage	Companion	Dried Material	Fragrance	Confection	Strewing	Repellent	Medicinal	ORIGINS
Angelica			×		×							×				×	×				×			×	Eurasia
Anise									×				×	×	×		×				×				S. Europe
Anise Hyssop		×	×						×				×	×	×				×	×	×	×			N. Amer.
Asafetida		×							×	×					×										S.E. Asia
Basil, Bush	×								×	×	×		×	×	×										
Basil, Camphor									×	×											×				E. Afr.
Basil, Cinnamon	×								×		×		×	×	×				×	×	×	×			
Basil, Crinkled									×					×							×				
Basil, Lemon									×	×			×	×	×						×	×			N.W. India
Basil, Sacred	×								×	×			×	×	×	×			×	×	×	×			S.E. Asia
Basil, Spice				×					×	×	×		×	×	×						×	×			garden
Basil, Sweet	×	×							×	×			×	×	×			×			×				ancient
Basil, Thyrisflora				×					×	×	×				×						×	×			India
Basil, Tree										×					×							×	×		
Basil—Thyme	×	×	×						×		×		×	×	×						×				Eurasia
Bay, Sweet				×	×	×	×							×		×	×		×	×	×	×			Med.
Bay, California														×					×	×		×			W. USA
Bedstraw					×			×											×						
Bee Balm		×	×		×				×	×			×						×	×	×	×	×		E. USA
Betony		×							×				×											×	
Betony, Wooly		×				×				×			×						×						Turkey/SW Asia
Bible Leaf	×					×	×									×	×	×	×	×		×			Eurasia
Borage		×	×		×				×					×								×			Eur./N. Afr.
Burnet, Great			×						×	×															
Burnet, Japanese			×							×	×														

HERB / COMMON NAME	Scent	Bee Herb	Flowers	Bonsai	Shade	Ground Cover	Hedge	Screen	Border	Potted	Rockery	Pond	Tea	Salad	Spice	Smoking	Pottage	Companion	Dried Material	Fragrance	Confection	Strewing	Repellent	Medicinal	ORIGINS
						LANDSCAPE USES										HERBAL USES									
Burnet, Salad					X	X			X				X	X			X		X						Eurasia
Calamint	X				X				X	X	X	X	X								X	X	X		S. Eur/Med.
Calendula		X							X	X	X		X	X			X				X				S. Europe
Camomile, German	X	X	X						X	X	X		X					X	X	X	X	X		X	Europe
Camomile, Lawn	X				X	X			X	X											X				
Camomile, Roman	X	X			X	X			X	X			X								X	X	X		Eurasia
Camomile, Dyer's			X						X										X						
Caraway									X				X	X	X	X	X		X	X	X				Europe
Cardoon		X						X	X					X			X		X						S. Europe
Catnip					X				X				X								X	X	X		Eurasia
Catnip, Lemon									X	X			X									X			
Catnip, Dwarf	X	X			X				X	X									X	X		X			Iran
Chervil					X	X								X	X	X		X				X	X		
Chive		X	X						X	X	X	X	X	X			X	X	X					X	Eurasia
Chive, Garlic		X							X	X	X		X	X				X	X					X	China
Clary		X							X	X					X			X			X			X	S. Europe
Clove Pink	X	X							X	X	X							X	X	X	X				
Comfrey		X	X		X	X		X	X				X											X	Eurasia
Coriander	X								X				X	X	X	X	X				X				S. Europe
Corido		X				X			X	X	X			X			X					X			Med./E. Asia
Costmary	X	X			X					X								X	X			X	X		Eurasia
Creeping Charlie					X	X				X	X	X					X					X			Europe
Cumin									X						X	X					X				Med.
Curry Plant	X	X				X			X	X	X		X	X	X	X			X	X	X				S. Europe
Dill	X	X							X	X				X	X	X		X	X	X		X	X	X	
Dittany		X							X	X	X			X	X	X		X		X		X			Greece/Crete
Dong Quai		X	X								X						X		X	X				X	China
Dropwort		X	X						X															X	
Egyptian Onion																			X						
Elecampane		X	X						X								X		X	X				X	C. Asia
English Daisy																									
Fennel	X				X			X	X				X	X	X		X	X	X		X			X	S. Europe
Fennugreek		X	X		X										X	X		X	X		X		X	X	S. Eur/Asia
Finocchio									X					X			X		X		X				
Garlic		X							X	X					X	X	X	X	X				X	X	
Geranium, Scented	X								X	X	X		X	X	X				X	X	X	X			S. Afr.
Germander, Wall		X					X	X	X										X						Europe
Germander, Silver		X					X	X	X									X		X					Asia
Giant Allium		X							X	X										X					W. Med.
Ginger, Wild					X	X					X			X	X	X					X	X			N. hemisph.
Goldenrod, Fragrant			X						X				X						X	X	X	X			
Good King Henry			X											X			X								

Columns 1–12 (Scent … Pond) are grouped under **LANDSCAPE USES**; columns 13–24 (Tea … Medicinal) are grouped under **HERBAL USES**.

HERB / COMMON NAME	Scent	Bee Herb	Flowers	Bonsai	Shade	Ground Cover	Hedge	Screen	Border	Potted	Rockery	Pond	Tea	Salad	Spice	Smoking	Pottage	Companion	Dried Material	Fragrance	Confection	Strewing	Repellent	Medicinal	ORIGINS
Hop						X		X					X						X	X				X	N. hemisph.
Horehound		X							X	X			X						X	X				X	S. Europe
Hyssop	X	X	X	X		X		X	X	X					X					X	X				S. & E. Europe
Indian Borage	X								X	X				X		X		X							S.E. Asia
Jasmine, Poet's	X		X		X		X	X												X	X				W. China
Jasmine, Arabian	X		X						X				X							X	X	X			
Lady's Mantle	X		X		X	X				X								X							
Lamb's Quarters									X					X			X								N. hemisph.
Lavender, Dwarf		X	X						X	X	X									X	X				
Lavender, English	X	X	X				X	X	X	X	X									X	X	X	X		Med.
Lavender, French	X		X				X	X	X	X	X									X	X				S. Spain
Lavender, Spanish			X						X	X	X									X	X				W. Med.
Lavender, Wooly			X						X	X	X									X	X				S. Spain
Lavender Cotton			X			X	X		X	X	X									X		X	X		Spain/N. Afr.
Leek									X					X	X		X								
Lemon Balm	X	X			X				X	X			X	X	X			X	X	X	X	X	X		S. Europe
Lovage					X				X	X			X	X	X	X		X		X	X				E. Europe
Love-in-a-Mist		X			X				X	X					X					X	X				
Lungwort		X			X					X															
Mallows			X	X										X	X		X		X						
Marjoram, Pot									X	X					X		X								SE Eur/Turkey
Marjoram, Sweet									X	X	X		X	X	X	X	X				X	X			SW Asia/N. Afr.
Marshmallow					X				X	X		X									X			X	
Marsh Marigold			X	X								X		X			X								
Masterwort		X			X					X								X	X						Bulgaria
Meadow Clary		X	X		X				X									X	X						Eurasia
Meadow Sweet	X	X	X			X			X	X									X					X	Eurasia
Mignonette	X	X							X	X										X					
Mint, Apple	X	X			X	X							X	X							X	X			S. Europe
Mint, Black	X	X	X		X								X	X					X	X	X	X		X	England
Mint, Corsican	X				X	X			X	X												X			Corsica
Mint, Coyote	X	X	X		X														X						W. USA
Mint, Curly	X					X	X														X				
Mint, Dotted	X	X							X	X									X		X				C. USA
Mint, Ginger	X						X			X	X		X		X						X	X			
Mint, Korean	X	X	X										X						X		X	X			N. Amer.
Mint, Mountain	X	X			X			X					X						X						N. Amer.
Mint, Orange	X	X	X		X	X				X	X		X	X					X	X	X	X			
Mint, Pepper	X	X			X	X							X								X	X		X	garden
Mint, Pineapple	X	X			X					X	X		X								X	X			
Mint, Round-leaved	X	X	X		X	X							X	X							X	X			N. hemisph.
Mint, Spear	X	X			X								X								X	X			ancient

HERB — COMMON NAME	\<LANDSCAPE USES\> Scent	Bee Herb	Flowers	Bonsai	Shade	Ground Cover	Hedge	Screen	Border	Potted	Rockery	Pond	\<HERBAL USES\> Tea	Salad	Spice	Smoking	Pottage	Companion	Dried Material	Fragrance	Confection	Strewing	Repellent	Medicinal	ORIGINS
Mint, Stone	X					X																X			E. No. Amer.
Mint, Water	X		X	X	X								X						X	X	X	X			
Mugwort, Common						X								X			X								Europe
Mugwort, Western						X													X						C & W USA
Mugwort, White	X	X			X	X													X	X					China
Oregano	X	X	X			X			X		X				X	X	X			X					Eurasia
Oregano, Golden						X				X							X								garden
Oregano, Italian	X		X						X	X	X		X	X	X	X	X		X	X	X	X			SE Europe
Oregano, Mexican										X							X				X				C. Amer.
Origanum microphyllum			X						X	X							X					X			
Pansy			X			X			X	X	X		X					X						X	
Parsley, Curly									X	X	X			X	X			X			X				Eurasia
Parsley, Italian									X					X	X	X	X								Eurasia
Parsley, Japanese				X					X				X	X	X	X	X								N. Amer./Siberia
Pennyroyal, Engl.	X	X	X		X	X			X	X									X	X			X		Europe
Pennyroyal, Amer.	X								X	X	X												X		N. Amer.
Pennyroyal, Holt's	X					X					X		X										X		E. No. Amer.
Pineapple Weed						X											X			X	X				N. Amer.
Rocambole		X							X	X				X	X		X	X	X						
Rosemary	X		X		X	X	X	X	X				X		X	X			X	X	X	X	X	X	Med.
Rosemary, Creeping	X					X			X	X												X	X		
Rue		X	X			X			X	X	X								X	X		X	X		S. Europe
Saffron		X				X			X	X	X		X		X							X	X		Turkistan
Sage, Bog		X							X	X								X							
Sage, Canyon		X				X			X	X															W. USA
Sage, Blue	X	X	X			X			X	X	X		X	X	X	X			X	X	X	X	X		
Sage, Dwarf		X	X			X			X	X	X		X		X	X			X	X	X	X			
Sage, Garden	X	X	X	X					X	X	X	X	X		X	X			X	X	X	X	X		Spain/Asia Minor
Sage, Golden	X								X	X	X		X		X	X					X				
Sage, Greek	X	X	X			X			X	X			X								X	X			
Sage, Pineapple			X										X	X	X										Mexico
Sage, Red									X	X	X		X		X	X			X	X					
Sage, Silver			X						X	X	X							X						X	
Sage, Tricolor									X	X	X				X	X	X				X	X			
Sage, Wood			X						X												X				Europe
Santolina			X		X	X	X		X										X						Med.
Santolina, Green			X		X	X	X												X						
Savory, Creeping	X	X				X					X														
Savory, Pygmy							X		X	X	X						X								
Savory, Summer	X								X						X	X	X					X			Med.
Savory, Winter	X	X					X		X	X							X					X			Med.

HERB / COMMON NAME	Scent	Bee Herb	Flowers	Bonsai	Shade	Ground Cover	Hedge	Screen	Border	Potted	Rockery	Pond	Tea	Salad	Spice	Smoking	Pottage	Companion	Dried Material	Fragrance	Confection	Strewing	Repellent	Medicinal	ORIGINS
Sesame		X							X					X	X						X				Africa
Shallot									X					X	X		X								
'Silver King'									X										X						
'Silver Mound'						X			X	X									X						
Skirrets												X					X								China
Sorrel									X								X								Eurasia
Southernwood	X						X	X	X		X						X	X	X	X		X			SE Europe
Sweet Cicely	X		X			X	X		X	X			X	X	X	X	X	X	X	X	X				Europe
Sweet Flag	X				X				X	X		X							X	X	X	X		X	N. hemisph.
Sweet Woodruff																									
Tansy, Garden	X	X			X			X	X										X		X	X	X		Eurasia
Tansy, Fern Leaf		X					X	X	X										X			X	X		
Tarragon													X	X	X	X	X				X				
Thyme, Camphor	X							X	X		X										X				Portugal
Thyme, Caraway	X	X	X			X			X	X			X	X	X						X	X			Corsica, Sard.
Thyme, Cat		X				X			X	X	X							X							W. Med.
Thyme, Creeping Golden						X					X			X	X										
Thyme, English		X				X			X		X			X	X										garden
Thyme, French	X	X	X			X	X		X	X	X		X	X	X			X	X	X	X	X	X	X	W. Med.
Thyme, Golden Lemon						X			X	X			X	X	X						X	X			
Thyme, Lemon						X			X	X			X	X	X						X				garden
Thyme, Marshall		X	X			X			X	X				X							X				
Thyme, Mastic		X				X			X	X	X			X											Spain/Portug.
Thyme, Miniature						X			X	X	X			X											USA
Thyme, Moroccan		X	X			X			X	X	X			X							X	X			Morocco
Thyme, Mother of	X	X	X			X	X				X		X	X	X						X	X	X		Europe
Thyme, Orange	X		X			X	X		X	X	X		X	X	X			X	X	X	X	X	X		
Thyme, Oregano	X	X	X			X	X				X		X	X	X										Europe
Thyme, Peter Davis		X	X			X			X	X				X								X			Balkan Pen
Thyme, Red-flowering		X	X			X			X					X											garden
Thyme, Silver		X	X			X	X		X	X	X		X	X	X										garden
Thyme, Tuffeted		X				X			X	X	X			X											Portu/Azores
Thyme, Wedgewood		X				X			X					X	X										USA
Thyme, White-flowering		X	X			X	X				X		X	X	X						X	X			Europe
Thyme, 'White Moss'						X					X														
Thyme, Wild	X	X	X			X			X	X					X										Europe
Thyme, Wooly		X				X			X																
Thymus zygis		X				X			X	X	X				X							X			Spain/Portug.
Valerian	X	X	X						X	X		X							X	X					Eurasia

HERB COMMON NAME	LANDSCAPE USES												HERBAL USES												ORIGINS
	Scent	Bee Herb	Flowers	Bonsai	Shade	Ground Cover	Hedge	Screen	Border	Potted	Rockery	Pond	Tea	Salad	Spice	Smoking	Pottage	Companion	Dried Material	Fragrance	Confection	Strewing	Repellent	Medicinal	
Verbena, Lemon	X	X				X	X	X	X				X		X	X			X	X	X	X	X		Chile
Verbena, Licorice		X						X	X							X			X	X	X	X			C & S Amer.
Violet, Florist's	X	X		X	X			X	X	X			X					X	X	X	X			X	Eurasia/Afr.
Wild Bergamot		X	X					X	X				X						X		X				E. No. Amer.
Wild Fennel		X						X	X	X				X	X				X	X					
Wintergreen		X			X	X			X				X						X	X	X			X	E. N. Amer.
Witch Hazel	X	X	X	X	X	X	X												X					X	
Wormwood	X			X	X	X			X	X								X	X			X	X		Europe
Wormwood, Beach				X	X					X									X						
Wormwood, Roman					X	X	X												X						S. Europe
Yarrow			X			X		X	X						X				X					X	N. hemisph.
Yarrow, Creeping			X			X				X									X						
Yerba Buena	X					X	X							X	X	X					X				N. America
Za'atar			X				X		X	X	X						X		X	X		X	X		Turkey/E. Afr.

Appendix III

Dictionary of Latin Names

(deriv.) derived from; (ref.) refers to

acetosa	bitter	caespititius	mounded, sod
acetosella	vinegar salt	calamint	excellent mint
achillea	Achilles (name)	calamus	reed-like
		calendula	calendric (ref. fl)
agastache	crowded ear of grain (ref fl.)	campanula	bell-shaped
ajuga	not yoked (ref. fl.)	candicans	white, hoary
		canum	grey, hoary
albus	white	capitatus	headed
alchemilla	alchemist's herb	cardunculus	thistle-like
		carnosus	fleshy
allium	garlic-like, pungent	carvi	Karawaya, Arabian
althea	Althaea (name)	caryophyllus	clove-like
anethum	Anethon (Gk.)	caudatum	of woodlands
angelica	angelic	cerefolium	waxy-leaved
angustifolius	narrow	chalapensis	fringed (ref. fl)
anthemis	flower	chamaecyparissus	ground cypress
anthriscus	Thrace (deriv.), rejoice	chamaedrys	on the ground
aquilegia	eagle's claws (ref. fl)	chamaemellum	ground apple
		chenopodium	goosefoot
arborescens	tree-like	chrysanthemum	golden flower
archangelica	Archangel Michael	citriodorus	lemon scented
argenteus	silver	coccinea	scarlet-colored
aroanium	furrowed		
artemisia	Artemis, elegant	coleus	sheath
arvensis	field grown, cultivated	communis	common
		coreopsis	bug-like (ref. fruit)
ascalonicum	Syrian (deriv.)	coriandrum	bug-like (ref. odor)
atropurpureum	dark purple		
aureus	golden	corsicus	Corsica
		cotula	small cup
balsamita	balsam-like	crispum	curly
basilicum	royal, princely	crocus	Krokos, Gk.
bellis	pretty	cryptotaenia	hidden band
borago	rough	cumin	Kumino, Gk.
byzantina	Byzantium (city)		

cyanus	blue	helleborus	to injure, poison
cyminum	cyme bearing	hirtum	hairy, rough
cyparissus	cypress-like	hortensis	of gardens
damascena	Damascus (city)	humilis	dwarf
dictamnus	Mount Dict (Crete)	humulus	earthy
		hyssop	aromatic herb
didyma	twinned	inula	helenium (deriv.)
dentata	toothed		
douglasii	David Douglas (explorer)	jasmine	Yasmin, Persian
dracunculus	serpentine, little dragon	labiatae	lipped
elegans	elegant	lactiflora	milk white flower
farinacea	starchy, mealy	lanata	wooly
ferula	cane or fennel-like	languinosus	wooly
fillipendula	thread-like and pendulous	lanicaulis	wooly stem
		latifolia	broad-leaved
		lavandula	to wash
		leucotrichus	white haired
fistulosa	hollow	lovage	Liguria (city) (deriv.)
flavum	yellow		
florepleno	double flowered	lupulus	wolf-like
floridus	flowery	majorana	greater
foeniculum	hay-scented	marrubium	bitter (Hebrew)
foenum-graecum	Greek hay		
foetida	bad odor	melissa	of bees
fragrantissimus	very fragrant	mentha	Minthe (name)
fructifera	fruitful		
frutescens	bushy, shrubby	micans	sparkling
fruticans (fruticosa)	bushy, shrubby	millefolium	thousand leaved
		mollis	soft
gallium	curdles milk, cheese renning	monarda	Nicolas Monardes
		monardella	dimin. Monarda
gentilis	of the family	moschata	musk-like
glacialis	icy	multifida	parted many times
glaucus	blue-green, grey	myrrhis	myrrh like
gracilis	slender		
gramineus	grass-like	nana	little
grandiflorum	large flowered	neapolitana	of Naples
graveolens	strong scented	nepeta	Nept (city)
gaultheria	Francois Gaultier	niger	black
		nitens	blooming
hamamelis	apple tree-like	nitidus	flourishing, luxuriant
hedeoma	sweet smelling	nobilis	noble, famous
hederacea	ivy-like	nudiflorum	naked flower

obtusum	blunt, rounded
ocimum	to smell
odorata	fragrant
officinalis	medicinal
origanum	joy of the mtn., mtn. beauty
oxalis	sour
panonicus	Panonicus
patens	spreading
patiencia	enduring
pedata	footed
pedemontana	mountain walker
petroselinum	mountain celery
pilosa	covered with hair
pimpinella	bipinnula (deriv.)
piperita	pepper-like
plumosus	feathered
pontica	Pontus (city)
poterium	claret cup herb (deriv.)
praecox	early, ripe before time
pratensis	of meadows
primula	early
prunella	prune colored (ref. fl.)
ptarmica	feathery, comb-like
pulchellum	very pretty
pulegioides	pennyroyal-like
pulegium	fleabane
punctata	dotted, spotted
purpurascens	purple
repens	creeping
requienii	to rest upon
reseda	to soothe
rosmarinus	delights in sea spray (der.)
rotundifolia	round leaved
rugosa	wrinkled
ruta	to set free, cure
rutilans	red
salvia	save
sambucifolia	elder-leaved
sanctum	holy, sacred

sanguisorba	blood staunch
sativus	cultivated
schoenoprasum	rush leek
sclarea	clear eye (deriv.)
scutatus	buckler-shaped, shielded
semperflorens	ever blooming
sinensis	chinese
solidago	to make whole, heal
spicata	ear of corn (ref. fl.)
stachys	ear of grain (ref. fl.)
stellerana	bright, shining
stoechas	Stoechade Is.
sylvestris	of woodlands
symphytum	unite, bring together
tanacetoides	tansy-like
tanacetum	immortal (ref. fl.)
teucrium	Tucer (name)
thracicus	Thrace (country)
thymbra	savory, Thymbra (city)
thymus	incense, fumigate
thyrsiflora	spirally wound fl.
tinctoria	dyer's herb
tomentosa	densely wooly
trigonella	three angled fl.
tuberosum	tuberous
ulmaria	elm-leaved
urticifolia	nettle-leaved
valerian	to be in health
vera	true
verbena	sacred herb, Vervain (deriv.)
vernalis	of spring
verum	true
villosa	soft and hairy
viola	Ione, Gk. (deriv.)
viridis	green
vulgaris	common
zygis	yoked, joined

Bibliography

This bibliography is provided to help you in your search for information on herbs or their use in the ornamental garden. Books that may give more detailed medicinal data are preceded by (M). Books that may be useful for garden design information are preceded by (D). Any book that constitutes a reference guide is marked with (R).

ANDERSON, E., *Plants, Man and Life* (52)
ARBER, A., *Herbals: Their Origin and Evolution* (32)
BAILEY, L. H., *How Plants Get Their Names* (Dover 63)
(R)_____ , *Hortus III, Manual of Cultivated Plants* (76)
(D)BILES, R., *The Complete Book of Garden Magic* (47)
(D)BIRDSEYE, C. & E., *Growing Woodland Plants* (51) (Dover 72)
(D)BROOKLYN BOTANIC GARDENS, *Herbs and Their Ornamental Uses* (83)
_____ , *Dye Plants and Dyeing* (64)
BROWN, D., *Encyclopedia Botanica* (78)
BROWN, A., *Old Man's Garden* (38)
BROWNLOW, M., *Herbs and the Fragrant Garden* (57)
(M)BUCHMAN, D., *Herbal Medicine* (79)
(R)BOERNER BOT. GAR., *Herb Information Handbook*, Ed. R. Wrensch (75)
(D)CHATTO, B., *The Damp Garden* (84)
CLARKSON, R., *Herbs and Savory Seeds* (72)
_____ , *The Golden Age of Herbs and Herbalists* (40) (Dover 72)
_____ , *Green Enchantment* (44)
_____ , *Magic Gardens* (39)
_____ , CLARKSON, R., *Herbs: Their Culture and Uses* (42) (71)
CONROW, R. & HACKSEL, A., *Herbal Pathfinders* (79)
(R)CRACKER, L. & SIMON, J. Eds., *Herbs, Spices, and Medicinal Plants*, Vol. I (85)
(D)CRISP, SIR FRANK, *Medieval Gardens* (33)
(D)CROCKETT, J., *Encyclopedia of Gardening*
(D)_____ , *Landscape Gardening*
CROW, W., *Occult Properties of Herbs* (69)
DARAH, H., *The Cultivated Basils* (80)
DIOSCORIDES, *The Greek Herbal* (34)
FITZPATRIC, F., *Our Plant Resources* (64)
(R)FLANNERY, H., *A Study of the Taxa of Thymus Cult. in the U.S.* (82) (monograph)
(D)FLEMING, L. & GORE, A., *The English Garden* (79)
(D)FOLEY, D., *Ground Covers for Easier Gardening* (61) (Dover 72)
FOSTER, G., *Herbs for Every Garden* (73)
FOX, H., *Gardening with Herbs for Flavor and Fragrance* (33) (Dover 70)
_____ , *The Years in My Garden* (53)

GARLAND, S., *Complete Book of Herbs and Spices* (80)
(D)_____ , *The Herb Garden* (84)
(D)GESSERT, K., *The Beautiful Herb Garden* (82)
GIBBONS, E., *Stalking the Healthful Herbs* (66)
_____ , *Stalking the Wild Asparagus* (69)
(D)GILBERTIE'S. & SHEEHAN, L., *Herb Gardening at its Best* (82)
(D)GIVENS, H., *Landscape it Yourself*
GORDON, L., *A Country Herbal* (85)
_____ , *Green Magic-Flowers, Plants & Herbs in Lore & Legend* (77)
GRANT, J., *Designing a Garden*
_____ , *The Fragrant Garden*
GREENAWAY, K., *The Language of Flowers* (1884 reprnt)
GRIEVE, M., *A Modern Herbal* (31) (Dover 71)
GRIMM, W., *Home Guide to Trees, Shrubs and Wildflowers* (70)
HALL, D., *The Book of Herbs*
HARRISON & MASEFIELD, *Oxford Book of Plants*
(R)HARRINGTON, H. & DURRELL, L., *How to Identify Plants* (57)
(D)HARVEY, J., *Medieval Gardens* (83)
(R)HAY, R. & SYNGE, P., *The Color Dictionary of Flowers and Plants* (82)
HAYES, E., *Spices and Herbs, Lore and Cookery* (61)
HEALY, B., *A Gardener's Guide to Plant Names* (72)
HEDRICK, U., *Sturtevant's Edible Plants of the World* (19) (Dover 72)
HEFFERN, R., *The Herb Buyer's Guide*
HVASS, E., *Plants that Feed and Serve Us* (73)
(D)IREYS, I., *Small Gardens for City and Country*
(D)_____ , A., *How to Plan & Plant Your Own Property* (75)
JACOB, D., *A Witches Guide to Gardening* (65)
JONES, D., *The Herb Garden* (72)
(M)KADANS, J., *Modern Encyclopedia of Herbs* (70)
KAMM, M., *Old Time Herbs for Northern Gardens* (38) (Dover 71)
(M)KLOSS, J., *Back to Eden* (39) (75)
(M)KROCHMAL, A. & C., *Guide to the Medicinal Plants of the US* (73)
KRUTCH, J., *The Gardener's World*
LATHROP, N., *Herbs, How to Grow, Select and Enjoy* (80)
LEHNER, E. & J., *Folklore and Odysseys of Food and Medicinal Plants* (62)
LEIGHTON, A., *Early American Gardens—For Meate or Medicine* (70)
(D)LEIGHTON, A., *American Gardens in the Eighteenth Century* (76)
(M)LEUNG, A., *Chinese Herbal Remedies*
LEVY, J., *Herbal Handbook for Everyone* (66)
LOWENFELD, C., *Herb Gardening: Why and How to Grow Herbs* (71)
_____ , & BACK, P., *Herbs, Health and Cookery* (67)
(M)LUST, J., *The Herb Book* (74)
(R)MARINO-RODRIGUEZ, M., *Plants and Plant Products, FAO Bul. 25-1* (83)
(R)MATHEWS, D., *Travel Guide to Herb Shops, Farms and Gardens* (83)
(R)_____ , *Herbs by Mail* (83)
MATHEWS, W., *Mazes and Labyrinths* (22) (Dover 72)
MELTZER, S., *Herb Gardening in Texas* (83)
(M)MERCK INDEX, 10th ED., *An Encyclopedia of Chemicals, Drugs and Biologicals* (83)
(R)MORTON, J., *GoldenGuide to Herbs and Spices* (77)
_____ , *Major Medicinal Plants*
NEHRING, A. & I., *Picture Book of Perennials* (64) (77)
(R)NUTRITION SEARCH INC., *Nutrition Almanac* (73)
(M)PARK DAVIS CO., *Manual of Theraputics* (10)
(R)OLIVER, P., *The Herb Gardener's Resource Guide* (83)

PELLEGRINI, A., *The Food Lover's Garden* (70)

(R)PIRONE, P., *Diseases and Pests of Ornamental Plants* (70)

PRUTHI, J., *Spices and Condiments*

RANDOLPH, V., *Ozark Magic and Folklore* (47)

REPPERT, B., *A Heritage of Herbs* (76)

RHODE, E., *A Garden of Herbs* (69) (Dover 83)

(M)ROBERTS, B., *Characteristics of Selected Controversial Nutrition Products*, Table I (83)

RODALE PRESS, *Rodale Herb Book* (74)

_____ , *Encyclopedia of Organic Gardening* (78)

ROSE, J., *Herbs and Things: Jeanne Rose's Herbal* (72)

SANDERSON, L., *How to Make Your Own Herbal Cosmetics* (79)

SAUNDERS, C., *Edible, Useful Wild Plants of the US and Canada* (20) (Dover 76)

(M)SCHAUNBERG, P., *Guide to Medicinal Plants*

SCOBEY, J. & MEYERS, N., *Gifts from your Garden* (75)

SILVERMAN, M., *A City Herbal*

(R)SIMON, J. CHADWICK, A. & CRACKER, L. *Herbs—An Indexed Bibliography, 1971–80* (84)

SIMMONS, A., *Herbs to Grow Indoors* (69)

_____ , *Herb Gardening in Five Seasons* (69)

(R)SIMONSEN, J., *The Terpenes, VOL. I–IV* (47)

SINGLETON, E., *The Shakespeare Garden* (31)

SQUIRES, M., *The Art of Drying Plants and Flowers* (58)

STUART, M., Ed., *The Encyclopedia of Herbs and Herbalism* (79)

(D)SUNSET BOOKS, *Lawns and GroundCovers* (81)

(D)SWANSON, F. & RADY, V., *Herb Garden Design* (84)

SWANSON, F., *How to Grow Herbs* (82)

(D)TALOUMIS, G., *Container Gardening Outdoors* (72)

TANNAHILL, R., *Food in History* (73)

TAYLOR, N., *Fragrance in the Garden* (53)

(R)TETENYI, P., *Infraspecific Chemical Taxa of Medicinal Plants*

TIEDJENS, V., *The Vegetable Encyclopedia and Gardening Guide* (43)

(D)TINKEL, K., *Rooftop Gardening*

(D)TIPPING, Ed., *Gardens Old and New*

TUCKER, A., *Potpourri, Incense and Other Fragrant Concoctions* (72)

(M)TYLER, V., *The Honest Herbal* (81)

(R)UPHOFF, J., *Dictionary of Economic Plants* (68)

WEBSTER, H., *Herbs, How to Grow and Use Them* (39)

(M)WEINER, M., *Weiner's Herbal-Guide to Herb Medicine* (80)

WESTCOTT, C., *Plant Disease Handbook* (71)

(M)WHEELWRIGHT, E., *Medicinal Plants and Their History* (35) (Dover 74)

WHITLOCK, S. & RANKIN, M., *Dried Flowers, How to Prepare Them* (62) (Dover 72)

WILDER, L., *The Fragrant Path* (32)

YANG, L., *The Terrace Gardener's Handbook* (75)

General Index and Cross Reference

Included in this comprehensive index is a cross reference for the many common names of herbs, as well as a listing of over 650 species and cultivars. Page numbers or listings preceded by the letter **C** indicate *Chemical,* and by the letter **F** a *Food* or culinary use of the herb. An **R** indicates a *Recipe* in which the specific herb is used. A species name enclosed by brackets implies a change and is followed by one that is more accepted. The names of the major herbs are bold-faced; page numbers indicating primary reference information are also bold-faced.